CRY THE BELOVED MIND
A Voyage of Hope

VERNON M NEPPE MD, PHD

Seattle, Washington

Seattle, Washington
Portland, Oregon
Denver, Colorado
Vancouver, B.C.
Scottsdale, Arizona

Library of Congress #: 98-67899
Library of Congress cataloguing in publication data.
Neppe, Vernon M.
Cry the Beloved Mind: A Voyage of Hope
1. Self-help 2. Brain Medications 3. Sciction (science through fiction)
4. Psychopharmacology 5. Neuropsychiatry 6. Psychiatry 7. Neurology
8. Depression 9. Seizures 10. Tardive Dyskinesia 11. Catatonia
12. Anger 13. Drug Interactions 14 Complementary Medicine.
15. Anxiety 16. Psychosis. 17. Unusual Spells.
18. Medical Social Dilemmas. 19. Brain 20. Neurotransmitters
Includes preface, prologue, glossaries, index and endnotes.
368 + xvi pages.
Author : Vernon M . Neppe MD, PhD

ISBN # 0-89716-823-2; Peanut Butter Publishing, Seattle.
Copyright: Brainquest Press, Seattle.

Printed in the United States of America.
First printing. 1999.

PUBLISHER: Brainquest Press (URL: www.brainquestpress.com)
in conjunction with
Peanut Butter Publishing,
Pier 55, 1101 Alaskan Way,
Seattle WA 98101
Telephone 206 748 0345

BOOK CITATIONS:
Neppe V.M. *Cry the Beloved Mind: A Voyage of Hope.*
Seattle, WA: Brainquest Press. 1999.

FRONT COVER ART: Warren Liebmann (wliebman@wwonline.com)
BACK COVER DESIGN: David Marty.
PORTRAIT OF DR. NEPPE: Christopher Conrad

Dedication

*To all those
who have allowed me
to share with others
this remarkable
voyage of hope:*

*my esteemed patients;
my honored teachers;
my precious family;
and other beloved minds.*

Acknowledgments

Certain people stand out in terms of the assistance they have given:

- Thank you to my patients, teachers and colleagues through the years.
- Elisabeth Neppe, my wife, has been a great bastion of support and a loyal proofreader, who has helped ensure the readability of this book for the curious general reader.
- Dr. Tom Trzyna worked long hours with me during the initial development of the concepts in many of these chapters.
- Warren Liebmann, the talented Toronto photographic artist, specially designed the front cover.
- Erich von Abele contributed not only with the typing, layout, proofreading and presentation of this manuscript, but also with numerous helpful suggestions and ideas.
- The editorial suggestions of Felice Loebel, Brandel Sundt and Elliott Wolf have made this book more readable.
- Christopher Conrad prepared the back-cover photographic portrait; David Marty overviewed overall cover design; able assistance was also provided by Albert Peres, and by my webmaster, Ray Eads.
- Authors Paul Loeb, Phil Mattera, Dr. Mel Morse, Dr. Michael Norden and Paul Perry have given important practical advice.
- Candace Kovner Belair, Dr. Jay Luxenberg, Dr. Jason Schneier, Lennie Frutiger, Dr. Ted Johnson, Dr. Ren-Chieh Lien, Rachal Rapoport, Janet Simmelink, Dr. Dale Sobotka, Marlene Souriano-Vinokoor and John Walenta also assisted with specific suggestions.
- Field testing proved particularly worthwhile. This feedback process allowed for structural changes to the book making complex areas simpler to read. This way I could cater to the general reader as effectively as possible while also receiving feedback from numerous specialists. I am particularly indebted to the valuable input given by Colette Bjorkelo, Jake Ehli, Dr. Glenn Goodwin, Joseph Isaacson, Ann Knowles, Norman Mainwaring, Molly Neppe, Edna Schachter, Dr. Stan Schiff, Dr. Ronnie Schneeweiss, Dr. Machelle Seibel, Jerry Sparkman, Dr. Kurt Steinbrecher, Dr. Gary Tucker, Linda Woolf, and Harry Zeitlin.
- I particularly appreciate the support of my staff including Dawn McConnell, Leslie Nolan and Carrie Skouge.
- Nova Development Corporation in California allowed me to use clip art on the brain. This has been modified for use in this book.
- Finally, I acknowledge with gratitude the genius of Alan Paton and his book, *Cry the Beloved Country*. The phrase "Cry the Beloved" beautifully expresses what I want to say, and this great author is being honored by its revivification in my title.

About the author

Vernon Neppe, MD, PhD, is a medical specialist in neuropsychiatry and psychopharmacology. He lives with his wife and two children in Seattle, Washington, where he practices medicine as Director of the Pacific Neuropsychiatric Institute. Dr. Neppe also has a more distant academic appointment as adjunct Professor of Psychiatry and Human Behavior at St Louis University, St Louis, MO.

Dr. Neppe trained in his native South Africa and also at Cornell Medical Center in New York. In 1986, Professor Neppe founded and became Director of the first Division of Neuropsychiatry in a Department of Psychiatry in the United States (at the University of Washington in Seattle, where he is now on clinical faculty). During his prestigious career, he has received numerous board certifications, specialist qualifications and professional awards in the United States, Canada and South Africa, and is a fellow or member of seventeen professional USA and international associations. He has published extensively round the world, received research awards, and acted as a consultant for the *DSM IV*, the official psychiatric nomenclature manual. He has also lectured extensively and has chaired scientific international conferences on four continents. He also is in-demand as a speaker on brain and medicines, and he has a special skill in communicating with different audiences.

Dr. Neppe has been listed in such publications as
The Best Doctors in America,
Who's Who in the World,
Men of Achievement,
Five Thousand Personalities of the World,
Two Thousand Notable American Men and
Five Hundred Leaders of Influence.

His previous books for colleagues include
Innovative Psychopharmacotherapy and
The Psychology of Déjà Vu.
This is Dr. Neppe's first book for the general reader.

His deep empathy, special expertise and important discoveries form the foundation of this unique book directed towards general readers, patients and families, as well as students in psychology, medicine and related areas.

About this book

This is a book about hope: optimism for those with even the most extreme conditions of the mind. Those in distress will benefit enormously by the positive message of success. But then so will those interested in psychology, medicine or even a new style of writing.

The author, Dr. Vernon Neppe has outstanding credentials.
He is an internationally recognized pioneer in the fields of neuropsychiatry and psychopharmacology, and communicates that real caring, humanity, knowledge, humor, respect and warmth that we all want in our physicians.

We can identify compassionately with every unique and fascinating patient, learn to respect them, and participate in an engaging medical detective mystery of finding solutions to the seemingly insoluble.

This is a book you do not want to miss. Every page educates and enthralls the reader—whether patient, physician, intelligent general reader, student or therapist—touching important social issues ranging from gun control to informed consent. The book's broad spectrum engages interest while fascinating and teaching all at the same time.

Far more than pharmacology, this book delivers meaning for those who have lost it. Viktor Frankl did so in an abstract sense, and Norman Vincent Peale more pragmatically in his theological directions. This book promises to be the medical and pharmacological equivalent, unfolding through twelve chapters the hope that, by careful evaluation, patients can, should and will get better.

The chapters form a series of linked stories blending several real patients together into one using the new style of "sciction"—science through fiction. Through these fictitious case histories, Dr. Neppe explores how correction of the underlying biology of the brain can do wonders for one's mind. The use of extensive dialogue simplifies complex areas and allows easier targeting of specific areas of the book such as depression and anxiety, seizures, psychoses and movement disorders. Dr. Neppe provides insights into drug interactions as well as fashionable alternative medicines like St John's wort, so that it feels like one is consulting with this master clinician.

Cry the Beloved Mind has the qualities of a classic—a new style of educating, a voyage of hope for those with difficulties and a wonderful introduction to the area for students of psychology, medicine, as well as members of family and friends of patients.

Contents
Preliminaries

Chapters

Glossaries

Preface
Science Through Fiction

Cry the Beloved Mind represents a series of voyages in the pharmacology of psychiatry and neurology, reflecting a single message: there is help for the anguished patient. People can be helped, provided we are aware of the exact biochemical or electrical abnormalities involved and we have the appropriate interventions to alleviate the problems. Each of the twelve chapters is a unique voyage directed toward the same destination of exploration and hope.

This book educates and stimulates. Didactic principles about understanding symptoms and restoring health are interwoven with patient portrayals to provide concrete examples of diagnostic and therapeutic dilemmas. These techniques allow a focus on medication options, which sometimes reflect important breakthroughs in pharmacological knowledge. I hope the reader will share with me some wonderful voyages of discovery. These include the first successful treatment of profound tardive dyskinesia, the awakening of the catatonic patient, the dousing of brain fires in both non-epileptic psychotic and aggressive patients, and the normalization of patients who have lost efficacy on antidepressants. However, the complex solutions in this book portray more than a medical mystery. Respect and hope are the key themes of *Cry the Beloved Mind*.

But the pharmacology of hope would be incomplete without the crucial spice of this book: deliberate diversions that allow discussions within each chapter to explore social issues such as normality, cause and effect, searches for meaning, gun control, informed consent, labeling of patients, generic substitution, alternative herbal medicine, jet lag, regulation of medications, drug interactions, historical perspectives in psychiatry, shock treatment, and techniques such as measurement of brain waves at home.

Cry the Beloved Mind targets a wide and diverse readership. Those seeking help for themselves or a family member should benefit. Health care professionals and students of psychology, pharmacology and medicine may profit greatly. Literary scholars may be interested in the new style: *sciction*—science through fiction. Even the inquisitive senior high school student may find the concepts embodied are applicable during the iconoclasm of anomic adolescence. But most of all, I have written this book for the curious layperson: You can take pleasure in an ongoing medical and psychological detective mystery spiced with the controversial and yet primarily aimed at education and showing caring for others in need.

This book reflects my optimism that most problems linked with brain abnormalities and behavioral difficulties can be treated. Detailed clinical evaluation over many different sessions ensures that each individual's numerous unique characteristics have been carefully evaluated. Brief medical exams may contribute to the truth, but turning a life around often requires more subtle appreciation of the complexities. It is in this sense that the sciction of this book reflects an approach that I have learned, and am still learning: My many patients have taught me to look, listen and apply whatever knowledge and skills I may have to help their recovery.

The ideas in *Cry the Beloved Mind* are intended to flow as the text within sections and chapters are connected closely with the themes of the preceding ones. Yet, each chapter is a distinct entity which can be read, and hopefully understood and appreciated, on its own. Extreme facets are dramatized, yet the lessons that emerge can be widely applied. A book such as this becomes a twelve act play with different scenes in each chapter. The play calls for an intensity that makes each patient atypical; but such unique attributes exist within everyone.

The voyages described in this book reflect unusual patients and therefore require unusual solutions. If these clients can be helped, how much more so can the average patient improve? The voyage of hope is an important one, but we should never lose a sense of perspective. Most people with neurological and psychiatric disorders reflect common problems with ordinary solutions which respond well to appropriate medications. Most patients do not need these innovative approaches.

No form of treatment is a panacea. While this book is intended to communicate how, by detailed evaluation, even the most difficult of patients may be helped by medication, it is not a comprehensive didactic exposition on pharmacology or on psychiatric disease. The appropriate medical specialist, not this book, should determine how, why and when to use a specific drug. Exhaustive detail can be found in standard texts.

All books have lofty hopes. So, too, does this one. My primary hope is to help many in need, enhancing knowledge of medical and neuropsychiatric conditions, and making way for further books in the *Cry the Beloved* series. Toward this end, I also offer for scrutiny the new literary direction of sciction.

Vernon Neppe.

Prologue
The Style Of Sciction

While writing this book, I was faced with a dilemma. How do I convey important scientific information on psychiatry, neurology, social issues and medications in a vivid and readable fashion? Science, at times, is too detailed and dry; and case histories plus factual information do not easily fit the fabric of a novel.

The solution was *sciction*—science through fiction.[1]

Sciction (pronounced "skikshun") reflects the literary vehicle for the voyage of exploration that is this book: I apply the methods of medical diagnosis and treatment to the cases, but the patients they represent are fictitious amalgams.[2] I have melded concepts with composite patients to portray my approach to helping another's suffering. The object is an education far more diverse than the management of the actual patient. The *end* is greater understanding of numerous different psychiatric and pharmacological areas; the *means* is the composite illustrative patient.

Sciction allows for a special style—a play embedded in prose—to facilitate comprehension and enjoyment. The teaching model of doctor and student is woven into the dialogue of the book, just as the treating model of doctor and patient is. These interactions represent a well-established interactional teaching style. However, the added prose amplifies, links, clarifies and narrates compassionate care.

Sciction necessitates three diverse didactic leaps: Firstly, providing helpful information sometimes necessitates actually detailing doses; this may compromise the literary flow, but helps to remind us that specific dosing is critical for success. Secondly, the medical student, Andrew, through his questions and especially through the responses of the Doctor, becomes a particularly convenient educational device to convey relevant information; but of course, in reality, almost all these interactions with patients are performed in the confidentiality of the doctor–patient relationship, and not with a student present. Thirdly, a large letter beginning a paragraph separates significant theme changes. This commonly reflects time-shifts or changes in the discussion. Signifying these separations creates more intelligible portions for the reader to digest; it also allows for targeting significant interest areas more easily. This balance of detailed complex pharmacology and intelligible simplification is a delicate one: Particularly complex themes or pharmacological detail are, in addition, punctuated by an explanatory footnote linked with the large letter beginning and ending the section.[a] This way, the reader is alerted to what can

---

[a] This is such a footnote (in letters a, b, c) reflecting style. Endnotes (in numerals like 1,2,3) reflect content and are at the back of the book.

be skimmed over. These techniques allow more comfortable reading: Appropriate comfort level is a priority for education and fascination.

Stylistically, maximizing education without sacrificing clarity proved a challenge solved by a series of global structural changes aimed at greater ease of reading: The dialogue style of italics for questions and regular print for answers enables you to more easily scan for specific interest areas. I have found the "em dash" (written "–") a valuable way to define medical phrases succinctly. Other techniques are also aimed at easier comprehension: Every chapter begins with a "Key Chapter Themes" summary.[3] Furthermore, I encourage you to make use of a series of reference glossaries at the back of the book. These clarify concepts and terms. They include a brief brain diagram, drug categories, lists of neurotransmitters, definitions of medical terms, specifics on the pier and bathtub analogies in the book, medical abbreviations, generic and trade names, indexes and endnotes.[4] By these means, difficult concepts become more comprehensible to the curious layperson.

Sciction produces its own dilemmas. As a scientist, I wanted to document every comment with a reference. I fought off that temptation to make this book more readable to the lay person. I have generally found it inappropriate to cite the text, as the cases themselves are scictitious— scientific fictional composites. I have restricted citation to a minimum, in endnotes at the back of the book, identifying only the essentials of the concept under discussion or sources for amplification. Sometimes these endnotes reference my work in order to share the personal and professional voyage of discovery that is the overall thrust of this book. This allows you to resonate a little with the historical perspective. Such citations are not meant to diminish the important contributions of uncited colleagues.

The sciction style of this book allows for two interwoven elements: The unique case histories in this book fascinate, the themes in the chapters educate. However, the factual areas dealt with may reflect exceptions, not the rule. Simplification may compromise extremely complex subjects and there is a danger of loss of perspective if specific patient experiences are too easily generalized. Most patients do not require extreme measures to improve; most physician consults yield beneficial results; and critiques of particular drugs do not imply the medications are deficient, just unsuitable for the portrayed scictitious patient. Individual bad reactions do not make medications globally inappropriate. Pharmacological interventions generally involve the subtle balance of beneficial effects far outweighing side effects; and profound adverse reactions are relatively rare in practice. "When you hear the hoof beats you should think of horses not zebras." *Cry the Beloved Mind* portrays the exotic mysteries of zebras, even as it teaches the general principles of horses.

Vernon Neppe

Chapter 1

Awakenings Revisited

Catatonic stupor—past and present.
Dopamine, informed consent, neurotransmitters, Pellagra,
schizophrenia. Sinemet and levodopa, high dose vitamins.
Voyage of new discovery.
(Priscilla, Jocelyn: patients; Madelaine: Jocelyn's mother),
(Edward, Andrew: students); (boat analogy) [3]

She sat like a waxy figure: mute, unable to communicate, yet seemingly taking in her environment, a wooden statue, eyes staring vacantly into space, arms planted in whatever direction we cared to move them.

I clapped my hands. There was a small blink. I tried to coerce her to follow my movements, pointing across from right to left. Her eyes moved slightly. She was responsive to her environment, clearly taking in some subjective aspect of her bizarre world, yet sitting like this immobile, inanimate object.

There she was, seemingly molded out of *marble*. Yet marble cannot be moved; and I could move these arms to wherever I wanted. With this passive movement and yet total inactivity in her own voluntary movements, it felt as if I was moving a pliable piece. Rather, one could say, she was shaped out of *plastic*. She had plastic tone, and this stiffness in the muscles, or the lack of it, is typical of the catatonic patient.

Edward, a gifted medical student, was with me in the examining room.

What's wrong with her, Doctor?
Priscilla has catatonia, a strange neuropsychiatric–neurological plus psychiatric–condition. She's aware of her environment, but unable to respond. She hears, sees and maybe even thinks, but remains in this bizarre reality where she cannot respond to her environment yet is conscious of what's going on. She seems aware of what's happening. No doubt, her thinking and emotions are distorted, but we cannot prove this because she's in a cocoon where we cannot intrude.

So how are we going to approach evaluating Priscilla?
Usually, we obtain clues on medical history from the patient and clarify information with the family; but we don't have this opportunity with Priscilla. So we're going to use the basic time-honored method of medicine: We'll make a diagnosis based on examining her.

Can we diagnose anything specific?
Yes. Because she seems to be aware and only her responsiveness is impaired, we first diagnose the catatonic syndrome–the symptom cluster. Next, we look for a cause of her catatonia. There are multiple reasons for catatonic states to happen, including the main causes listed in most textbooks–schizophrenia and manic-depression. But we have found a special clue with Priscilla: Her malnourished presentation suggests a deficiency of a chemical in the brain and this may have caused her strange behavior. Priscilla could have a psychiatric presentation due to a neurological condition in the brain. If we can isolate the chemical and replace it, Priscilla will respond dramatically.

It was the early 1970s. The scene was a hospital for the less privileged in a poverty-stricken area of South Africa. I was a young medical intern. My patient, Priscilla, was to be my introduction as to how appropriate therapeutic interventions can profoundly and positively impact the brain. Priscilla's catatonia molded my career.

We examined Priscilla.

Her skin has these little flaky lesions that are falling off!
Yes, and it's rough. We call this dermatitis–a complicated medical way to portray a skin condition. But strangely, this dermatitis is one of the "Ds" of an unusual condition.
What condition?
Pellagra. This disease is due to a profound B-vitamin deficiency. It's a condition seldom, if ever, found today in our Western cultures.

2

What are the other "Ds" of pellagra?
We talk of the classic triad—the "3 Ds": dermatitis which you've seen; diarrhea which she has; and dementia—a chronic brain condition associated with memory and intellectual deterioration.[5]
Does she have the dementia, Doctor?
No, Edward. Priscilla does not seem to exhibit the "D" of dementia. However, her mute state and bizarre non-responsiveness despite the clear consciousness don't allow us to assess her memory or intellect for brain deterioration. In any event, the "D" of dementia may be a misnomer because catatonic states are more common in Pellagra than dementia is.

How long has she been this way?
For a couple of days. She was at home until this evening. You can see she is dehydrated—look how dry her skin is. Part of this fluid deficiency is her not drinking water and the other side is her diarrhea. I think her diarrheal soiling may be because of her non-caring.
What do you mean, Doctor?
She's in a state where she totally neglects herself. She doesn't move and cannot care even for such functions as excretion of body fluids. Without treatment, Priscilla would die in a week or less.

So what should be done?
We will give her very high doses of the specific B vitamins that she's deficient in—thiamine and nicotinic acid in large amounts, several thousand milligrams through an intravenous line.
We need to give her nothing else? What about strong psychiatric drugs?
No. Ed. We're treating the actual cause. Watch for a miracle. [b]

It was like the waking of the dead.
Priscilla had presented to us at 11 PM. By the next morning, she was talking, coherent, moving about, no longer a statue, and no longer exhibiting the catatonic plastic tone. I had cured my first case of Pellagrous encephalopathy.

Priscilla was delighted.
Doctor, I feel human again.
How can someone the night before be completely non-responsive and unable to talk, and in the morning, after receiving only vitamins, become a beloved human being again?

I looked at her in amazement.

---

[b] Single letters in large font indicate either a short advance in time or a shift of theme. Using the theater analogy, the next section would be Act 1, Scene 2.

I'm so pleased for you, Priscilla. This need never happen to you again. Let's ensure that you receive sufficient vitamin supplements to prevent it.

> Priscilla swung her arms out in front of her, in delight, as if to say "Look what I can do."

I will never let this happen to me. They tell me I was like a statue. It's hard for me to even understand how I was!

> Edward, the student, was also astonished at Priscilla's overnight recovery.

This is remarkable, Doctor! But why does Pellagra happen?
Because the brain's biochemical pathways are not able to perform what should be done. The specific deficiency is niacin, and previously in the deep south in the United States, where it was prevalent in the 1920s, this B vitamin was actually called "pellagra preventive factor". As you saw, Edward, Priscilla had totally slowed down to an absolute statue, until we could give her the right fuels to re-invigorate her.

It's amazing.
Yes it is and, although these vitamins reflect standard care for this condition, the response is certainly impressive.

> Priscilla was so much better that we were able to discharge her into her sister's care that very day. She went home along with enormous doses of vitamins and appropriate dietary supplementation. Medical follow-up was scheduled for a few days later. My introduction to the wonders of finding the right medicine for the right condition left an indelible imprint. Suddenly, my intention to do pediatrics moved away and I became a neuropsychiatrist instead.
>
> I had deliberately chosen to work with underprivileged patients in South Africa. This reward of seeing people such as Priscilla responding so dramatically to appropriate medication could not be measured in words. It opened up the ultimate practice of medicine: the caring angle, the framework of trying to help for no other purpose than to allow another person to re-experience health. To me, the gift was the awareness that, given the right biochemistry and the correct underlying lesion, we could manage the great majority of problems that present themselves. At the miracle of Priscilla's reawakening, I wanted to cry: from joy. I had had personal experience that a beloved mind could be saved.

That early experience, of perceiving a catatonic patient responding so completely to vitamin therapy, was the precursor not only for a career in psychopharmacology and neuropsychiatry. It also was revisited many years later by a fascinating re-experience of catatonia.

It was fifteen years later—the late 1980s. Great changes had occurred in all our lives. Priscilla, the catatonic with Pellagra, had not relapsed. Ed, the student, had become Edward, the physician and, in fact, Edward, the Psychiatrist: Like me, he too had been intrigued enough from that experience with Priscilla to enter the discipline of the *mind*. He realized the brain was insufficient; there was a person behind the brain—a soul, a human, a mind.

However, for me, not only had the decade changed, but the country had as well. I had relocated from South Africa to the United States. Countries and decades had shifted: the setting was different, yet the same context remained. Years of experience in neuropsychiatry had deepened my understanding of my initial impression: People can be helped and handled with the respect that they deserve. We need only find the underlying biological problem. If we can do this, we can treat, and lives will improve dramatically. Hope is a door away. But the door may be camouflaged. Such a search may not be easy, and it may require several mid-course corrections where we have to rethink what had been thought before; yet the rewards, to the patient and to the doctor, are illimitable.

Priscilla and Edward had, by circumstance, been paired together so many years before: a catatonic patient in torment evaluated by a medical student experiencing his first introduction to the area of significant brain disturbance. Now with Andrew, my new American medical student, I was embarking on a fresh educational voyage. Ironically, another catatonic patient, Jocelyn, would serve as Andrew's first introduction to brain disease.

She sat there, an attractive, blonde lady, disheveled though well nourished. I tried hard to attract her attention, yet, nothing seemed to do so. Between times, I had this subtle impression that, maybe, she was following my movements with her eyes, despite her absolute mutism and her waxy flexibility. She could have been the Mona Lisa, so quiet, and yet so intriguing to everyone around. Jocelyn brought back the picture of Priscilla of so long before.

But Jocelyn did not have the stigmata of Pellagra, with skin lesions and gross vitamin deficiencies. Hers was a more subtle biochemical condition, but the label was the same: catatonic stupor. Here I was, on a different continent, America, with a different student, Andrew, in a different decade, the 80s, facing the same dilemma: How do I handle Jocelyn? How can I make her life better? How do I instill hope into her very being? Will her family light up with the pleasure of seeing this beautiful lady functional again? Could it be that I will have the opportunity to impact on her life? I hoped this would be so, because I had a treatment planned for Jocelyn: very different from high-dose vitamins, but all the same, a powerful and logical, yet pioneering intervention at that time.

Andrew, the tall, dark-haired, bespectacled medical student assigned to me, began what was to become a long line of well-reasoned questions.

Does catatonia always involve this waxy statuesque presentation?
No. Remarkably, catatonia is a disease of extremes. The catatonic state manifests as either extreme excitement where the person is moving all over, or as extreme retardation. It is this retardation, this catatonic stupor, that's associated with the waxy, passive flexibility and the waning of tone in the muscles. [6]

When people have catatonic excitement, how do they present?
They're extremely active, always doing things, never stopping.

But are they not then manic?
This is why some argue that catatonia is closer to manic-depressive psychosis—which we now call bipolar affective disorder—than schizophrenia; but, no, they're not then manic. The major difference is purpose. The manic patient is very active and remarkably alert. They do purposeful actions, even though these acts may land them in difficulties, like spending sprees or sexual promiscuity. The manic may have a grandiose self-perception: a supreme being, or the richest person in the world. Patients with catatonic excitement, on the other hand, are totally disorganized in their thinking. There's no basis for their actions. They may toss objects about the room, tear up chart notes randomly, laugh inappropriately or talk so illogically that their conversation sounds like and is actually called "word salad". Mania is a relatively common condition, seen many times a year by psychiatrists. Catatonic excitement is very rare, seen maybe once

or twice a decade. Sometimes patients vacillate between catatonic stupor and catatonic excitement.

The condition sounds fascinating!
Yes, Andrew, it is intriguing, but we should always remember the human behind the condition. You are entering a very rewarding profession where we can help people.

Andrew had begun where Ed had left off: I was to learn how his fascination moved him to assiduously explore all options to a greater knowledge and understanding in his chosen profession of medicine.

So is Jocelyn's catatonia, which is unassociated with vitamin deficiency, linked with schizophrenia?
It could well be, Andrew. At one point, catatonia was perceived to be a primary feature of schizophrenia. This catatonic state opened the way to a diagnosis. Other conditions can cause catatonia, but having reviewed Jocelyn's history, examination and investigations, I believe she has schizophrenia.

Doctor, I know that I should know, but what is schizophrenia?
Andrew, I'm glad you ask and don't just assume; knowing that you don't know is sometimes closer to knowledge than we think. Never feel, Andrew, that you cannot ask even the most basic of questions, because such questions are seldom simple; and, often when you think you should know, there is no way you can actually know. Just because you're a medical student doesn't provide you with a fount of special medical erudition. This needs to be acquired, just like the curious layperson could acquire such knowledge, if they could sit in on our sessions.
So in this instance, you've asked what may sound like an easy question, but in reality, it refers to one of the most complex of all psychiatric conditions.

Schizophrenia is a major psychotic condition.
Psychotic? Is that the same as psychosis?
Yes. The adjective and the noun. Psychosis refers to a state of out-of-touchness with reality and impaired insight—the patients do not realize they are ill.

But why the name, schizophrenia?
This refers to the *schism* between emotion and thinking.

What does the schism refer to exactly?

There's a separation of cognition from affect—thinking from emotion. The schizophrenic may laugh at a funeral: the inappropriate conduct and incongruous emotionality may be due to crazy thoughts that only he can understand.

Is this the key to schizophrenia?
No. There's also a disorder of thinking associated with illogical internal connections of thought. Two disparate topics may suddenly become enjoined together in a way that only the patient understands—idiosyncratic ideas are hallmarks of the condition. We use the term "thought disorder" to describe this. The patient exhibits other distortions of thinking characterized by delusions—fixed false beliefs, and hallucinations—perceptions without stimulus.

Like?
Like delusions of aliens controlling his brain, or auditory hallucinations in which the poor patient hears non-existent frightening voices. But these hallucinations are not as characteristic of schizophrenia as the disorder in thinking with the abnormal linking of thoughts, their special meanings and the illogical conclusions—the delusions—based on realities that are impaired. Schizophrenic hallucinations are usually exclusively auditory distortions of their perception—hearing voices which do not exist.
However, they are commonly linked in content with the delusional ideas that the patient has.

Aren't there other components besides the delusions and thought disorder?
Yes, schizophrenia manifests not only with the disorder in thinking, but also with the progressive "blunting of affect"—a diminution in range of emotion.

Anything else?
Yes. A neglected but important characteristic is a marked withdrawal into one's own cocoon—technically called "autism". You may recognize the word from the rare childhood condition with this name, but actually autistic withdrawal—retreat into one's own reality—is a primary feature of schizophrenia. This symptom is frequently linked with profound apathy and a marked lack of motivation so that even when we control the schizophrenic hallucinations and delusions, often these patients cannot function because of this amotivation. However, catatonia, at one point perceived as a primary feature of the schizophrenic illness, is no longer regarded as necessarily characteristic.

How is it manifested?

Again, we see the catatonia in schizophrenia in its two different extremes: extreme agitation, and extreme retardation reflecting the catatonic stupor with the waxy flexibility and the waning of tone in the muscles.

Does Jocelyn have the symptoms of schizophrenia?
Yes, Andrew, it appears so based on her psychiatric history. I have invited Jocelyn's mother to join us, to fill in the gaps prior to this episode.

Andrew wished to link our discussion to Jocelyn. We could do this more easily because of the third person, Madelaine, Jocelyn's mother, who had just entered my office.

Welcome, Madelaine. Would you be able to help us?
Madelaine smiled, but not happily. There was a wistfulness in her voice and an all too obvious sadness.

I can clarify a great deal, Doctor. I'm a psychologist and have worked with mental illness, so I understand more than many people what my precious daughter has been through. Still, I confess, at times, to being overwhelmed by the retrogression that my husband and I have seen with Jocelyn.[c]

I could only empathize with this poor parent.
I'm listening.
Doctor, Jocelyn was such a normal child. She worked hard at school, though she could be described as a loner. She graduated from high-school on the honors roll for academic achievement. I always believed she would fly through College. But it was not to be.
In her late teens, she began to change. Jocelyn became progressively more withdrawn into herself, and socialized very little. She was previously an avid reader, but complained she couldn't concentrate much. She neglected her appearance. She seemed to go progressively downhill, with no interest in others.
She obtained a job at a fast food restaurant that lasted less than a week: She would arrive late for work, and her employers reported she would stare into space.
She was probably hallucinating.

The day before she was fired she did not even attend work. She was exhausted having been up all night "on guard."
I knew no drugs were involved, and I feared the worst.

---

[c] This is the only section of this book where the regular (non-italicized font) in the dialogue section does not involve the Doctor but the temporary narrator of Jocelyn's psychiatric history, Madelaine.

At that stage, I tried to persuade her to see a psychiatrist, but she refused.
"There's nothing wrong with me."
I cannot but remember my initial distress when she, suddenly, looked at me with disgust and sobbed:
"So you're part of it as well."
> Jocelyn had clearly had a sudden delusional awareness of an unfounded truth.

> Madelaine continued to talk about her daughter, Jocelyn:
What "it" was, was unclear to me at the time, but later on, I realized it had to do with the Nazis.
Jocelyn then had a period of acute out-of-touchness with reality, which the doctors called a "psychotic break". Initially, we were mystified as to what she was thinking, because she refused to discuss her thoughts with anyone.

Eventually, she whispered to my husband:
"They are putting rays into my mind"

And then the whole story, came out, piece by piece.
"We're being controlled from afar by waves being propagated through the radio. They're trying to take over this country. Only I can stop them!"
I remember asking her: "But who is doing this terrible thing?" She had looked at me, surprised.
"But don't you know? How can you defend yourself if you cannot apprehend them? It's the Nazis. They've been trying to rape me during sleep."

I had tried to reason with her. "But this cannot be, they're not here."
"They do it from Europe! That's why they're so dangerous. You don't know how exhausting it is not being able to sleep, always being on guard!"
Naturally, she was worried about going to sleep, but she never could stay awake for 24 hours and be completely energized.

> I interrupted briefly:
So Jocelyn did not have a presentation of mania as her sleep disruption exhausted her and she could not stay up beyond a day, without utter fatigue?
That's right, Doctor.

Instead, hers was a disruption of sleep because she was too suspicious to sleep—paranoid—and needed to be on guard. We call this excessive state of being on guard, "hypervigilance". It's rather ironic that she is now not vigilant at all, in her nonresponsive and mute—absence of speech—catatonic state.

There's one more element, Doctor.

10

What's that?
At times, she would laugh inappropriately, responding to the voices she heard; she could not quite make them out yet she found them somehow extraordinarily funny, even though they were the voices of Nazis.

Madelaine, you're describing the typical "incongruous affect"—emotional schism with thinking—that we see in early schizophrenic illness.
Yes. Indeed, Jocelyn was then hospitalized in her twenties with symptoms diagnosed by her doctors as "schizophrenia".

I appreciate your psychological insights into this tragic story, Madelaine.
Thank you, Doctor.

Madelaine could not hold back her tears.
Would you please excuse me, Doctor?
Of course. Thank you so much for giving us these insights into your daughter.

Andrew had been listening intently to this interchange. He had been intrigued by the reversal of roles. Madelaine had been so concise with Jocelyn's psychiatric history that she could have been a doctor speaking. I had listened, almost like the student. But then much of the practice of medicine is listening to one's patients and their families, learning from them, empathizing with their traumas and rejoicing with them when improvements occur.

It was two hours later. I had had the opportunity to obtain further information from Madelaine, which I shared with Andrew. [d]

Jocelyn was hospitalized four years ago for the psychotic break that her mother described. She was treated with antipsychotic medication—neuroleptics—for what was, in retrospect, correctly diagnosed as a schizophrenic condition. She improved considerably, and even returned to college where she studied economics for two years.

That sounds promising.
Yes. She initially took her medication regularly and very carefully. All this time, however, she abhorred social contacts and would sit alone in her little office.

---

[d] For the rest of this book: The Doctor's comments are in regular print; Andrew or the patient's shorter comments or questions are in italics.

11

She would speak to no one unless spoken to and answering monosyllabi-
cally, seldom with any face to face contact. She took her Navane—a potent
antipsychotic—and, outwardly, she seemed to cope for two years.

So she was okay while on medication?
Yes, but unfortunately, about a year ago, she realized that there was
nothing wrong with her. She stopped her medication. She did not talk
about how her family had all now secretly joined the Nazis because she
felt it was important that they do not know that she knew the truth. Instead, she ceased all social contact. Gradually, she became more withdrawn. She had been working as a bookkeeper for six months at the time,
but she was dismissed from her job. Jocelyn realized this dismissal was
perfectly logical because it turned out her employers were also Nazis.

How did Jocelyn present this time?
Three days ago, she was found sitting disheveled in her home in a puddle
of urine. She had clearly not washed for days. She had soiled herself. She
reeked. She was quite statuesque and utterly mute: an observer who was
barely alive, yet physically had no signs of organic illness.

Is she psychotic during this time of immobility?
Only in the sense, Andrew, that psychosis means out of touchness with
reality. However, I think catatonia is really a state of altered consciousness so technically, it is different. Psychosis, strictly speaking, should be
limited to states in which the consciousness is clear, where patients are
aware and can respond.

Does that mean that psychosis is permanent and hopeless?
Certainly not! Sometimes labels like psychosis imply that the patient is
already condemned and the only place to go to is a mental hospital. This
is a small minority. Almost invariably, we find we can treat psychosis. We
have to understand differences: There's mild or moderate or severe flu.
Also, the flu gets better quickly, but some infections, like tuberculosis,
may persist. This is the same with psychosis, catatonia and schizophrenia.
We aim at managing the remediable, not missing treatable causes and
recognizing the chronicity of some conditions.

How do we treat?
Generally with psychiatric medications.
We call this discipline "psychopharmacology".

*Had Jocelyn's previous psychiatrist used psychopharmacological interven-
tions, like antipsychotic medication?*
Yes. Every time Jocelyn has been ill, she has been loaded with antipsychotics.

12

What's the rationale of antipsychotics?
They're a particularly fascinating group of drugs. They're based largely on a theory of psychosis that focuses on a specific neurotransmitter, the chemical "dopamine". Once you understand neurotransmitters, brain conditions and their treatment become simpler.

T hat word "neurotransmitter" had triggered it. By the sparkle in Andrew's eye, I knew we were in for an important teaching session.

I had, in fact, allocated several hours a week of one on one time with Andrew, so that he could learn about peripheral issues relevant to patient care, medicine and life itself.
Ultimately, we would always return to the patient's problems, and sometimes, I even preferred the patients to actively participate in our interchanges. This allowed him to develop a perspective. Using patient symptoms and treatment options as jumping points to peripheral medical diversions has proven an excellent way over the years of educating students and patients, and Andrew was no exception.

And what are neurotransmitters?
Neurotransmitters are a technical medical term for a group of several different chemicals that are transmitted through the nerves and produce a response each time they pass from one nerve ending to another. You can imagine there's a little bridge they have to cross, and we call that the "synaptic cleft" because the connection of these nerve endings are termed "synapses". When these chemicals cross at that point, they will produce results.

Which chemicals?
You ask an important and difficult question, Andrew. Bear with me on this because you will be applying this knowledge to most drugs that act on the brain. So I will summarize here: One major chemical is this dopamine, which is linked up with motivation, planning and movements; but dopamine is also associated with disease states like psychosis, catatonia, Parkinson's disease, and a terrible disabling condition due to medication, tardive dyskinesia. [7] Another critical chemical is serotonin, and this is the great controller of a variety of different complex behaviors and psychological experiences, as well as simple physiological regulatory functions, such as hormone influences and breathing. A third neurotransmitter is norepinephrine, also called noradrenaline, and this is more involved with such immediate effects as the "fight, fright or flight response". [8] Is that enough for you, Andrew?

No, Doctor. I want to hear about the others, too.

13

> I was beginning to see that Andrew had an unrelenting desire for knowledge.

All right, Andrew. There's acetylcholine, which seems to play more of a balancing role, but it's certainly involved in memory, and also has linkups with strange movement effects such as those in Parkinson's disease. Of increasing importance is the opioid system which is involved in pain control. You wouldn't think morphine-like substances are located in the brain itself, but they are; you may have heard of endorphins. There are a variety of other neurotransmitters as well, some of which are relevant in electrical transfers as opposed to chemical ones, and these are linked up with seizure disorders.

Which neurotransmitter chemicals are linked with seizures?
Those linked with seizures have particularly complex names, like GABA and NMDA.[9] GABA is predominantly inhibitory; NMDA mainly excitatory, as is the major excitatory seizure-linked neurotransmitter, glutamine. [10] Don't worry too much about these names: Remember only that special neurotransmitters exist in electrical reactions and that they are at this point not as well understood as many of those for chemical reactions. So this is an overview: Neurotransmission is an extremely important part of brain function and basic to psychopharmacology.

> Andrew, having bit off a bit more than he could chew, looked a little overwhelmed. I consoled him.

Don't worry. The important point at this stage is the principle. There are many different chemicals controlling the brain, and they all "talk" to each other in the context of a remarkably unified whole.

Do all these neurotransmitters arise from the same spot?
No, in fact, the cells that manufacture these neurotransmitters generally predominate in different parts of the lower brain, the so-called "brain stem". In turn, they send their chemicals to different areas of the brain where they exert their influence. So, for example, dopamine...

Yes. Where is that localized?
It originates in the highest part of the brain-stem called the mid-brain. Dopamine controls motor function—movements. Dopamine also impacts via nerve connections to the emotional brain, which we call the limbic system. So it affects emotions and movements.

So this is why dopamine is important in schizophrenia and catatonia?
Exactly, Andrew. This compound, dopamine, is perceived to be in excess in the conventional psychoses that we refer to as schizophrenia-like, or schizophreniform.

14

How are these conditions treated?
We treat psychosis with medications that lower the amount of dopamine. But I wish it were that simple. Dopamine signals are used for multiple very different purposes in the brain. Our medications are unfortunately not specific enough. A drug may decrease the levels of dopamine in one area to a normal level, but at the same time decrease the levels of dopamine in another area to a subnormal level.

And this results in ...?
Sometimes this produces a new imbalance which looks like Parkinson's disease. We call this "extrapyramidal symptoms"—the patients become stiff and rigid, tremulous, and limited in facial expression; they walk with small, rather deliberate steps, but almost looking as if they're out of balance. This drug-induced Parkinson's condition is associated possibly with too much dopamine depletion in relation to a second neurotransmitter, acetylcholine. Multiple neurotransmitters balance particular functions by complex interactions. These interactions or conversations are technically called "cross-talk".

I can see it's no simple process.
Indeed not. It is this interaction of these different chemicals that makes psychopharmacology so complex and so difficult, because no receptor or receptor subtype is an island. They all inter-communicate in so many special ways.

Could we say that receptors are the receptacles at which all these chemicals act?
Yes, Andrew, and you could further perceive these receptors as the various piers on a dock. The chemicals arrive on their boats and moor there. Sometimes passengers climb off to do their business, in which case the receptors produce an action, which we call "agonism" or activation.
Sometimes passengers cannot climb off because competing boats—other body chemicals or medications—are occupying the pier and blocking them from mooring: in other words, there's blockade, and the regular boats cannot come in. We call this "antagonism" or prevention of the activation; in this context, inhibition. [11]

Are antagonism and inhibition the same?
These are important, difficult concepts. You'll use them again and again. So let's clarify them. You can imagine that some of these receptors work not by stimulating but by preventing. They are, in effect, acting as negative receptors, by controlling. There needs to be a brake as well as an accelerator. Cross-talk occurs all the time. So you can see how they might stimulate negatively, ultimately producing inhibition of the whole system: To borrow from arithmetic, a negative times a positive remains negative.

But stimulation and agonism are not necessarily the same?
Correct. Agonism activates a receptor, but that receptor could act posi-tively—producing an action by stimulation, or negatively—preventing ac-tions by inhibition.

We could use the boat-pier analogy again, right?
Yes, Andrew. The dopamine boat comes into the dock and tries to moor itself at the pier—the receptor—in order to have influence there, but it can-not. The specific pier is occupied by another competing boat which de-pending on its properties might either cause passengers to climb off the boat and go to shore—it stimulates the receptor—or if it's an antagonist competitor boat, it will occupy the pier—the receptor—and in so doing block the dopamine boat from attaching itself and working.

Is there just one dopamine, serotonin and norepinephrine receptor?
No, Andrew, it's even more complicated. You can imagine every one of these receptors have their own families. So, for example, there are fifteen or more different serotonin receptors, and we keep discovering more do-pamine receptors, although two fundamental ones are dopamine-1 and dopamine-2.

So there is more than one dopamine receptor?
Correct. We call these "receptor subtypes", and they, too, communicate with each other and control each other. Each subtype is distinct not only by its actions, but because of its location in the brain, and its molecular structure.

I shifted gears.
But enough on receptors. Let's apply our knowledge to our patient, Jocelyn.

Andrew looked at Jocelyn and then up at me, quizzically.
Do you think Jocelyn knows what's happening around her?
That's a difficult one. Based on my experience of other catatonic patients, I suspect that she is at least partly aware of her environment: Patients coming out of these catatonic stupors are generally able to tell me what's going on and are able to remember events in great detail.

Does Jocelyn want to get out of that state? Do you think she wants to be like this?
Again, I think there's no easy answer. Certainly, there may be certain profound psychological causes that have shifted her to such a state. Maybe the Nazis have told her not to move otherwise the world would be blown up. These psychological causes are very much linked up with un-

16

derlying abnormalities at the biological level, producing chemical imbalances. Consequently, her perceptions of reality may be difficult and whether she would want to return to the more conventional responsive reality would be debatable.

Is she remembering this experience?
When I've asked other catatonic patients about this after they came out of their stupor, some implied that they remembered everything, but didn't feel constrained to respond to anything. Others recall with amazement what was happening to them with the implication that they would like to have returned to responsiveness, but could not. I suspect that the truth may well lie with deeper internal psychological motivation.

This stirred up an interesting question from Andrew.
Doctor, would you not want to put yourself into a catatonic state, maybe by taking some drug to see what it's like, so that you could actually record what's happening after you come out of the experience?
Personally not, Andrew. First, it's unlikely the drugs would produce such a catatonic state, because there are many other adverse effects which would happen before such a condition developed. Second, even if I became catatonic, the drug might cause more harm than anticipated: It might be just a short-lived harm via the direct effects of the drug, but it could be maintained for a prolonged period because I do not biochemically need the drug and my body may produce changes which could long outlive the drug. In addition, this experimentation may destabilize systems that may well have been stabilized before, so the risks would be enormous.

Any other side to the argument?
Probably not. You're right that it would be fascinating to be able to experience this first-hand; I can do without such fascination!

Is there any parallel that could shed light on this?
There is. Regrettably, some people indiscriminately use "non-prescribed drugs of abuse", euphemistically referred to as "recreational drugs". A small sub-group have deliberately gone on these so-called "trips" to understand what it's like. They have even scientifically recorded their experiences with hallucinogens—drugs that induce hallucinations—like lysergic acid diethylamide (LSD). This is something I strongly discourage because even one "trip" may destabilize functioning, not only short-term, but even potentially long-term. However, there are numerous such records, sometimes by experts, or their students, who have experimented under controlled conditions. [12]

17

Madelaine entered the room once more, and looked at me, her eyes sad.

Do you think she's suffering, Doctor? Is this a painful experience? I noticed there is music playing. Can she experience any pleasure from that music?

I looked at Madelaine empathically.

I don't know. I have no evidence that catatonics experience any pleasure. On the other hand, I suspect that this is almost like a bizarre dream state, where the patient does not perceive anything to a profound degree. It's further complicated by the underlying condition, such as the schizophrenic thinking. This, in turn, is often associated with a distortion and a blunting in emotions, such that many of these patients do not experience the appreciable range of emotions that most people experience.

The sadness in her eyes softened a bit.
At least she probably isn't suffering.

Andrew, too, was interested, but intellectually and less so emotionally: It was early in his career. He had yet not yet reached the level of real caring prerequisite for good medical practice; but that would come.

How long has Jocelyn been in this state, Doctor?
She has been in this mute, wakeful, yet non-responsive state for ten days now. She came into the hospital a week ago and she has been receiving antipsychotic medication since then.

What do these antipsychotics portend for Jocelyn's treatment?
Her antipsychotic drugs—her neuroleptics—should treat any hallucinations and delusions which may be linked to her catatonic state and we believe these psychotic features are likely submerged deep in her consciousness. We therefore use these "neuroleptics" because we know that she likely has an underlying psychotic condition and if we impact this, then maybe she would begin talking and come out of her catatonic state.

Are conventional antipsychotic medications the logical first treatment for catatonia?
Strangely, not, Andrew. There's an interesting anomaly in this regard. When animals were studied to discover new antipsychotic medications, one way to determine if those drugs had antipsychotic effects was through an indirect observation. You cannot diagnose psychosis in a rat, but what can be done is to notice whether or not a chemical produces this same waxy flexibility state of catatonic stupor, which in the animal model is re-

18

ferred to as "catalepsy". If the drug produces this cataleptic state, it's likely that it produces an antipsychotic effect.

That sounds like a strange paradox!
Indeed it is: A patient presenting with a schizophrenia-like illness with a catatonic type state; yet on the other hand, the antipsychotic drugs used to treat schizophrenia produce the same catatonic state in animals. These neuroleptic drugs work in psychosis because they block up the dopamine system yet catatonia is linked with this very blockade of dopamine.

Is there an explanation for this strange dopamine paradox?
Possibly. You'll remember how neurotransmitters may work in different areas. Dopamine could be deficient in relevant lower regions of the brain producing the immobilization of catatonia and yet it could at the same time be excessive in the higher brain producing psychotic thinking.

So you should, in reality, not expect antipsychotics to work in catatonia?
You're right, Andrew. Jocelyn has continued to be non-responsive to conventional neuroleptics and this is not unexpected: In fact, this lack of response is almost invariable in catatonia. Nevertheless, in the customary medical management of this condition, neuroleptics, paradoxically still remain the first line of treatment because physicians are trying to improve the deeply submerged psychotic state that may also exist.

Andrew and I settled down for another didactic session together. Such meetings would become common over the next few months, and, in fact, my mentoring of Andrew would continue intermittently over a decade into his medical career. This is what medical education is all about: continuing to learn, refreshing oneself with new ideas and ultimately contributing to the patient.

> We applied the typical common student-physician interaction. I verbalized this to Andrew:

The ancient Greek philosopher, Socrates, initiated the question-and-answer method of teaching as a means of achieving self-knowledge. His theories of virtue and justice survived through Plato, his most important pupil.
In ways, in medicine, we still try to practice Socratically, applying integrity and compassion. But even more so, the style of medical education is Socratic. The student or the patient asks the question, the doctor answers. The teacher stimulates the student or patient to learn and learns from him as well.

This time Andrew stumbled inadvertently on a controversial area.

What are the known acute treatments for Jocelyn's catatonic state?
The predominant one is electroconvulsive therapy–ECT–so-called "shock therapy". Shock treatment, possibly because of its name more than anything else, has become synonymous to the lay person with something which is an insult to the patient's brain. Imagine passing a direct electrical current through the patient's brain!

Yet isn't it harmful? All I know about shock treatment is the negative way it was portrayed in that movie "One Flew Over the Cuckoo's Nest."
People at times will raise their hands in disgust and amazement that psychiatrists can be so cruel as to contemplate shocking patients. I truly do not like the term "shock". This has become an extremely inappropriate, denigrating lay term for a scientific, relevant and safe procedure. It's unfortunate that most people do not have appropriate information on this, at times, miraculous procedure.

But what is its success record?
Strangely enough, ECT has proven to be the single most effective treatment for getting patients out of the catatonic state and also for intractable depression.

Does it have problems?
Ones which we can solve. For example, anesthesia is necessary. Also, in the patient with depression, there might be some memory impairments. These can continue for several months after the procedure; but the poor memory is usually more than balanced by the degree of cognitive improvement–of enhancement in thinking–that follows on the amelioration of the depression. Consider that conventional antidepressant responses in the severely depressed occur in only three out of four patients; ECT is extraordinarily effective in the refractory agitated depressed patients–the group who do not respond to antidepressants–some would say 90% or 95% effective.

Even more effective than our antidepressant medications?
Yes, this is a truly remarkable statistic considering that ECT is often only performed on the most intractable of patients where even a 20% response would be considered good. Certainly, we see the need for ECT in the more difficult depressive who often presents in a university setting because of previous response failures.

W e shifted back to Jocelyn:

Is electroconvulsive therapy indicated with Jocelyn?
I don't think so. I have decided to hold off on electroconvulsive therapy, despite knowing that it should help her catatonic state, because I want to treat the cause rather than the symptoms alone. We can always use ECT as a last resort, the way it's used in depression, in the refractory—the non-responsive—patient. We may see an immediate response with ECT in catatonia, though because ECT is not treating the cause, we would be achieving only a temporary, though effective reprieve.

How then can we can take Jocelyn out of her catatonia?
If we apply the models we have discussed, Jocelyn's state seems to be associated with dopamine deficiency. Consequently, a logical approach would be to be to allow her brain to produce extra dopamine.

How are you going to do it?
One way would be for Jocelyn to receive a dopamine agonist drug. Let's use our boat–pier analogy, a metaphor you will repeatedly apply, Andrew. We will move Jocelyn out of her catatonic state by occupying and stimulating the dopamine pier.

But if schizophrenia relates to too much dopamine, won't it just make her worse?
Yes, it may. It's likely she will then manifest the psychotic condition that is probably camouflaged by her catatonia at the moment, but we cannot avoid that, and if that happens, we can treat it with antipsychotics. [13]

Then will you give dopamine to Jocelyn?
Not quite: We cannot give straight dopamine itself because it does not pass through the special blood-brain barrier that allows access to the brain. One solution is to give levodopa, a so-called "precursor drug"—it doesn't work itself, but becomes chemically active when converted in the body. In this instance, levodopa becomes dopamine. However, there is a problem when we use levodopa alone: Levodopa may make the dopamine in the brain that we want, but it also produces dopamine in the peripheral body—outside the brain.

And this results in…?
This produces major side-effects: nausea, raising of the blood pressure, and headache. This restricts its use to a relatively low dose and therefore its brain effects may be inadequate.

How can we solve that?
The solution reflects one of the wonders of modern combination pharmacology. The drug Sinemet, marketed for treating Parkinson's disease, allows some of the levodopa to cross into the brain, then quickly disables

the remaining part that stays in the periphery and so alleviates the side-effects. It is a brilliantly conceived combination drug: The portion of levodopa that does not pass directly into the brain is neutralized by another similar, but inactive chemical, carbidopa, which like dopamine cannot itself pass into the brain. Thus nausea, the main bodily side-effect of the levodopa, is ablated and yet more levodopa can go directly into the brain. The name "Sinemet"–from the Latin: sine = without, and the Greek: emein–to vomit–is therefore particularly appropriate.

Today was a special day, because Jocelyn's mother had come to visit her in the hospital, with a special purpose. I was explaining our further course of treatment with Sinemet, and I was performing the important medical litany of **informed consent**, which was the heart of my consultation with Jocelyn's mother, Madelaine. I had asked her permission for Andrew to be present during our discussion, and shortly thereafter, he entered the room. He was clearly interested in the issue of informed consent.

But Doctor, she's never quite been like this. What has happened is so different. I know that she has been very much out of touch before, hearing voices and talking about persecution with the Nazis, and being very suspicious. Of course, she's never bothered to take her medication of late, despite my trying to push this. Now, she sits there not saying a word, yet it's as if she understands everything, Doctor. Yet she takes on these strange postures. When I moved her hand to hold her, it just sat there.
Yes, this is traumatic for you and for her. We have been considering certain management options. Although Jocelyn is present and has not indicated by her actions that she's refusing this kind of treatment, we wanted to obtain a more definite assent. You, as her mother, are her closest living relative, and I wanted to let you know what we're doing. She has been receiving the more conventional treatment for her underlying psychotic condition, which will help with the thoughts and the voices and the bizarre ideas. However, we don't really know what she's experiencing now. What we do know is that she does not move and looks stiff, somewhat like a waxy portrait.

What does it mean, Doctor?
We believe that this is partly linked up with her condition because we would see this condition commonly occurring before the advent of these antipsychotic medications. On the other hand, medications such as these sometimes produce this state in certain animals like rats. We therefore want to give her an antidote by giving her an opposite kind of medication, which we believe may help her.

What are the risks, Doctor?
It is likely that Jocelyn will show symptoms of psychosis once she comes out of this catatonic state, but we can treat these symptoms. Additionally, because we have limited data on this form of treatment, we do not know what other consequences could potentially occur. Therefore, a risk factor is the entering of realm of the unknown, but I have used this treatment before with success. Of course, the other risk factors are the relatively minor side-effects of the drug, such as nausea and vomiting.

And so it was that I discussed the informed consent process with Jocelyn's mother. We looked at possible benefits and risks and compared these with other options, such as electroconvulsive therapy. We decided instead to go ahead with this treatment of Sinemet, which was new and therefore experimental, to assist in Jocelyn's recovery. We were, of course, not experimenting on her for intellectual curiosity: The intention was for her to become better. This, based on the knowledge we had available, was the logical approach.

Andrew asked a deep question which had no easy answers.
Doctor, how do we reconcile the whole area of informed consent in the psychotic patient?
It's extremely difficult to reconcile, Andrew. We want the patient to be able to fully understand what we're doing, particularly in a procedure which is unusual. On the other hand, the patient's perception of reality is so different that this might preclude such understanding, even though she might consciously have heard what's being said. The interpretation may be extremely colored by her own illness. Jocelyn may believe that her doctor is trying to poison her or make her worse or is in cahoots with the Nazis. Consequently, even though she may tacitly agree by not disagreeing, and may under certain circumstances even sign consent, it's difficult to know if she has, in truth, agreed.

When do doctors assume the responsibility for the decision of consent?
We doctors, at times, make such decisions in this regard. We may chart that we believe the patients understand what has been told to them. If we have the least doubt, we want their guardian or a parent or a spouse to agree with the procedure. Sometimes, in an emergency, we do not have such options. The exact requirements vary from state to state: Laws have been enacted to protect patients from over-zealous physicians. Medications can be poison as well as food.

What's the bottom line, then?
The fundamental point is to practice medicine as best we can. In truth, there are issues even with regular approved medication. Possibly half of the inpatients in psychiatry may not be receiving medications within la-

beling—specifically approved in the package insert for their particular condition. Alternatively, the dose may be different from the official package insert. For example, often there are stipulations for a short duration of treatment. This could be because when a drug comes to be approved by the FDA—the Food and Drug Administration—it frequently may not have been researched over periods of years.

Why?
The costs to the pharmaceutical company or the discomfort to the patient may have been too prohibitive. However, in reality, many symptoms last years.

Any other examples?
Yes. Studies may have been performed on average doses of medications and sometimes, realistically, patients may need higher doses than are found in the package insert.

I presume that the original studies have at least been done on the average patient with that condition?
Not always, and often not at all. Frequently, the studies have been on patients receiving only the experimental medications and not taking anything else. This might be an ideal situation for studying the drug, but not for examining and monitoring possible drug interactions. Similarly, patients with specific medical conditions such as kidney disease may have been deliberately excluded from the study population. Yet, real people may have significant medical illness.

So exclusions make some studies less than ideal?
Exactly. But the opposite may also apply.

In what way?
Because, some of the original patients studied may have been a special non-responsive minority resistant to conventional treatments for their condition. Alternatively, patients may volunteer because they want medical care. Consequently, they may even be prepared to acknowledge or deny symptoms to ensure they are admitted into the study. These situations do not reflect the real world: It's only after approval of a drug, that we begin to obtain significant experience of its strengths and weaknesses.

And many of these patients have been on combination medications?
Yes. Many patients are quite appropriately receiving more than one medication for their psychiatric or neurological condition. However, you can imagine that it's rare for the FDA to have officially approved combination treatment. The combination of medications are not approved together, even though the individual drugs being used are in the correct

dose, for the correct duration and for the appropriate diagnosis. Amongst the few medications that have been officially approved in combinations—developed as combination tablets—is Sinemet.

Should we also include chemicals not generally thought of as medication?
Yes. For example, patients might be using non-prescribed recreational drugs, herbs, vitamins, minerals and health food store products. They also might be smoking, and most commonly, using caffeine. In reality, when we prescribe medications, there may be interactions with the cigarette smoke, as well as with the nicotine, the alcohol and the marijuana, not to mention the vitamins and the herbal preparations.

Does this mean that medications and non-prescribed drugs may produce varied responses in combination?
Yes. In this regard, we can be dealing with results different from what the drug is manufactured for. In a certain way, our practice is: first, not to poison; second, try to use the most appropriate logical approach to treat the extremely difficult patient.

Do most patients then need the imaginative treatments such as what you're contemplating with Jocelyn?
Most certainly not. The great majority of patients do not need these innovative procedures. Our pharmacotherapeutic approaches to medication use on the brain in psychiatry and neurology are sensible and generally simple. At times, however, we encounter patients who do not obey the rules. These are the exceptions, whose predicaments encourage us to look at the balance of effects and side-effects in a special way. In so doing, we are led to insights that may apply to the general patient.

M adelaine, having followed our interchange with great interest, looked at me and voiced her concern:
You know, Doctor, you're quite right. Clearly, my daughter can't fully understand what you're saying; but then, even I don't comprehend all the complicated information about pharmacology, either, and even if I did have a grasp, I'm sure I wouldn't have your kind of knowledge. Can I, in fact, sign consent when I don't really know enough about these drugs? There's always so much to learn about them!
You've asked an excellent question. We can never know everything, and if we did, maybe there would not be a need to practice medicine, as we could all cure ourselves. However, we do make the valiant effort to get people to at least one basic level of understanding: that a drug may or may not work, and may or may not have side-effects. This may not sound like much, but it is very different from the situation where you would have the choice to decide without much information at all.

Like the voting process.

Maybe! How many voters know exactly what each candidate stands for, and how many voters know all the intricate details of some proposition that's being decided? In fact, even if the voters did know, how many would know whether that candidate can carry out what he stands for and is of an appropriate emotional and mental mettle to be able to perform the duty he's representing?

Sometimes, Doctor, it seems the ordinary person like me, expects and almost wants the doctor to say all this complicated stuff that goes over our heads, even though we don't understand it. It's comforting and reassures us that you know a whole lot more than we do and so you must know what's best for us.

Well, I hope it's not quite so one-sided. I think we can have faith in the ability of the "ordinary patient" to grasp certain basics about their treatment. I regard them as competent enough to take part in the decision-making process with their doctor, without expecting to transform them into medical experts.

Thus, we began Jocelyn on small doses of Sinemet—levodopa plus carbidopa—and by so doing, she received levodopa, which was converted into dopamine in the brain. She was still on her antipsychotic medication, because she was being covered for a possible exacerbation of her psychosis. We built up the doses every four hours, giving tiny doses, beginning at a quarter tablet of the smallest size.

Within hours, we could begin to see that the catatonic state was subsiding. We built up gradually over time. The dopamine activated her motor movements and, despite the small pre-existing coverage with antipsychotic medications, Jocelyn came out of the catatonic phase within a day. Gradually, she improved, first eating spontaneously but remaining mute, then becoming more responsive to her environment and finally, actually spontaneously initiating conversation.

Within two days, Jocelyn was out of her catatonic state. Her coverage with the small doses of antipsychotic medications allowed for a situation where her psychosis did not exacerbate initially.

Jocelyn was not fully recovered, but was eating and even talking when spoken to.

I remember your moving my arms. It was strange being in that state, Doctor. I feel much better now.

We continued treating her with Sinemet for ten days until we were entirely clear of her catatonic features. But I knew Jocelyn's new-found normality was only temporary. Based on my experience with this treatment of catatonia with Sinemet, I knew the pointer of too high a dose would be the dopamine excess state of psychosis.

After ten days she began to hallucinate her voices again and develop strange thoughts about these terrible evil entities, the Nazis.

You must be careful, Doctor. They're invading. They're trying to infest my brain by radio waves and kill me.

This was my sign to taper the Sinemet: She was now in a state of do-pamine excess. We pushed up the dose of antipsychotic and within days, Jocelyn's hallucinations of voices of the Nazis and her bizarre thoughts disappeared. She continued to improve over the next week and she was discharged from the hospital. Arrangements were made for careful follow-up.

I needed to emphasize the key to Jocelyn's future.

Jocelyn, you have a biochemical imbalance that is treatable. We know that based on your condition and your past history. But it requires a commitment from you: ensuring that you continue taking your antipsychotic medication.
I want to, Doctor. But you must understand it's difficult because those voices tell me not to, and I must obey.

Jocelyn, we will give you long-acting injectable medication. This way the voices will not be there to tell you, and the responsibility of your taking medication will be shifted from you to the mental health clinic.
I'd like that, Doctor.

Andrew wanted to obtain a perspective of what he had learnt.
Where historically does this treatment fit in? Did you develop this?
Yes and no. Yes, because I developed levodopa or Sinemet treatment in schizophrenic catatonic stupor. [14] No, because levodopa was used in the late 1950s for a different kind of catatonic like state.

Andrew's forehead wrinkled in puzzlement and interest.
Tell me more, please.

The neuropsychiatrist, Oliver Sacks dramatically describes in his book *Awakenings* [15] a condition with some similarities. The book was later made into a movie and the dramatic story became far better known.

What condition did Dr. Sacks describe?
He portrayed the treatment with levodopa of a little known and now apparently extinct medical condition called "encephalitis lethargica" or "Von Economo's disease". This was a bizarre condition thought to have been due to a world-wide viral epidemic. The condition presented in the 1920s and 1930s and seemed to disappear thereafter.

Presumably this condition was not like Jocelyn's catatonia?
Probably not. Like Jocelyn, the patients were absolutely non-responsive to their environment, fitting the description of a stuporous catatonic state. However, encephalitis lethargica was, in theory, regarded as a form of Parkinson's disease. It affected part of the mid-brain called the substantia nigra–the same area affected in Parkinson's disease and the site of production of the chemical neurotransmitter dopamine, which was evidently depleted in this condition. Amazingly, this lethargic brain condition went on for twenty or thirty or even more years. The patients were so slowed in their movements (or should I say "non-movements"?) that they were part of the living dead. They were unable to perform even their most basic functions of hygiene as a consequence. Yet in the peculiar way reserved for catatonics, they were in some way aware of their environment.

And how were they treated?
These patients responded for some months to what at the time was an experimental drug for Parkinson's disease–the same remarkable levodopa! Carbidopa had not yet been developed in the late 1950s, so the potential side-effects were problematic for these long-term mental hospital patients. Ultimately this treatment of encephalitis lethargica lost efficacy after some months. Fortunately, with Jocelyn, we will need to use levodopa for only about two weeks.

So knowing history helped you develop this treatment?
Unfortunately, not. In fact, I developed this treatment long before I learnt about encephalitis lethargica or its historic treatment with levodopa, so it literally became a case of *Awakenings Revisited*. In any event, in *Awakenings*, we learn of the exciting treatment with levodopa of what has been regarded as a variant of Parkinson's disease. In Jocelyn's instance, we are talking about a different pioneering treatment which has nothing to do with Parkinson's disease, namely using Sinemet in the catatonic stupor linked with schizophrenia.
But is Jocelyn the first such case?

No. Actually, Jocelyn is only a later part of the story, because she followed on numerous patients I had treated with Sinemet for catatonic stupor. The Sinemet brought patients out of their catatonic state, though invariably, the psychotic symptoms that were probably dormant all the time, exacerbated themselves somewhat. These were easily controlled with antipsychotic medications; and, of course, the Sinemet treatment was for periods of days only.

A month later, Andrew wanted to know about Jocelyn.

Doctor, how is Jocelyn?
She is doing well, Andrew, but it's a more difficult area than it sounds. She, like many patients, did not have insight into her own condition—she didn't realize she really was ill. This meant that she was at risk to stop her medication and become overtly psychotic again, developing uncontrolled hallucinatory phenomena and delusions—which she did.

What did you do?
Shortly after leaving hospital, we changed Jocelyn's oral perphenazine antipsychotic medication into equivalent doses of injectable neuroleptic–antipsychotic. As you know, she was at risk for relapsing again by stopping her oral medication, and this way every four weeks, she received a long-acting injection of the antipsychotic, Prolixin Decanoate. This drug and another long-acting injectable drug—haloperidol decanoate—has revolutionized the management of schizophrenics in the community. These are the only two major long-acting psychiatric drugs available in the USA.

Was this useful with Jocelyn?
Yes. Once Jocelyn was receiving this long-acting medication, she did not need to remember to take her medications. In addition, she did not have the delusions that prevented her from taking her medications: She no longer believed the Nazis were trying to poison her and that her medications may be the poison they were using.

It's now five years since we treated Jocelyn with Sinemet for her catatonia. She has been maintained on the Prolixin Decanoate in small doses— 25 milligrams (mg) every four weeks. She attends regularly for follow-up at her mental health clinic. She has not relapsed in any way and, in fact, has returned to work and is functioning well as a bookkeeper.

Jocelyn had some news at our recent appointment.

Doctor, I want to tell you that I recently met another patient while waiting for a follow-up appointment. We intend to marry, but we have made the decision that we will not have children. In fact, last month, I voluntarily had my tubes tied.

I think you made an important decision, Jocelyn. There is a complex potential genetic risk and the baby's child-rearing environment would have been less than optimal. Moreover, there would likely have been an added psychological risk for yourself: You did not need the added strains of motherhood at this point. But I am pleased *you* made the decision. This determination could not have been made by anyone else, and I would have helped support you psychologically, even if you had decided to have children.

I looked at Jocelyn with genuine pleasure.

I'm so pleased that you're better, Jocelyn. We have balanced your imbalance of chemicals. Provided you continue your medication, I anticipate that you will continue to remain well.

Thank you, for the opportunity to help you become better.

Jocelyn's return to normalcy echoes Priscilla's wakening to life, and reflects the story of continuing innovative success: There is hope for the future using appropriate chemical manipulations in the brain on real biological illness.

Chapter 2

More Is Better?

Medication toxicity.
Epilepsy, EEGs, generic substitution, infrequent grand
mal seizures, labels (disease).
Dilantin, new anticonvulsants.
(Harry: patient), (Andrew: student ^{e}); (boat analogy)

The shrill squeal sounded like a 130-decibel alarm going off.
Buppopbuppopbuppop! Everyone in the library heard this sharp, repetitive sound caused by the spasm of the muscles inside Harry's larynx—
laryngeal stridor. This heralded to all around that he was having a
grand mal seizure—a generalized tonic clonic episode of epilepsy.
They saw Harry, lying there, unconscious, not knowing the trauma
he was causing to the group that had accumulated around him.
There he was, on the floor, shaking and flailing, but no longer making a sound. At first, he had a phase of utter stiffness—a tonic phase—
lasting about 30 seconds. This was followed by an even more frightening minute of rhythmic, synchronous shaking of all four limbs—the
clonic phase.

A little puddle accumulated. He had been incontinent of urine—
another ignominy for this poor, unconscious, usually perfect gentleman. Gradually, his eyes opened, just briefly, and he got up on his
knees for a few seconds, just long enough to throw up. Then he lay
back down and went to sleep. He had no alert bracelet with *seizure
disorder* written on it, so people could not have known that he was
epileptic. This would have saved him a significant amount of distress.

Already one of the kind spectators had gone to phone for an ambulance, and another quickly came forward to help. Others assisted in
carrying him, lying on his side, across the hall to an office where
there was a couch. Fortunately, nobody tried to force an airway into

---

^{e} From this point, the only medical student is Andrew. He participates in every chapter.
However, the patients and sometimes the family members differ in each chapter.

his mouth so he could breathe. It was not necessary and could only have broken his teeth.

Harry, in fact, did not commonly have grand mal seizures. This was, by history, only the tenth in his lifetime. This time there was a clear but strange precipitator. As part of his higher Master's degree studies, he was in the University library working with a photocopy machine and the light seemed to be defective. He remembered it flashing, but that's all he remembered.

What had happened to Harry was the trigger of the so-called "photic stimulation" of the copier machine, in this instance, possibly three cycles per second. This synchronized with his brain and produced a buildup of a sharp series of discharges that ultimately led to a grand mal seizure.

Harry had also presented with a disorder of his muscle tone, but his was not plastic, like Priscilla's and Jocelyn's. Harry's tone during the seizure was rigid and stiff; he had an entirely different condition, epilepsy.

P oor Harry woke up an hour later, after his deep sleep following on the grand mal seizure. For a moment he wondered what had happened. His wife was there to comfort him.

She whispered in an empathic voice.
You had a seizure, Harry.

But even before she spoke, he knew the answer. He was able to recognize the typical confusion features, with that awful headache and that sense of nausea.
Not again! It's not fair. I had pushed up my medication, and I thought that would have prevented it!

Harry was taking the anticonvulsant—medication to prevent seizures—Dilantin (phenytoin). He was taking it alone for his sometime, but infrequent, generalized tonic clonic seizures. Every so often, maybe monthly, he would have what he regarded as minor attacks, with little blankouts. These events had severely compromised him: They made it impossible for him to drive, and he felt a little ashamed to interact socially.

At that moment, I came into the room.

Doctor, you know, it's not fair. Two weeks ago, I felt as if maybe I was going to have a seizure, so I pushed up my dose of Dilantin, and what happens? This is the third seizure I've had in two weeks! And this time I ended up in the hospital, because it happened in the library, where people saw me and were amazed at my shaking! How can I tell them that I don't need to go to the hospital; it costs a fortune and all I was having was a regular seizure and they've just got to accept that? But of course, I can't communicate at all during these episodes.

It's always difficult. Have you contemplated getting a little bracelet, which may help?

Yeah, that's a good idea, Doctor.

Let's see if we can find out what may have been a cause for these seizures.

Well, I can't explain it, Doctor, because, after all, I pushed up my dose of Dilantin.

Yes, you pushed up the Dilantin. I suspect we already have a good solid reason for your having had that seizure.

What's that?

Your Dilantin level—your phenytoin level—was in the toxic range. It was 26. It should have been between 10 and 20.

Toxic? But all I was doing was trying to give my system more of my cure. Surely that's good? Surely that would prevent the seizures? Surely more is better?

No, in fact, we must be careful that we don't overdo it, that we don't give you too much anticonvulsant medication—antiseizure drugs.

Does that explain why I was feeling so funny?

In what way do you mean?

Well, you know, I found that I couldn't really walk straight, that I was unsteady on my feet, and at times, particularly in the morning, I would have double vision. Also, I felt nauseous quite a bit over these past couple of weeks.

These may all have been signs of Dilantin toxicity.

That's strange, Doctor, because I only pushed up the dose by 50 mg. I was taking 300 mg per day and I only went up to 350 mg. Surely that wouldn't be enough to make me toxic?

Strangely enough, there are certain medications that actually produce significant toxic reactions by small increments of doses. The liver had to break down the Dilantin, but couldn't.

Why's that?

33

The Dilantin is lipid-soluble, meaning fat-soluble. This means it dissolves not in water, but in alcohol like liquids. This is a characteristic of many psychiatric and neurological drugs as they need to pass into the brain through a barrier that only allows fat-soluble substances to pass. These brain drugs usually need to become more able to dissolve in water before they can be excreted through the kidneys in the urine.

So does the liver do this?
    Impressed by Harry's awareness, I explained further.
You're right, Harry. The liver does this job through substances called enzymes. These liver enzymes break down the Dilantin, but at a certain point, reach a limit and cannot handle any more. We call this different kind of metabolism "zero order metabolism" and more correctly, it reflects non-breakdown. Suddenly, a small incremental increase in dose will produce an enormous increase in the blood level and toxicity at the level of the brain.

Are you saying that the additional 50 mg I took became transformed into a quantity of more than 50 mg?
Yes. Let me give you a perspective. With almost any drug, if you increase the dose of some medications, the body level is going to be higher, in general. With occasional drugs, unusual adaptations occur, where certain medications, like one called Tegretol, even speed up their own metabolism, but only to a certain new plateau. Sometimes, higher levels are linked with a decrease in absorption, as with iron tablets. However, with a drug like the Dilantin you have been taking, the liver, at a certain point, says "I can't handle beyond this dose." Consequently, the drug level rapidly escalates. This may originally have been 17 or 18; then with that small daily increase of 50 mg, the blood level suddenly rises to 28, because the liver cannot handle the difference.

    Harry seemed interested.
Can you give me another analogy?
Yes, I can. The chemical factory of the liver is busy breaking down the substance and saying, "Give me more, I can handle it." It has ten workers—the enzymes—busy breaking down the Dilantin. The workers toil through 8-hour days spending all their time handling the Dilantin that's coming in, say 300 mg. You then up the dose to 350 mg, but those workers—the enzymes—only work eight hours a day; after that they punch out their time clocks and go home and never work overtime. So, if 350 mg starts coming in every day instead of 300 mg, the Dilantin is not down to zero after each work day, but down to 50 mg.
The amount builds up every day, so that three days later, suddenly there may be up to 150 mg of extra Dilantin which, instead of being broken

down, lies around unprocessed. Eventually, the workmen work a little overtime so the extra amounts don't greatly increase.

The interchange sparked a question in the mind of Andrew, always a keen-minded medical student.

But how does this extra Dilantin have any effect, let alone a bad effect, if it's not being broken down by the workers? Wouldn't it just lie there, inert?

No, Andrew. You're missing the point. The workers are in the liver. The Dilantin is still passing into the brain and in excess quantities. That's why it's causing toxicity.

Harry was clearly concerned.

So Dilantin is not so good?

It's good, provided we know what we're doing. Dilantin was one of our earliest anticonvulsants, and it still is a useful medication. But, at these high levels, it messes up your mind. So this is why it's important to modify the status quo.

Does this liver overload happen with other drugs?

Yes, it can, but seldom at a therapeutic dose. Dilantin is one of the few brain drugs with this tiny range between high therapeutic level and toxicity.

Well, Doctor, you tell me my side-effects are due to the Dilantin, and I believe you. But my last physician told me that my side-effects were all psychological.

What side-effects?

My wife told him about how irritable I had become and I told him about my thinking which was just lousy. I could not concentrate and I would do things twice because I had forgotten that I have already done them. I would play a poor game of chess, even though I was a champion. I couldn't focus for long, and worst of all, my kids told me I had changed as a father and not for the better.

And these were all regarded as psychological?

Yes, Doctor. My specialist told me he was not interested in all that psychological stuff. He told me to pull myself up, turn over a new leaf and stop being a hypochondriac.

I took a deep breath. I felt I was letting Harry know a well-kept secret.

You need to understand that when some doctors cannot find what's wrong, they may unconsciously feel intimidated and they attribute the

35

symptoms to the patient's psyche. In other words, if they cannot find what's wrong, then it has to be in your head; it has to be purely psychological. To me the label "psychological" must be linked with several positive diagnostic features: It's not simply the negation of "not physical". *Thank you Doctor for saying so!*

My attitude is that this psychological label can stress people out and ironically make many symptoms worse—psychologically! Then this justifies the doctor's diagnosis which has become a self-fulfilling prophecy.
I'm glad to hear this, Doctor.
All I say is, "Okay, we cannot find this, but that doesn't mean that there's nothing there. It means only that we cannot diagnose the cause at this time. For the time being, we have to live with this unknown and if necessary, treat the condition symptomatically. With persistence, we usually have some clues about how to treat it."

Harry wanted to learn more.

Does Dilantin in the correct dose control all seizures?
No. We always choose our anticonvulsant prescriptions carefully because most do not work globally on all seizures. For example, Dilantin does not usually help those children who have "petit mal"—a seizure type with blackouts lasting seconds, sometimes beginning, without warning, in midsentence. Suddenly the patient switches his consciousness off, looking blankly into space as if in a daydream. Equally suddenly, like a light, he switches back on, without confusion, but unaware of the precious moments that have been lost, and continues to talk as if nothing had happened. We can sometimes diagnose petit mal by its specific brain wave pattern on EEG. Even in the most appropriate dose, Dilantin not only does not control these petit mal seizures. In fact, it makes them worse.

I turned to Harry.
Harry, what kinds of seizures have you had with too much Dilantin on board?
I had more grand mals. However, the most common blank-out seizure I had with too much Dilantin was what I call the "little attacks", as opposed to the generalized tonic-clonic seizures. My wife tells me they also involve blank outs, but I stare and am out some thirty seconds. I have a warning— an aura—lasting maybe a fraction of a second: An inexplicable sensation that it's beginning, then I lose contact for the half minute, all the time remaining standing, if that's how I was before the little attack. Then afterward I have a headache, and feel perplexed and a little disorientated.
Harry, these are likely to be temporal lobe seizures not true petit mal, based on your description. We'll evaluate you shortly. For the present, I

think it's worth your while listening in to a teaching session on seizures that I have planned with my student, Andrew.
I'd like to, Doctor.

Andrew was looking a little perplexed. This was the first patient with a **seizure disorder** that he had come across in his short career as a medical student.

Is there always a cause for a seizure?
No. However, in some ways, medicine can be an amusing specialty. We doctors use peculiar terms in medicine for when we don't know the actual cause, and that's in the great majority of cases of epilepsy.
Possibly this is a way of remaining empowered.

Example?
Have you ever heard the term "idiopathic"? When we don't know the cause we say, "the cause of this is that it's idiopathic." Now idiopathic means we don't know the cause. If that doesn't satisfy you, in medicine we have another term, "cryptogenic". Same principle: "Cryptis" is the Greek for hidden—it has a hidden cause. In other words, we tell patients "there's a cause, but it's cryptogenic." Now we have explained it all, you see. That way everyone feels good. The patient feels good because they now know the cause: its cryptogenic; and the doctor feels good because it's cryptogenic. We may have put a label on it, but we still don't know what it's called. Reality is about putting a label on diagnoses even if they don't deserve one or the cause is unknown.

I see what you mean by amusing. Are there any other examples?
Sure. If you have a sore joint, your doctor says, "You have arthralgia"—which only means a sore joint, which you already knew, but it sounds official. It's interesting that we don't have a proper medical term for a flushed cheek. So I present you with a new label: "gena rubra." Now it's a disease!

Is there another component, then, besides labeling illness?
Certainly. There is health as well as illness.
Most of the time, the aspect that's ignored is the healthy part of the individual as opposed to the ill part of the individual. We should be working with the functional engine.

So does the label seizure disorder accurately portray the condition Harry has?
Labels are, at times, simplistic. Some diagnoses may be clear-cut, but not as often as you would think. I suspect there's an enormous submerged group of seizure disorder patients out there—maybe even five or ten fold

more than those we conventionally recognize because of their obvious grand mal attacks. Yes, Harry has a seizure disorder, and because he has had several seizures in his life, the label "epilepsy" is also used.

Harry had listened intently to our labeling discussion and now actively participated.

All the same, I experience the label as a stigma. Has epilepsy always had a stigma?
Let's look at it historically to see. I'll create a non-rhyming poem to help you:

Epilepsy, the anthropologic: the shaman's communication with the gods.
Epilepsy, the belittled: the "epileptic insanity" label of Emil Kraepelin.
Epilepsy, the dangerous: the "lunatic asylums" of the nineteenth century.
Epilepsy: the linguistic: ancient Japanese derivations of seizures and psychosis being similar.
Epilepsy, the neurological: the "Falling Sickness" of the Middle-Ages.
Epilepsy, the psychological: the rigid, irritable "epileptic personality".
Epilepsy, the religious: the "Sacred Disease" of Hippocrates.

The past has taught us a great deal about what seizures are not. Most importantly, you can see how different disciplines and cultures have viewed it through the ages. Seizures have been both abused and respected.

W e shifted to specifics about epilepsy.

Doctor, what exactly is a seizure?
A seizure happens when the nerve cells—the neurons—in an area of the higher brain—the cerebrum—begin to fire together uncontrollably. We use the term *paroxysmal* to describe this synchronous brain firing, and when the firing is over both sides of the brain, unconsciousness often results.

Does one seizure make you epileptic?
No. A person is only epileptic when he has seizures recurrently without obvious reason. So seizures can occur in alcohol withdrawal, diabetic coma or high fevers. That does not make the patient epileptic. However, two or more seizures at different times without an obvious medical condition would qualify.

How do the seizures manifest?

Grand mal with the shaking that goes with it is the most obvious. Simple blackouts due either to petit mal with blank looks lasting seconds, or certain episodes from the temporal lobe of blackouts which last longer and are followed by confusion, are also well known. [16] Sometimes, however, we see just strange behaviors, or movements localized to an area like the arm, or the person has bizarre experiences.

These are the ones that are missed?
Right, and also far more difficult to diagnose. These events most commonly arise from the temporal lobe of the brain.

And do they have specific features?
Yes, but there are numerous symptoms. For example, they may manifest with distortions of sensation or thinking or even of basic bodily functions like sweating or with stereotyped movements like chewing. Sometimes no vocabulary can describe them: They don't fit any usual experience; they're indescribable.

Can these therefore look like psychiatric disease?
Indeed, yes. In psychiatric presentations, they can manifest as subtle episodes of behavior, as well as affective (emotional) or cognitive (thinking) changes. Because they most commonly derive from the temporal lobe, we frequently use the term "Temporal Lobe Epilepsy". This indicates the anatomical origin of the firing. However, today we prefer a functional term so we talk about a broader non-anatomical description of "complex partial seizures". "Complex" is actually a misnomer: All it means is there's some impairment of consciousness–full awareness is gone; originally it was used to reflect complexity and the term has stuck.

And what if there's still full consciousness?
We talk about "simple partial seizures".

Can you always distinguish a simple partial seizure from a complex partial one?
No. Often this call is difficult to make. You can imagine that an epileptic patient who experiences special symptoms while fully aware of everything around him may be having simple partial seizures. But these symptoms, which usually last seconds, can be varied: a buzz in his ear, burning rubber smells, distortions in size, sudden sweating, uncontrolled weeping, sudden right arm jerks or a rising stomach sensation.

So when is it a complex partial seizure?
When a patient with these identical symptoms also experiences alterations in his awareness he may, be having subtle consciousness distortions. These symptoms would then be "complex partial seizures".

39

These alterations may show themselves as a strange sense of depersonalization—feeling not quite himself—or of derealization—unreality about the world. They may even be a sudden profound mood change over seconds, or a sense of disorientation or a loss of time, or a frank absence of consciousness with no other manifestation.

And does the term "partial" mean that it's only part of a seizure?
No. These are still full seizures, although they may be minor. "Partial" refers to the fact that the origin of the firing is localized—we call it "focal"—to an area of the brain.

Surely all firing must be partial then?
Not so. Some derive from below the cerebrum. They originate in lower areas of the brain like the brain stem. The firing then is "generalized" as they fire right across the higher brain of the cerebral cortex.

For example?
The most classical and common epileptic seizures are the "grand mal" kind, technically called the "generalized tonic-clonic seizure".

So do these always start off "generalized"?
Excellent question, Andrew. No. They can be focal somewhere in the higher brain initially. They then start off as a complex or simple partial seizure which "secondarily generalizes" itself as opposed to the ones deriving from below the higher brain which are "generalized from the start."

Where do these complex partial secondarily generalized tonic-clonic seizures usually come from?
Usually they come from the temporal lobes or the frontal lobes, and they can come from either side of the brain.

A̲ndrew probed further.
But where does epilepsy fit in to the greater scheme of medicine? Is epilepsy regarded as a psychiatric or a neurological condition, Doctor?
You've asked an important question. Is there a separation between brain and mind? If people are suffering do we empathize with the Cherished Brain or the Beloved Mind?

Today in psychiatry, a great void exists concerning seizures. The so-called bible of psychiatric classification called DSM IV does not even address the links of seizures and psychiatry. [17] In the past decade, we have used several non-specific, diagnostically inadequate or inaccurate labels including "organic delusional disorder", "atypical psychosis", "organic hallucinosis" or "organic mood disorder". Now, in DSM IV, we have "mental disorders due to a general medical condition", with seizures having no special pride of place. Epilepsy has remained a predominantly neurological and not psychiatric condition; the handful of psychiatric epileptologists–psychiatrists who are epilepsy experts–worldwide have not allowed this situation to correct itself.

Is this a pity?
It's more than that. It's astonishing. Neuropsychiatrists, in fact, frequently recognize that significant behavior disturbances may correlate with firing episodes–you'll remember the term "paroxysmal discharges"–in the brain (particularly the temporal lobe and the emotional brain area called the limbic system). These patients would not be considered to have a seizure disorder by many neurologists. Many neuropsychiatrists believe these patients represent a form of *episodic electrical cerebral firing* which we, for non-prejudicial reasons, have called *Paroxysmal Neurobehavioral Disorder* or simply PND. We characterize the individual events as "atypical spells" to avoid the debate as to whether these are true epileptic seizures. [18]

So you have to introduce new terminology?
Yes. The spectrum of epilepsy and psychiatry is couched in controversy and in diagnostic labels that are ambiguous, uncertain, non-existent or invented based on pragmatic experience.

What causes these atypical spells of the PND condition and the seizures?
Both proven seizure phenomena and PND may follow an acute brain insult such as a blow to the brain, artery blockage or bleed, encephalitis–brain infection, anoxia–too little oxygen, or tumor–a benign or malignant growth.

Anything more?
Yes, conditions precipitated by chronic exposure to recreational drugs of abuse like cocaine, LSD, and amphetamines and possibly cannabis are important. Also, some epileptics have loaded family histories of seizures or other anomalous events like subjective paranormal experiences–what they regard as psychic experiences. These may correlate with a different kind of temporal lobe functioning.[19] However, for the most part, the cause of the epilepsy is not easily determined, so we can use that term for hidden–cryptogenic.

I suppose most people with epilepsy have psychiatric problems?
Most certainly not! Most epileptics are healthy: They do not have any psychiatric stigmata, and the only difference between them and a general non-epileptic population is the occurrence of their seizures.
Wow! I didn't know that.

41

Actually, I have divided seizure disorders into two. Possibly 90% of epileptics are in the group of what I call the "epilepsy standard patient".[20] These patients have no more psychopathology than the average patient. The epilepsy standard patients, without additional psychopathology, are functional within the community, and should be differentiated from the "epilepsy plus patients".

So the second group consists of the epilepsy plus patients?
Yes. This minority of epilepsy patients have significant behavior or psychiatric abnormalities relating to the organic aspects of their seizure disorder. These patients frequently present psychiatrically, or may be evaluated commonly in an academic setting. They may have been misdiagnosed or be more resistant to conventional anticonvulsants alone, needing psychiatric drugs as well. As many as one-half require hospitalization for this. These patients may have a broader coarse neurobehavioral syndrome—a technical term I use to describe behavior due to hard line brain conditions. Some of this group may be mentally retarded. The epilepsy plus patients also include a group in which psychoses and seizures coexist. Finally, probably the most common population with severe psychiatric problems is what Dieter Blumer calls "interictal dysphoric disorder patients."[21] These patients have depression between episodes of seizures and so require anticonvulsant plus antidepressant treatment.

Andrew needed now to prioritize what he had learnt.

Does everyone accept these disorders?
No. These conditions remain controversial, particularly the debate whether these are linked with temporal lobe foci or relate to seizure disorders in general. A number of confounding variables, such as dosage, number of anticonvulsants prescribed, severity of seizures, impairments in seizure control and number of seizure types, may play significant roles in making interpretation even more difficult.

Is "epilepsy plus" therefore unusual?
Right. The epilepsy plus patient probably is a small minority—possibly a tenth—of the total number of epileptic patients. They may be intractable, difficult to manage, and have behavior disorders superimposed on, or co-existing with the epilepsy.
Is the "plus" of "epilepsy plus" directly related to the seizures?
Sometimes, but often not. The behavior disturbances or the psychoses may or may not be causally related to their epilepsy. Sometimes the psychiatric history is easier than the epilepsy diagnosis. For example, an alcoholic with psychiatric problems happens to have several withdrawal

seizures: He's not epileptic because the seizures are due to a specific reversible medical cause—he has a psychiatric condition without epilepsy.

What about when psychiatric patients are perceived as having epilepsy when, in fact, they do not?
Andrew, you're really on the ball, today! Their previous labels of epilepsy may be wrong: for example, a single seizure is often caused by alcohol withdrawal or other medical conditions.

Anything else?
Yes. Alternatively, they may have had an acting-out episode, incorrectly interpreted as a seizure instead of a pseudo-seizure—also called hysterical epilepsy—and this is not epilepsy at all. Some patients may be on anticonvulsant medication for mood disorder like manic-depressive illness or for paroxysmal episodic behavior disturbance like anger episodes, and the medication may be misconstrued by a new treating physician as for seizure control.

So misdiagnosis is a problem?
Certainly. Patients may wrongly be put onto anticonvulsant medication for black-outs which have not been proven to be epileptic.

But surely that's sometimes done to be safe?
Yes. It's not necessarily incorrect to do so. The patient's well-being must be considered and sometimes diagnoses can't be definite.

Any other causes of wrong diagnosis?
Yes, an abnormal electroencephalogram—EEG—does not make the patient epileptic. Epilepsy is a clinical not purely a brain-wave diagnosis. It's probably best to limit epileptic psychiatric patients to those having a confirmed history of epilepsy associated with at least two documented seizures which were not linked to withdrawal phenomena or fever or other acute events.

Does it work both ways? Can seizures produce behavior disturbances?
Indeed. Patients who are epileptic may have periods of altered or impaired consciousness following on their seizure. The resulting confusion may manifest behavior disturbances. This should not be interpreted as psychiatric; it's clearly what we call a "post-ictal confusional state".

In English?
Even better, I'll let you know in Latin, because as you know, many medical terms are from Latin. "Ictal" is medical jargon for seizure. "Post-ictal" means the time right after the seizure.

43

And post-ictal features relate to confusion?
Actually, one of the most important post-ictal features is headache that follows on any seizure, usually grand mal or complex partial events. Also, patients may have other post-ictal features like disorientation, sleepiness or general body fatigue. After grand mals, muscle pain and nausea are also common. So these are the typical post-ictal features and they sometimes help to make the diagnosis when they're present following on an atypical spell event.

What about the rest of the terminology?
Knowing about ictal helps. "Pre-ictal" is the period before the seizure. Some people use the term "peri-ictal" to include the whole area between pre- and post- including the seizure. "Inter-ictal" refers to a time between seizures and I even like to use the term "non-ictal" for when there's no relationship of events to the seizures. Got it?

Yes. Just: pre-, post-, peri-, or inter; then you hook on the ictal.
Right.

Any more problems with diagnosis?
Yes, one more. I mentioned patients diagnosed with pseudoseizure phenomena—the hysterical ones whose seizures are not epileptic. The problem is the majority also may be having real seizures which have been missed, along with their non-epileptic events.
It sounds complicated.
Yes. However, fortunately, these basics will serve you well.

At this stage, Harry, who had been listening carefully, interjected.
Thank you Doctor. That's fascinating. I feel better knowing I'm an "epilepsy standard" patient. But I must tell you something.
Yes?
I know when I'm going to have a seizure, so I think my experience must be pre-ictal.

How do you know?
I get this same roller coaster feeling every time. It lasts a few seconds and it's like nothing I've ever otherwise experienced. Then I have either a blackout or a grand mal. It's always the same.
So what you describe is something peri-ictal—round the time of the seizure. In fact, it's not pre-ictal because this roller coaster is actually part of the seizure. Because there's no distortion in awareness, many epileptologists would describe it as a simple partial seizure. It then progresses, it generalizes to loss of consciousness. We call this...

Simple partial seizures with secondary generalization to tonic clonic or absence events.
Harry, you're amazing. How did you learn so quickly?

He turned away a little embarrassed.
Doctor, since you ask, I'll admit I saw it in my chart! But tell me more about my roller coaster.
We call the sensation starting the seizure an aura. The origin in the brain of your kind of aura—your roller coaster feeling before the bigger seizure—is not well demonstrated, but obviously, there's an origin and that's why it consistently begins your episodes. For your roller coaster sensation, firing begins from an anatomical area, probably deep within the temporal lobes, as most strange episodes derive from there.

How does it happen?
Sometimes feelings can be strange during or before a seizure. This is because the area of firing in the brain might not be a commonly used area of the brain. Consequently, people could have seizure-like experiences which they don't have at any time in their waking life, and they find it difficult to find words to describe it.

When did you first start having seizures?
It may have been in my teens, Doctor. But I don't think so, because recently I remembered my childhood experience. I would repetitively encounter the same taste hallucination of "horse-flavored candy"; there's no such taste, but that's the closest. It was always the same and lasted a few seconds.
Could that be linked?
Likely, yes. Given your history, it may have been a simple partial seizure.

Does that help you in your assessment, Doctor?
Yes. Any unusual episodic phenomenon, such as momentary strange tastes like "horse-flavored candy" help us. As this used to happen repetitively as a child, I have an added perspective on the seizure elements. It's consistent and stereotyped over time suggesting a likely seizure phenomenon. So, what you tell me is most intriguing and most relevant, as well. It could be coincidental, because when you look through the retrospectoscope, it always looks different.

Harry was clearly intent on understanding as much as he could.
Well, how are you going to evaluate my symptoms, Doctor?
First, we'll do an EEG—an electroencephalogram.

What does an EEG consist of?

A routine EEG involves monitoring your brain waves for about an hour while awake. During this time we will use special procedures which we know sometimes bring out abnormalities: namely, hyperventilation–overbreathing, and photic stimulation–flashing lights at varying frequencies.

Do you always do this overbreathing?
Yes, unless there's a medical reason not to do so, like with breathing problems. Similarly, if there's an intolerance to flashing lights, we won't do that.

So is that the whole routine?
No. We also measure sleep for an hour–a sleep EEG.

Andrew took the opportunity to learn more about EEGs, as well.

Why do an EEG, Doctor?
An EEG examines brain waves. So it's the key test to detect abnormal episodes of firing in the brain. This firing sometimes produces seizures or local abnormalities.

Are these local abnormalities then due to tumors?
They can be. However, this is only a rare cause. Sometimes they may be due to tiny areas of scarring, but most times we cannot find a specific reason.

When do you order an EEG?
EEGs should be ordered in possible seizure disorder and whenever patients report any strange symptoms which could be linked with brain firing. These include any symptoms lasting seconds or any atypical or unexplained events. These may, at times, detect specific local–also called focal–abnormalities, like those in the temporal lobe.

What actually is the temporal lobe?
The temporal lobe of the brain is that portion of the higher brain that's associated with a great deal of functions, particularly functions of integrating various experiences. It blends perceptions coming in from all the five senses–seeing, hearing, smelling, tasting, touching. It combines these senses with emotions; and even possibly links up to the experience of intuition, among others. When it doesn't function as well, a great deal suffers as a consequence: In effect, instead of "integration" we see "disintegration". One of the reasons why the temporal lobe may not function as well is that it's the most primitive part of the higher brain. Consequently, it may be the most vulnerable to injury such as brain trauma, drug abuse, fevers and infections. We often see this abnormality manifesting on measures of brain waves–in the EEG tracing–where there may

be marked slowing in one or both temporal lobes or even abnormal sharp waves.

So what exactly does an EEG detect?
EEGs examine the brain waves for a short period of time, like an hour or two in the patient's life. During this time we look at every fraction of a second to decide whether there are any abnormal episodes lasting seconds going on inside the brain. In typical medical jargon, we call these very short cerebral–brain–firing episodes "paroxysmal discharges." We also look for unusual rhythms lasting minutes or even occurring throughout the tracing. Both the paroxysmal discharges and the abnormal rhythms may reflect the cause of underlying neurological or psychiatric problems and sometimes, the same symptom can produce different EEG pictures.

Like?
Memory impairments are an example. The lack of registering events may show up on EEG with abnormalities of slowed rhythm sometimes reflecting altered consciousness or impaired brain function. However, they may manifest as EEG firing in the brain suggesting epilepsy.

        Harry was a little worried.
What if we find abnormalities?
We can treat these by treating the cause of the abnormal rhythms, or if there are seizures, we can put out the fires in the brain with medication. EEGs look at the electrical side, while most conditions like Parkinson's or depression are treated purely on the chemical side.

I'm not likely to have a seizure during a two-hour EEG, am I?
No, it's unlikely when you have the regular EEG that any "target symptoms" would happen. However, we can detect a great deal even during phases when you're not having a seizure.

Why even do a sleep record? Isn't that just more work?
Sleep records will pick up a local abnormality four times more often than waking EEGs. However waking EEGs also have a high pick-up rate and sleep EEGs cannot be interpreted without the wake EEG, so both should be performed.

But how can I get to sleep in the middle of the day?
We give a sleeping aid like chloral hydrate as this does not change the EEG much and does not prevent the demonstration of focal abnormalities.

Should I take my medicines?

Yes, carry on as normal. We want to obtain information about how you are today. However, there's a big exception: Certain medications should be particularly avoided in EEGs. The worst offenders are the benzodiazepine group.

What belongs to that group?
Drugs like Ativan, Xanax, Klonopin, Librium, Valium, Halcion, Tranxene and Serax.

What do they do?
They have strong anti-epileptic effects, and profoundly normalize the EEG.

So they must be powerful anticonvulsants?
They're superb, but it seems only for weeks, not months or years. The body adjusts and then all we're left with is possible physical dependence and seizures if we withdraw benzodiazepines. So we should use them preferably only when we want to break an epilepsy cycle.

Andrew was back to his intense learning style.
If people are on them, they can just hold a dose for their EEG?
I wish. Unfortunately, benzodiazepine's effects on brain waves may last weeks even with the ones that are very short acting. This means the yield of demonstrating epilepsy after the patient has had benzodiazepines administered decreases a great deal, but we still need to research how much.

How long should patients be off them then?
A good rule is three weeks. However, if you need these medications, the danger of withdrawal just for an EEG is too great to worry. Doctors just live with the lower yield knowing the EEG does not exclude anything.

Does the same apply to anticonvulsant medication?
Yes, but strangely enough, possibly not to the same degree. We seldom recommend holding a dose of anti-epileptic drugs in people with epilepsy because we don't want them to seize.

But can we be clinically without seizures and yet firing a great deal on EEG?
Yes, people may think they're seizure-free, but actually they could be firing fifteen times at night.

What's happening to that firing?
It's rather like water boiling, but just simmering on the top, as opposed to the water at a rolling boil.

Then it's less of a problem?

48

Well, that simmering probably doesn't help the memory. Furthermore, many believe that seizures beget seizures. In other words, the more you have, the more your radio frequency is tuned in, so it's better to try to eliminate them.

Harry was keeping up with the flow of the discussion.
This can't be healthy for our mind, can it?
No. If you have twenty episodes during the space of two days, you can imagine what it does to your mood and to your irritability. It's like having a grass patch where there has been a fire and the grass has recently burnt. It has to re-grow all over to recover the healthy grass. Your memory is sometimes really impaired, and at times, there might be headaches or fatigue, and it can leave you entirely and utterly exhausted. One cause of chronic fatigue, therefore, might in fact be a fire that's occurring in the brain, and all we need to do is put out that fire and we will have treated the underlying cause.

Could firing be a cause of psychiatric problems that don't respond to conventional medication?
You've got it! But strangely sometimes the seizures may help. There's this paradoxical balance when one has a seizure. All that electricity builds up, causing irritability and mood swings over seconds. Then, with the seizure it washes out and sometimes severe depression clears up in seconds. It's one of the dilemmas we have. Do we want to take the seizure away totally? In your case, Harry, yes, we do. However, occasionally, we have to compromise with this buildup. I think the change in Dilantin dose will help your irritability quite a bit: maybe too much is being suppressed.

It was five days later.
We had just performed the EEG on Harry, delaying so that the toxicity could be eliminated as a confounding factor.
We examined his waking EEG tracing.

Do you notice, Harry, how your brain waves synchronize with the frequency of the light flashing?
I showed him how when the lights were at five per second so were his brain waves, when they flashed at ten per second, his waves synchronized. They continued to do so at thirteen cycles as well as at twenty.

I heard two voices at once, Harry's and Andrew's.
Amazing, Doctor!
Yes, it is. We see this regularly and it's quite normal to synchronize. We call it "photic driving". This may be the same effect that triggered your

seizure near the copier machine, but this time it didn't trigger any abnormal event.

What about the overbreathing, Doctor? Did that show anything?
Yes, it did, Harry. Do you notice that about two minutes after you finished hyperventilating, your waves change?

I pointed out an abnormality in the right temporal lobe in the form of a slow three second run.

We examined Harry's EEG further. By this time his blood levels of Dilantin, which we had monitored daily, had become non-toxic and reverted to the upper normal range at 19. His EEG showed normal background activity though there were two episodes showing profound slowing both localized to those EEG channel placements that reflected the temporal lobe.

And overall, what's the verdict?
It's abnormal, but not too bad. The Dilantin is probably doing a good job covering you for your seizures.

When we talk about seizures, Doctor, what do we see on EEG?
Classically, an EEG may show generalized "runs" lasting a second or two or even ten, with high voltage sharp waves which look like spikes and linked with tall, but rounder slower wave forms. You don't have any of that.

Can you make psychiatric diagnoses on EEG?
Not now, but maybe one day. Historically, we always talk about these sharp spikes as the prototype epileptic phenomenon. This is and is not the case. These sharp episodes may well reflect classical seizures. However, commonly, particularly in psychiatry, we see behavioral abnormalities associated with the slowing, and it may be that electroencephalography has lagged behind, because it has been predominantly the bastion of the neurologist and not the psychiatrist. Of course, sometimes we don't detect anything on EEG even though there's firing in the brain.

Why?
Simply because our electrodes are located around the skull. If the electrical changes do not extend to the surface of the brain, we cannot detect it. Of course, we could drill a hole in the skull, and put electrodes right inside areas of the brain, but this is dangerous and seldom done.

You mean it's sometimes done?

Yes. If a patient is being analyzed for possible surgery of the brain for their epilepsy, we want to know exactly where the abnormal firing is coming from. If we cannot detect the exact localization from scalp electrodes, depth placements may help.

So how can we demonstrate for sure that a symptom is actually a seizure?
The only definite way is for the symptom, like an unexplained smell, to occur at the same time as a seizure on EEG.
If the EEG seizure is localized in the brain, we may even locate the area in the brain causing the symptom.
Will the EEG will demonstrate that?
It can, but usually it doesn't. An EEG is such a short period of a patient's life-cycle that it's unlikely the patient will actually have a seizure. However, even if he did, the EEG may not necessarily show it, since it will have already spread all the way from the area of firing to the scalp. This is a long way from any firing in the midline or deep structures.

But if my minor events—the burning smells I get and the roller coaster feeling—are rare, should I even take medication?
If you were having four or five atypical spells a day, that's easy. We would need to control it. But you're having events every month or two. So you may say, "well, let it happen." But you must look at the balance of how disabling the spell is compared with the inconvenience and costs of taking medication.

And in my instance?
In your instance, Harry, we're not talking minor events. Grand mal seizures, even if only one per year, need adequate control. Additionally, you have those absence blackouts.

Do you want me completely seizure-free, Doctor?
Certainly, I do. I want you seizure-free without side-effects if possible.
When a person becomes seizure-free for a year or more, it makes such a difference compared with even only having, say, one seizure a year.
I know. It keeps me from driving.

Yet, did you know that everyone has the potential toward having seizures?
Seriously?
Yes. We know that through ECT–shock treatment. ECT is given under controlled conditions: Muscle relaxants markedly relieve the shaking, and anesthesia allows greater comfort. Nevertheless, the object is still to induce a grand mal seizure and everyone is vulnerable. There is a range of sensitivity to seizures–thresholds–for different people so a range of stimuli can be used in ECT. The same applies for spontaneous brain firing.

51

Harry, all we're trying to do is to raise up your threshold so that you won't have a seizure.

So is that what anticonvulsant medication does?
Yes: We should give enough to raise the threshold, but not cause significant side-effects.

Harry, after all this, was still interested in listing his medication side-effects.
In that case, Doctor, Dilantin affects my memory as well.
Not surprising. At those high levels, even at 20, we frequently see more thinking type side-effects than at lower levels. People may become more rigid in their ideas, slowed in thinking, irritable, sleepy, clumsy and slowed. However, this only happens in some. One difficulty is that we're never sure if it's the medication or the seizures that may be responsible. It may even be the underlying brain condition, for example, some scarring that may cause seizures and may be an area of damage in the brain, as well.

What happens if I took an additional drug?
If you ever went onto a second anti-seizure medication, you would take lower doses of the Dilantin.

Are there any vitamins or minerals I should take?
Yes. I like all my patients on Dilantin to take one of the B vitamins that may become depleted, because Dilantin speeds up certain metabolic reactions in the liver. This vitamin, folic acid, is required to act in these chemical reactions. Strangely, another vitamin, Vitamin D may become deficient because its level might drop, as it is broken down quicker in the liver by these reactions, and Vitamin D is also involved with calcium absorption. Consequently, I suggest you consider taking small amounts of calcium and Vitamin D plus folic acid.

Doctor, there's another minor problem I have. Dilantin effects my gums.
Indeed, on examination, Harry had thickened gums, a common side-effect of Dilantin. It's worthwhile asking your dentist for an opinion, Harry.

If necessary, we can change you around to another anticonvulsant medication, like tiagabine (Gabitril) or topiramate (Topamax).

Would you tell me a little about Gabitril and Topamax a bit?
Sure. Briefly though, because we're not yet changing you around. Both of these are newly approved in the USA. This is good and bad.

Good because we have even more outstanding options, bad because we're still unsure what they do in the real world. Technically, they were approved as "add on therapies" to be used only in conjunction with other drugs like Dilantin, Tegretol and Depakote.

Why the restriction?
Because it was too risky to study new anticonvulsant drugs on their own. What would have happened if they didn't work? People would have been seizing.

So they are approved only as add on medication, but sometimes used on their own?
In practice, yes, but they need to be studied more in the real world. However, provisionally, topiramate (Topamax) seems a good anticonvulsant, indeed. When you look at the statistics of decreased seizures when patients are on it, it's impressive. However, my patients, at times, have reported uncomfortable experiences on Topamax. So this needs to be further studied. Its effects on behaviors might well vary depending on the individual, and possibly on too high a starting dose, but if it can be tolerated, it's outstanding.

The other new anticonvulsant is Gabitril. We like it, because it solidly diminishes the incidences of seizures and seems to be consistent in doing so; and it seems to be well tolerated. However, again it's early days.

Harry seemed to be enjoying his lesson on anticonvulsants.
How do all these drugs work?
They involve a variety of different chemicals called GABA, NMDA and Glutamine: These are the three major neurotransmitters involved in electrochemistry. Neurotransmitters are like boats which attach to their own specific pier. They have influence when the passengers climb off the boats to do their business—in which case the transmission across the synapse occurs. They could also create a distant shadow on the shore—impact other bodily functions at a distance rather like a hormone does. Finally, just occupation of the pier does something even if no stimulation occurs: it makes sure other boats don't moor there—that other chemicals will not influence the receptor.

It sounds like a good analogy. Could you explain further?
These long-range shadows cause inhibition—it may be colder on the shore. Other times, the changes may lead to passengers climbing off the boat. There is excitation occurring and eventually the impacts may be felt distantly as the passengers move further away. Those passengers are "messenger systems" in the jargon of biochemistry: They go ashore and

53

may impact what's happening anywhere in the town—called the human body in our jargon!

What about the boat?
The boat stays moored so other boats—other neurotransmitters—cannot get in.

And what do the medications do?
They help the boats come up to the pier in the right proportion. Sometimes, but not always, they actually occupy the pier acting as boats. In treating seizure disorders some of the boats like the glutamine boat are stimulating neurotransmitters; others like GABA, are inhibitory—they prevent firing, but at a different pier whose job is to do that. This is a simplification, but a comprehensible one. So ultimately, therefore, medications like Dilantin put out the firing, but they're also acting on these base level chemicals.

Harry's questions brought us back to his compelling personal concern.
So what are we going to do now?
Dilantin is a good drug so I don't want to change you to another, given that adequate control of your seizures mainly occurs with only occasional episodes.
However, what we will do is diminish your Dilantin. We will see whether we can't get a new level of control, at a lower level, where you don't have any signs of toxicity. However, we would still want to adequately control you as best we can with one anticonvulsant.

If you changed me around to another drug, could I easily withdraw off the Dilantin?
Not easily. It's a major problem going off any anticonvulsant. In my experience, Klonopin and phenobarbital are the most difficult drugs to withdraw patients from without them seizing a great deal; then comes Dilantin; much easier are Tegretol and Depakote. We don't know as much with the newer ones—Neurontin, Lamictal, Felbatol, Gabitril and Topamax—with regard to ease of withdrawal. Generally, I like patients to be on one anticonvulsant at a time, but I don't just stop the one and start the other. I taper the first gently over many months, sometimes even over a year.

Why?
So that the patient runs the smallest possible risk of a withdrawal seizure. Of course, in between, I actually increase the new medication to what I regard as a therapeutic level. It's difficult.

Why?
Because I only know when I've not succeeded if the patient has a seizure and that may take months. So I aim at better statistical control than before although very much wanting my patients to be seizure free.

How then would you do it with Dilantin?
If I did not want you on Dilantin at this point, I would not just say: "Let's stop the Dilantin. I'm going to give you tiagabine or topiramate instead." If I did this, you would probably seize a great deal, because your body has become used to the Dilantin. So the trick here would be to change you around, but ever so slowly so that the whole process might take six or even twelve months, or even longer: time is unimportant. We would taper so gradually that your body would hardly even notice. Usually what I do is I load up a little on the new drug like tiagabine or topiramate, so that there's some coverage while we start tapering the Dilantin. We would continue to taper as we slowly increase the other medications.

Could I consider phenobarbital instead or in addition? I know it's sometimes combined with Dilantin.
I certainly don't recommend phenobarbital alone, or in combination. It impacts badly on higher brain function, causes depression and interacts markedly with many different medications making their breakdown so rapid that you have to profoundly increase their dosing. Phenobarbital also causes personality changes that can make beloved minds into irritable souls. But phenobarbital is cheap–that's partly because it's generic. Phenobarbital is at the bottom of the rung. I believe it's a drug that should seldom be used in Western countries where economics cannot easily justify the sacrifice of functionality. Yet, because it is so cheap, it is the most used anticonvulsant agent in the world.

On hearing that the generic drug issue was raised, Andrew rattled off a wealth of questions.
So you recommend generics?
Certainly not generic anticonvulsants. Some generics are okay.
Please help me, Doctor, in that regard. What makes a generic drug an acceptable alternative to the brand name drug?
Generic drugs are approved when they're "therapeutically equivalent" to the standard–generally brand name–drug. In other words, they conform to several strict criteria.

What criteria?
Generics must contain approximately the "same" dose of the equivalent active ingredient. Also, they should be of similar quality and purity. They must produce the same effects on the body, and be as safe as the original

brand name product. So, in practice, generics usually work like the original brand name products and they save a great deal of money because they're much cheaper.

It was clear Andrew was not going to be satisfied with the simple answer.

The way you've said it, it sounds like we could always use generic; but isn't there dispute?

Yes. Sometimes, I will use the brand name drug when dose is critical. I want the dose to be as controlled as I can get in some conditions and in some patients. In fact, ideally, I would like to see the production of a medication being so consistent that we would find the same dose every time if we analyzed it.

You said the "same" dose. Who polices the "same" dosage idea?

The FDA. [22] They have strict controlling regulations to try to ensure that the chemical parts of the drug that are relevant are equivalent. Generic drugs must, of course, be produced using acceptable standards of control. Although, technically, there may be quite a wide variation, a drug which was just in the acceptable range would probably not last long in the marketplace or be marketed at all. Most generics are not too bad. In fact, they're reasonable replicas of the original at a fraction of the cost.

You mentioned the word "same" dosage. What's the range the FDA allows?

The technical term used is bioavailability. This must be the same. The essence is that the active generic drug must be absorbed and become available in the brain (with neuropsychiatric medications) at a speed and degree comparable to the original standard brand name drug.

Andrew was getting quite insistent.

But what's the "same"? I want to understand this.

Bioavailability is a complicated concept; simplifying it may make you interpret it wrongly.

Well, what's the bottom line?

You don't give up do you, Andrew? The FDA criteria may superficially seem rather liberal for generics.

Figures exist for what's equivalent. As a concrete example, let us take 100 mg of the trade drug Elavil and use that as the standard. Technically, the rate and extent of absorption for its generic, marketed under the chemical name of amitriptyline, would need to be between 80 mg and 125 mg to be generally considered "bioequivalent". This is called the -20 %/+25% rule.

It does seem to be a big difference, doesn't it?

Yes, and it may be, but we have to have some cut-off range. Usually, this wide range is considered okay. But you can imagine that's why I don't like generics in critical situations. With antiseizure medications, for example, I don't want my patients to receive 550 mg of carbamazepine when they should be getting 600 mg. The risk of seizure is too high. Similarly, I think people with potentials towards irregular heart beat may be impaired if the drugs that normalize their heart rhythms were off by such a range. Alternatively, some drugs have a small range between therapeutic and toxic dose. You've seen, Harry, how a tiny increase in Dilantin, your anticonvulsant, can make the person who was under control become toxic: suddenly he becomes confused, sleepy and unsteady on his feet. Even worse, he may start to seize because the brain levels are too high. Generic variations therefore may cause problems in this kind of patient.

But Doctor, why is the FDA not imposing a 100% equivalence on drugs, instead of an 80% equivalence?
At a certain point, we have to be reasonable in setting standards, and this approach allows for variations. There are variations even in the parent compound, which means that if we had close to 100% equivalence on generics, what would we compare it to? The parent compound itself might still fluctuate a little bit. The -20/+25 rule is based on the broad idea that this kind of variation, in most conditions, will not be harmful to most patients. In reality, the range of acceptability works out narrower than this and there are fewer variations and frequently drugs fit a -10/+10 profile. This is particularly if the drug is regarded as potentially toxic: Specific rules guide individual drugs with the ultimate responsibility involving the manufacturer not the FDA.

So when can I prescribe generics?
For some conditions, such as depression, the greater variation with generics will not usually make much difference. The variations I've outlined may seem liberal, but they're based on a medical decision that, for most drugs, the difference in the concentration of the active ingredient in the blood does not make a significant difference clinically. Moreover, this difference reflects the limit of range, and the detailed statistical criteria that are also required make it unlikely that any drug with the most extreme limits of variation allowed could be approved as equivalent. In fact, not infrequently, the generic drug is from the same company as the original drug and meets the same production standards.

Why would they produce a generic and compete against themselves?
Because they have lost the patent on funding. It means other companies can copy their drug and although their profit margins may drop considerably, the original company still has the machinery in place to make a smaller profit and compete easily with other generic companies.

You mean sometimes patients going to the same pharmacy may not even get the same generic each time?
Persistent aren't you? You're right. When the generic is prescribed the patient may get any of many different equivalent medications. There may easily be twenty or more different preparations for the more popular drugs. You can imagine the cheapest one may end up being dispensed. This may differ from one time to another, which may make the variation even more.

Can generic drugs differ in any other way from the original ones?
Yes, they can and at times do. Several differences are acceptable. Their shape can vary. Moreover the configuration may not be the same, for example, capsule or tablet. They may be packaged differently and their color and even flavor may not be the same. They may have varying preservatives which at times makes their expiration time different. These are all acceptable variations according to the FDA.

And so, it seemed, Andrew was finally satisfied.
So I won't use generics on my epileptics?
That's right.
But for patients with depression, I can use generics, always?
Only sometimes. You must consider each case carefully. Some people are very sensitive to small changes in dosage. If so, I would use the same brand name product. On the other hand, if finances area concern, and the dose the patient takes does not seem critical, then I would use the generic. I wish I could make sure that the patient would get the same brand of generic each time, but I can't, so the risk is always weighed with the financial benefit.

But Harry was not satisfied.
Sometimes, Doctor, I need to take a specific medication because I can't afford another prescription drug.
That's a good reason.
One time, I was prescribed some Lamictal, but it was just too much, so I was put back on Dilantin.
Yes, this reflects another side of it. Even when we're talking brand name drug, the newer medications are often more expensive than the older ones. It's always a dilemma trying to balance the value of the new medications with the old.
The old ones aren't obsolete are they?
Not at all. Many are well researched and work perfectly well. Often these newer medications differ only because of lowered side-effects. If we have good control without side-effects, then the old ones are fine. If we don't, we sometimes need to go in a newer direction to get better control.
What do you think in this regard?

A day's hospitalization usually costs more than six months' worth of medication. Consequently, it's cost effective going with the newer medication if the newer medication makes a significant difference.

But Doctor, now that I've heard a little and read a lot, I don't want to take any other anticonvulsant, only Dilantin.
Why is that?
Because it's the only one I can take as a once a day dose.
You're right and wrong. All the older anticonvulsants require multiple dosing during the day, a real hassle. Once a day dosing is a major advantage of Dilantin against these older anticonvulsants. However, two of the newer ones, Lamictal and Topamax, probably can be given once a day.

I understand Dilantin comes as a liquid as well, so we can adjust the dose exactly, right?
That's a possibility, but usually not necessary.
Moreover, Tegretol made me sleepy and Depakote made me fat when I tried them both for short periods.
So you had side-effects on them and prefer Dilantin in the correct dose?
Right! So Dilantin is for me?
Maybe. Let's see. Two major criteria are: "Does it help as much or more than other drugs?" and "Does it have side-effects that are problematic?" I would like to see you free of seizures without side-effects.

T he winter had shifted to spring; the spring to a glorious summer. Harry returned for his eighth follow-up appointment during this period.

Harry, it seems that everything is going extremely well for you.
Yes indeed, Doctor. We cut down the dose of the Dilantin and I'm now consistently taking 260 mg a day, along with the extra supplementation you recommended. I take some folic acid, some vitamin D and calcium, because of Dilantin's effects on liver metabolism. Did you know, Doctor, I haven't had a single grand mal seizure since that awful time when I was hospitalized for toxicity?
Yes, I was aware of that.
And the best news is, I no longer have difficulties with my memory. I'm as sharp as I used to be! I can think, I can focus, I can concentrate, and I'm even winning regularly at chess.

We had ensured that he receive appropriate vitamin supplements and that he had regular sleep times, because, by history, sleep deprivation had aggravated his seizures. The importance of regular meals had also been impressed upon Harry: He was not going to seize because of inappropriate fluctuations in blood sugar. He had cut out his alcohol: even a tot of wine once a week seemed to trigger temporal lobe absence seizures. Harry was one of a small minority of epileptics with this problem.

It was ironic that, on his left hand, was an alert bracelet, "seizure disorder, Dilantin, see wallet," and in there was a sheet of paper listing when it would be necessary to call his doctor and his wife's number. The sheet gave a brief description of status epilepticus—one seizure superimposed on another—an occasion when hospitalization would be necessary; mentioned nursing unconscious patients on their side; and emphasized that Harry's tongue would not be swallowed during a seizure. The irony, of course, was that since the advent of that bracelet, he had never needed to use those instructions.

It's better to be prepared, Doctor, and I actually kind of like the look of it.

I looked at Harry and smiled. His Dilantin blood level was now 15. I had not meant to be Procrustean[23] about it: the usual range is 10-20. It was a pure accident that his last three levels had come back consistently between 14 and 16. His symptoms were controlled without significant side-effects. Our taper had been slow, and my monitoring careful.
But there were other minor changes that had assisted Harry in achieving an absolutely perfect record—no seizures, not even minor ones—for the last five months. Instead of him taking his whole dose at night, I had discovered that some of these small blankouts, which turned out to be complex partial seizures, would occur in the evening. So, we subdivided his dosage to twice daily to maintain an adequate therapeutic level through the day.

More revealing, perhaps, was Harry's demeanor.
You know, Doctor, I'm not irritable anymore. People don't perceive me as the "big bad wolf". In retrospect, I should have recognized the slowing and my rigid thinking and my moodiness. I thought it was just something I had to live with, but probably I was a little toxic even before I increased the dosing.
Harry, people like you enrich my life enormously. I'm so pleased that you're feeling better. It helps me to appreciate how beloved life can be for you and vicariously, through your improvement, for me. Thank you so much.

60

Chapter 3

The Woman Who Predicts Earthquakes

Strange events.
Ambulatory EEGs, cause and effect, labels (psychological),
normality, resistant focal seizures.
Lamictal.
(Lucy: patient; Martin: Lucy's husband)

It was an ordinary day and Lucy was conversing with her husband, Martin. Suddenly, the change occurred. She recognized it immediately as she had thousands of times before: that typical weird feeling, one of those unexplained sensations, which she could never put into words.

She knew what would follow, and like an observer she witnessed the symptom progression in her own body: that strange little movement always of her right thumb, then her hand forming that familiar pointless grip, and then that progressive jolt up her right arm.

She felt helpless when the next stage followed. Her mouth became numb, then her tongue, lips and chin. She listened to her husband carrying on his conversation. Martin seemed to have no awareness that Lucy had undergone any kind of event. She could hear him speaking to her.

She wanted to respond, but couldn't: That familiar sensation of not being able to speak for some sixty seconds had begun. She tried to shout out: *"I'm having another one of those episodes!"* But no word could reach up to her mouth: She was experiencing yet another speech arrest. She knew what was happening because it had happened so many times before.

Then, thirty seconds later, she was coming around, a little confused, as if she had lost some time. By that stage, something more must have happened, because Martin was no longer across the table from her, but was right by her side. Her special epileptic attack with complex partial seizures affecting one local area of the brain, causing a minor change in her consciousness, and the progressive march of her symptoms, had run its course.

Are you all right, Lucy? Are you all right?

She blinked, opened her eyes, and looked around a little perplexed. *Yes, I'm fine.*

She recognized that usual confusion that followed on a seizure.
This is the fourth one today! You know what that means: an earthquake must be close.

The following day, Lucy was drained of energy—typical after her series of seizures. From previous experience, she knew the event should be happening.

Martin turned on the TV to watch the news. At 11:05 AM, the story was broadcast: Southern California had a relatively small earthquake, 5.4 on the Richter scale. Lucy was a thousand miles away from there but, as always, seemed to have detected it.

A few minutes before she had come to me for her regular follow-up visit, I discussed her case with Andrew, the perennially inquisitive medical student. He seemed to be looking forward to meeting her for the first time and encountering a subject that intrigued his ever questioning mind.

I felt Lucy's story was an opportunity for Andrew to learn about patients that fall outside the bounds of most medical practice, and I began filling him in a little on Lucy.

Andrew, some of the patients we meet in a complex neuropsychiatric practice, are outside the limits of normal medicine. A confluence of psychological trauma, organic disease, religious dilemmas and even the ostensibly paranormal can appear, which you may be tempted to treat as madness alone. Sometimes, the doctor needs to listen deeply, to untwist the threads of the narrative and find what may be a combination of causes at the core. Lucy is such a case. It is a fact—a fact demonstrated by observation of her behavior and by statistical analysis of her predictions—that Lucy can predict earthquakes. She can't tell you where they are, and she has grown at times to hate the experience through which she gains the insight. However, almost every time there's an earthquake within a thousand miles with a magnitude over 5 on the Richter scale, Lucy will know about it at least a day in advance.

I could see Andrew's skeptical eyes narrow ever so slightly.
Surely what you're talking about is a coincidence?
In the strict sense that Lucy's seizures are co-incidental with the occurrence of earthquakes, yes. In her life, they seem to happen at the same time. That's a reality. It represents a cry calling for us to help alleviate such suffering even when we don't fully understand why.

W hen she entered the office, Lucy told us about her latest experience:
I knew it was fairly large, because it was worse than usual, but not half as bad as it could have been. The time we had one a hundred miles away, even though it was a 4.5, was really hard for me; and that one wasn't like the one in Japan, where it was somewhere between a 7 and 8.

Her scientist husband had meanwhile been doing his usual calculations.
Here's the latest breakdown of geomagnetic variation around the world: I picked it up on the Internet.

Martin had told me about this hobby of his, developed because of Lucy's strange seizures. I had some concern about the possibility of **cause and effect** where, if Lucy might have knowledge of when earthquakes had occurred, she could trigger the seizures based on that knowledge.
But how could there be any question of cause and effect, however, when the earthquakes always happen a day or two *after* the seizures? Or do they?

This time I asked.
Do you tell Lucy about what you've found on the Internet?
No. In fact, the only time I really go on is when Lucy has a cluster of seizures, and I start wondering, is something happening? So I take a record of seismic activity all the way through. You can see that 6 weeks ago, Lucy was completely clear for three weeks, and there was little earthquake activity. Sure, there's always a tiny amount all over the world—3s and 4s—but during that period, nothing close and nothing big. Then there seemed to be little clusters, and she started to get worse.

Andrew had been listening to all this with great interest, but all the same with some guarded skepticism.

But, Doctor, how do you know that Lucy's seizures are linked with earthquakes? Couldn't they be entirely unrelated and just accidentally simultaneous?

I cannot be sure, Andrew. We believe it's likely they're linked, because we did a detailed statistical analysis. We were shocked to discover that her seizure phenomena correlated with the earthquakes at a statistical level greater than one in a hundred thousand against it happening by pure chance.[24]

Has this area been studied much?

Not really. Published research on this topic has only begun: Michael Persinger in Canada, for example, has been investigating the possibility of a relationship between geomagnetism and the temporal lobe. Dr. Persinger's studies follow on my work analyzing correlates of subjective experience with the temporal lobe.[25] At any rate, in a hundred other patients, no relationship existed between their seizures and geomagnetic fluctuations, even measuring several days before and after such marked changes. Whatever else, Lucy's case is unusual if not unique.

But why would the other epileptics not have any response? Could there be some other factor—maybe psychic—accounting for Lucy's capability?

Maybe there's some common element. Maybe it's something in the atmosphere or some pulsation detected from beneath the surface of the earth; these phenomena could be the link with seizures yet all we detect is the correlation with earthquakes.

Are you prepared to say that the one causes the other?

Not necessarily. We always try to use the most parsimonious, fruitful and logical explanation for events. Sometimes we do not have obvious answers.

Do your seizures differ depending on the kind of earthquake?

Yes, Doctor. It seems that they're bigger with a larger earthquake, and smaller with the smaller ones, and the farther they are from where Lucy is, the less likely the seizures are to occur.

It seems one has to take into account two aspects of physics: distance and intensity of the earthquake.

Andrew interposed, addressing me.

Should we always have to prove events?

Not always. Sometimes it's impossible, but we must understand the experience: Sometimes we can measure it, while at other times we need to make conceptual leaps.

For example?
When an apple falls from a tree and lands on the ground, we can hypothesize that it was pure gravity. On the other hand, how do we prove gravity statistically? How do we quantify gravity? We can't see it. There's no control test we could do, involving objects falling upwards. Or alternatively, what happens if the wind carries that apple sideways? That's a confounding factor in the real world. How do we prove that gravity as a pure force exists? The practice of medicine, at times, is soft. We base our information on the best available knowledge, but sometimes establishing cause and effect relationships is difficult.

You mean it's not always a "hard" science?
No. Medicine is as much an art as a science; physicians "practice".

Lucy spoke softly looking down at the floor.
Doctor, I have a simple question.
Feel free to ask it. The simplest questions are always the most difficult to answer, and invariably elicit the greatest truths.

I want to know if my experience is normal. In fact, what is normal? Am I normal?
I told you the simplest questions are the most relevant! Normality implies coping at every level: psychologically, biologically, at a family level, at a social level, at a cultural level, and at an ethical level: **Normality** is based on a, wait for it... biopsychofamiliosociocultural model! Coping implies causing no impairments that would produce deterioration or diminished function. Coping also requires not disrupting other people's functioning as well, which happens sometimes in people with personality disorder, for example.

So am I normal?
Lucy, your seizures interfere with coping. That's abnormal, but we're trying to normalize you. Your possible detection of events is okay because it doesn't impair your coping. However, indirectly, these may be linked with your seizures. These cause problems so that side of it is abnormal. So you can see normality is relative to how you define it.

How would you measure this?
I use behavior as a measure, because it is the end-point expression, at an action level, of a person's thinking and emotions. The coping concept of normality manifests as normal behavior as opposed to just internal dynamics, such as those of thoughts, feelings or biological processes. Normality is quantified by behavior.

65

This time it was Andrew's voice that was almost challenging.

So I can think what I want and be as bizarre as I can in my dreams? That's okay?

Generally, we allow people to think and have emotions as free as they want, provided that it doesn't impair their functioning or the life of those around them. The same applies to dreams. When such personal subjective experience shows itself in impaired behavior disrupting the life of the dreamer, then this is abnormal.

That's when you're consulted, Doctor?

Yes. This becomes a catalyst for the meeting between the doctor and the patient, and this catalyst—the visible, measurable, quantifiable behavior—is at the same time an important source for the diagnosis and the search for a treatment.

That answers my question.

   Andrew appeared satisfied, but I wasn't.

Not quite.

Why?

Because you asked me two questions about subjective experience. I answered that I quantify normality only on the resultant behavior. I didn't answer your second question.

Which was?

You asked: "That's okay?"

Well, if no-one else is affected, is it okay to think what I want and be as bizarre as I can be when taking drugs?

That's a source of much debate. You can see it's different from the normality question. Effectively, if you're hallucinating on a recreational drug, but it doesn't disrupt anyone's life, is that okay? No, it isn't. You may not objectively be exhibiting behavior abnormal to others at that time even though your hallucinations are unusual for you.

The normal behavior definition would apply, but I would characterize the use of the recreational drug as abnormal socially as it contradicts federal law and is also socially deviant. So overall, that too, is abnormal as our socio-cultural parameter comes into effect; it impacts adversely on the functioning of the society. Moreover, biochemical changes in the brain may ultimately not produce normal behavior.

So when are someone's symptoms crazy?

There are certain happenings in the world, we don't fully understand or even conceive of. The easy way out is to say, "it doesn't exist and it doesn't happen, and if it does happen, the person must be mad or faking."

However, the right way out is to say, "I may not understand why this is happening, if it's happening, but I will try to find a rational, reasonable explanation for it." If a person is able to reproduce these kinds of phenomena, I will not label them as "mad", I will label them as "different". Again, we use our yard-stick. It's only if it's impairing their coping at the biological, the psychological, the social, the family, the cultural level, or at the ethical level that we then will say, "Hold on. We must treat this abnormality!"

But the issue was not merely academic. Besides the seizures, there were some negative aspects to Lucy's earthquake detection ability, her special "gift" which caused frustration.

Doctor, you know what's interesting but also annoying?
What's that, Lucy?
Sometimes I miss: sometimes, when there's an earthquake, I don't always have a seizure. In fact, sometimes I just get this absolute fatigue and I'm knocked out and I sleep the whole day and I have a headache. Could it be that this is the equivalent of a seizure?

Again, the grass fire analogy seemed an appropriate response.
You ask a good question. It could well be that you were having seizure phenomena in your brain and not being aware of it: so many of them, in fact, that it had made your brain fatigued. In other words, it was like a grass fire, which your brain then put out, leaving the smoky after-burn of fatigue and the other symptoms you mentioned. The grass has to re-grow and this takes time.
It's true, Doctor. Because sometimes the ones that are the closest or most powerful just make me utterly exhausted for two or three days before. It's almost like I don't even have the energy to have a seizure; and yet within hours of the earthquake happening, even when I don't know about it, which is most of the time, I begin to feel better. It's weird!

Lucy stopped, quietly mulling over her comment, shaking her head and then came another, perhaps even more personal question.
I don't want to lose this ability to feel when an earthquake is happening, Doctor, but it seems to link up only with my seizures and this terrible burned-out feeling. Do you think I could maybe just have the ability without the seizures?

I empathized with her, as I knew she was asking a pained question.

It would be wonderful if you could, Lucy. Unfortunately, at this point, it seems that we may well be dealing with something that necessarily correlates in the brain. I cannot absolutely prove that it correlates 100% or even 70% or 80%. We might even be dealing with an entirely different cause and effect, but at the moment, it's best to hypothesize that you're detecting some kind of geological phenomenon.

And that's earthquakes?
Not necessarily. Maybe there's a third common outlying cause like fluctuations in the earth's magnetic transmissions. Maybe it's purely coincidental.

But Doctor, I want to ask my question again and this time I'm not being funny: Could it be, that I might ever get to a point where I will predict earthquakes healthily?
Only if the underlying brain link-up is normalized and yet at the same time this does not impact your ability. As your ability seems to based on your pathology, it would be difficult to conceive of this. It's like the window outside your mind will be shut if we control the events in the room that's your brain.

Andrew had listened quietly to this point.
Can you refresh my memory about how you first noticed the relationship, Lucy?
A few days after a series of massive seizures that over-rode my medication, I read in the newspaper about a large earthquake in California. Silent weeks would then pass without seizures and normal activities. Then I would again have a terrible cluster of disabling attacks that would wipe out a weekend; and again the news would report an earthquake in Alaska or even as far away as Nicaragua.

So when did you establish the link?
It was a strange story, but the way we discovered the link was even stranger. I didn't figure out the connection myself. It was only when the researchers serendipitously analyzed these effects statistically that it became clear.

At this juncture, Andrew turned to me, finally shifting topic a little.
Do you think we might find some clues in Lucy's in-depth medical history, Doctor?
I have taken Lucy's history already, previously. However, I had planned to devote the second half of Lucy's visit today to a more in-depth review

of key areas to see if there was relevant new ground to cover, so it was a well-timed question.

Lucy, why don't you tell us about the first time you had a seizure. What happened, and what led up to it?

Well, Doctor, in the winter when I was 22 and in college, I became deathly ill. My temperature reached 105 degrees, I was hospitalized with symptoms of vomiting and the most terrible headaches, my spinal fluid was taken, and I was diagnosed with viral encephalitis, which they told me was a viral inflammation of the brain. Then, shortly after I recovered, I began to experience these unusual seizures.

Before this illness came upon you, do you recall any significant traumas in your life?

Absolutely not. I had a happy childhood, came from an affluent loving family and was educated at private religious schools. I have searched for unusual events in my life that I could latch onto, but I must tell you everything from my normal birth through to my happy marriage has been without major traumas. I was fortunate enough to complete my college degree after my encephalitis and as you know I've worked for many years as a computer software consultant since then.

Andrew wanted to complete the picture.

How did you discover the seizures, Doctor?

When I first met Lucy, she was suffering from clusters of six to seven seizures every day. On her second visit, my assistant called me into the exam room: I found Lucy partially undressed and in the midst of one of her seizures. Luckily, her feet were bare, and we found that during the seizure she displayed an upward curling up of the toes when her soles were stroked.

You mean the Babinski response?

Very good, Andrew. Now, in anyone but the newborn whose brains are still relatively undeveloped, a Babinski response always indicates a problem with neurological deficits. She also lacked a corneal reflex response during her seizures: Her eyes did not blink in response to a cotton stimulus on its edge. All of these diagnostic features are important to keep in mind because they prove that, however bizarre her story, Lucy has an organic medical problem. Without such documentation, these frontal lobe seizures could have been misdiagnosed as hysteria.

How do we know the frontal lobe is involved?

We know that because of her kinds of symptoms. She has a speech arrest as a consistent part of her seizures. The speech arrest indicates a problem in the dominant hemisphere of the brain.

69

Specific characteristics of the arrest allowed us to pinpoint the damaged area further. Her seizures do not keep Lucy from understanding instructions–she can understand language. Her disability is speech output–expressive speech. She can understand but cannot vocalize even though when we observe her seizures, her muscles of speech–which, of course, she can control under normal circumstances–seem intact, and she actually tries to talk sometimes. This function is located near the posterior part–the back–of the frontal lobe in the dominant hemisphere of the brain. Technically, because of her sensation change around her mouth, an area next to this, in the anterior part–front–of the parietal lobe must also be involved.[26]

What about the rest of her seizure sequence?
This has varied a little over the years in the exact character of the muscle movements that they begin with. However, they have consistently been on her right side with speech arrest.
I have observed Lucy having a fully-fledged frontal lobe seizure. This begins with a rapid rotation of the head, then follows the "Jacksonian march" of symptoms–a tremor developing in her right hand that gradually became a jerking of the forearm and finally movement of the whole arm and shoulder.
Finally, the seizures end with impairment of responsiveness with speech arrest, followed by confusion.

Why is it called "Jacksonian march"?
The phenomenon is named after a late nineteenth century British expert in epilepsy, Hughlings Jackson, who first noted this crescendo of movement during seizures.

So this kind of seizure means that the encephalitis had damaged Broca's area?
Exactly. The Broca's area of the brain is responsible for expressive speech and that is in the posterior frontal lobe. Her seizure movements are also consistent with this diagnosis–rapid and aversive head movements and a gradual progression with Jacksonian movements. These features also fit the same broad locality.

Was there any other localizing information?
Yes. A final clue is that Lucy cannot write too much with her right hand as her arm grows quickly tired; this happens at times unrelated to her seizures. These symptoms, also, suggest frontal lobe involvement, and are commensurate with scarring we have found in the left posterior frontal area on a Nuclear Magnetic Resonance Imaging–MRI–test of the head.
From what you have told me, I assume her laterality is purely right sided?

Andrew was sounding like a doctor.

You're correct. Lucy has pure right laterality. This means she writes, bats, throws and kicks with the right side of her body being dominant. She even looks down a monocular microscope with her right eye. This means, of course, that the left side of her brain is the dominant hemisphere. We expect this to be so as her seizure events make sense: She has a left frontal lobe seizure focus and she has speech arrests.

Andrew shifted gear just slightly.

What was the opinion of her previous physician?

Before we saw her, Lucy had been treated with anticonvulsant medications to help control her daily seizures. Her doctors had begun to wonder whether she needed this medication. This was so because while in hospital for a period of observation, she had no seizures at all: All the sophisticated video-telemetric monitoring of her actions and specialized measures of her brain waves by round the clock EEG monitoring could not produce a seizure if it was not going to happen. When we trace back the dates of her hospitalization, this correlates with a quiescent earthquake period.

And she never had any seizures?

This is not uncommon. People in hospitals lie in a bed without real-life anxiety. We know stress increases the possibility of seizures, incidentally. Many patients with epilepsy do not seize while in the hospital because of the environment, controlled temperature, enforced rest and inactivity.

Outside of a hospital environment, is there any harm trying to see what would happen to her condition if she were off medication?

I'm afraid there is. As an example, a patient of one of my colleagues had her "seizures" labeled as purely psychological. She was taken off all medication, and lived for a full year without a problem: one full year. At the end of that year, she was brought into the hospital by ambulance with full blown status epilepticus, an unending cascade of seizures with each new one superimposed on the last. She couldn't be controlled, and within hours of the onset of her seizures, she died.

Yet you say that Lucy's previous physician wanted to take her off all her anticonvulsants?

Yes. Because of her lack of seizures on regular EEG, her last doctor had stopped all her medication. This was the puzzle she presented. Her referring physician thought she had hysterical epilepsy—so-called pseudo-seizures.

Why?

71

Based on the diagnosis of what I call positive negation—the most dangerous form of medicine. Seizures had not been found while in hospital, so obviously there were no epileptic seizures; however, she was having events which were unusual: She must be hysterical.

But I'm still missing part of the story, Doctor. How did this diagnostic difference become resolved?
Let's go back a little in time.
After Lucy had consulted with me on two occasions, I received a call from her previous neurologist. He asked how Lucy was doing, but seemed to have a secondary educational motive to the call. When I said she was doing well on anticonvulsants, he disagreed. "You're being fooled," he said. "You might as well have her on placebo. It's just your faith in the drugs and her faith in you. That's all it is."

What did he do?
Apparently, he had also contacted Lucy, and she soon announced to her husband that she didn't need any medication. It was making her sleepy; she had side-effects; and besides, she was cured. First she cut the medication in half, then she stopped it altogether over a period of two months. A week after she quit her anticonvulsants, she finally called me to report that she was doing just fine and that she had decided to stop all her medication.

And how did you feel?
I was far from comfortable with that decision.
I told Lucy that I was pleased about her feeling well, but I was very concerned about her condition and that the vacation from her seizures would inevitably end, probably sooner than later.

So what did you do?
I was worried enough to contact her husband and ask him to persuade his wife to restart her medication. I drew the parallel of diabetics, the majority of whom, at some point out of denial of their illness, abandon their insulin, occasionally with disastrous results. Lucy was not, of course, diabetic, but epileptics also sometimes deny the reality of their seizures. Even worse, because seizures occur episodically, the deluge can occur at any time.

That was Monday. On Wednesday, she was brought into the Emergency Room with frontal lobe status epilepticus, a life-threatening state where one seizure is super-imposed upon another. Instead of a spark here or there in the tinder, Lucy had a forest fire in her brain.

That's a vivid and rather unsettling image.
Yes, Andrew, it is. We brought Lucy to the emergency room by ambulance and worked for half an hour to bring her spells under control. She was not fully aware of what was happening to her, but she knew that some "episode" was occurring. People around her would tell her about strange head movements, the long minutes when she was unable to respond to questions or talk, and her tendency to drift off to sleep complaining of a headache—a typical sequel to a seizure. One episode superimposed upon another during this, her worst period.

So what did you do at that point?
We hooked her to an electroencephalogram–EEG–right there. She was seizing so much that we had difficulty attaching the electrodes. Over her eyes in the left frontal lobe there was constant neural–nerve–firing. We gave her intravenous anticonvulsant medications and gradually she came out of the spell. Yet the EEG data looked ambiguous because muscle movement over the eye muscles can be read as seizures.

Were you reading a seizure in her brain or only the twitching of her face?
That, of course, is an important question. Several experts felt the tracing showed genuine seizures.
But can a person fake an EEG?
No.

Is voluntary twitching picked up as a seizure, too?
It should not be. However, muscle movements can so distort readings that the genuine brain waves underneath cannot be read. So this muscle artifact sometimes makes readings more difficult.

What are you getting at with these questions, Andrew?
What I'm wondering is, couldn't even positive findings on an EEG be construed as inherently inconclusive in ruling out a psychological cause?
It's not quite as bleakly ambiguous as that, Andrew, and as you know, there are different kinds of EEG. Somehow, we had to settle whether her seizures were real or imaginary.

Why? Was there still dispute?
Lucy's other doctor—the same neurologist, who incidentally was not present, during this episode—was convinced that the breakdown must have just been "hysterical". He wanted to take her off her anticonvulsants again. He even threatened to commit her to an inpatient mental ward and told her flatly that her medications were all placebos. He was prepared to make a big gamble: if he was wrong, Lucy might have another episode of status epilepticus, and with one seizure being superimposed on another,

she could die. Fortunately, now that Lucy was under control, she finally realized that maybe something was truly going on.

Lucy entered the office.
I've stopped denying these seizures, Doctor. But it would be useful if I could demonstrate one of my episodes during the EEG. I want to prove that I'm not a hysteric. Can you increase the chances of my having episodes?
As you know, in a regular EEG, the flashing lights and overbreathing may bring episodes out, but they haven't in the past for you. Some people use particular placements of electrodes, for example, down the nose and under the skin near the ear or cheeks. However, the statistical yield does not justify the inconvenience here.

I looked directly at Lucy.
I have a far better idea.
What's that?
Home ambulatory EEG.

I've never heard of it. What is it?
It's an important recent advance. If you have some of the target symptoms that you've described, we may be able to pick up some firing that's occurring in the brain while it's occurring.

What does it involve?
Home ambulatory encephalography is basically the same as a regular EEG, in that you're hooked up to various electrodes. The ambulatory EEG machine is portable so that you can wear it at home to monitor brain function every minute of the 48 or 72 hours it is worn during all activities. Consequently, it permits a much more complete analysis of complex symptoms than the usual regular office EEG. It's the latest technology available for out-patient monitoring—you go home plugged into a small but sophisticated computer. In your own natural environment events may be more likely to occur than in a hospital.

What do I need to do?
You should press a "push-button" for any events that occur.

Explain?
You've already mentioned how you frequently find yourself having several different episodes which last seconds and come on suddenly.
Let's list a few: your sudden burning smells; your irritability that springs up out of nowhere; your fluctuations of mood over seconds; that rising sensation in your stomach; and your actual blankouts.

If any occur, you press a special push-button, and chart "strange smell" or whatever happened. The ambulatory EEG then correlates the episode with any recorded abnormal brain firing at the time.

What exactly does that imply?
This way we hope to determine exactly where the firing is arising, how frequently it's happening and what kind of firing is happening. We're also able to establish whether the events you recognize by push-button may be linked with seizure firing.

What if I'm unaware of an event?
A member of your family can press the button. In fact, people are often unaware of their seizures, so a family member has to press the push-button.

If I have an episode but realize it only after it's over, what's the point in pressing the button?
We'll obtain a reading: The push-button has the capability of going backward in time a bit–it will actually allow us to detect what happened up to two minutes before. Consequently, it is, in effect, a marker for what has happened.

What other symptoms should I look out for?
You'll remember we have used a paper and pencil and computerized screen test–the INSET [27]–looking at your symptoms. We then amplified these symptoms. Let's go through your positive answers so you can understand the kinds of symptoms that may be linked with firing of the temporal lobe.

Yes, I gave several positive responses.
We have listed some like the strange smells. You also have the episodes of speech arrest. You mentioned several rare symptoms that may or may not be relevant like confusion episodes, the sensation of moving and the spots in your front vision. You also told me about ear ringing, weirdness distortion, acute anxiety which switches on or off in seconds, and sudden compulsive thoughts. Other symptoms seem to occasionally occur as well with episodes of intense religious feeling, distortion of word order, slowing of speech, momentary difficulty concentrating, nausea lasting seconds and some paranormal–psychic–experiences.

So what do these mean?
These are examples of what I call "possible temporal lobe symptoms". If any of these happen episodically–changes occurring in an instant or in seconds–even if it's the most minor of things, like the sense of déjà vu, or a major event like an explosion, press the push-button as we might be

able to pick up something on EEG. On the other hand, it's possible the firing waves may not surface in the scalp, as they derive so deep in the brain. Alternatively, the symptoms may be non-specific and have no seizure firing, not correlating with any brain wave.

Do I do anything special other than marking down my episodes?
No. Just carry on your regular routine.

What if I don't end up pressing the button at all?
Is there any value to the test then?
Yes. Even if you don't press the push-button, we may detect silent episodes—events you're not necessarily aware of, unassociated with any symptoms you know about, but which also reflect firing. These may occur during the waking day or during natural sleep.

So we obtain measures of sleep?
Yes. In fact, we obtain good physiological measures of sleep in the usual environment of your home and we frequently pick up numerous abnormalities during sleep.

Do we measure anything else?
Indeed. As an extra, besides the sixteen (and in some models twenty-four) brain channels, we're able to detect abnormalities of heart rhythm, of muscle movements around the eye and jaw, and periods of apneic respiration—where you stop breathing for a half or one minute during the night.

Does the ambulatory EEG interfere with my activities?
Not really. As you go from room to room in your house, you will unplug yourself and re-plug yourself in. You obviously cannot shower with the apparatus on—it's not waterproof.

So I could do anything other than get it wet?
Yes, you can theoretically. However, in practice, most people look a little like astronauts and they don't go out much. I've never had a patient who said, "Don't worry, Doctor, I'll be going off to work wearing this!" One patient who was a little bit of an exhibitionist would deliberately order pizza, and she really got a kick out of shocking the pizza delivery man, but that was an exception.

Is there a difference between a regular and an ambulatory EEG hookup?
Yes, though you're hooked up to the same kinds of EEG electrodes in an ambulatory EEG, they're stuck on far more securely so they can last several days.

But surely one day of monitoring is enough?
Not really. You could be fairly clear one day, and then the second day, you may have fifteen episodes. So we can determine how consistent or variable your seizures are from one day to another.

Do I have to be plugged in electrically for the whole two days?
No. There's a battery source for short periods. So if you are in a car, or out in the garden, and an episode happened, you could press the push-button and activate the tracing. We have found this resource valuable.

What if the times I did press the push-button all turn out to be normal?
Sometimes the electrically normal episodes are important. For example, you mentioned an attack of a music sound in your ear, and separately that your thoughts fluctuate over minutes. You also described that you have episodes of disorientation for date and time, as well as distortions of the sense of time, your word order and your pronunciation. Additionally, you listed slurring of speech, not being able to understand things, and difficulty concentrating. These could turn out not to correlate with the EEG: They may not be seizure phenomena.

Why not stick with a regular EEG?
We must be lucky to pick up specifics. We have two hours on an office couch with regular EEGs and two days at home with ambulatory EEG. Also, regular EEGs have "noise", which we have to get beneath to read the relevant data. The ambulatory EEG computer filters out most of the artifact.

Artifact?
Yes, the "noise": It's the technical term for disturbances that have nothing to do with the brain. The most common problems are muscle movements over specific areas like the temples, forehead, jaw or eyes. Another problem is when an electrode–the attachment of the electrical measure to the head–becomes loose. The tracing may be distorted also by electric blankets or waterbed heaters. These are often difficult to differentiate from real EEG tracing in regular EEGs. Sometimes the movements are so great that it's hard to find a genuine brain wave underneath.

But my regular EEG was normal before, so should I even bother?
The parallel that I like to draw is the following: Sometimes we will come across normal EEG waves despite expecting to pick up some
abnormality, and the person will say, "but nothing happened that weekend!" It's rather like saying, "we're going to do an EEG tracing while monitoring a baseball star's home-run swing." But he doesn't hit a home-run. From that do we conclude that there's no home run swing or that we

have not yet ascertained what the EEG waves would be like while hitting home-runs?

When do you decide this ambulatory EEG test is necessary?
When we have not obtained sufficient data from a regular office EEG tracing and we have a suspicion there may be some seizure firing in the brain. Although ambulatory EEG is a neurological procedure, not infrequently we find episodic psychiatric problems have been misdiagnosed. It's critical to recognize this, as the abnormality may require medication, and such firing would not respond to conventional psychotherapy, although the support may be useful.

If there's only one event, would it be cost effective?
If you have only one occurrence in two days, it might be like saying there's this new currency sitting in the mint. If you have twenty occurrences one day and then only one the next day, then we know your seizure firing in the brain fluctuates. If you have fifteen the one day and fifteen the next, then we know it's likely consistent and we have an index of severity.

What if I have no episodes of firing in the brain?
Then we will base our opinion clinically. It's still possible that something is going on in your brain, but that's less likely and unproven. Sometimes, negative results indirectly support another hypothesis by exclusion, as when, for example, the electrical test has not confirmed the firing. This allows other hypotheses like the events are in the abnormal chemistry or in a damaged structure in the brain. On the other hand, some of the experiences may be due to non-specific medical reasons; or they may be due to psychological causes...

Like which symptoms?
The episodic sense of weirdness, the sense of time being slowed down or speeded up and the sense that you're just watching yourself or not part of yourself; also, when these happen episodically, the sudden unreasonable thoughts that come into your head. In these instances, we will detect no change.

So even negative tests are valuable?
They can be by exclusion. At least we're reasonably confident that nothing profound is happening inside the brain.

> Lucy's flood of questions just did not end.
> She had suffered a long time.
> This time she wanted to make sure everything was right.

Surely we don't need this test if people know they're having episodic events?
We do. First, some people can recognize an episode each and every time on an ambulatory EEG. If they're not having any episodes other than those that they're recognizing, we probably don't need to repeat the test (say) six months later on treatment: We can rely on their subjective detections. However, sometimes, patients may be having several episodes a day which they don't even recognize are occurring.

But how can people not know they're having seizures?
Because even though there may be firing in the brain, there may be no clinical correlate: In other words, the person doesn't experience anything. You can imagine that there are many "silent" areas in the brain—so if firing goes on there, it just fires. In order for you to experience something, it has to impact a brain area that your conscious mind can recognize as relevant. For example, when it suddenly hits the area pertaining to the arms, you might experience arm jerks; or if it hits an area pertaining to smell, you might perceive strange smells.

But do all areas of the brain do something, Doctor?
Not always. Sometimes, firing in a silent area—and this is a vast part of the higher brain—produces no subjective experience in consciousness, but may be doing insidious damage all the same because seizures are not usually healthy. So people often don't know they're having little seizures.

Could we just monitor me during the day, Doctor? It may be uncomfortable at night.
Actually, people are able to sleep rather easily while hooked up to the ambulatory EEG apparatus. That's important because sleep sometimes allows us to detect many seizures; maybe the brain is quieter, so we can detect events in the scalp more easily, but certain events seem to happen predominantly in sleep. One reason why regular EEGs may not pick up what monitoring over two or three days does is because we have only a tiny amount of chloral hydrate induced sleep and no REM—rapid eye movement or dream—sleep. If the abnormality happens exclusively during those phases, we won't detect them on regular EEG.

Surely, it's better to be admitted to the hospital for this procedure?
No. This is an out-patient procedure.
You'll remember the inpatient—in the hospital—procedure where your EEG is monitored while you lie in bed and simultaneously a video is run so that events can also be analyzed by videotape. This is good, although ultimately the decision is not usually based on the video, but on the brain waves, so the value of the video is to see if you have psychological non-epileptic events.

So if the video is useful, why not just hospitalize?
The problem is you're not likely to have any episodes there; it's a different environment with less stressors.
So it may take weeks of monitoring sometimes to obtain an answer, and, in any event, some people's psychological problems co-exist with genuine seizures, anyway. Instead, home EEG monitoring has no video, but has a real life situation where episodes of symptoms may happen.

So will all my symptoms in my head be detected?
No. A headache for a whole day is not going to produce change on ambulatory EEG. On the other hand, headache just suddenly occurring for one or two seconds may produce change.
If you had persistent strange smells occurring throughout the day, we generally are not going to find a change. It's the episodic phenomena that we're looking for on ambulatory EEG.

Lucy's flood of questions was finally ebbing.
Most people can't have this test, right?
Right. I don't know how to answer if yours is a rare condition, because you are fortunate to have ambulatory EEG available. It's an apparatus that's not available to 99.9% of the American population at the moment; there just aren't enough facilities around, as it's too expensive to be readily available. However, without it, we may miss the diagnoses of undetected seizures and with it the opportunity to turn around a life.
Let's go for it.

And so we performed an ambulatory EEG on Lucy, monitoring her in her home environment for two days, using state of the art computerized EEG hardware and software.

We also had the tracing independently assessed by an expert on the East coast.

Well, what did you find out?
Over a period of 48 hours, you had absolutely no abnormalities except under one circumstance: You pushed the button fourteen times when you felt your typical episode associated with the speech arrest coming on. Thirteen of the fourteen episodes were definitively assessed as true left frontal lobe seizures. The fourteenth was difficult to assess, but also appeared abnormal.
 It seems you not only may have a capacity to detect strange earth phenomena, Lucy. You have a remarkable skill to pick up each and every seizure you have. This can serve you well in future evaluations.

80

Surely that's common?
It should be, but it's not. Many people who have seizures have far more silent episodes on ambulatory EEG than they have real events corresponding to the times they pressed the button.

Andrew, as usual, had his own series of questions.
Are these abnormal results on ambulatory EEG an answer?
I would assume so. When two events correlate, we should ask: Is it coincidence or a relevant correlation? The medical approach has always been to associate symptoms and signs when appropriate. When we find a test that's abnormal which potentially fits the clinical framework of symptoms, we assume that the two are related and have relevance.

And Lucy should not have another episode of status epilepticus like you described earlier or is it an ever-present danger?
Status epilepticus is a dangerous condition, but it is unlikely to occur again with Lucy taking medication.

What's your plan of action, Doctor?
First, we'll put her back on anticonvulsant medication. I have chosen to look sequentially through several of the main anticonvulsants, if necessary to mix and match, measuring change by seizure frequency, even with any earth movements. I will temper this with trying to find the lowest amounts of side-effects and the highest efficacy. I think we will achieve our goal of fully controlling Lucy's seizures, although it may take a year or two because of the complexity of her condition.

Lucy went back onto anticonvulsants: Almost immediately, her life stabilized again.

It was nearly two years later. Andrew stopped by and asked me about Lucy, and I began to pick up where we had left off.

So, Doctor, what have you done about Lucy's seizures?
We have tried a series of different anticonvulsant medications to establish which one is the best for Lucy.

How do we know the medication is controlling the episodes?
This is a difficulty for most people: We may know when people have episodic events of seizures or atypical spells; but we do not know if patients are completely under control when events are not occurring. We know

they're better than they were, but are they at risk for a seizure? That's the essence.

But such monitoring of seizures is easier for Lucy?
Maybe, as we have records of major earthquakes, and we're finding that Lucy is surviving these periods with far fewer seizures than before. This suggests much better control.

What have you prescribed?
We have given Lucy several different anticonvulsants sequentially: Tegretol, Dilantin, combinations of the two, then Depakote. At one point, she was on small doses of all three. Lucy did well at one point on Felbatol, but unfortunately, had such significant side-effects that we had to stop it. She has also received a benzodiazepine like Klonopin, but this had little impact.

You've been able to do all this?
We have been able to do these assessments relatively quickly because of the failed control and the quick effects of anticonvulsants compared with the three weeks it takes for antidepressants to become effective.
Incidentally, one of her physicians even gave her some antidepressants: Lucy, at times, had been distressed about her experiences.

What do the antidepressants do?
Most antidepressants characteristically increase the frequency of seizures, and that's exactly what happened in Lucy's case.

But what about the anticonvulsants that were tried?
They helped, but not when any significant geomagnetic fluctuations occurred. Lucy would then have eight or sometimes even twenty of her complex partial seizure episodes in one day.

Well, is Lucy better like you promised?
> Andrew's tone was almost a challenge, but a concerned one:
> He clearly did care.
Yes. I'm pleased with how she has done.

What are you treating her with now?
Finally, we have settled on the drug Lamictal (lamotrigine). It's one of the newer anticonvulsant medications in the United States, although it has been around for several years in many other countries. It's an outstanding anticonvulsant.

How does it work clinically?
Lamictal seems to have two effects: We're using it to put out the fire. However, as an added bonus, we are noticing a gradual stabilization in

mood. That effect has been much slower–it can take up to six weeks. Whether or not this mood normalization relates directly to putting out fires, which then gradually stabilize the beloved mind, or whether it's a separate effect, we don't know. I think the easiest hypothesis relates to putting out the fires which allow for gradual physiologic stabilization.

Are you satisfied with the Lamictal?
Yes. I perceive it as at the same kind of efficacy level as Dilantin, Tegretol and Depakote: I regard it as a primary anticonvulsant, even though it's marketed as an "add on": You'll recall that all the newer anticonvulsants are approved by the FDA only as add on anticonvulsants as studies couldn't be done with them on their own. The physician, however, is allowed to make a judgment choice and can choose to use these drugs alone.

So are you using it as an add on, Doctor?
Yes and no. We're using Lamictal [300 mg per day] as the primary anticonvulsant. However, Lucy happens also to be taking tiny doses of Tegretol [200 mg daily], which seems to help take the edge off the intensity of some of the episodes when they happen.

And have you repeated the ambulatory EEG?
Yes, and one episode, recognized by Lucy, occurred in a two day period. This is added confirmation.

A few minutes later, Lucy entered and shared an experience that brought us back to pragmatism.
I have noticed, Doctor, that if I decrease the Lamictal, I start to get seizures again. I get a hazy state like a memory of a dream that makes no sense and secondary impressions go along with it: like an extreme sense of wrongness and a misapplication of the laws of physics, if that makes any sense to you; but it's an extremely odd experience and has its own set of physical symptoms that go with it.

I confess Lucy's description didn't make full sense to me, but neither, for that matter, had Lucy's experiences with earthquakes. I understood the gist of what she was saying. Sometimes when events happen in rather unused areas of the brain, they're difficult to describe because we don't have a vocabulary that fits.

I responded circumspectly:
When you have a seizure, do you feel you could access parts of your subconscious which otherwise you could not access, almost in a kind of dreamlike state?

83

That's exactly it, and there are times when it's so colorful that it sucks me in and it's hard for me to know where I really am.

Your kinds of episodes could easily have never been diagnosed. Many specialists might never realize that these are actually seizure phenomena. You aren't being moody or impaired or not understanding what is going on; you actually are having seizure episodes. They say that seizure episodes occur among only one in two hundred of the population. My impression is that we're probably dealing with a frequency possibly five fold greater, as many events go completely undetected: People think of seizures as grand mal seizures, when in fact, these aurae are seizures as well.

Lucy was also always a person who held out great hope.

When can I be allowed to drive a car, Doctor? You don't know how traumatic it is for me not to drive.

I truly feel for you, Lucy, but you know the answer: Unfortunately you cannot. You're not seizure-free and you run a risk not only to yourself, but to anyone on the road, even pedestrians.

How will we tell when I am ready?

Basically, when you are seizure-free. We also use other information. We make the assumption that the chances of an event are small the longer control exists. So often physicians or licensing departments use a period of twelve to eighteen months of seizure-free time to decide whether the patient can drive. Obviously, the risk even then is higher than the general population; but then the risk is also higher after heart attacks, in the very old, in narcoleptics, or in anxious patients, to name but a few groups who are not as scrutinized as the epileptic.

Anything else?

Yes, we can repeat the procedure. Ambulatory EEGs are particularly useful to establish that no silent firing episodes are occurring: if they are not, we know we have achieved even better control—certainly over the days of the procedure.

With you, it's unnecessary possibly, as you seem to be aware of all your seizure events.

So that's it?

Not quite. Clinically, we distinguish episodes of loss of consciousness from seizure events without impaired consciousness—simple partial attacks. These are obviously far less risky for driving except that they also can progress to full blown seizures.

We also carefully look at events that appear psychological, but may actually be firing, such as explosive outbursts.

Any other relevant points?
One final consideration: there's the role of the sedation caused by the medication. This is more general for many types of prescriptions, but something to note particularly with driving long distances, in poor ventilation or with great heat.

At this point, Andrew renewed an old theme.
What about the earthquake connection, Doctor?
Andrew, you never give up. Our object here is to treat the seizures and diminish suffering. Whether or not the earthquakes are or are not linked could always be a source of debate, because it's controversial and unusual. It's not highly relevant except in the context of impacting seizure control; that seizure control can be measured by using anticonvulsant medication.

I thought that would close the issue, but it didn't quite; Andrew turned to me.

Seizures linked with variations in earthquakes? I've finally solved it! Doesn't the Earth vibrate at a particular frequency? Could this be the link?
Good question, Andrew. You're referring to the "Schumann Resonance". This frequency, generally stated as about eight cycles per second (Hz)[28], in fact varies quite a bit depending on atmospheric effects in the ionosphere. Positive and negative ions shift rapidly, at the speed of light, producing a vibrational frequency with potentially numerous further harmonics. The problem is that the Schumann frequency occurs only under certain conditions, like lightning. However, you can see how this impacts on brain-waves. Certainly many alternative help groups have tried to utilize this effect to improve skills or to meditate. It's interesting that our resting alpha waves are at 8 to 13 cycles per second.

Could it be that Lucy links up with these cycles and resonates, and in this way is picking up the geomagnetic variations?
Maybe this is what's being picked up, but it's highly speculative. Does it just happen that these variations, some of which may be precursors to seismic activity, synchronize in a way that makes her seize, just like some people seize when exposed to particular kinds of photic light stimulation?

Fascinating. A sonic corollary to the photic phenomenon!
Well, what's the answer?
Debatable: It's easy to explain events post hoc—after they happen—but whether that's the true explanation, I do not know.

85

Do you think Lucy was becoming increasingly sensitive to every change in her environment that might cause a seizure?
It's not atypical for epileptics to experience a gradual worsening of their conditions. Seizures beget seizures. Damaged or hyper-sensitive areas of the brain can become more damaged, producing more extreme symptoms. Focal seizures in one hemisphere may be followed by "mirror" local damage in the same area of the other hemisphere. Eventually, some patients have generalized events like grand mal.

I may not have been fully able to appease Andrew's dogged inquisitiveness or his furrowed brow, but I suspect he came away from our consideration of Lucy with a deeper appreciation of the superb efficacy of anticonvulsants, with an awareness of the responsibilities of the physician, with a feel for the dangers of making ill-considered medical decisions, and with an insight that we may not know everything about the world.

And in that regard, Lucy still loses control, but only before some major quakes. When she does, it's to a lesser degree. It requires a large quake or one that's nearby to evoke responses. The control on Lamictal is truly remarkable. Still, month by month, the confirming evidence comes in, usually as a call from Lucy or her husband. "She's out of control, Doctor," and then, a day later, a whacker of a quake occurs somewhere in the Western United States.

Andrew smiled kindly.
So Lucy is doing well?
She has never done better. In fact, she doesn't have too many seizure episodes, even with the earthquakes. It could be said that our earthquake detector is failing.

Lucy came to see me last week. She was radiating the warmth that I've always known she had. Her golden locks and brown eyes glistened as if to say "I am better." She exhibited not a trace of depression. Her seizure control had made the difference. She brought a record of her seizures for the past month: Quite blank, except for two clusters. Penciled in were comments—a small quake in California produced a mild seizure and some disorientation, while a larger quake a nearby state had produced a very bad weekend.

She smiled.
I've come to accept the things I cannot change. Maybe some day they'll pay me to predict earthquakes!

86

Chapter 4

Defying The Norm

Epileptic psychosis.
Hypoglycemia, levels of function, normal variation,
targeted prescribing.
Depakote. (Eileen)

I was writing notes on my patients in a small office just off the inpatient ward of the hospital. Picking up Eileen's chart, I began to write: *She has not yet demonstrated green skin*. There was a knock on the door, and there she stood.

Doctor, my skin's turned green!

I wasn't surprised. We had seen it all before, every stage of the rigid delusional stereotype that followed after a cluster of epileptic seizures.
Nor was I surprised when she came back a few minutes later making several disconnected statements.

You know, I'm worried that I'm becoming homosexual. My skin, you know, my skin isn't real. They've made it completely of leaves.

And then she continued with the non-sequitur that always followed the skin story.

Did you know my husband is having an affair?

I expected the next phase, which came about three minutes later. She knocked on the door again, softly, and leaned her head in through the partially open doorway.

That Russian lady out there. I don't know why they sent her to spy on me, but I know she's working for the CIA. You Doctor, I trust you, but that lady and the head nurse and the cafeteria lady, they're all CIA agents!

87

She ended her declaration with a convinced if extravagant look in her eye, and closed the door politely to leave me alone. I nodded momentarily as if to communicate that she had run the full course of her delusions, and nothing more would occur.

Andrew, who had been sitting with me, looked a bit incredulous.
Who was that?
That was Eileen, a patient of mine. She has an almost unique kind of seizure disorder which began following a mountaineering fall at age 26. By that stage, she had a PhD in Physics. Since her seizures began, every few months she has had these intermittent episodes, always following a cluster of two or three seizures on the same night. Every one of them has exactly the same bizarre thinking—almost like an area of the brain starts firing a repetitive video. These have been scattered between her regular seizures. She carries on her personal relationships, and functions reasonably between these events. However, you can imagine that her uncontrolled epilepsy has led to unemployment. To give herself a sense of self-worth, she has occupied her time with volunteer work.

Andrew was intrigued.
Will you tell me more about Eileen's seizures?
She has a grand mal seizure about once a week and other than some confusion does okay after it. However, every few months, Eileen has a cluster of full blown grand mal epileptic seizures, possibly two or three together during the night. This cluster is frequently linked with this fixed series of events which follow.
It always begins the same way, usually on a Wednesday night. The following morning, Eileen feels distressed and agitated, and her thoughts start to become disorganized. She can't concentrate at all; and she feels as if she's swimming in a twilight sea, where real objects merge with fantasy. As the hours pass, she would become more and more overwhelmed, until her husband realizes it's time to bring her to the hospital. These events are so regular and stereotyped they may as well be a movie clip.

And that, I assume is what brought her here this time?
Yes.

How long do these episodes last?
Generally, they clear within two days; and afterwards, she's usually amnesic for the events of the past fifty or so hours.

You mean she doesn't remember anything?
That's right. It's as if a repetitive movie plays out in front of us all—always identical, down to the most basic detail. She later on deduces she's been

in hospital and friends or family or I tell her what was happening, but she's incredulous and denies any direct knowledge of it.

And then after the episode?
She behaves quite normally. So we know that three days in the hospital is adequate. In fact, now that we have involved her husband we hope to totally abort these hospitalizations by initiating high dose antipsychotic medication as soon as the events begin.

Does she always have these delusions after her seizures?
Fortunately, a delusional episode—a period of fixed false unalterable beliefs—does not follow every seizure only the cluster. The single grand mal seizures she has about once every week leave her a little confused and fatigued the next day. When she has a cluster of several grand mal seizures at night, her cycle of delusions begins. If she's lucky, they strike only after a three month hiatus. Eileen's husband has become expert at evaluating her symptoms and even at forecasting which are likely to be accompanied by disorientation, paranoia, and the strange notion that her skin is turning into a sheet of leaves. This is one good reason why I hold out enormous hope for controlling these episodes as an outpatient.

Is there anything else besides the seizures themselves that could help prevent these episodes?
Yes. With the earliest clues—seizure cluster, confusion on the first day—we increase her antipsychotic medication to abort an anticipated delusional episode.
But in the early days of her treatment, we didn't know this. We only knew that we had a strikingly unusual case of epilepsy with psychotic thinking, a case that defied the norm. Fortunately, we have been able to demonstrate the seizure disorder on EEG.
What does the EEG show?
We see sharp spiking episodes lasting several seconds in the temporal lobe of the brain. Most times it's on the left, sometimes on the right. We think these are two independent sites of brain irritability.

And during this state of delusions, what's her EEG like? I suppose it must be much worse.
Strangely enough, no and yes. Let me explain: Usually when I look at her EEG during one of these phases, it looks just a little slowed at times with no specific focus of abnormality becoming obvious. It's actually much more normal than when she's not having a psychotic episode.

Why?
We sometimes see this normalization of a tracing during a psychotic phase: It's become known as the "Landolt drive-in phenomenon". Drive

in the psychosis, drive out the abnormal EEG. Some argue that the abnormal EEG is the normal compensation.

Do you believe that?
Not in this case. We think these bizarre thoughts may be post-ictal—a sequence following the seizure—although it may be an extended unusual seizure equivalent.

And isn't it also true that EEGs in general don't pick up everything that could be in the brain? So an EEG may be normal when actually firing is occurring?
Yes. An EEG will tend to pick up neural "firing" at superficial levels of the brain. If a patient's seizures occur deep in the brain, they may not show up. Sometimes before surgery for epilepsy, a surgeon can open the brain and insert electrodes deep in the sub-dural cavities or still deeper to pick up deep firing of this kind.

So her brain waves during this time are normal?
Usually, but not always. That's why I originally answered, "No and Yes." During her first visit to our hospital, we hooked her up to an EEG monitor while she was having her florid delusions. Strangely, her brain waves seemed absolutely normal, until we asked her to hyperventilate—over-breathe. This is a routine part of the EEG procedure and it often helps to bring out abnormalities that are dormant. This overbreathing certainly produced a change: Three minutes into the deep breathing, she went berserk and tore down the EEG lab. After Eileen hyperventilated, she jumped off the couch, broke free of all the connections, and began to destroy the EEG department, trashing machines, breaking furniture, emptying shelves of books and equipment. She had gone utterly berserk. But she finally calmed down, after two minutes, and it was all over. Later on, she had no memory at all of what she had done.

What did all this mean?
Before she disconnected her EEG through her wildness, she had given us an important clue: The EEG record showed the sudden appearance of slow delta waves at a rate of about two to three cycles per second. These waves continued for twenty seconds. They suggested that she was entering some strange twilight of consciousness.
The expert who read the EEG was not immediately impressed. "One in a thousand patients have such profound extended delta waves after hyperventilation, so we regard it as a normal variant," he pontificated, "and they don't mean anything." I thought that one in a thousand could not be defined as "normal," and that Eileen's attack on the department wasn't "normal" either.

My colleague disagreed, and said that he didn't take behavior into account in reading the EEG. Often, it seems, our disciplinary boundaries blind us to reality. So we have only tested this once!

What do you think caused this behavior?
I think the overbreathing changed her alkalinity level of her blood slightly. This predisposed her to a seizure in the brain and also, therefore, to the confused behavior that came with it. So I'm proposing that she had an atypical seizure phenomenon superimposed upon her current post-seizure or post-ictal state.

Andrew now had settled into his groove for obtaining legitimate and important details.

I assume Eileen is an ordinary person between these episodes?
Yes. She describes herself as a somewhat introverted, mildly submissive follower, who avoids the center of attention. She has few goals in her life, gives up tasks quickly, and avoids arguments if she can. She's trusting, despite the bursts of paranoia that accompany her delusions.

How long have you been seeing Eileen? How did it all begin?
I saw her for the first time during her third hospitalization, two years ago. On that occasion she explained all her symptoms as the result of a homosexual rape, but at the same time she said she was not certain if such an assault had ever happened. At times, she said, her fear of rape made her aggressive. In fact, her records indicated that on an earlier visit to a hospital in another state, she had attacked a male medical student who was interviewing her. Staff members were also at risk.
Yes, I just heard her mention something about that.
They seem to have played a constant role in a strange story in her mind: Someone from the erstwhile Soviet Union had helped her start a restaurant, only to accept bribes from the CIA to spy on the food. Sometimes, late at night, she would try to cut herself to remove the leafy skin she believed they had enclosed around her body. Fortunately, her attempts to remove this layer of leaves were generally carried out with equally imaginary knives.

Andrew continued asking particularly difficult questions.
Was her use of imaginary knives part of her delusions? Or was she actually being lucid and rational enough to avoid hurting herself?
That's difficult to know. I suspect it was all part of a dream state she gets into during these phases and this is an altered state of consciousness where our reality is not the same as hers.

Often, she would sit during an interview cutting her arm with her index finger, sawing away at her forearm over and over again.

And what is the origin of this leafy green skin, Doctor?
Deep in her past, she said, she had tried to save a friend from a fire. "I was burned all over," she said, "and then they put this skin on me. But I failed. I didn't save her. My friend died in there." No evidence ever came to light to support these stories. She hadn't served on a volunteer fire department, or lived or worked in any other place where there had been a conflagration or any other disaster that might have been the root of this delusion.

Did she ever say who "they" were, who put the green leafy skin on her?
The CIA.

Do epileptics often have her symptoms?
Eileen's symptoms are probably almost unique for a victim of epilepsy.[29] What remains unusual is the link between epilepsy and delusional psychotic symptoms, where the symptoms are so stereotyped and are so directly preceded by a cluster of epileptic seizures the night before. This kind of neurological connection is very unusual.

Andrew's look began to acquire a philosophical glint:
The fact that these delusions are, in effect, caused by brain chemistry gone haywire makes me wonder if all our normal thoughts, reflections, imaginations and aspirations are not just reducible to brain chemistry—albeit a balanced brain chemistry? What do you think, Doctor?
You've asked the supreme philosophical question. What's mind? What's brain? Are they the same or different and if so in what ways? Are we trying to help a beloved brain or a beloved mind?
I have many thoughts in that regard, but they're extremely complex, so I would refer you to the numerous debates on the mind-body problem. [30]

But why is Eileen's psychosis so unique, anyway?
Technically, seizures and psychosis are often contradictory: psychosis improves with seizures. As you know, the history of electro-convulsive therapy—ECT—was based on the successful idea of inducing seizures to control the delusions of schizophrenia. Yet in Eileen's case seizures are directly linked with delusions. This is because it's linked around the time of the seizures—it's peri-ictal. So when psychosis is peri-ictal clearly this contradiction does not apply.

Has Eileen ever had a conscious, sober and critical awareness of her delusions when she's not having them?

No. She cannot recall them.

However, people have told her about them and that's why she has tried to explain the contents based on her past experience.

If the anticonvulsant was controlling the seizures, and if you say the seizures were causing the delusion, then why wasn't the anticonvulsant medication sufficient to control the delusions? Why was antipsychotic medication necessary at all?

It's a good question. Presumably, if we could totally control these clusters of seizures, antipsychotic medication might not be necessary at all. It may be that Eileen has an underlying predisposition to strange kinds of thought, but these may be directly linked with the seizure phenomena. The fact is that once she begins having this cluster of thoughts, it goes beyond a seizure phenomenon and it enters into the realm of bizarre behavior, which antipsychotic medication routinely controls.

What about the risk of tardive dyskinesia?

Andrew had brought up the big one. This side-effect of antipsychotic medication is the most frustrating condition in all psychiatry because of its frequent irreversibility. The condition manifests, at times, in terrible movements which the patient cannot control.

It seems perfectly logical to talk about risk factors of any medication, Andrew. We should use the correct dose rather than a higher wrong dose. This may lower risk factors, particularly in a patient such as Eileen who has an organic condition in her temporal lobe which may make her more sensitive.

Andrew's interest was piqued even more.

So Doctor, do people who have seizures in effect give themselves shock treatments?

Yes, their grand mal seizures are the equivalent. However, everyone has a threshold to have a seizure. Epileptics just have a lower threshold—the synchronous firing that produces the seizure occurs more easily.

Why don't seizures then end up actually treating the problem?

Probably because we're talking about numerous different areas of firing and kinds of seizure type. Sometimes, one grand mal seizure will immediately stop an episode of depression that has gone on for a month in an epileptic patient. Occasionally, we see episodes like with Eileen where seizures seem to be linked with strange experiences. Many times, there does not even seem to be a link of the behavior and the seizures. Then there are the changes in thinking linked with toxic side-effects of the medications or other co-existing brain damage to take into account, or two separate genetic conditions, or stress in the environment.

But remember that the great majority of epileptics are as *normal* psychiatrically as the rest of the population.

The word "**normal**" opened a flood-gate: Knowing Eileen was only due to see me a half-hour later, Andrew took advantage of our student-mentor relationship to probe an extremely relevant area.

Doctor, what's normal? I'm still not sure.

I was tempted to give Andrew the same answer as to his mind-body question, namely, avoidance; or "do you have a year to discuss it?" But it was so important, we considered the issue there and then.

You will remember I talked about coping at the biological, the psychological, the familial, the social and the cultural levels. Then I introduced the ethical level as worthy of consideration.

When you say, "cope", at what level ought one to be coping?
I think I understand where you're coming from. Does "coping" mean that you have no problems, that you are, in other words, simply neutral? Does it mean that you're handling the world in an average kind of way? Or does it mean that at every one of these levels you have to excel? Or does it mean something else?

Yeah, that's the kind of question I'm getting at!
Well, Andrew, I have debated this issue a great deal. At one point, I regarded coping as merely an adequacy of being able to function without developing symptoms which are adverse at every one of those levels. Now, possibly, I like to conceive of a phenomenon of "superior coping." Do you remember from your psychology classes what the most basic level of functioning is?

Security?
Correct! This security at its most fundamental level is expressed by the survival instinct.
One level higher, possibly other basic instincts—such as sex—should be adequately fulfilled.
At a higher level, we could be coping without pain.
At an even higher rung, there may be a facet of expected growth emotionally and intellectually.
Even higher still, is the emergence of the ethical and moral level.
However, many people argue that the highest level of attainment is *actualization of self*—reaching a pinnacle where we're able to perform at our

best. Many believe this reflects the highest level of coping. For some years, I, too, believed that the actualization of self was the highest pinnacle.
Then I realized that there's yet another growth level above this—a completely different conceptual level. That level is *transcendence of self*—going beyond the individual into some kind of collective reality, where we're going above what's needed at an individual level.

Andrew immediately interjected.
Only when the level of self-transcendence is attained is the individual allowed to discover "altruism", at the moral and ethical level. This way we can help others in a disinterested way and by so doing paradoxically allow supreme benefit to ourselves.
I see you have read the philosophies of the seventeenth century German mathematician, Baron Gottfried von Leibniz, Andrew?

He nodded proudly, but his brow began to knit up again.
Can you give me a concrete example here?
There is one strange, yet concrete example. It's one which many people object to and which certainly doesn't really reflect self-transcendence, and that's the argument that a person's country comes first, for example in war. At that level, we're sacrificing ourselves for a higher or broader reality. Perhaps a more philosophical example, and one that I find more consistent with my thinking is the following: After we achieve our aspirations and actualize ourselves, we then inspire others to grow by our achievement, contributing at a larger level even if this might entail our own suffering.

So again, there may be religious implications here?
Possibly. There are certainly philosophical implications and inklings of ethics and higher purpose.

Which you would embrace under the term "quasi-religion"?
Precisely, because if it does not necessarily imply a formal religious view, it does embrace meaning and relevance to life.

But Andrew, that's enough philosophizing for the present. Let's return to discussing Eileen so you can be prepared when you formally meet her.
Yes, that would be good.

Eileen's condition is called a peri-ictal psychosis. It's a psychosis because she has a fixed, unchangeable set of beliefs that interfere with normal reasoning; and since the psychosis occurs around the time of her seizures, it's peri-ictal—which can be before, during or after her seizures. Sometimes this is called simply an epileptic psychosis. From our first examination of

Eileen, we suspected that her epileptic psychosis was associated with electrical firing in a particular area of the brain.

What Andrew had learnt led him to wonder:
Was anything else triggering Eileen's delusions?
We had only one other clue, her tendency to have a few beers every Wednesday, and clusters of seizures often coming on Wednesday nights.

Did you counsel her to cut out her drinking?
Yes, we did, and, in fact, she had about 50% fewer seizures; but this isn't the whole story. She also complained of forgetfulness, and postulated early on that her standard anticonvulsant medication was partly responsible for her memory problem. However, we changed her medication and it made no difference.

Why was she so different?
Well, could it be that she was having far more seizures than we were able to detect through an office EEG?

Why didn't you start out with a take-home ambulatory EEG? I remember how helpful that was in Lucy's case—the earthquake lady.
Ambulatory EEG is a fairly recent innovation, and it was not yet available when we were first seeing Eileen. When it did become available, we decided to try it on Eileen to look for any signs of abnormalities that could account for her strange post-ictal delusions. We sent her home with twenty electrodes on her head and waited.

What did you learn?
The results were remarkable. Although she was free of abnormal behaviors between her episodes, when she slept at night, she would have ten or even fifteen small episodes of firing on EEG. She would complain sometimes in the morning that she had slept poorly, or that she did not remember the previous day well, but that was all.

What was the significance of that?
That failure to remember was a fascinating clue in itself, because memory theory suggests that it's during the night that the memories of each day are organized into "engrams" and stored in long term memory. Eileen's seizures in a way limited her to short term memories for the affected periods. Eileen also experienced occasional definite seizures during the day. She would also have other questionable daytime events like failing to recall any part of a TV show, or suddenly feeling dizzy. Most remarkable were bizarre and intense déjà vu experiences, where she would become certain that she had had combed her hair before.

But she had!
Indeed she had. But her déjà experience made her aware that "this was different!" [31]
Alternatively, she would flash back—parts of her life would seem strange, or she would see her life passing like a movie before her eyes.

All this sounds like a strange concatenation of symptoms. What did you make of it?
Some of these symptoms were probably epileptic. I was reasonably sure because, for example, her déjà vu episodes were associated with headache, sleepiness and some disorientation straight afterwards—you'll recognize these as post-ictal symptoms which occur frequently after even many minor seizures. [32] Similarly, her flashbacks had post-ictal features.

And some may not have been epileptic?
Well, Andrew, her odd changes in her memory bear further analysis. Yet, she never recalled her delusions. I suspect she could not recall the delusional episodes because they were so linked with the seizures.

Why do you say that?
Because Eileen has always kept an impeccably complete diary describing even her most minor attacks and also her toxicity side-effects like daytime dizziness on Tegretol. Diary writing is found to be so common among epileptics that a Harvard neurologist, Norman Geschwind, considered hypergraphia—excessive writing—a symptom of temporal lobe epilepsy. This conclusion is controversial.

And you don't think it's true?
No, I don't. This is based on my personal experiences across several cultures. Also, patients with seizures often record data so that their physicians may be helped! We shouldn't label them for so doing. However, there have been some famous writers who apparently had temporal lobe epilepsy. Two from the nineteenth century are the Russian, Feodor Dostoyevsky, who wrote the epic *Crime and Punishment*, and the British poet laureate Alfred Lord Tennyson. [33]

Should we then just regard symptoms that we cannot easily explain as psychological?
The more involved I am with neuropsychiatry, the more I realize that I must not directly and immediately and without substantiation attribute a patient's symptoms, no matter how bizarre they initially sound, to psychological causes. There may, commonly, be underlying psychological motivations and reasons why the patient's particular features or pain may be occurring in the particular area. However, almost invariably, if we seek hard enough, we will find a direct and relevant organic cause for that

97

patient's pain, whether it be a simple spasm in the upper abdomen or a bizarre sense that ants are busy biting her in her right lower calf area. There frequently is a significant accentuation of these symptoms because of added psychological elements.

So attributing symptoms to psychological causes should not be a "cop-out" to avoid seeking an organic etiology?
Yes. It should be as positive a diagnosis as the rest of medicine. If we begin at this level we will be far more able to find the direct causes, and in epileptics these are sometimes extremely complex, relating to bizarre firing in various parts of the brain.

It was time to concretize the information Andrew had learnt. The conversation returned to Eileen's condition.
What do you think caused Eileen's epilepsy? For that matter, what causes epilepsy in general?
Most epilepsies–probably 70%–are idiopathic, which is the medical way of saying that we don't know why they occur. But among the common known precipitators of epilepsy are birth trauma, head injury, stroke, high fevers during infancy, infections, brain tumors, Alzheimer's, or multiple sclerosis.

What about Eileen?
The uniqueness of Eileen's symptoms suggested a unique and perhaps traceable origin for her disease. In Eileen's case, the mountaineering fall or maybe just a minor skiing accident which occurred about three years before that, may have been the root of her problem. In both, she may never have lost consciousness; perhaps she was woozy for a few seconds or a minute, yet there may have been enough damage to a key area of her brain. A year after that mountaineering accident, she had her first seizure.

Could she have had a seizure that caused these accidents?
That's also possible. We try in medicine to attribute causality to logical events. Sometimes they're actually irrelevant, or we get the order wrong. The chicken may be the seizure; the egg one or both of the accidents. But what came first?

Are there any other pieces to Eileen's puzzle?
This may be another clue: Eileen once had a grand mal seizure in my waiting room. We immediately collected blood and urine samples so that we could form some hypotheses about the chemistry of her body during a seizure attack: Her blood sugar was a little low.
Could Eileen be experiencing hypoglycemia during or before seizures? Could her alcohol consumption throw her sugar balance off just enough

to trigger an attack? I sent her downstairs to arrange for a standard four-hour glucose tolerance test, which consists of an overnight fast, followed by a measured dose of sugar, followed by blood draws every thirty minutes over a period of four hours.

We reviewed her blood glucose results from this episode.
Eileen's fasting blood sugar was normal at about 90; after the sugar meal, it rose to 115, as expected. Then gradually it sank as her body utilized the meal. Normally, we would expect a low of 70 or 80, which is where Eileen's blood sugar rested two hours into the test. The lab then urgently called through Eileen's three-hour blood sugar: it was 32, a precipitous drop. For the month following, we had asked Eileen to prick her finger every few hours and use blood sugar sticks to test her blood glucose. However, we were not able to establish any meaningful connection between her insulin balance and her delusions or seizure clusters despite her apparent low blood sugar—hypoglycemia.

But can you link Eileen's hypoglycemia with the temporal lobe?
Maybe. An abnormal physiological state may make you more predisposed to trigger temporal lobe phenomena.

Example?
A common example theoretically is hypoglycemia. Dysfunctions—abnormal functions—of the temporal lobe which do not occur under normal circumstances become triggered under this abnormal circumstance of low blood sugar. But this is only one metabolic cause. In others, it might be a porphyric state or limited blood supply to the brain with anoxia—insufficient oxygen in the cells—that might be inducing the dysfunction. In other words, if you're biologically dealing with a significant metabolic imbalance, it may be that this disproportion is predisposing towards the added sensitivity of the temporal lobe, the most primitive area of the higher brain.

You mentioned that Eileen has two foci—areas of firing—in the temporal lobe. Could the temporal lobe be the brain area connected to delusions?
Clearly, the higher brain—the cerebral cortex—is associated with thinking. We generally perceive the temporal lobe as the great integrator and the frontal lobe as the great executive. Such a complex function as a delusion clearly involves an interface of numerous different brain functions so it's unlikely that we will ever locate one area that's linked with delusions. This is one reason why I believe Eileen's bizarre thought spells are post-ictal—linked with the time period after the seizure and not actually part of the seizure. In simpler language, I think that her seizures in some way set up a pattern of altered consciousness that brings unconscious psychological matter to the forefront rather like having an extended dream.

Andrew wanted a broader perspective.
Are there any other patients with strange psychoses and seizures that you've treated?
Many, Andrew. Let me give you an example of a patient with a chronic inter-ictal psychosis—persistent, ongoing hallucinations between seizures.

I'd like to hear more about this patient.
Brian had auditory hallucinations several times a day for months but, unlike Eileen, was acutely aware of them and thought they were real.[34]

And Eileen knows they're not real?
Yes. During her normal phases, she's actually embarrassed when told of her behavior.

What about Brian?
Brian began to hear voices, chiefly male voices that suggested that he do odd things, usually minor acts like tying his shoelaces. He told his doctor about them and met with a skeptical response. This frustrated him. His faith in their reality was so strong that he tried to record them on tape, because obviously the people around him were lying when they said they could not hear these voices, and he wanted to prove them wrong. To his utter shock, when he played back the tape recording, there was nothing but the hiss of the tape head.

That must have been something of a wake-up call for him.
Yes, it was. Brian drove to an emergency room, where he reported, "I hallucinate." And this story ended happily: On low doses of antipsychotic medication, he stabilized completely, receiving in addition one of the new anticonvulsants, Neurontin (gabapentin).

How has he done?
Splendidly. The important point here was that the correct diagnosis was made. Brian was having on average one seizure per year, but with the Neurontin has been completely under control for two years now. He has again been licensed to drive, and he is now happily married.

Does he still need antipsychotics?
Yes. As a precaution, we have maintained him on tiny doses of Mellaril. He takes 10 mg daily; the average antipsychotic dose is 300 mg per day.

Why does he not take more?
Because higher doses exhaust him. He becomes heavily sedated. It shows that biochemically he's not the regular dopamine excess type psychotic. [35.]

Andrew needed the reality check that medical students often miss: A sense of priorities.

Do Brian and Eileen reflect the average story of the epileptic?
Most certainly not. They're both rare. These cases are far beyond the norms of epilepsy, which almost never coexists with delusional or hallucinatory experiences. However, they may point the way to unraveling some of the mysteries of the brain and its relation to complex seizure types. Typical, however, are our detailed attempts to help and the success we have had.

So, did you settle on the same kind of treatment for Eileen as you did for Brian?
They have similarities: Anticonvulsant on the one hand, small doses of antipsychotic on the other. However, there are differences in the detail. For example, we originally prescribed the anticonvulsant Tegretol for Eileen, but that only reduced her seizures to a pattern of one every ten or twelve days. Every two or three months she still had a major cluster with a full psychotic break. We kept Eileen on a small dose of antipsychotic medication to try to control these outbreaks. She and her family were instructed to increase her dose of antipsychotic if there was the least sign of delusions following a seizure.
Because she had these major cluster attacks, we also gave her a supply of Ativan, a benzodiazepine that has powerful short-term anticonvulsant properties, for when seizures are occurring. She also slightly increased her Tegretol dosing during these periods.

So is she still taking the Tegretol?
Yes, but only temporarily. Although we had initially started with Tegretol, it did not fully control her seizures. However, the hypoglycemia and alcohol factors had not been fully isolated either at that point. In addition, Eileen's common complaint had been: "Can't we do something about the sleepiness?" As I've indicated many times before, I don't like my patients to have side-effects. This is one reason why we are changing her around to a well tried anticonvulsant medication, Depakote. This also helps these focal abnormalities, sometimes with a higher and sometimes with a lower success rate than Tegretol, depending on the specific area of firing.

How will the change around occur?
We will work carefully in shifting her over to anticonvulsant monotherapy—off the Tegretol and onto the Depakote. I have allocated six months for that change-over. Because of this slow taper, I hope to avoid withdrawal seizures.

Eileen entered the room. We interchanged basic follow-up information and were ready for the instructional part of the consultation.
Let's discuss your new anticonvulsant, Depakote—technically called divalproex sodium or valproate.
Depakote is a useful medication for seizure disorders. It can also put out many fires, and we don't see the allergy that we do with Tegretol. Depakote has a common but not publicized problem: some people complain they get fat on it.
That's not good, Doctor.
I don't particularly like people to get fat on a medication, because that's a side-effect.

What are the advantages of Depakote for me?
There are several. It seems to help cycles—certainly it does in manic-depressive illness—and you have a cyclical variation to your seizure clusters. So it may or may not help abort some psychotic episodes. We'll wait and see. Secondly, you described to me rather classical migraine headaches which seem to be linked up with times of your regular seizures. Depakote often helps these. Thirdly, it's a solid, tested anticonvulsant with few side-effects other than the weight problem, which only sometimes happens, and usually when people don't watch their weight. In fact, a major advantage of Depakote is that it is generally well tolerated with few side-effects and it's far less sedative than Tegretol.
Well that's good. I don't like getting sleepy on medication.

Should I be watching for any side-effects?
Important side-effects are nausea in a small minority of people so I give it with meals.
Secondly, you may develop a coarse shaking of your hand—a tremor. To me, that means you're taking too much.
Thirdly, as with all medications, we see the potential for drug interactions. Many medications will push up the Depakote level and conversely, the Depakote will raise up the level of several other drugs because it competes with them for breakdown at the liver level.

For more technical stuff, please always consult the package insert of any medication you take. [36]
I do, Doctor. But I confess it makes me frightened.
That's why I like to educate my patients about their medications in terms they can understand and prioritize because frequently, the package inserts include so much that's irrelevant and rare that it's hard to understand what's important.

It was three weeks later. Eileen was attending her first follow up appointment after release from the hospital.

I've not put on any weight, Doctor.

Excellent, Eileen. Since we initiated the Depakote while you were in hospital, I know you've watched your diet carefully. You've worked through this inconvenience without any weight gain. In any event, you must make this awareness of your weight a part of your life and that would be a good principle in any event even without your medications.

Nor have I fo und the Depakote sedating me.

Good. It shouldn't usually, but everyone is different.

Do I need my bloods taken today, Doctor?

Yes, you have taken Depakote now about ten days in the current dose [500 mg three times daily]. So you would usually have achieved a steady state level, but it's complicated by the Tegretol you have in you which we're tapering slowly. We can use your valproate levels a little to assist us in dosing and, in general, blood levels are also useful to monitor compliance when patients are not taking their medications. We will monitor both your Depakote and Tegretol levels today and at subsequent visits until you're stable on Depakote alone, and then every six months or so, unless there are prescription changes.

Eileen looked away, embarrassed.

Doctor, I have a confession that will come out in the blood test. I truly want to take my medication correctly, but is there a way I can better remember my medicines? I'm afraid I sometimes forget to take them, and at times, I can't remember if I have already taken them so I may take them twice.

Yes. The simplest is to buy a week pill planner set like a Mediset. That way, you can set up all your medication for the next week separating your three doses each day into the appropriate compartments.

Andrew, a little impatient to hear of some sign of resolution to Eileen's case, pressed on:

Are there any other directions you have taken, Doctor?

We have used several different measures: anticonvulsant and antipsychotic medication; but there are additions.

Which ones?

We have taken precautions to assist the hypoglycemic episodes. We cannot prove that they're directly related, but it's likely that they are. First, we investigated to establish that Eileen does not have an insulin-producing tumor, which could be lowering the blood sugar. We're satisfied that she does not have a tumor. Instead, it's likely that in response to a high refined sugar load, Eileen sometimes drops her blood sugar considerably by pushing out too much insulin.

103

How does this impinge on her health?
This is probably not healthy for her, and may, in fact, be a trigger either for her single seizures or for her cluster of seizures. Because of this, we have introduced a rather rigid diet.

What about Eileen's medications?
Andrew, while we were controlling the hypoglycemia, we obviously were aiming at our major direction, which was controlling the seizure phenomena and the psychosis.

So what antipsychotic do you use?
I've prescribed risperidone (Risperdal). This is one of the newer antipsychotic medications, and there are several that are now on the market: Zyprexa and Seroquel are two other examples. It's hoped that these medications will diminish the risks of the terrible condition of tardive dyskinesia, without other increased risks.

What kind of risks?
A medication called Clozaril is an example of a drug where bone marrow "depression"—suppression of blood cell production—is common enough for us to have to monitor the blood cells regularly. We don't want that to happen, and with risperidone, the risk of bone marrow depression is not there, and we hope that, just because it's somewhat different biochemically, there will be a lower risk of tardive dyskinesia.

How much have you been giving?
I use two different doses, Andrew. During the normal phases, I give Eileen tiny doses—the smallest possible size, half a milligram. During the acute psychotic phases, we go up to 3 to 5 milligrams per day which, in general, will knock her out.

It was four months later. Eileen had returned to see me for follow up. Again we went through the important routine facets: Seizure control, which was clearly much improved; the Tegretol taper, which was proceeding well; and the small dose of the antipsychotic Risperdal, which was not producing any problems. I was pleased to find that Eileen had no side-effects on the Depakote and, in fact, had noted a slight mood elevation. We had aborted the psychosis quickly and adequately following one cluster of seizures by increasing her Risperdal temporarily for three days. It seemed a good plan was in place.

Andrew was still curious.

But what about the hypoglycemia?

      I addressed Eileen directly.
Do you remember how we told you to treat yourself like you're a diabetic?
Yes, I remember, Doctor.
In effect, what we suggested is that you do not have highly refined sugary foods, so that your blood sugar won't go up and down precipitously.
I've been doing that, Doctor.

Do you want to tell Andrew the result?
Yes, Doctor. My frequency and number of seizures have been cut down by another half, by cutting out alcohol and by watching my blood sugar.

And you will remember we did other interventions as well?
Yes, Doctor. I take the chromium picolinate and the zinc that you suggested.

      I turned to Andrew.
There's some alternative medicine data arguing that chromium and zinc may be involved in shifting glucose into the cell. Whether this is so, I'm not sure, but I felt it could do little harm in small doses for Eileen to try it, although, as with any alternative medical approaches, this is Eileen's choice.

      I faced Eileen, again.
Eileen, what did the additional chromium and zinc do for you? I ask that because initially you were only watching your blood sugar.
It seemed to help, Doctor. I think my seizures decreased down even more, by maybe about 20%.
So, Andrew, this is what we did about the hypoglycemia.

      I turned back to Eileen.
And Eileen, presumably you and alcohol have divorced?
Most certainly, Doctor. We discovered that correlation nearly a year ago and it's obviously real. Small amounts of beer trigger my seizures, maybe because it produces hypoglycemia—I don't know.
All I know is I stay off any alcohol and once when I tried it again at a party, I had a seizure that night.

But Doctor, may I ask you something else?
Go ahead.
I hear one can now use all sorts of special techniques to help epilepsy. What about vagus nerve stimulation?
Vagus nerve stimulation—VNS—is a new technique. It involves stimulating the vagus nerve—a nerve outside the brain that is involved with automatic

105

functions of the body—in the hope that this will decrease the frequency or severity of seizures. It sounds promising, but like the first edition of a computer software its potential should be balanced against the unknowns. It seems to be reversible, but it still requires surgery and taking other anticonvulsants. Current thinking is that effects are maintained over years and that if the stimulation is discontinued later, the body will not be like an addict. VNS may be useful in uncontrolled epileptics and in that group about a third improve significantly, so in a way, the statistics may be similar to a new anticonvulsant drug. So let's stick with your medication, Eileen.

A year passed. Eileen had attended for follow-up.
It sounds like Eileen is under good control, Doctor.
Indeed she is. She's no longer taking the Tegretol. We have established an average dose of Depakote [at about 1000 mg a day], and Eileen's seizure frequency has dropped to approximately one episode every three weeks. On the last ambulatory EEG, she had only three episodes of firing on one of the two nights, and none on the other. We haven't seen a psychotic episode now for six months, and that one was quickly controlled.

And before, would she have required hospitalization for that episode?
Yes, but we have learnt to recognize these episodes. As soon as they begin, we add in our antipsychotic regimen: We increase the dose of the risperidone. Also, we add in small doses of Ativan for four days after a cluster of seizures.

It sounds like you have had excellent success.
Yes, it has been highly gratifying to deal with patients whom we can help. Maybe that's what self- transcendence is all about.

Chapter 5

Explosions In The Brain

Psychosis and diagnostic dilemmas.
Atypical spells, brain firing and atypical "schizophrenia",
kindling and chindling, medication compliance,
neuroleptic toleration, schizophrenia, temporal lobe disease.
Antipsychotics, Clozaril, Trilafon, Risperdal,
Tegretol. *Voyage of new discovery* (Steven)

He sat there, his eyes fixed upon mine, his gaze intent and interested. He looked around the room, as if to incorporate everything into his troubled mind. He forced a smile, because he was clearly actively distressed at what he had become. After all, he was only fifteen and had only three months before dropped out of school, unable to concentrate, not able to focus.

Doctor, it's not as if I've used any drugs or anything. I've been a good boy. I just don't know what's gone wrong.

Steven's interaction was so sincere and clear. It puzzled me. I was perplexed because there were ominous conclusions that could be drawn from looking at his presentation.

Andrew showed a particular interest in Steven. I was pleased to see how he was beginning to empathize with the his patients' suffering.
What do you think is going on, Doctor?
It's too early to make a diagnosis but there are pointers that we should usually follow.

Like?
When a young adolescent steadfastly deteriorates over the previous nine months, dropping out of school, becoming impaired in social habits, sometimes not even dressing during the day and being pushed to take baths, and there are no recreational drugs involved, schizophrenia is a strong possibility.

107

Is there other support for this diagnosis?
Yes. Steve has been hearing noises in his head that communicate something incomprehensible. He has never quite made out what these voices are saying, but he knows they are there. He told me: "I hypothesized that they were from the Devil, but I don't believe that." Given these frightening symptoms, Steve's presentation could classically be perceived as a schizophrenic illness; and his prognosis, given his early presentation, appears to be anything but rosy. And yet...

Yet...?
There is something different here about this presentation. Here is a young man who can interact in a special, warm kind of way. Patients with schizophrenia cannot do that. Often, schizophrenics exhibit a frosted glass communication: When they verbalize information, it's rather off-beam, unclear and vague. Steven was not sitting in the corner of the room, eyes scanning in a paranoid fashion, afraid to verbalize and communicate. He was directly interacting from the center, taking into account his whole environment, maintaining good eye contact, and desperately seeking help for something he knew had befallen him.

I pursued my suspicion relentlessly. There had to be something else going on. I was determined to find it and help save a beloved mind.

Indeed, when I took his history, I discovered certain clues:

So you had a little viral "'flu" episode about 18 months ago?
Yes, Doctor. My temperature was high—up to 104—but it came down in a day. Mostly, I remember the intense headache during that time. By the time my family took me to the doctor, I felt much better, except for marked fatigue and a lesser but lingering headache.

Looking through a retrospectoscope is always difficult. However, I felt that Steven had had an episode of infection of the brain—of encephalitis—and it may have left him with some scarring. This finding could occasionally be visible to the naked eye if we viewed the brain. More likely, however, it could not be seen at all. Instead, some subtle, physiological change, possibly in the **temporal lobes** of his brain, could be producing a potential towards firing, and maybe a mimicking of Steve's schizophrenia-like presentation.
Perhaps this denial of a schizophrenia label was important to me. I did not want this handsome, kindly young man to have to experience the trauma and the suffering of an early presentation of severe schizophrenia. I wanted to find another cause. Maybe I needed to find another etiology—cause. I did not want to cry for this suffering fellow human. Whatever my motivation, more and more, I became

convinced that we were dealing with a temporal lobe condition that was mimicking an underlying schizophrenic condition.

I began my diagnostic probe.
Do you get irritable?
Not really, Doctor. But I am afraid of myself. I fear I cannot control myself with others, so I stop socializing. It's one of my biggest problems. At that point, I don't feel well at all. Strangely, I have another experience with this lack of control feeling: Sometimes before this happens, I get this horrible smell, almost, but not quite, like burning rubber. I can't describe it, it's different from anything I've experienced before.

This was so typical. He could not quite put his finger on his olfactory hallucination. Why? Because it was, possibly, like nothing he had experienced in reality. It was just an area of the brain that may have been firing, an area possibly located in the mesial aspect—the middle part—of the temporal lobe. This little firing was producing a sensation which was unreal for him.

He seemed to be describing an event that was ictal—epileptic-like—possibly involving firing inside a deep part of the temporal lobe—the area of the brain usually involved with integrating experiences. Consequently, his experiences were the opposite; he manifested the typical disintegrating symptoms that characterize temporal lobe dysfunction.

I probed a little further to better understand Steve's change in functioning.
I had always been a good student. I was on the first rank of the top quarter of my class. I scored mostly As with occasional Bs. I seemed to have a particular aptitude for mathematics. I loved to read.
Why the past tense?

Steve looked at me, tears running down his face.
Because "loved" is right; because I can no longer do these things. I've changed, Doctor. I still would like to, but I can't concentrate anymore. I don't know what's gone wrong. I just can't think.

Chronic disproportionate concentration disturbance is a common phenomenon we find in schizophrenic-related illnesses, and invariably it's disproportionate to other kinds of symptoms. So here too, he correlated with what would conventionally be diagnosed as a schizophrenic illness. I even noticed a blunting in his affect—a diminution in range of emotion. This is a progressive feature in schizophrenia-related illnesses.

Steve moved his chair toward me; whispering, as in confession, he spoke about his auditory hallucinations.

You know, Doctor, I don't enjoy these voices of the Devil. I know they're abnormal, because I shouldn't be having them. I can't really hear them well at all in certain ways, but they seem to be instructing me to do things, but I don't do them because I know it's wrong and I know it's weird. Is there a way to treat this?
Indeed there is, Steven. You're fortunate that there's a powerful group of antipsychotic drugs, also called neuroleptics or major tranquilizers. These are absolutely remarkable in treating the problems of hallucinations. We ought to be able to take away these hallucinations in a matter of days.

Andrew, the medical student always keen on showing his knowledge, wedged in here:

Isn't there a debate about this, Doctor, whether the hallucinations, treated with antipsychotics, will go to the back of the brain or the back of the mind, or will just disappear? In other words, are they just transferred from the conscious mind to the unconscious mind, or are they eliminated completely?
That question may be a philosophical one, Andrew, more than anything else.

I faced Steven.
For you, Steven, the important component is that, with the voices going away, you may find your thoughts are more ordered and you're concentrating better.

But again, in this atypical manner, Steven was able to verbalize:
I don't experience as much pleasure as I did before. I can't find myself interested in things. My friends seem to be rejecting me, but I don't seem to be able to care.

I realized this change in emotion was, in fact, not the blunting of affect in schizophrenia, but potentially a part of his temporal lobe disease. This change in emotion was, in fact, almost a loss of caring. The cause could have been a secondary phenomenon of his encephalitis—which, when looked at in a more detailed historical way, seemed actually to go on for several days, not just the day he had remembered.
Steven had insight into his condition and experienced this change rather intently, He had told me:
I knew that something was different.

Andrew wanted clarity.

What would be a lack of insight?

I can contrast Steve's insight, with the lack thereof of Milton, a classical schizophrenic patient, I once had. The conversation had run:

It's completely unfair that I'm in the hospital. I'm only in the hospital because I'm honest.

In what way, Milton?

I told people about the unseen voices I was hearing. I know everyone hears these voices, but only I was honest enough to admit it. What did I get in return? Getting hospitalized!

What a contrast with Steven. Milton truly had no insight into the fact that he was ill. Steven was fully able to comprehend his illness.

How are we going to proceed with Steven?

Andrew, we must fully investigate him to fully establish whether there was an obvious medical or neurological cause.

And what does that consist of in this instance?

More of the same. We take a detailed history, do an appropriate physical, neurological and mental status examination and integrate all this information. We already know his blood tests are all within normal limits.

But obviously his brain waves are critical?

Right. The big test is his electroencephalogram. We performed that yesterday.

What did you find?

There, on his EEG, is a subtle but definite focal abnormality. He has a temporal lobe focus—an area of physiologic change in the temporal lobe of his brain on the left side, predominantly towards the front. This left anterior temporal abnormality shows up on two or three occasions during the EEG. Such a finding is a possible clue for treatment, based on our previous research.

Andrew was intent on following my line of thought.

What previous research was that?

It was some interesting work that I originally did in South Africa on a group of patients who had been labeled as having a chronic psychotic condition, generally schizophrenia, and who had not responded to conventional anti-schizophrenia medications. They were still, sometimes after many years, sitting in a mental hospital, and had not shown any progress.

111

We looked at every patient in this hospital who, on EEG, showed up with a focal abnormality in the temporal lobe of the brain.

What were you looking for?

We hypothesized that maybe some explosions were occurring in the brain, and if we could put these explosions out, the patient would be better. In other words, it was thought that, in addition to receiving their antipsychotic medication, if they received the antiseizure drug Tegretol, we would extinguish abnormal brain firing and improve the patients dramatically. This, in fact, is what happened, in the first and only double-blind study of its kind. The patients responded remarkably well. [37]

They found real relief from the Tegretol?

Yes, indeed. This carbamazepine treatment is now in general use on people with these episodes of explosive disorders: Perhaps tens of thousands of people have benefited from it. I believe it may be because Tegretol is putting out an electrical fire in the brain.

So is it a seizure it puts out?

It may be a seizure or seizure equivalent given the firing: However, we do not perceive firing in the brain as epilepsy unless the patient also exhibits classical clinical seizure manifestations. So I like to look at the discrete episodes as "atypical spells", avoiding the debate of whether these are actually seizures.

And it won't work without the fire?

Right. So obviously, it doesn't work in regular schizophrenia. In fact, when Tegretol is given to pure schizophrenics, they get worse, because the Tegretol causes the antipsychotic medications to be metabolized—broken down—more quickly, cutting the amount available in the brain. [38]

Andrew proceeded to ask possibly the key question about the abnormal electrophysiology of the brain.

What do you think is the mechanism?

I suspect the mechanism may be similar to a special example of electrical physiology gone wrong—what the Canadian, Graham Goddard, called "kindling". [39]

What's kindling?

"Kindling" implies the lighting up of a fire in the brain. It relates to a rather fascinating phenomenon: At first, tiny direct electrical stimulations of certain areas of the brain initially do not produce a response—they are sub-threshold. However, repetitive electrical stimulations may suddenly result in a seizure or equivalent happening. So the sub-threshold non-response changes permanently to a threshold response. This has been

112

demonstrated in various animals, like the rat and the guinea pig. However, with each shift towards greater degrees of encephalization—developed brain—as the animal scale is climbed, it becomes increasingly difficult to induce this phenomenon of kindling. It can be debated whether kindling happens in people, and if it does, whether it is relevant in practice.

What's the basic element?
Fundamental is that a tiny stimulus that does not produce a response—the sub-threshold electrical stimulation—when repeated ten, twenty or thirty times, eventually produces a response—it becomes threshold.

What kind of response?
The response depends on where in the brain the stimulus occurred. However, basically, the response that occurs is a seizure phenomenon.

So these poor animals develop seizures?
Yes and, depending on where they fit on the animal scale, these seizure phenomena start off as local movements, like jerks. They then eventually progress to full grand mal. However, as we advance up the evolutionary scale to more highly developed brains, certain differences in the sequence begin to happen. So, by the time the cat is kindled, strange behaviors are preceding the local movements, not following them. Extending this movement up the animal scale, if this sequence occurs in man, we should kindle odd behaviors, long before the actual grand mal seizures happen. Whether kindling happens in man is still disputed because fortunately, we don't experiment like this on humans.

What's your view on such animal research?
I, personally, am ambivalent about experiments on any animals in any area where harm can be done. On the one hand, important data has been obtained and there usually was no other way to obtain it, yet I cannot but feel desperately sorry for the pain and loss of life to helpless animals. I cry for their suffering. But let's return to kindling.

So the phenomenon of kindling was what motivated your study?
No, it didn't. I had not yet learnt about kindling in 1979. The idea of firing certainly drove my thinking, but I thought that more relevant may be not an electrical but a chemical stimulation. So, long after my study, I introduced a new term, "chindling"—chemical induced kindling. [40]

Why the difference?
Kindling classically refers to the unlikely mechanism of seizures induced by *outside electrical* stimulations. However, because similar effects can be caused by chemicals such as cocaine, chindling is probably a far more

113

important mechanism of induced abnormal brain firing in man. The end point may be very similar although the exact chemical mechanisms differ slightly.

Why did you introduce "chindling"?
Because, given the number of people who abuse recreational drugs, chindling could potentially be an important mechanism of producing a tendency to abnormal brain firing. Drugs such as cocaine quickly induce chindling, yet nobody actually uses an electrical probe to stimulate a specific area of the human brain as occurs in kindling. Instead, lower doses over a period of time produce changes in the brain akin to seizure-related firing. When chindling occurs in the rat, this phenomenon rapidly causes death because cocaine quickly chindles generalized grand mal seizures which cannot be halted.

Is chindling the same as kindling?
No. Theoretically, there are certain fundamental but subtle contrasts between kindling and chindling and I realized that in humans this chemical-induced phenomenon was a more likely explanation than the classical kindling phenomenon. Again, whether chindling or kindling are the legitimate explanations for the firing in humans may be less relevant than the principle of gradually induced abnormal brain firing from any stimulus, *internal or external*. This producing abnormal behavioral fires which can be put out with anticonvulsant medication—with drug treatment for epilepsy.

Did you extend your studies thereafter?
Yes. Given this background, and much of this was developed after my initial first study, it seemed logical to look at people who had explosions in the brain, manifesting as irritability, agitation and anger. These could have been linked with firing. What would Tegretol do to these people, particularly those who were exhibiting features of being somewhat impaired and those who were linked up with drug-related phenomena?
What was found?
Many different studies or case reports, by numerous researchers, showed again the value of Tegretol in explosive anger seemingly due to a brain cause. However, these are based on clinical case reports not the special highest level, double-blind studies.

That's interesting, Doctor. Can we talk some more about these studies?
Indeed we can, and we will, Andrew. [41]

Andrew, let's return to discussing Steve. I felt it's important to establish whether the episodes in the temporal lobe that we found on regular EEG have any clinical correlate. Could it be that these strange smells that he experiences are directly linked with his EEG changes? Could we find brain wave changes directly correlating with these smells? I had hopes, but not high ones, of finding this out during home ambulatory EEG monitoring.

Why the pessimism?
Andrew, this is based on our previous experience. Patients must have the symptoms during ambulatory EEG monitoring and sometimes they don't.

Well. What did you find when monitoring Steven using that home EEG?
We did not find anything out of the ordinary, except to confirm and even better localize the original intermittent EEG abnormalities in the temporal lobe of his brain. These were, in part, accentuated during his natural sleep cycles at night, but we also found eight episodes during his waking periods over the two days. He had pushed the button on the EEG several times, indicating that he wanted us to correlate his experience with the EEG at that moment. Unfortunately, however, he never had the specific target features we were looking for—the strange smells, for example.

Why not continue monitoring until such an episode occurs?
I don't believe it's necessary. We have a diagnosis here, and prolonged monitoring escalates expenses. It was useful, however, to observe that Steven had a similar number of episodes on each of the two days of monitoring.

And now?
The key here will be if Steven responds to this appropriate anticonvulsant medication. He's not going to respond totally: We're still going to need to clear those strange voices—the sounds he experiences and can never quite make out—with antipsychotic drugs—neuroleptic medications. However, we should need far lower doses of these neuroleptics to normalize the bizarre thinking, allowing him to integrate his thoughts and make sense of linkups of one thought to another.

Why will he only need lower doses of neuroleptic?
Because biochemically Steve does not have schizophrenia. We should be able to correct his dopamine balance with a small amount of dopamine blocker, namely neuroleptic, not the large amount required in real biochemical psychoses.

So in summary?
At this point, we will treat him sequentially with low doses of antipsychotic medication, and we will then add in the Tegretol if it's necessary.

What antipsychotic did you choose?
I've prescribed a favorite antipsychotic medication for Steven, perphenazine (Trilafon) in very low doses [4 mg daily]. The usual minimal
antipsychotic dose is about 12 mg daily; commonly patients are on 24
mg.

Why Trilafo n?
My preference for the perphenazine had been based on accumulated experience of thousands of such patients.
Some of the other antipsychotics have side-effects that are untenable, such
as the stiffness associated with drug-induced Parkinsonism in Stelazine;
or the sedation, the sleepiness and the tachycardia—rapid pulse—in
Thorazine. Trilafon could also cause these side-effects. But my experience
has been that these side-effects would only occur at a higher dose than is
necessary. Consequently, if we encountered these side-effects, we could
actually lower the dose of the perphenazine. This, in fact, has correlated
with some research that was done in the 1970s in Europe.[42]

Andrew had been itching to ask,
But Doctor, don't we want to use the latest antipsychotic medications?
Each in its own time. They all have their value. Strangely enough, even an
old drug like Trilafon impacts on the serotonin-2 receptor by blockade,
just like some of the newer ones do. The difference is that the newer
ones, in general, impact far more, on serotonin-2 than the dopamine receptors.

What's an example of that?
A drug like Risperdal is a typical example of one of these newer antipsychotics.

I've heard about Clozaril. Isn't that the key drug?
Clozaril (clozapine) is an important drug. However, I have mentioned
that dangerous side-effect of bone marrow depression. Although this is
relatively rare—maybe one in a thousand patients—it is something we have
to be acutely aware of. We should monitor the patient carefully, sometimes even as much as every week or two, depending on the particular
jurisdiction, circumstance and possibly dosage. So we have to balance
risk and benefit. The particular benefit of Clozaril is in the patients who
are withdrawn and have so-called negative features, and who have not responded to conventional antipsychotics. It may be that its mechanism is a
little different. Some of these newer antipsychotics, such as Risperdal,
have allowed us to use less Clozaril.

What about the risk of tardive dyskinesia with these drugs?

116

Tardive dyskinesia is, of course, the major long-term risk with antipsychotics. We continually assess the risk of this condition with its sometimes irreversible disease process involving rather glaring, bizarre movements of the lips, tongue, face, arms, hands or legs. Occasionally, instead, we see a related disabling condition, "tardive akathisia" in which the patient cannot keep still. The risk of these conditions with any of the neuroleptic drugs is important and we hope that, but don't know whether, the newer drugs will lower that risk. The antipsychotic drugs fundamentally embody the principle of balancing benefit with risk.

When does the benefit outweigh the risk?
Well, Andrew, sometimes it's no competition. Imagine the suffering in a patient who is hearing voices, thinking aliens are controlling his mind, and is in the utter torment of Hell because the Devil is instructing him to perform certain acts that are against his conscience. Such a poor, tormented individual can get amazing relief from these antipsychotic medications, and the object is to give the correct amount under the appropriate circumstances for the correct duration of time. This may not eliminate the risk of tardive dyskinesia, but logically, it should reduce it. We cannot entirely prove this hypothesis, but this has been my experience. If patients receive too high a dosage, they're at stronger risk. On the other hand, we want to administer the correct dose for the patient, and they will do well indeed.

But is tardive dyskinesia always irreversible?
No. We sometimes find that it seems to go away after six or nine months. It's complicated by the fact that each time we increase the dose of antipsychotic, we may find a temporary improvement as a biological adaptation to this change. Strangely, we may have found a useful cure for this condition.

What's that?
High-dose buspirone therapy. [43]

Then when, Doctor, do you use the newer antipsychotic agents?
You're persistent, aren't you, Andrew? You know, *new* is not necessarily better, even though we have seen certain significant advances. Also, being new does not necessarily guarantee there won't be side-effects. So, for example, one of the limiting features we at times will see with Risperdal is of the patient complaining of being sedated and sleepy. Our hope, however, is that these newer drugs may lower the risk of tardive dyskinesia, or may eliminate that risk entirely. This is based on their specific neurotransmitter properties of a mix of far stronger degrees of serotonin-2 antagonism compared with their dopamine blockade. On the other hand...
Yes?

117

I was going to give you a mouthful, but it's too complicated.
No. I want to hear.
Well, briefly, the limited degree of dopamine blockade may produce less antipsychotic effects relative to its impact on serotonin blocking. This serotonin effect may be linked up with relief of anxiety, depression, and possibly aggression. These could be appropriate target symptoms for the newer antipsychotic drugs or maybe we should use them routinely and gamble on eliminating tardive dyskinesia. Alternatively, we could restrict use to resistant psychosis. You can see, it's a matter of personal choice.

Can we discuss these biochemical features?
You can see they're complex, Andrew. So we will set aside a time to talk about it.[44]

But Andrew wasn't finished.
You haven't mentioned Haldol yet. Is that not the standard? If not why not?
Haldol (haloperidol) is a commonly and useful medication in psychosis. It was generally the first choice medication in the USA, Canada and Israel long before the newer era of antipsychotics, beginning with risperidone, began. However, my impression is that haloperidol has two problems. First of all, it is so extremely potent that low doses need to be given.

Can you give an example?
Well, one famous example was the first patient treated with haloperidol, many years ago in Belgium. The patient apparently presented with a manic episode. Because he was the first to be prescribed with this experimental drug, the exact appropriate dose was unknown. He was given one milligram daily. His manic episodes settled and he was maintained on this dose for many years. He married, became an architect and raised a family. Many years later, he was taken off Haldol; immediately, within a week, he relapsed. I can tell a similar story.

Please do.
Our experience, in the early 1970s, was to use low doses of haloperidol—doses like 1 or 2 milligrams daily. I remember a patient who actually was receiving 5 milligrams a day, and this was so unusual that other physicians came to consult with this patient.

When did this low dose Haldol treatment change to higher doses?
In the mid-1970s, when rather suddenly, physicians went to the other extreme. It became the fashion to increase the dose to 150 mg of Haldol a day; but this produced side-effects, not the least of which was called the "neuroleptic malignant syndrome". So the dose was dropped. Theories

developed that once the dopamine receptors had been blocked, there was little point in going higher, and this may be so. Realistically, we need only use small doses of haloperidol, and when we do, we might find that even those small doses are too much. A patient, particularly someone who is not psychotic, may develop drug-induced Parkinson's symptoms on 1 mg a day, but it is difficult to obtain smaller doses than that. It would be useful if we had a liquid form, where we could use 0.1 mg in some patients.

Dosage was one problem, but you alluded to a second problem: Where does dopamine fit in?
The second problem may be more subtle. You will understand that there are different receptor subtypes. Well, Haldol works more selectively on one of them, dopamine-2 compared with dopamine-1 and this may have some subtle impacts on increasing the risks of tardive dyskinesia, but it's complicated and speculative.[45] We have spoken generically about the neurotransmitter dopamine and that dopamine excess might be associated with psychosis.
Which would mean that dopamine deficiency would help with psychosis?
Well, more accurately, it would mean that dopamine depletion would decrease the psychosis, and this is one mechanism the antipsychotic drugs have.

Andrew looked at me quizzically.
I don't understand. Why is it, Doctor, that some patients' bodies respond to tiny doses of medication, while others require enormous doses?
There are several different issues here: Those taking large doses of medication might be taking it because, in fact, that medication is not being absorbed—it's going right through the gastrointestinal tract and being excreted as feces at the other end. Some people just do not absorb medications as well, and this may be particularly so if they're having their medications with drinks like milk, or taking antacids. These could change the acid-base balance in the stomach. So, this may be one explanation: decreased absorption.

What else?
A second may be that their liver is working so much overtime that they're metabolizing these medications rapidly through the liver.
With most of the medication being lost?
Yes. Drinking a great deal of fluids might sometimes wash out medications somewhat prematurely through the kidneys, so higher doses are needed. Also, thin people don't have great areas of fat for fat-soluble medications to go to, and almost all of our psychiatric and neurological medications are fat-soluble because they have to pass through the so-called blood-brain barrier. So metabolism of drugs will vary, particularly

119

in the extremely obese compared with the very thin, because the fat-soluble drugs will go into fatty tissue.

Why does the blood-brain barrier only allow fat-soluble drugs to pass through?
Because part of this barrier has a lipid—a fat—membrane.
Are there drugs that can pass into the brain even though they're not fat-soluble?
Yes, there are: Tiny molecules like lithium. Lithium does not need to be fat-soluble, because it passes through by a different mechanism.

The reasons you give, Doctor, relate to the patient's body not actually using the full amount of the medication he's taking because of poor absorption or rapid metabolism. But are there instances where a remarkable differential in dose has endogenous biological causes?
Excellent question, Andrew. Yes. Some patients need more drug, sometimes much more drug, than others even though they have, theoretically, the same diagnosis, and even though the differences are not related to different absorption, metabolism or excretion. The difference is probably at the receptor level—how sensitive the patient is to medication and how many receptors need to be filled.

In other words, how many boats need to be moored and how many passengers get off each boat or are prevented from doing so?
Exactly. Andrew, you've integrated that metaphor perfectly.

But Andrew was on a good wicket.
He wanted more information.
Doctor, I know that people with schizophrenia are sometimes diagnosed with depression. Do schizophrenics get depressed, or could we say they're sort of "sub-depressed"?
That's an area of debate, because, as you know, the schizophrenic patient over a period of years may become blunted somewhat in emotionality; and yet that blunting may not be perceived as much in the context of their delusional thoughts. So, for example, when aliens are invading their mind, they may experience enormous movements of emotion.

So that's a delusional thought?
Right. It's a fixed false belief for our culture.

Steven's mother had a question:
Isn't schizophrenia a split personality?
The schism is really between the mood—the emotion—and the thinking. So, it's not a split of personality, or for that matter, a multiple personality,

a Jekyll and Hyde; in schizophrenia, the abnormality shows itself in the single disintegrated personality.

Andrew elbowed in:
What about prescribing antidepressant medication for the schizophrenic?
During the earliest schizophrenia phases, the patient may notice that something is going on–some intangible is wrong. Under those circumstances, we sometimes diagnose a depressive episode, situationally linked with the distress, but separate from the schizophrenia itself. The problem here is, when we prescribe antidepressant medication on its own, the schizophrenia usually gets worse. The trick is to prescribe both antipsychotic medication, and that generally first, as well as some antidepressant medication.

But are there patients who have both conditions?
Yes. We have an entity called "schizoaffective illness". I sometimes look at this as the diagnosis of the diagnostically destitute. The label of "he's not quite schizophrenic or manic-depressive; he's somewhere in-between." There's no reason why we should not have further biological entities. There are several good reasons why we should. So, for example, a male schizophrenic patient goes to the local mental health center and happens to meet a manic-depressive lady: It would be logical to hypothesize that the resulting genetic combination may be schizoaffective illness.

Any other terms?
Yes. In the same way, we could hypothesize several other conditions: "Schizopath" for patients with some schizophrenic tendencies and some psychopathic tendencies. Or what about "psychophrenia" which may be a version of the reverse? Obviously, we don't use these terms. However, we do use the term "schizoaffective illness" quite commonly, and I believe it is a legitimate entity. These patients do not tend to deteriorate as much as in schizophrenia. They often can work and be productive to a point, and can be maintained on appropriate medication. In this subpopulation, it may be particularly useful using drugs such as Risperdal or Zyprexa which act potently on the serotonin-2 receptor as well as on the dopamine receptor. Several such antipsychotics have recently been marketed and others are being clinically investigated.

What of the many who have used recreational drugs and become ill?
True. When someone has used PCP or LSD, for example, and develops a psychotic condition either shortly afterwards or even years later, there are two diagnostic options: Either say that a hallucinogen drug mobilized an underlying schizophrenic or manic illness which may have come anyway but maybe later, or that this is a drug-induced psychosis. The way I

differentiate it is clinically and pharmacologically. I ask: "In what way does he appear to have non-classical elements to his schizophrenia?"

Clinically?
Most people with drug-induced psychoses have the positive symptoms of schizophrenia, but not the negative ones. They hallucinate, they're deluded, and they're thought disordered at times with the positive symptoms; but they are not apathetic, amotivated and withdrawn with negative symptoms.

And pharmacologically?
Drug induced psychotics do not respond to antipsychotic medication alone. They need something extra, often anticonvulsants.

A̲t this point, Steven, who had listened intently but without a word, rather suddenly entered the discussion:
So it seems like it would be logical for me to have a combination of antipsychotic medication with the Tegretol?
You're most likely correct, Steven. Good thinking! It may be so, but I have a rule about that: Would you like to hear it? It is important.

Yes. I want to share in my treatment.
My rule is one medication change at a time. In your particular instance, it would be logical to begin with low doses of antipsychotic medication first, to see how you do, because this would be the more conventional approach to your particular condition.

And so I started Steven on 2 milligrams of perphenazine—Trilafon—a day. I watched carefully for clues for improvement, reviewing him on a weekly basis. He seemed to concentrate minimally better, but there was no real change. We went up on the dose to 4 mg per day. Again, the voices were still there, and he still couldn't really focus. By 8 mg per day, he had developed a little bit of stiffness, suggesting we had gone beyond his tolerance. This to me was an exciting finding, because, if he had a conventional psychotic condition, he would likely have been able to **tolerate antipsychotic doses** of medication. But he did not. This meant, possibly, that we were likely dealing with a different kind of condition. We checked that his compliance was appropriate.

We certainly did not add in an anticholinergic medication like Cogentin or Artane to counteract these side-effects of too high a dose. Instead, we dropped back to 4 mg of Trilafon daily. The side-effects settled, but we still had residual problems because Steven still had symptoms. This process had taken a short but possibly adequate initial period—three weeks: enough time to allow some degree of psychophysiologic stabilization, but not enough time to allow for the full workings of the Trilafon.

It was unusual that Steven had required such low doses of neuroleptic. One possible reason may have been the episode of encephalitis he apparently had suffered, which ostensibly had triggered his illness. To me it was biochemical evidence that he was not schizophrenic: This group tolerates high doses.

Andrew shifted forward in his chair. He adjusted his glasses. He looked ahead at me intently. I knew the big question was about to come.

You've implied that Steven could easily have been inappropriately labeled as schizophrenic. Are diagnostic labels useful?

Of course, medical practice is based on diagnosis. On the other hand, we must be careful. I sometimes find labels put on people are limiting and even traumatic for the patient. "Doctor, you know I'm manic-depressive, but I'm doubly unlucky, I'm also schizophrenic." Over years, different medical colleagues will sincerely and sequentially apply all these labels onto one patient; of course it's one illness. All it means is that everyone has a different opinion. Additionally, what these labels don't describe is the healthy core: They focus only on the illness.

I turned to Steven.

So having said all that, let's voyage down the road of history so you can understand how labels have changed and what we can legitimately call you.

I'm listening.

Please do so although I'm going to be a little technical, too, so Andrew can also learn from this.

In the early 1900s, the great neuropsychiatrist, Emil Kraepelin had a historic subdivision of major psychiatric illness. He divided psychotic illnesses into three: "dementia praecox", which we now know as schizophrenia; "manic-depressive insanity", which we sometimes call bipolar affective illness or bipolar mood disorder; and "epileptic psychosis". Those were his three conditions.

The psychiatric community then eliminated epileptic psychosis, wrongly because it exists, but also rightly because it's a heterogeneous condition. These same nomenclature experts argued that the other two—schizophrenia and bipolar illness—were homogeneous, so these conditions were retained. In fact, the great unifying contribution of Kraepelin to psychiatry was that he recognized that all these different conditions, once regarded as heterogeneous, were actually homogeneous.

This time it was Andrew who interrupted.

What do we learn from this?
The trouble is we're not dealing with real homogeneity. Many of these conditions are still heterogeneous. We have facetiously described terms like schizoaffective, schizopath and psychophrenia. We wonder about genetic combinations that we now are seeing, possibly different from times gone by, because of successive drugs and the local mental health clinic waiting-room.

What has changed?
You see Andrew and Steven, years ago, schizophrenics didn't have available neuroleptics and so were withdrawn, they were autistic, they were asocial, and they seldom married. In fact, when you took a history and you found they were married you would ask, "Are they really schizophrenic?" because we did not expect them to be sociable enough to marry.

What impact does this have on the next generation?
With medication we're producing a symptom complex that's enormously difficult to conceive of, and entering an unknown realm. Fetuses might receive brain modifying medication during their mother's pregnancy, and we don't know what effects these drugs have on their later development. It may be good or bad or neither. You could argue that giving neuroleptics to the fetus of a schizophrenic mother, might, in fact, prevent the child from developing schizophrenia. However, it may make the condition worse. Alternatively, maybe there could be a bimodal result: Those not genetically predisposed may suffer severe biochemical brain insult and those who are genetically potentially schizophrenic may have their illness halted in utero. Add in the possibilities of the many movement disorders neuroleptics cause and the complexity builds enormously.

What should we do then?
We do not know the answer, but it is a critical area to research and find out. So we're in an exciting time in psychiatry, where there's a major need for epidemiologic studies over periods of generations. Of course, these studies are expensive and difficult to perform. Nevertheless, certainly one responsibility in medicine is to collect information for the next generation on a database, but it's seldom done.

Are labels good?
Andrew was back to his original question.

124

The worst part about labels is people may generalize their condition and think, "Well, this is what's going to happen to me" and they begin to perpetuate a prophecy that may be based on a pessimistic outlook.

I directly addressed Steven.
So Steven, I want you to understand that you can be helped, that our findings have suggested that you do not have the condition of schizophrenia, and that we have powerful medications to help you.
That's a great relief, Doctor. I must tell you that since you've been teaching me about my symptoms, I've been convinced I could be helped. In fact, I knew it.

This comment was a remarkable affirmation of Steve's positive thinking. However, strangely, because of Steve's symptoms with his delusions, I had to hold back from misinterpreting his obvious positive normal affirmation as a psychotic lack of insight. I held back and accepted Steve's comment in the spirit in which it was declared. I looked at him compassionately.

How would you describe my condition? I know you don't like labels, but which one would you use?
Temporal lobe syndrome with psychosis.

Andrew, the typical medical student, meanwhile continued his medical voyage of exploration.
Is this temporal lobe syndrome with psychosis diagnosis common?
In a way, I think the condition is common, not the diagnosis. It depends how it is perceived. Sometimes, I consult with patients who were labeled schizophrenic the first time, then on their next admission "drug induced psychosis". "Atypical psychosis" follows, then "psychosis not otherwise specified", and then "bipolar illness", "borderline", and "schizoaffective illness". Finally, we arrive at "none of the above", the correct diagnosis because many of these patients have temporal lobe foci. Many physicians are not sophisticated enough to pick it up. Some even say, "for your bipolar illness, we'll give you a bit of Tegretol or Depakote or even Lamictal," but they may not realize that the anticonvulsant was actually eliminating local areas of brain explosion.

So is it the explosion in the brain that's the cause of the illness?
It would be easy to say "Yes, it is," but then I'm being simplistic. I'm uncertain what role the firing actually plays. It is interesting that these three anticonvulsants all seem to help conditions like manic-depression, suggesting there's a link with firing, as the chemical mechanisms of action of these anticonvulsant drugs are not the same.

125

Andrew looked up at me from his notepad and observed:

You always talk about "firing in the brain," Doctor. Is there such a thing as good or healthy firing?

Indeed there is. Electrical firing is occurring in the brain every moment of the day in every micro-second of time. What's happening is that all our nerves and many of the cells of our body involve tiny currents shifting sodium and potassium across the cell membrane; generally it is sodium out of the cell and potassium into the cell. These currents are stabilized by other cations like calcium. All nerve conduction occurs because of this fundamental principle, with the consequence that electricity is part of our basic bodily experience and obviously healthy.

How do we then distinguish healthy firing from pathological firing?

Clinically, if the fire causes problems, that's unhealthy. If it helps, that's healthy. Firing can be excitatory or it can be inhibitory. You can imagine that the brain (and the whole body) has to have various controlling elements. Sometimes, indeed, some anticonvulsant drugs seem to act, at least in part, by stimulating the inhibitory circuitry; and firing occurs all the time in the most miniscule fashion as various biochemical phenomena. They produce extremely important tiny electrical currents. At a higher level, when electrical currents in cells mobilize themselves and synchronize themselves, we may potentially get seizures, because those currents fire and become threshold. In other words, there comes a point where this synchronizing induces a response.

Explain?

Imagine stimulation level 3—no response; level 4—no response; level 5—clangs and whistles: enormous response causing great change. Threshold is level 5.

Andrew, always curious, continued with another typical deep question.

What about episodes that cannot be proven to be seizures on EEG, but seem likely to respond to anticonvulsants because they have some kind of firing? Can we classify this?

We like to call these "atypical spells" and we extend the label of firing beyond seizures to the term "paroxysmal neurobehavioral disorder"—PND. [46] We find this terminology useful: the actual phenomena may not have been proven to be seizures yet many of these patients with short episodes have disturbances in their behavior that respond to anticonvulsants.

So appropriate neuropharmacological response is an important diagnostic indicator?

Exactly, Andrew. You're using solid medical terminology. In other words, improving on medication sometimes helps us understand the underlying problem.

126

Andrew paused a moment, thoughtfully.

Clearly this PND is important and often mirrors brain firing detected on EEG. Did the EEG change psychiatry in any way?

Yes. Prior to the development in the 1930s of the EEG by the neuropsychiatrist, Hans Berger, all seizure disorders were classified as mental disorders.

And now?

Epilepsy is not generally covered in psychiatric textbooks. Moreover, the EEG has become the domain of the neurologist and the linkage of psychiatric disorder to the EEG is still in its infancy.

Why?

Because analysis of brain waves from the perspective of psychiatric behaviors has not been well researched.

Can we do anything about it?

EEGs are possibly under-used in psychiatry partly because electroencephalographers have a broader range of what constitutes normality. They search mainly for focal and seizure phenomena. They're generally not psychiatrists and potentially valuable research and clinical information may be lost. For example, one testable hypothesis is that relatively flat EEG tracings may be more common in certain personality disorders, with certain psychotropics—brain active drugs—or in a subpopulation of schizophrenia. Seldom is this kind of background even reported on.

Andrew smiled and made what appeared to be an inspired comment.

Clearly there's a greater need to pay attention to unusual episodic symptoms. This will ultimately lead to a workable classification and the recognition that certain seizure-like features need to be treated by psychiatrists.

Andrew, I would have said the same!

I know! I overheard you talking about it yesterday!

So not only are you retentive, Andrew, you're honest!

Again, Steven spoke up appropriately, demonstrating the integration of his new knowledge.

But I have an abnormal EEG.

Yes, Steven; and this is one important clue to your condition. Clinically, you have features different from schizophrenia and similar to temporal lobe dysfunction—a malfunction in this primitive higher brain area. Moreover, your EEG supports this.

I discussed the use of Tegretol with Steve and his mother, giving them a chance to ask whatever questions they wished.

Steve began with the most fundamental question.

What do you think is wrong with me, Doctor?
Let's look at your situation, Steven. You have an atypical presentation for schizophrenia. You present a little younger than usual. You relate and interact quite differently from the way a typical schizophrenic does. You have insight into your condition. Moreover, you have some symptoms suggestive of a temporal lobe condition and EEG confirmation of these symptoms.
So, on history, examination, and testing, you're different from the conventional schizophrenic. However, we have a further biological pointer: You do not tolerate antipsychotic doses of medication. This suggests a biological difference, implying probably a biochemical difference. This gives us alternative medication clues, too.
At this juncture, we are ready to add in Tegretol.

The always querulous Andrew, again in attendance, had some questions of his own.
But why don't you wait? It's only been three weeks. It might be that we might see continuous improvements for periods of several months?
Yes, indeed, this might be so. However, it's only speculative. We balance success versus failure and side-effects versus therapeutic effects. I estimate the degree of change we may expect over the next few months may be about 10% or, if we're lucky, 20% if we were to wait. I want to add in the new medication, the Tegretol, because I'm expecting changes of 80% or 90%, particularly if our diagnosis is correct.

What happens if he simply has schizophrenia?
Under those circumstances, the Tegretol will probably lower the level of the antipsychotic, Trilafon, he's taking: I'm afraid he may actually get a little worse.
Can you risk it?
Yes. We must. We have the possibility of Steve recovering significantly.
I looked at Steven.
We can always reverse the process, Steven, and take you off the Tegretol, if we need to.

So the worsening would be temporary?
Yes, it should be. All it would require would be an adjustment of the Trilafon dose. The risk should be low.

What chance will this have of helping me?
I think it ought to be excellent. We have recently evaluated a group of patients admitted for short hospitalizations, but like you, resistant to their small doses of antipsychotic medications. Also, like you, they had some

temporal lobe symptoms. However, strangely we could not even detect their abnormalities on regular EEGs and we did not have available the technology for ambulatory EEGs. Our measure of change was only during their hospital stay, but the improvement was absolutely dramatic. [47] Based on my experience with this population, as well as with an outpatient population, I suspect our chances of seeing a significant improvement in you are outstanding.

Based on what, Doctor?
Mainly my observation and our knowledge of other's reports in situations such as yours.

I'll go with that experience anytime! But will all my temporal lobe type symptoms be helped, Doctor?
Some will. Some won't. There are two kinds of problems in the brain that can be linked up with firing: The first is the episodic phenomena, which we identified. This will usually respond to anticonvulsant medication. The second component are the symptoms pertaining to "scarring", but no firing. This "scarring" is seldom visible as dead fibers of tissue— "gliosis"; usually there is just physiologic non-function where the cells don't work properly. We find that these cells can improve when the surrounding firing diminishes as this provides a healthier environment for recuperation.

Does Steven have the same predisposing factors as other temporal lobe disease patients?
No, Steven has had a previous encephalitis. Many of our other patients with temporal lobe disease did not give any clear history of any obvious brain injury like infection of the brain, head injury, or tumor, for example. Some, however, had a history of significant drug abuse.

At what point do we contemplate using Tegretol without a clear precedent like prior encephalitis or head injury?
The pointer here appears to relate to other relevant accessory symptoms which seem to derive from the temporal lobe: These symptoms, like anger explosions, usually occur episodically over seconds. If you treat a patient with schizophrenia and add in Tegretol and they do not have some of these other accessory symptoms, it is likely that their condition will deteriorate. One of the reasons why it will deteriorate is that the Tegretol, just because of its action in speeding up some of the enzyme pathways in the liver, will lower the level of the antipsychotic; and the antipsychotic is necessary. In the instances where the Tegretol is needed, often the patients will feel dysphoric on the higher dose of antipsychotic, so the lowering of the dose is useful if other symptoms are controlled.

But what about just giving a lower dose?
We have tried that as well, Andrew, and it seems that the active intervention of the Tegretol is all-important.

And when do we use the Tegretol? What kinds of accessory symptoms?
The major consistent accessory feature that seems to help in patients with a schizophrenia-like illness, or who sometimes have been labeled as having a chronic atypical psychosis, seems to be irritability and explosiveness. When that symptom complex occurs, we know that the patient is likely to respond to Tegretol as adjunctive medication to their antipsychotic. Please remember that the Tegretol is not antipsychotic and will not help the psychosis itself.

So we can't use it on its own?
That's right. We have to use it with the neuroleptic—the antipsychotic medication—whether it be Trilafon, Thorazine, Risperdal or Clozaril.

> Successful treatment usually requires educating the patient about the basics of a medication, even exact dosing patterns. I proceeded to do this, inviting Steve's participation. [f]

*H*ow do I start taking the Tegretol, Doctor?
We build up the dose of Tegretol slowly. If you initially needed half twice a day, in a month you may need one three times a day. It's the same body dose, it's just the liver has speeded up the breakdown. So if you find yourself sleepy before, it may not make you sedated a week later. In other words, you will tolerate higher doses without side-effects and yet notice therapeutic effects. You can build up every third day by 100 mg till an initial target dose of 600 mg per day is reached.

Will I then have to keep taking more and more?
No. At a certain point, it gets more stable.
This may happen when you're taking one 200 mg tablet three times a day. It might sound unnecessary to talk in this simple way, but in fact, discussing each little facet of medication and compliance is the fabric that will allow you to be successful. Some people require different doses, but if you do, I will let you know.
Why must I build up the dose of the Tegretol, Doctor?
Tegretol possesses a rare property among drugs: it speeds up it's own metabolism in the liver. In other words, a month after you're taking it, you will need more Tegretol than you needed before.

---

[f] These rare footnotes will alert you when the text between two large letters reflects more complex areas or specific detail which the general reader may want to gloss over: This deviation focuses on principles and concrete areas of Tegretol prescription.

Oh, I see. How long do these liver processes go on for?
Technically, this so-called "liver enzyme induction process" might continue with slight changes for three months. However, probably about 90% of those changes have occurred in that first month, and then another 7% in the next two months, and then maybe 3% thereafter. In other words, once your liver has stabilized this process, you're at the correct dose.

Does all the liver get speeded up or is it just part?
It is likely that just a part gets speeded up, as certain enzymes increase and others don't. I believe the GGT—the gamma glutamyl transferase—is the key liver enzyme to measure, as it seems to parallel the speed-up process. This enzyme works with a B vitamin called folic acid. If you don't have enough folic acid you can become deficient in it, and this deficiency could be particularly relevant even in heart disease, maybe even as important as a raised cholesterol. A correlation was found, but this is not necessarily a cause-effect relationship.

Why should folic acid work?
Theoretically, because it contributes to the breakdown of certain toxic chemical compounds in the body.
So I should take folic acid supplements?
Yes.

Does the speeding up occur the same in everyone?
No, it varies a great deal with each individual. This means that on the same dose, a blood level of 11 at week 3 may drop to 8 once the speeding up fully kicks in at, say, week 5. Fortunately, Tegretol works within a broad therapeutic range—possibly 6 to 12.

Any side-effects to watch out for?
If you get unsteady on your feet with a little nausea or sedation or double vision, then you're taking too much Tegretol. If that happens, we would cut down the dose.

What about an allergic reaction?
About one in every seven or ten patients of mine develop a rash.
This may or may not go away. Far less common is an allergic sore throat, fever or mouth ulcer. You should stop the medicine pending urgent discussion with your physician. Finally, the occurrence of "bone-marrow depression" is extremely rare—maybe one in forty thousand patients on the medication, maybe even less than that. When we do a blood count, we will, almost every time, see a drop in the white cell count. Sometimes this will be below normal. This is not linked with bone marrow depression and doesn't seem to increase the risk of infection.

Can I get generic?
Yes, but I never use plain generic Tegretol, or for that matter any generic anticonvulsant, but I may use other specific brand names like Carbatrol.
I need exact dosing in conditions such as yours, and I'm more likely to be guaranteed that with the same consistent, well-established preparation.

> Steven was clearly extremely interested. This young man had already experienced life's torments. He was determined to do everything right. He was full of important questions.

So you've suggested Tegretol. Are there different kinds? What preparations should I take?
Tegretol comes in several slightly different preparations–the regular 200 mg tablet, different longer acting versions (Tegretol XR and Carbatrol), a chewable preparation and even a liquid. You must be careful to just substitute the one kind for the other as they may not be exactly equivalent.

Why?
Because chewables, if they're truly are chewed, are better absorbed, so more becomes available to the brain.
Long-acting preparations may be absorbed at slightly lesser rates. Liquids may be highly absorbed, but will depend on what's in your stomach. So each might be a little different, depending on absorption. This important principle can be applied with many different medications.

Is the liquid for a really low dose?
Yes. A few people are exquisitely sensitive and need the tiny amounts that can only be dispensed in liquid form. Higher doses knock these medication non-tolerators out. So if you're experiencing side-effects on the low starting dose, I don't want you to decide, "I better not take it, I must be allergic to it." You're not allergic to it: It's just that you're taking too much: like taking twelve aspirins when you only need one. There's an advantage to being so sensitive, because it keeps your medical bill down!

Any special tests to do?
We usually do blood levels and start by monitoring your blood count and liver enzymes particularly the one I mentioned earlier, the GGT–the gamma glutamyl transferase. I also like to know your electrolytes, as sodium–your salt level–may become too low on Tegretol.

Will I have to take Tegretol for the rest of my life?
Not necessarily, because theoretically, if you put out the fire, there might not be a recurring cause for it to keep springing up again; when the grass-fire is extinguished, it may not reappear. However, most people with full-blown seizure disorders have recurring reasons for their grass-fires, so they usually require a lifetime of medication.

Is there a chance I could ever not have to take it anymore?
There are certain circumstances where this fire can be doused for good and then we can taper the medication down to zero, without the fire ever recurring, but this is a fairly infrequent scenario. [48]

Well, Doctor, I'm really glad you've gone into such detail about taking my medication.
Yes, I like to do this with every medication I prescribe. Even though some aspects of medicine are routine, this basic advice is important.

And yet, Steven had not quite finished with his questions.

Doctor, I have to admit, I have difficulty remembering to take medication, let alone three times a day. Are there any tricks you know that could help?
Steven, you're asking about what we call "compliance with medication." This is one of the most important and difficult parts of your treatment. There are ways that may help. You could consider buying a watch with multiple alarms. This way you will be reminded when to take your medication. Also, weekly tablet dispensers are helpful. You can prepare your medication once per week in these Mediset dispensers, so you don't have to worry each day about the dosages.

Anything else?
Yes: try to cultivate regular medication patterns at *specific times*. These should be linked with specific actions like taking with meals at breakfast, lunch and dinner or taking medication before bed.

And how should I take the tablets?
Take your medication with water. This allows consistent absorption. Avoid chocolate milk, cola drinks, fruit juices, coffee or tea for about half and hour before and after: Otherwise, alterations in absorption pattern may result.

But I'll also be taking the folic acid you recommended with the Tegretol, and I take many vitamins, too. When should I take them?
As long as you're consistent and take the same brand name each time, you need not worry. The body will establish its own blood level for the Tegretol and we can always adjust the dose as necessary. If you take something new temporarily, like antibiotics or antacids, preferably do so at a different time so as not to modify absorption too much. Remember: consistency is important.

What if I miss a dose?

133

You ask important questions, Steven. If you have missed one dose, in general, take that dose as soon as the error is discovered; this may mean taking one double dose. If you have missed several doses, take one double dose with the next dose, then with the following dose a dose and a half, then go back to your regular prescription.

Can I apply these principles to other medications or do they just apply to Tegretol?
There are always exceptions, but in general, these guidelines can serve as excellent rules for other medications.

And so, Steven started on the low doses. He built up his dose of Tegretol, slowly over time, increasing every three days by another 100 mg. This way he avoided the unwanted side-effects of sleepiness, unsteadiness on his feet, as well as the more common dizziness and nausea that too high an initial dose might have produced. He watched carefully for any allergic reaction, but fortunately he did not have any.

Within a week, Steven reported some mild side-effects and some improvisation with his dosage:
Doctor, I'm finding that I need only 300 mg per day at this time. When I take 400 mg daily I'm a little sluggish; my thinking is slowed.
Those are likely symptoms of mild Tegretol toxicity. Not surprisingly, similar symptoms could happen if you took too much of some of the other anticonvulsants, like Dilantin. So that's why I gave you some flexibility on your dosage. You're the one taking it. I'm not experiencing the side-effects. You did well to notice, and I'm pleased you recognized these symptoms as it shows you paid attention when I discussed them with you. But do me a favor, please?

What?
Next time you cut down your dose, please just check with me. That way I can ensure that it is a drug-related side-effect. In this instance, we'll do a blood test to check that you have an appropriate therapeutic level for the medication.

Do you treat blood test results?
Not generally. I treat people. The blood test will at least allow me to know that you're not toxic and are taking the medication appropriately. I will be able to decide whether I have the latitude to minimally change the dosage if I believe it clinically indicated.

W ithin a month, Steven rated himself as a nine on a scale of one to ten, with ten being the best. His mother argued that he was a ten! *I'm not perfect, but maybe I was never a ten in my whole life anyway.*

Andrew still remained the scientist.
I know that we always try to use one drug at a time. Why does Steven need both medications, Doctor?
Because we cannot achieve control with just one of these medications. If a single drug does its job, that's fine. However, frequently, it does only part of the job. The principle is to be rational about our additional medications. Tegretol reflects the firing that was put out in Steve's brain. The Trilafon reflects the chemical modulation. There is a subtle commonality between the two. The electrical control is often modulated through the chemical facets, and if there's more electrical stability, there's more chemical stability. The converse also applies.

So chemical stability is "critical"?
Indeed, it is. However, the different receptor subtypes reflect remarkable chemical complexity. Each impacts on another. To misquote the 17th century English metaphysical poet, John Donne: "No receptor or receptor subtype is an island entire of itself." They influence each other not only from subtype to subtype, but also across the various receptors of the different chemical neurotransmitters: for example, serotonin, norepinephrine, acetylcholine, dopamine, and the opioid receptor all influence each other.

But there are also indirect effects?
Exactly. Added to this is the other component of influence: At some point a series of steps, called a "cascade" effect occurs. It's like a string of dominoes each falling down when knocked by the previous one, and modulation at the electrical level is also an important influence here.

And just what is modulation?
Modulation is best perceived in a parallel metaphor. If the lights are too bright, they're dimmed. If too dark, they're lit up, but all to a moderate or correct degree. Modulation avoids the extreme and is a physiological way the body adapts up and down.
In effect, we're talking about multiple feedback loops, is that right?
Yes. Invariably, the body has chemical and electrical ways to signal: "I've got too much, drop the level." Or it reports: "I have insufficient, I need some more." Sometimes, food cravings may be relevant here, like the pregnant lady needing to drink milk to supplement her calcium.

135

Does modulation imply appropriate bodily controls of mechanisms which could relate to nerve transmission but which could also even relate to heart rate or eating?
Exactly.

It was six years later. Steven returned for a follow-up visit.
Doctor, I'm doing things so well! I feel more alert; and a nice bonus is that the headaches I used to have seem to have disappeared. I can understand people more than I used to. In other words, I can focus on what others are saying and I can concentrate. I'm a senior in college now, and it's going well. I do my homework, I don't find it stressful, I work with other students, and I particularly like English. I'm thinking of a career with children.

Like a movie on fast rewind, I remembered in a series of moments the early parts of Steve's illness. Some five and a half years before, Steven had returned to school shortly after we had started him on the Tegretol. Initially, he had attended one of those special schools that allowed him to take one or two subjects with time flexibility. He gradually increased over a period of six months the number of hours he could allocate to schooling, to the point where he was able to return full-time. He had continued with a therapist he had been seeing, which I felt was important, because some of the disharmony he had been experiencing was the conflict of returning to normal. He even worked in a department store on the weekends, where he made a little over the minimum wage. He had no side-effects and had been continuing to take his medication. He exhibited no features of tardive dyskinesia.

He had done well, but recently felt even happier.

I learnt one reason for this.
By the way, Doctor, I have a girlfriend now. When I was ill, I never thought this would be possible!

Steven had done well on his combination of medications: The Tegretol had helped with the *explosions* in the brain, and his dysfunctional system was biochemically normalized with, in this instance, the Trilafon. The combination of biochemistry and electrical modulation had proven all-important.

Chapter 6

Tomorrow
I Will Kill Myself

Suicidal hopelessness.
Anger, atypical episodes, borderline, chronic fatigue,
gun control, meaning, out of labeling use, religion and
psychiatry, suicidal ideation.
Tegretol. (Wendy)

Wendy sat in my office, squeezing her fingers nervously, a strained look on her face.

Doctor, I don't know why I'm seeing you anyway. You doctors are all the same. My mother insisted I come, but this way I can die tomorrow in peace. Not really in peace. I'm going to kill myself. But don't bother to ask me how, Doctor, because I'm not going to tell you. You can be sure I've got a plan. I've been thinking about it for years.

Why haven't you killed yourself before?

Because I wanted to live. But now I know I should die. It's the only fair thing to do for my husband and my children. I can't have my children remembering me as I am. They probably will, but I'm frightened that I'm going to kill them. You're about the 28th doctor I've seen. They all tell me there's nothing wrong with me, or there's something wrong with me that they can't do anything about. I'm sick of doctors. Maybe I'll take one with me.

This was my introduction to Wendy. Frustrated, honest, in urgent need of help. When a person presents with acute suicidal symptoms, you have to hospitalize.

Wendy was ready for that suggestion:

Don't put me in the hospital, Doctor, because I'm not going to go, and if you try to get a commitment, I'll swear there's nothing wrong!

Usually, in the first interview, I try to obtain a patient history and an account of the problem, so I can figure out where the patient is coming from and how I can help. But in Wendy's case, I was literally playing for time.

137

I ended up trying the standard approach of entering into a contract with the patient:

We have two choices, Wendy. Either you promise not to do anything to yourself—and I have to believe you—or you're going to have to enter the hospital.

It seemed to work. After a cagey negotiation, she agreed to give me a chance and promised not to kill herself, or anyone else, for the time being. Her history, meanwhile, yielded interesting, though not entirely surprising details.

Wendy was only 29. She had dropped out of high school at age 16 when she had had a brief interlude with recreational drugs. She had been married since age 17, and she had two daughters, aged two and twelve. They were the best "things" in her life.

Wendy seemed to be somewhat ashamed of herself.
Oh, I'm just a housewife.

I raised my voice slightly, but emphatically.
"Just a housewife?" Just an unfortunate phrase.

Why do you say that, Doctor?
It represents an unfair perception common in our society. You're not a less valued member because you're not working outside the home. American culture sometimes does not perceive the homemaker as a bona fide worker. Clearly, you're performing a particular kind of work.

So you understand that I do things, Doctor?
Certainly. We should all recognize it. When you put it in perspective, however, you are working: It would cost an absolute bundle to replace that. Day care, house cleaning, cooking, banking, doing all the mundanities that sustain the "home economy". In fact, this phrase involves redundancy when you look at the original Greek meaning of economy—"managing the household." The well-ordered home is, in its own right, an important and viable contribution. Moreover, your greater availability at home more easily provides the special softness of high quality mothering.

And you do feel for us housewives?
I feel for you the homemaker! Societal changes have resulted in the diminishing and disparaging of the importance of the home and one of its principal managers: the housewife. This is the last bastion. The women's movement has, in an ironic way, discredited the woman at home in favor of the "working woman."

138

It was a little later. Wendy had left the room for some blood tests. Andrew did some probing:

How did Wendy come to you?
The psychiatrist who had seen her last referred her to me with the diagnosis of borderline personality disorder.

What's that?
Psychiatry has developed a complex and often useful set of categories for talking about the different kinds of mental illness or behavioral disorders. The term "borderline" has been popular for the last decade or so. The idea of the borderline type entered the mainstream bible of psychiatry—the DSM 4—from the vocabulary of psychoanalysis. Borderline does not mean of limited intelligence, or on the border of being psychotic. It means that the patient seems to have a character disorder that's disrupting their own lives and the lives of others, because they live a life of black or white, wonderful or terrible. They're living constantly on the border between extremes. There are no grays in their perception of experience. People around them are good or evil, happy or unhappy. Life is either exciting or a living death.

Does Wendy have any relevant characterological features?
Plenty, actually. I have had the opportunity to review a great deal of background notes. Wendy's character disorder has focused to some extent on her perception of her own sexuality. She is an attractive woman and knows that she's alluring: She enjoys attracting men and yet at the same time becomes angry with anyone who likes her. In fact, she talks about hating men because of their seductive behavior. She also has a deep contempt for women, whom she regards as stupid, as belonging in the home, and as ugly.

Were there other features of relevance?
Yes. Besides this low self-image of her life as a housewife, Wendy regards herself ugly as well, even as she simultaneously thinks of herself as both beautiful and seductive. Wendy sometimes refuses to eat for days at a time and then binge eats for hours. She has mutilated herself by cutting her wrists, burning herself with cigarettes, and hurting herself in other ways. At times, she would confine herself in her room for days, the door locked, not eating and not talking to a soul.

So she has had a great deal of past trauma?
Indeed, so. Wendy did not trust anyone enough to tell about all the events that went on in her life. Her willingness to trust her doctors was low. Among the puzzles in her life was the disparity between her grades in school and her obviously good intelligence. Perhaps she had mutilated

herself in that way, too, by consistently failing to live up to her abilities. Perhaps, though, she had an organic brain disorder—a firing or a scarring somewhere in the depths of her mind.

Sometimes she has trouble expressing herself; sometimes she even has difficulty telling the difference between left and right: But these are common complaints among many otherwise normal people.

Are there any triggers for an organic hypothesis?

Yes. I suspect the short lived, but intense contact she had with recreational drugs during her teens was highly relevant. She would snort cocaine, twice a week for some months, as well as using significant amounts of marijuana and the occasional hit of LSD. However, she has never had a significant head injury or infection of the brain and she was a normal birth. Her school difficulties may also have been linked with a brain-based specific learning disability like dyslexia. The sad fact is that she has never had a test for brain function or for neurological disorders.

What was done during this period instead?

Over the years she had drifted from one psychotherapist to another for a variety of talk therapies. She had experienced classic Freudian therapy, cognitive therapy, directive therapy, aversive therapy, hypnosis, behaviorist approaches, existential challenges and perhaps others as well. Additionally, she has taken virtually every group of conventional psychiatric drug. Every one of these approaches has failed. At times, there may have been marginal improvement, but that's all.

Well, what did the therapists work on?

Her symptoms gave the various therapists plenty to work with. At times she seemed to have become fully psychotic. The face of the "alien" sometimes appeared to her right, but never spoke. Symptoms of these kinds can have several sources, but in Wendy's case, I suspect childhood sexual abuse.

Why?

Because she spoke in guarded terms of several puzzling episodes when she was ten years old: A teenage male cousin had spent the summer with them. Wendy does not seem to have much recall about the incidents, but apparently some lurid detail came up on hypnotic regression, although this could have been her unconscious playing tricks on her.

What specifically may be linked with sexual abuse, here?

These visions of all-powerful, overwhelming, and alien forces may be the only way patients can visualize and express the experience of a parent or sibling turning into an alien, entrapping, abusive force. How many of these stories begin with bright lights at night, abduction from the comfort of a bed, strange physical examinations and probings, disorientation and terror? How many end with the final unexpected return to the comfort of the child's own bedroom, every image an almost transparent image for an unexpected visit in the night from a normally friendly relation, who suddenly behaves in an alien way, only to return to the normal, smiling brother or uncle or mother the next morning?

Certainly that might explain some of the newspaper articles?
Yes. The pages of the sensationalist tabloids may hide any number of disguised stories of familial abuse. UFO abductions may be metaphors for sexual attacks. Similarly, voices from heaven demanding the construction of pyramids or temples may merely be enormous talismans to protect a victim from further abuse. Wendy's hallucination of the "alien" might well have been a distorted memory of a sexual abuse experience, where she may have focused her eyes elsewhere while she struggled both to free herself from the attacker's hands and to fix her attention on anything but what was, in fact, happening to her. Some people with visions of this kind are beyond reach and never seek help.

Does her childhood also fit her current presentations of aggression?
She apparently never learnt the pattern in her childhood. She was never beaten as a child, and her parents were always protective towards her. So that leads to considering problems with the wiring in the brain. When the psychological dynamics don't fit, we should always look organically.

I reviewed the notes further for Andrew:
Wendy recollected many nightmares, tantalizing and frightening at the same time, in which the alien face came into her room, always on her right, looked threateningly at her, and then proceeded to touch her. Men attacked her in these dreams, too, and she imagined herself as one of the stupid, helpless women she so often condemned, the women who in her judgment deserved whatever happened to them.

So what was the result?
These and perhaps other incidents had left her with a crippling legacy of rage. Early in her marriage, she had stabbed her husband, and although she whispered urgent denials of child abuse, it seemed evident that her own children, whom she treasured above everything, had also been the objects of her anger. Whatever had happened in the privacy of her home, she had passed a death sentence on herself.

It was an hour later. Wendy sat there, staring intently ahead.
I looked her directly in the eye.
Do you own a gun?
Whether I do or I don't, it's my own personal business.

It may well be, but you're consulting with me, and I want to help you.
I appreciate that.
That's why my question is important. Do you own a firearm?
Well, not exactly.
What do you mean by "not exactly"?
Well, my husband has one, but I don't use it.
Do you have access to that firearm?
Well, yes, but he keeps it locked up.
Do you have access to the key?
Yes, I suppose so, but I would never use it.

> Stage 1 was established. Wendy was aware of my covert theme. Stage 2 involved the soft confrontation phase.

But you've talked about the times you've thought about ending it all.
That's true, but I'm not going to tell you how, Doctor. Maybe it wouldn't even be with a gun.
It's not a case of "maybe it wouldn't be with a gun." We're going to have to work through several elements here. One is, I don't want you to harm yourself in any way, by any means. A second element relates to the gun.
Okay, so maybe I might have thought once or twice about shooting myself.

> Stage 2 of soft negotiation was over. Stage 3 involved communicating the facts.

All right then: what do you want to do about it?
It doesn't make any difference anyway, because if I didn't have a gun and I wanted to kill myself, I could always do it some other way.
Well, actually, it does make a difference. The gun is, unfortunately, an extremely effective means for taking your life—four out of every five such attempts are fatal. It may even be that a few of the non-fatal attempts were not actually attempts at suicide. Moreover, some people may not have intended to kill themselves and were just acting out a cry for help, but ended up ending their lives with a firearm.

But aren't there a hundred ways to kill yourself, Doctor? Aren't they all just as effective?
In truth, the other methods of attempting suicide are, fortunately, less effective, like overdosing or gassing. However, although they may not end in death, they can cause enormous problems for the survivor.
For example, gassing oneself in a car by carbon monoxide poisoning can cause the most awful neurological side-effects. Then the person has to live with their deformities and brain damage constantly as a reminder every day of their past suicide attempt. It's literally a situation of "act then and

142

regret for the rest of your life." At least there's a life to regret. With a gun, that would be highly unlikely.

> Wendy's facial expression reflected both the pain of a new dilemma, and an anger at someone daring her deeper intentions.

Again, you're going on about guns. Why don't you speak out about the evils of knives also?
A firearm is literally a suicide machine. It's an extremely effective means of suicide. We should look at the design of a gun: What's it manufactured for? For target practice in a few, but basically guns are expressly for one purpose: to kill or deter others through the threat to kill.

But that's the whole point, Doctor. My husband and I need our gun for self-defense.
It's a rather odd point you make here, living as you do in the United States. We have the world's worst record of firearm violence in the so-called civilized world, and not by a little but by a lot, possibly several hundred times worse than Britain, after converting to an equivalent population size.

You know, Doctor, maybe I have thought about hurting myself, but even though I talk about striking my children, I'm not sure that I would ever hurt another person.
I'm pleased to hear that. People don't usually intend to use guns in violent acts; they do it impulsively. Controlling access may reduce the ease with which the small but dangerous minority, who may use it violently, can get hold of them.

But Doctor, I don't ever plan to use my gun violently.
Nor, incidentally, do the great majority of people who find themselves in a violent situation. Most violence does not occur between strangers; most violence is occurring in the home, at a domestic level, between people who know each other, sometimes closely.

> Wendy was softening just that little bit. If she wasn't she would have terminated the discussion. It was obvious she was hearing what I was saying, but the resistance was still there. No longer was she denying her access to her husband's firearm.

There's another issue here, Doctor: You know, I'm a woman, and sometimes I'm out on my own and I've got to protect myself against strangers: I've got to protect myself against rape and assault. What happens if I'm in a dark alley?

143

In fact, these are extreme rarities. When we start looking at statistics, we will find that a firearm may be used only once in five hundred times in self-defense. Unfortunately, the risks of handgun ownership far outweigh the benefit by two hundred fold, particularly in your own home.

Yes, Doctor, I know about that. We have been there, my husband and I.
You see, this raises up your risk even more.

> I was getting through to Wendy. Stage 4–the personal side–was beginning. But rationalization would creep in, periodically.

But Doctor, isn't it true that the people who kill themselves with guns are mostly men?
That's not really true. We're finding that most women who kill themselves do so with firearms.

> Wendy still played the game of denial of the personal issue by shifting the topic a little.

Well, Doctor, does this mean people shouldn't own cars? More people die in motor vehicle accidents than with firearms!
You're right. Auto wrecks killed 35,000 Americans in 1995. But within a decade, guns will kill more than cars.

> At this point, Andrew, who had been unusually quiet, seemed to feel a need to join in to vocalize something he had been holding in. I was not delighted that my specially developed theme was being interrupted. I was battling a patient's death wish and here was my medical student arguing abstractions. He was treading where angels feared, a sign that he still lacked the special skill that students need to learn: when to keep quiet and when to act. I had to ensure that I could maintain my momentum, but I knew this would be easy because, to me, the issue was so cut and dried.

Just a minute, Doctor: I have a gun, and I feel I have the right...
> I quickly interrupted.
Andrew we'll talk about your rights later. At the moment, I'm talking to Wendy.

> Wendy seemed relieved at this interruption. She had relaxed somewhat and had stopped leaning forward in her chair. She wished to add something, though she spoke softly and somewhat insecurely.

Doctor, I really don't know enough to debate this issue. But I do have a question: Don't statistics lie? Don't they tell you what you want to hear? Don't they all just add up to a pile of irrelevant gun control figures?

Good question. There's no easy answer. Statistics are valuable when used properly. However, they should be applied in the context of common sense. The common sense here is that gun use may be impulsive and lethal.

I could see by her inadvertent nod that I was getting through to Wendy!

Is it really as bad as all that?

I'm afraid so. Amongst my patients, firearms would often have been impulsively used if they had been available. So many have told me, "You know, doctor, you told me to get rid of my firearm, and if I would've had one, I wouldn't be here today."

You know, Doctor, I think you've made your point. I'm going to speak to my husband about this. Do you think it would be all right for us to give our gun to somebody for safekeeping?

Yes. One recommendation, which may or may not be easily available, would be to consult with the police, and they could help you in this regard.

This way, my husband, if he really was serious about target practice (and he often talks about it, but never goes out to the range) would be able to have access to the gun when he needed it.

W e had solved one basic crisis problem: the firearm. Now there was a second one: Her thinking about **suicide**. I knew guns were just the concrete method. I was entering a similar but different battlefield, again with no holds barred. I wanted to battle the concept of suicide.

Have you ever thought about what might happen to you if you killed yourself?

Yes, sometimes. I just feel that when you're dead, you're dead. Like a piece of wood, like a doornail, there's nothing there anymore. It's over.

Let me not in any way impact on your belief systems. "Let me not to the marriage of true minds admit impediments." [49] But let me raise important questions: What happens if you're wrong? What happens if, when you die, you're not just dead? You're in some way existing in another form? What happens if you suddenly find yourself feeling extreme remorse for your actions? What happens when you suddenly realize that you may have been in this world for some special purpose in self-development, and that you had failed, and that you're going to need to try again?

145

I could impose all sorts of other views. Some would say: What about karma or reincarnation? But others would throw in: What about hell or damnation or purgatory? I'm not going to be too philosophical about these possibilities, Wendy, but I want you to be aware that maybe there are more things between heaven and earth than we can fully conceive of. Possibly, death may not be a finality.

Well, I'm prepared to take that risk, Doctor. I don't think I really believe in all that mumbo-jumbo anyway. The life I've got now is enough for me to handle without having to worry about another life.
Maybe before you take that risk, you ought to take a look at the literature in that area. You might suddenly find that risk to be a big one indeed. You might discover a great deal of cogent support for the likelihood of some form of survival of the human personality after bodily death.

Doctor, you're frightening me! I don't think it's fair. Here I have my own thoughts about this, and, frankly, it would be just as well if I didn't have to worry about other conflicting ideas.
I'm deliberately setting up a conflict with your thoughts. I call this the "no-holds barred debate", because this is serious enough for no holds to be barred. I can help you feel much better, but you must allow me the opportunity to help you. We cannot have that opportunity if you destroy yourself before you're allowed to improve.

If death isn't the end, who is to say that killing myself won't actually result in a happier existence in some other life?
That's an interesting speculation and it leads to philosophical biases. I like things to make sense. It seems to me unreasonable to expect happiness when we have not succeeded in caring for ourselves adequately and left a trail of guilt and despair with others: with family and friends who remain alive.

But what about people who get away with all sorts of crimes, even murder, and seem to live a charmed existence? Life shows us that not every last person gets his just desserts. If people can get away with it in this life, who's to say they can't in the next life?
A theological dilemma? Maybe there's a higher dimension and at times we cannot conceive of it.

Please explain that, Doctor. I've come to you, and I guess that means I must want help.
The ancient Greek philosopher, Plato, used the analogy of how the occupants of a cave would only see the shadows of those passing by outside, not the real passersby. Those shadows were for these occupants their false reality. Maybe it's the same here. To debate issues of good and evil, of

justice and reward without looking a dimension beyond what we conceive of, may make life less meaningful and our existence less true.

So maybe there's a deeper meaning to all this?
Yes. There are always two sides to an argument, and bear in mind that you may be sorely disappointed if you killed yourself. Isn't that a strange thought, to think it would be the end? Maybe it's not the end at all.

> Andrew was keen to make his point. I was concerned he would again unintentionally mar my venture to keep Wendy alive, but this time he supported it.

What about "Pascal's Wager"? The French mathematician, Blaise Pascal, argued that even the most resolutely skeptical agnostic has to logically weigh the possibility of a horrible afterlife because of suicide.
I can see you're a philosopher, Andrew.
Yes, it was my major.
I suppose you will tell me that Pascal's prescription was to weigh this horrible afterlife against the temptation to indulge in nihilistic atheism.
Yes, and we could arrive at a logical conclusion at the very least.
What?
That it would be a safer wager to try to cultivate a reverence and interest in the afterlife, rather than risk the possibility of damnation, or regretting at leisure or even reincarnation as a cockroach.

> Wendy had been trying hard to hold back her emotions, but she was now clearly wounded.

You mean it's kind of like a gamble?
Yes, but it's the most important bet you will ever place.

> My student had fully joined the no holds barred debate. It seemed Wendy was even more persuaded.

I don't think I want to be a cockroach!

> Again, we reviewed her past incidents of anger and rage, sometimes acted out on family members, sometimes at herself.
> She related several overwhelming episodes of distress:

I struck my five year old in the jaw for no reason other than "blind rage" and once I purposefully burnt my own hand with an iron. Then there was the time I crushed a wineglass in my hand causing bleeding.

> I had come to believe, however, that Wendy was treatable.
> Her alternating fits of rage at others and at herself, that rapid vacillation between masochistic and sadistic acts, were accompanied by a deep need to find help. The first task was to establish whether her episodes of anger and rage had an organic base, whether in other

words she had a brain disorder as well as a deep psychological trauma. Clearly psychological treatment alone had not helped her, if after seeing twenty seven specialists she was still at the point of committing suicide. I wondered whether there was a temporal lobe disorder accompanied by irregular firings or electrical discharges, a fire in her brain that was literally enraging her. If she had seizures of this type, perhaps I could find a pharmacological fire extinguisher to bring the symptoms under control.

At her next visit, we continued our foray into this avenue of treatment. In fact, Wendy occasionally spoke of herself as if she experienced seizures.

You know what's wrong with me, Doctor? I have a wire that's loose. It's never been connected in the right place in my brain. I can't predict when I'm going to blow. I don't even recognize when it starts. Just suddenly I get angry with anything or anyone around me. I broke my arm once punching it into the wall. I've punched holes in walls three times. Sometimes I don't even know what I've done. I forget it all. People tell me about it later. It all builds up for about ten minutes, and then it happens, and later I feel so guilty I just want to kill myself. I want to apologize, but it's hard because then I have these terrible headaches; and then I get so sleepy: I just want to go to bed. Sometimes I don't know what day it is, or what time of the day it is, or even the month of the year.

Wendy was describing the typical post-ictal symptoms following an epileptic seizure: headache, clouding of consciousness, disorientation, confusion, amnesia, the build up to an explosion. The loss of control and the non-directness of her outbursts were also typical: that need to lash out at whatever target was handy. When no other target was available, she would stab herself instead: with scissors, razor blades, even ball point pens; anything sharp. The amnesic element could easily be part of the complex partial seizure equivalent where the person does not remember all of what they have done. But if these episodes were linked with seizures, we were dealing with a rare condition, indeed.

I continued obtaining historical detail.

Wendy, can you tell me when these symptoms first appeared?
About in high school, My grades started to fall. I had been labeled learning disabled. I think stress seemed to worsen my performance.

She looked down at the ground, and in a sorrowful whisper added:
And, of course, I had started taking drugs.

What did your doctor do?
My mother took me to a doctor who prescribed Librium. But I hated it. I hated being sedated. I hated the idea of being a mental patient on a tranquilizer.

Did you take the Librium?
No. Instead of taking my dose, I stockpiled it for several weeks and then, I made my first attempt at suicide.

What happened then?
Well, when I recovered from the attempt, I told my parents about what I was seeing—my visual hallucinations.

What visual hallucinations were these?
I would see horrible distortions of the "alien". Always just to my right side and only the head with horns.

And what was done for you?
I was given some antipsychotic medication, Hal...
Haldol?
Yes, Almost immediately, I swung into an acute medical crisis. My eyes almost popped out of my head: real weird, where my eyes moved to one side and were held in, like, a paralysis. What was amazing was it happened on the first dose and the doctor said it was a small amount.

Andrew, had been listening in quietly till then:
What do you suppose that is, Doctor?
That's a condition known as an "oculogyric crisis". An oculogyric crisis is a rare response to high doses of antipsychotic medication that occurs more commonly in men than in women and in the young rather than the old.

What triggers it, exactly?
Within the brain, the balance between dopamine and acetylcholine is thrown off by an overdose of antipsychotic, requiring an immediate intravenous infusion of anticholinergic drugs.

I felt a deep empathy for Wendy. In spite of what she may have done to her children and her husband, she had chosen to make a heroic effort to remain moral in the face of an uncontrollable and probably deeply organic brain disorder.

Time after time she had sought help, and time after time each therapy she tried had failed.

149

I understood her frustrated attempts to be a good person when every therapist she had met had labeled her as disordered, borderline, defective in her character, and because of her childhood visions of the "alien" head, psychotic.

I don't want to be written off, Doctor. I'm a person. I'm a human being.
And we will not write you off, Wendy. I want to do everything I can to help you. You will become a more serene human being.
What are we going to do then?
Have your brain waves ever been tested with an EEG?
No, Doctor, I've never had that.

I continued to be amazed that over all her years of treatment she had never been assessed by a simple EEG. No one had considered that she might have an organic brain disorder. Wendy was the typical "psychiatric patient" who should be monitored with an ambulatory EEG to demonstrate her disease of the "mind" was indeed a treatable disease of the "brain".

I educated Wendy, just as I had numerous patients before. As always, I was asked new questions about the device.
Wendy, we're going to arrange for an ambulatory EEG, which is an improvement on the regular EEG. It does not involve a routine office visit, but is actually a device you will wear for two days at home.

What's the purpose of this device, Doctor?
It will enable us to look for odd wave forms anywhere in your brain. The superiority of ambulatory EEG over regular EEG lies not only in the additional length of the test, but because you can be monitored during all the usual stresses of normal life: dinner, TV-watching, dreams, nightmares and explosions of anger.

What does the device look like and how does it attach?
An ambulatory EEG monitor is only the size of a Walkman cassette player, and we attach it to your scalp by electrodes. You can wear it anywhere you don't feel self-conscious with it on.

Do you mean that someone is reading the results "live", at the same time as I'm wearing it?
No. Your brain waves are recorded onto a computer for us to analyze later.

So when am I supposed to start with this home EEG? This weekend?
Unfortunately, there will be a delay of a few days till the apparatus becomes available.

Is there any other testing you can do before that?
Yes, in fact, I want you to complete a formal screening device to elicit symptoms of seizures and the temporal lobe disease. I call it the INSET screening device. [50] After that, we will go through your answers because I want to see if you have symptoms.

What kinds of questions do you ask on the INSET, Doctor?
I try to screen with pertinent questions; I don't want people just to fill in a vague description, like "I had this unexplained smell." We want to ascertain details of many different symptoms.

And with the smells?
We analyze the exact description of every special smell hallucination: how long it lasts, its pleasantness degree, associated symptoms occurring with it or just before or after, triggers, frequency, time of day it occurs and exact description. By so doing, we're able to ensure that the smell you're describing, to you anyway, is of a certain special kind. We then try to establish whether this could have correlates in the brain.

What's the significance of smells?
These strange experiences reflect an area of the brain which is firing if there's no stimulus to their occurrence. With smells, it's the so-called mesial temporal cortex that's being stimulated, an area that's really hard to record on EEG because it's so deep. It's complicated because the specific area may vary a little for different people, but at least it's usually consistent for each individual: The same area causes the same firing each time. That's why seizures are so consistent in their aurae—their warnings.

But I have other strange symptoms like nightmares.
Surprisingly, nightmares often occur in people with a history of particularly temporal lobe seizures. In some way, they're often linked up with the seizure phenomena. As you experience more seizure control, the nightmares improve.

> So, Wendy completed the INSET test. She reported a varied group of unusual experiences. Andrew was intrigued, but chose only one of fourteen different positive responses to ask about.

Did she have any of those smell experiences, Doctor?
Yes, she did. She describes the perception of unexplained burning wood and this is particularly common as reflecting a possible symptom of temporal lobe firing deep in the brain. Almost daily, she has other distortions which she calls "hallucinations."

For example?

151

She has a momentary distortion of objects and with it a sense of intense déjà vu—that it was happening all over again. Déjà vu is another symptom potentially associated with epileptic firing, but which could be quite normal. We must be careful to interpret these symptoms in the context of her clinical condition.

How do you know she doesn't just invent the symptoms?
Because, we have certain special items in the test that do not reflect brain disease, but do reflect a vivid imagination.

Wendy already had made her own diagnosis, again.
I've already told you what's wrong with me, Doctor. I have a wire that's loose in my brain.
She then proceeded to weep uncontrollably. I comforted her.
What's wrong, Wendy?
Nobody believes me. The doctors say my wiring is okay!

W hile waiting for her ambulatory EEG, I wanted Wendy to feel we were doing something for her. I was confident that she would wait at least until after she completed her tests before potentially exhibiting an act of self harm. While there was hope, she would grab it. I did not want to prescribe inappropriate medication unnecessarily. To make her future-oriented, to get her to begin to think about her life as if it would have a future at all, I suggested a modest first step.

Wendy, how much coffee would you say you drink a day?
Oh, between ten and twelve cups a day; and some of those are double espressos. Why is that important, Doctor?
Because your daily intake amounts to a dose of 1500 or more milligrams of caffeine. Now, 1,000 milligrams of caffeine, the equivalent of seven or eight cups, will induce anxiety in the average, healthy adult. In fact, these levels are used to induce anxiety in laboratory experiments, and it's well known that anxiety is part of a feed-back loop.

What do you mean by a feed-back loop?
Anxiety produces hostility which produces more anxiety which gives rise to greater hostility, until the whole cycle accelerates to an explosion.
What are you suggesting I do?
My advice is to start treatment by cutting your coffee by half a cup a day. We don't want you to stop completely and get withdrawal headaches. However, I don't expect you to start immediately. We can wait until we have the EEG results.

That's fine with me, Doctor! If I have a normal EEG, it's all over anyway, so I might as well wait to stop the coffee!

The following week, Wendy arrived to be hooked up to the machine, and quite casually announced:
By the way, Doctor, I'm off coffee. I thought about what you said, and I just stopped it. Did I have a headache those first three days! And I still have headaches almost every day.

This was, of course, typical of her impulsive behavior. She could have prevented withdrawal headaches by a slow taper over weeks. But, she could not tolerate the idea of the gray area, the gradual reduction of coffee. She was either addicted or coffee-free, cold turkey. On the other hand, it demonstrated her remarkable inner strength.
Like I say, I have really bad headaches, and I can't stay awake, but I'm not as irritable. Who knows, maybe I won't have enough anger for the machine to notice.

In fact, Wendy only had three minor episodes of anger during the 48 hours she was on the monitor. When she returned to the office and we went over the results, she was upset.
I've failed, Doctor. I've failed myself and now I can kill myself. There's nothing on the EEG. This must mean I'm just a psychological nut-case. You can't cure me. Anyway, I don't deserve to live.

I knew that this was a potential major trauma for Wendy. Initially, the results looked bleak, paradoxically, because of their sheer normality.

> Andrew, at this point in his career, still tended to see the results as a piece of paper, not as a patient who had enormous investment in life and death.

So what are her EEG results, Doctor?
Well, Andrew, we reviewed Wendy's record. The ambulatory EEG, in theory, could be interpreted as normal. However, there was a tiny bit of firing on both sides of the temporal lobe of her brain: One or two second episodes of sharp waves occurred several times deep in a primitive zone of the brain closely related to the limbic system, with all its connections to human emotion and sensory perception. Traditionally, we read this kind of tracing as within normal limits because it could reflect a normal variant brought on, for example, by fatigue.

What significance could this have?

153

It could conceivably reflect a chemical imbalance or minimal physical scarring deep in the temporal lobe. This could create profound symptoms such as the sensations of bizarre sounds, strange tastes, or visual spots. Wendy doesn't have these. However, she did mention sudden uncontrolled mood swings like a "yo-yo" occurring literally over seconds. She also has episodes of experiencing unpleasant odors. The EEG was normal during the three periods of anger she had during those two days, However, if the firing were deep in the brain, it would not have been recorded on our scalp electrodes. In any event, she describes her episodes during the ambulatory EEG as "minor, not a big one," so we may not have detected the real explosions.

What do you think?
Something doesn't fit. Although the EEG findings technically could be read as normal, in this instance, given Wendy's history, I think the temporal lobe findings actually reflect abnormality. It's possible that she has discharges deep in her brain that we could not detect without surgical implantation of electrodes.

Which is not an option, right?
Not at this point. Such invasive neurosurgery is out of the question unless I have further support data where we would potentially be operating on the brain to cut out an area of firing.

Why can the anger attacks not be psychological?
Because "psychological" is also a positive diagnosis. Her dynamics could fit this framework, but she has had psychotherapy without any result. There is also no supporting pattern of learned aggression from her childhood. Her symptoms also eminently fit a temporal lobe hypothesis.

Could it be that the two are linked?
You're correct, Andrew. Strangely, we commonly see significant stressors like sexual abuse seemingly aggravating temporal lobe disease.
But how?
The parallel is a catastrophic event, sometimes with repeated frequency, lowering the threshold for a firing event in the brain. It's like tuning in a radio receiver and getting straight to the channel you're looking for. We require a lower degree of stimulus to arrive at the firing, the tuning in, rather like the mechanism of a conditioned reflex. I think this must be the normal physiologic equivalent, and such traumatic stress is the psychological side of the conditioning gone wrong. Another concept, the "kindling phenomenon" that we have discussed briefly, is the psychophysiologic electrical side of this, reflecting firing gone wrong.

Does Tegretol work on this kindling?

Yes. It's extremely potent.
And does it work on this kind of post-traumatic stress?
Yes, again. There is some support for the idea that Tegretol does.

So what will you do?
I have looked at the clinical symptoms predominantly. I have combined this with the ambulatory EEG findings, which using pure EEG criteria could be interpreted as normal, but which using the patient context symptoms certainly suggest firing. I have decided to control whatever electrical firing she may be experiencing. So given all this, it's reasonable to pursue Tegretol with Wendy.

*T*ell me more. What has led you to this strategy?
Firstly, Andrew, Wendy's attacks reminded me vividly of a group of patients I knew in the late 1970s when I first began to study anticonvulsants: I treated three patients who had hallucinations. They heard voices that would torment them and threaten them, would sometimes see ghoulish objects, and they had other frightening delusions as odd as those any schizophrenic might have, and yet they did not respond at all to antipsychotic medications. Their paranoid ideation included all the thoughts typical of schizophrenics: devils or other all powerful beings were conducting elaborate plots against their lives, and yet these experiences were different.

What was different about them?
When I reviewed their records, one common thread stood out from the fabric of those lives. They had all abused hallucinogenic drugs. In place of the withdrawal, even the autism of schizophrenics, these patients were communicative. They offered long explanations of their conditions; they talked endlessly about political plots; and they were confrontational. My first attempt at therapy was to prescribe Dilantin, which you will recognize as an anticonvulsant drug, and together with the antipsychotics these patients were already taking, it brought their symptoms under control.

Where did the Tegretol figure in?
Well, later I did that double-blind study on Tegretol, which, as you know, is a related anticonvulsant. [51] I preferred Tegretol for formal study because it seemed to have less effect on the underlying personality traits of my patients. For example, a Scandinavian study had reported that substituting Tegretol for other anticonvulsants resulted not only in equally good control of the seizures, but less anxiety, hostility and thinking difficulties than some epileptics experienced using the other drugs.
In other words, Tegretol was a sweeter drug; it brought out what good there was in people.

155

Does that mean it was a more physiologic drug than the others?
Not actually. It meant it had less side-effects. However, maybe that had to
do with controlling abnormal firing right at the point of origin, not allowing any spread even for millimeters.

Why was your study relevant?
We have touched briefly on my own double-blind study.[52] This historically became important because it's the only one that explored the reactions of psychotics who also had clear evidence of temporal lobe firing.
These patients had been sitting in mental wards for years and years, most
of them beyond reach and utterly unresponsive to medication. I started
the group on either placebo and antipsychotic or Tegretol and antipsychotic. Since it was a double-blind study, neither the patients nor I knew
who was taking Tegretol and who was taking placebo.

Why didn't others repeat the study?
Because double-blind studies are difficult and expensive. Moreover, because this is not specifically in the true sense a seizure, it was not an indication approved by the FDA—it was **"out of labeling"**. [53]

*W*hat does *"out of labeling"* mean?
The Food and Drug Administration—the FDA—in the United States exhibits careful controls on medications. They become approved after a
lengthy and careful process with certain restrictions. The dose, duration
of treatment and official diagnoses in which they can be used are stated.
This refers to their "labeled indications".

When would Tegretol be used within labeling?
In conditions such as seizures or special kinds of pain.
But then it's sometimes prescribed for other conditions?
Exactly. That's an "out of labeling" prescription. It's quite legal. This way
the FDA allows the physician discretion to decide when the drug should
be used in other conditions.
I see. But, why would a physician want to use a drug out of labeling?
Because we want to help our patients. Sometimes, the standard treatment
fails. Other times, there's no standard treatment. So, for example, as far as
I know, there's not a single drug anywhere in the world approved for aggressive outbursts.

If we stayed within labeling, then we could not treat aggression?
Right. Nor could we treat many other conditions. Physicians have to be
responsible and careful, and use the best available treatments.
Drugs approved for one use, may never develop a formal approved indication from the FDA for another use, because formal new studies may

156

cost hundreds of millions of dollars. The pharmaceutical companies may decide not to bear the expense of something that already is commonly known anyway.

So was your study successful?
Very much so. The treatment turned out to be so important that colleagues began to use it on their patients. However, the extended benefit is not just the Tegretol, but the broader use of anticonvulsants for episodic brain related atypical explosions in the psychotic and ordinary person which this study pioneered. It opened a whole new world for psychiatry. The electrical as well as the chemical. This is what makes medical research so exciting.

I've always been interested in the double-blind study. How much is a double-blind study really blinded?
Less than you think. A difficulty with double-blind studies is that sometimes the results are so obvious that it's impossible to keep up the illusion that the doctors and patients do not know which drugs particular patients are taking. I can illustrate my answer with one patient: He reported to me two weeks into the study that he was better. The dramatic change strongly suggested her was the carbamazepine—the Tegretol—not the placebo at the time.

Did you ask that patient in what way he was better?
I did.
And what did he say?
"You know," he said, "whenever I talked to people before, I had to keep myself from punching them and hitting them. The only way I could control myself was to withdraw. Now I can actually have a conversation."

Such a description says it all. What was the overall outcome?
When placed on Tegretol, almost all the patients came under control. Like Wendy, their violence was initially out of control, but deep within their personalities were human beings doing everything in their power to be moral, even if it meant complete autistic withdrawal.

Wendy had listened to all this with enormous interest. I was pleased that I could indirectly educate her like this because I knew that this third party type conversation was less threatening to her. She was now ready to participate.

But these people all had abnormal EEGs. What about me Doctor? My EEG was within normal limits.

Good question, Wendy. We can help you, too. I know that because of some further research we did on anger episodes like yours with the clinical temporal lobe type features. In fact, in one series, all the patients just turned out to have normal EEGs, but I was firmly convinced of my diagnosis. They responded dramatically to Tegretol. I suspect these patients, like you, had an area of firing so deep in the midline of the brain that we could not easily locate the focus of firing on conventional scalp EEG recordings.

Have you used Tegretol on people who have explosions without the psychotic features?
Yes. We have seen it work on both psychotic and non-psychotic patients. With you, Wendy, there is, of course, no need to use antipsychotic medications as well, because you are not psychotic.

And these patients fo und real relief from the Tegretol?
Yes, Tegretol helps prevent these episodes. However, we do not use anticonvulsants like Tegretol as a panacea to treat all problems of anger. These medications usually work only with the specific, selected criteria I am outlining as these reflect possible electrical firing in the brain.

What are the key symptoms?
Several. I list a few: the loss of control and the sudden unexplained, disproportionate explosions of anger lasting a few seconds (as opposed to a gradual stress related build up). Then there is the out of character elements in the anger behavior. Seizure-linked features like headache, confusion and fatigue after the event with sometimes the amnesia for part of the events are particularly important. Then there are the special pointers like the temporal lobe EEG firing and the lack of response to both traditional psychotherapeutic and chemical manipulations. When taken together, these criteria form a strong case.

What would the diagnosis be?
I regard such anger explosions as "atypical spells in the condition of paroxysmal neurobehavioral disorder". This way I avoid the debate whether they are actual "seizures". I regard these spells as related to abnormal electrical temporal lobe or limbic system firing in the brain, but this does not make them seizures.

You have implied this is a rare condition?
Yes. These criteria are specific and do not mean that people with planned or prolonged impulsive aggressive acts or under the influence of drugs can be regarded as having this condition. The great majority of people with anger do not have these criteria and should not respond to anticonvulsant.

158

As is my custom, I like to discuss with my patients the potential values and difficulties of using a new drug. At this time, Wendy brought up another problem she had. Again the burnt grass analogy was relevant.

Doctor, I find myself so tired all the time. I feel like I'm dragging myself around most of the day. Do you think I might have chronic fatigue syndrome as well?
Chronic fatigue is not one condition: It's the end-point of many conditions. The person is fatigued, and that symptom might well be due to many different forces, ranging from a well-defined physical cause to a psychological root. In your case, we have not found any other reason other than firing inside your brain. If this is the case, it's possible the Tegretol might help with your fatigue.
How?
If the firing burns up the grass that's your brain, it must take some time to regenerate new growth. The burnt grass produces utter exhaustion. It sounds strange, but I've seen people become energized on Tegretol too often for us to reject this mechanism, in people such as yourself,
So it's not the atypical spells themselves?
Correct. Instead, it's the consequences of them.

Acquiring energy again would be wonderful, Doctor! But I've also heard that too much sodium can cause chronic fatigue.
Strangely, CFS—chronic fatigue syndrome—is sometimes linked to people who, partly because of lay propaganda, think they need to limit their sodium intake and they end up with low blood pressure because their sodium is too low. I always am recommending not limiting sodium intake unless patients have specific heart conditions that require it.

Not limiting it? Isn't sodium bad?
Sodium is a necessary part of our world. In addition, the use of Tegretol here makes it even more relevant because a side-effect is to lower your sodium level.
Well, Doctor, what's your opinion? Should I be treated with anticonvulsant medication?
In your instance, we have the firing in the brain, and if I had just this alone without any clinical features, I would say, "Too bad. It doesn't matter. It's probably silent or of no great relevance." But we do have several pointers here. Your anger episodes with amnesia and post-ictal symptoms; your mood fluctuations; your rather unusual headaches; your strange smells; your chronic unexplained fatigue. Not all of these will

necessarily respond, but the anger and mood fluctuations are target symptoms that I would hope would be cleared by the Tegretol.

And the Tegretol will clear my headaches up?
I cannot say that the medication will clear them, because when you pressed your push-buttons for headaches, no correlate of firing occurred. However, if the headaches actually follow on deep firing in the brain, then they will be helped, and I've seen numerous cases of exactly this happening.

But I don't want side-effects. You'll excuse my saying so, but I'm cynical about medication.
I really don't want you to have any side-effects either. I want you to have the benefits without the adverse consequences. So sometimes we may even slightly underdose, but that's usually okay, because if you're having bad side-effects, you probably wouldn't want to take the medication anyway. There's a difference between hating to take medicines and taking the right medicines. Tegretol is the right medicine for you at this time, and I think with your special sensitivity, you will find a small amount of Tegretol useful.

Is this common, Doctor?
I think a lot more people have this problem than we're aware of. I think it's often misdiagnosed: under-diagnosed much of the time, and yet sometimes over-diagnosed without proper criteria. We see many of these problems linked up with a history of recreational drug abuse, because this often tends to have mobilized underlying tendencies. We can fix this problem with appropriate medication and put out the fires inside the brain.

And so we proceeded to discuss the use of Tegretol, just as I had for Steven. Wendy listened carefully and asked several questions, and she made one special point that Steven couldn't!

One more thing, Doctor. I'm on the Pill.
That's important to know, because Tegretol speeds up the metabolism of some drugs in the liver; by so doing it may impair control of conception by oral contraceptives. One solution is to increase the Pill dose slightly if that's not contra-indicated. Obviously everyone is different so your pregnancy risk may be higher all the same, and you may want to use some other form of protection. This is something for you to bring up with your gynecologist.

160

I launched Wendy on Tegretol on a Monday, with half a tablet, twice each day so that her liver would adjust. Too much at once would produce dizziness, vertigo, and imbalance. I was concerned that she might take all her tablets at once, the way she had cut her coffee all at once, so I gave her only ten at a time, seeing her every few days at first. To keep her mind off the drug, I suggested another change in her life-style. She was a chain-smoker with a two and a half pack a day habit.

Wendy, would you consider cutting back a few cigarettes each day?
I don't know about that. The coffee was one thing, but my cigarettes are something else.
Would you consider seeing a psychotherapist again?
I've seen twenty of them, and I hate them all.
This is going to be different. You're going to re-learn how to live.

B y Friday of that week, she was reporting real changes in her life, and with those changes an openness to discuss symptoms that had remained submerged came to the surface.
That afternoon, she made an important observation.
I'm not so much of a perfectionist. I'm spending more time with the children. My nightmares are better. I feel human again.

A fter the second week, she conveyed a clearer and brighter sense of self-reflection:
I'm not thinking about killing myself any longer. My kids still bug me, but you know they bug me like anyone's kids do, not the way they used to.
Suddenly she was able to talk about the physical abuse that must have been going on all the time.
The other day my daughter did something, and before I would have grabbed her by the neck and shoved her against the car and started to shake her, and I would have been lucky if I didn't kill her. But now... now, I just told her to stop and go to her room. I've never done that before.
She was beginning to be able to tolerate the many shades of gray in life.
I've arranged to see a therapist, too, because I want to talk about this, and about my cigarettes. I'm down to eighteen a day now, and I think I can get off them, eventually. I don't even need to set a deadline for myself; you know, I feel I can tolerate not having to have so much control.

B y three weeks after we started the medication, Wendy was ready to discuss a new issue.
She made a surprise announcement.

Doctor, I've developed some religious faith, and I think it's helped me.
Good for you. I think that's important.

Andrew, in attendance again, had an observation:
It's interesting, Doctor, I've noticed that you never directly discuss religion with patients.
There is a good reason for that. Most of the time I think it's important to be a "tabula rasa" [54]—a blank book—in which people can reflect their thoughts. It's not generally my function to impose ideas on them. When the subject is brought up, it's different. Ultimately I want my patients to make their own choices, though I may offer to guide them.

Wendy cleared her throat and spoke up assertively.
You discussed gun control with me pretty strongly, Doctor: Remember the "no holds barred debate"?
Yes, but that's a little different. I like to have a full perspective on what positive elements I can utilize in treatment. Also, you were an important exception. Events potentially were critical with your impending threats of suicide. Other than that, my function is to support your own healing, and allow you to develop your own ideas. I will try to support them when possible. This way you can use your special choices in your sojourn through life.

Andrew interrupted.
But when a person attains a powerful religious identity, how can he or she know this is not abnormal?
I think the abnormality in this regard is far less common than the normality. If the religious experience is interfering directly with the individual's ability to cope, then it's a problem, but not otherwise.

Wendy joined in, to share her own experience.
You know, Doctor, I can say now that God occasionally touches me in my deepest moments. I have had—not often, mind you—these peak experiences of ecstasy where I feel I can communicate directly.

Andrew was pleased to have a concrete example to illustrate his question. He waited till Wendy had left the room.
What do you think, Doctor? Is Wendy's experience normal or abnormal?
I have no evidence that it's abnormal. It would only be abnormal, as I see it, if it were to impair functioning in some way. If it actually enhances her functioning, then it can, quite possibly, allow her a broader participation in reality. This is Wendy's subjective experience. It may be controversial, but I do not perceive this as in any way abnormal.

What about the Bible, Doctor? You can find all sorts of stories in there, such as Abraham sacrificing his own son: Isn't that a schizophrenic action?
Again, we can debate using psychiatric terms like the "command hallucination": Abraham heard a voice that he interpreted as the Divine Being talking to him, and he went off quite prepared to kill his own child. In today's context, this could have landed him very easily in a mental hospital. Without more detail, it's difficult to determine whether this should be perceived as abnormal or not.

What kind of detail?
You have to look at actions in the appropriate context of times, culture and circumstances. This snippet may allow greater clarity. A patient once told me he was not religious and never attended church. Later on in the interview, he told me he was God himself. I asked him, "you mentioned you never attend any kind of religious gathering, and now you tell me you're God?" He replied, quite indignantly: "Of course: God doesn't need to attend church, you know."

But why do you think psychiatry is so seemingly opposed to religion?
I don't know if it's all that opposed to religion. I think that there are just certain differences in perspectives. The approaches of each use a different system. In other words, medication and psychological techniques on the one hand, and religious meaning and reflection on the other. I think all these can work well together. Religious views are based on a perspective that includes another reality, higher and deeper, that cannot be reduced to pure pathology. There is another side to psychiatry as well.

What's that?
Much psychiatry has become a secular practice where the attempts have been to substitute for the frameworks of established belief systems. It may have started with psychoanalysis, which in a way is its own belief system, as is Jungian theory. Meanwhile, I suspect the people with the best prognosis are those that have true religious feeling.

Does that mean that people have to become formally religious?
Certainly not. I don't think that formal religious conviction has anything to do with it, necessarily. We may be talking about distinct change at a moral level—a change of heart or a change of mind—without having to couch it in the structures of a formal religious context. Certainly, the drug addict and the alcoholic will improve substantially more, in my experience, if they have embraced some kind of higher identity.

What identities are you referring to?
In alcoholism, such groups as Alcoholics Anonymous can be a meaningful quasi-religious exercise, and certainly may be a serious substitute

for a formal religion. I use the term "quasi-religious" not in any derogatory sense, but just meaning an identification or awareness of something greater than oneself, akin to that cultivated in the more formally recognized religions.

Some would say that religion is really a psychological substitute for our feelings of inadequacy.
That could be one of several explanations. The great psychoanalyst Sigmund Freud perceived that there may be deep sources of inadequacy in those embracing the religious framework.[55] However, I've found that people are far more likely to give up their addictions, like a cocaine habit, if they have some kind of meaning, and without it, successful psychiatric treatment is that much more difficult. Utilizing higher meaning as easily implies embracing positive achievement as it does compensating for inadequacy needs. Elements of both may also occur.

> With what seemed to be some distress in his voice, Andrew
> brought up a recent experience in the library.

Doctor, I thought about that myself, and so I began reading some conventional psychiatric textbooks—comprehensive textbooks on psychiatry. I read their chapters on religion and psychiatry and I was amazed, because all I would find in their discussions were the ways in which religion was seen to be an aggravating factor in pathology. I could not find one word about the value of religion or meaning in helping the alcoholic and establishing more therapeutic attitude systems or being aware that maybe there are other reasons in life to recover.
Yes, some books, regrettably, only discuss the inadequacies of personalities, the obsessional rituals and the religious delusions. Often the implication in these books is that the mentally ill sometimes use religion as part of their psychopathology: the psychotic believes he's the Messiah, God Himself, dramatically communicating with God, or has special all-powerful solutions and codes to the world. These delusions are relevant, but rare. They are miniscule in relevance compared with the positive, healthy, functional side of theological support.

But what's normal in religion?
In essence, I have no problem with somebody who does not exhibit any coping impairment due to her religious beliefs, no matter how bizarre they may appear. If someone tells me she communicates directly with God in her religious experience, that's absolutely fine and even special. However, if that communication with a higher being is causing problems, by say, reflecting an out-of-touchness with reality, then it begins to be less than fine.
So, again, if the religious experience is interfering directly with the individual's ability to cope, then it's a problem, but not otherwise.

164

Right.

Andrew's vexation at his experience with his psychiatry textbooks had still not entirely left him.
*It was strange. When I read that chapter and another article like it, I was
dismayed, because I wasn't finding the positive side to religion I was looking
for. I thought that, surely, religion must be applicable in some kind of con-
structive way. In fact, I started to wonder whether psychiatry and religion are
not inherently antagonistic. Could it be, as Freud argued that religion, at
best, represents infantile fantasizing; and at worst, as the current psychiatry
literature I was looking through implies that religion only finds expression
in, or even aggravates, psychopathology?*

Andrew always amazed me with his breadth of knowledge
and capacity to apply it to the current setting.
I can assure you, Andrew, that this is not the case. I suspect, however,
that partly due to all the theoretical knowledge and ritual that surrounded
early psychoanalysis, psychiatry became a belief system just like religion is
a belief system. I'm not targeting psychoanalysis, but using it as an example here of the therapist attributing actions purely to unconsciously motivated self-destructive behavior, instead of looking at the positive side as
well. Because of this, we suddenly found that there were divergent directions we could follow: religion or psychiatry. Clearly, there are many
positive facets to psychiatric practice, just as there are to religion.

*It seems though, Doctor, by the same token, that psychiatry has tended to
ignore concepts such as good and evil. Surely these are concepts important
enough for everyone to be concerned about?*
You're right about that. I suspect this is an area that should be carefully
researched and one that may well yield results fruitful for the world of
psychiatry.

I think this area is so important. Would you briefly elaborate, Doctor?
One of the strange aspects in the area of psychiatry, a facet that's rather
fascinating, is that we tend to ignore good and evil. We tend to perceive
evil often in the context of pathology—of abnormality or defect, not as
some separate, concrete entity. The model we use in medicine is predominantly a biological model. Evil is then perceived as biochemically or
biologically based.

Do you think this?
No, I don't. First, we may encounter five different systems—the biological,
the psychological (involving emotion, thinking and motivation), the family system, the social system (of interactions within society) and the

broader cultural framework. In the past, I have used the umbrella term of the "biopsychofamiliosociocultural" approach to highlight this.

However, there's another facet we ought add in here: the ethical element, the element pertaining to real good and real evil. Possibly, we ought to be talking about an "ethicobiopsychofamiliosociocultural" approach, because all five systems influence ethical behavior.

That would certainly be the longest word in English!

Yes, it is, Andrew, other than a lengthy disease of the lung which as a name is capitalized anyway.

But can evil sometimes determine behavior even in the psychiatrically ill?

I believe so. One patient can have a profound delusion that the neighbors are aliens from Mars trying to kill him, and she can go out and kill those neighbors. A second patient, with the same delusion, might end up killing himself. A third may feel that she cannot do either because both are evil acts.

Don't we see the same fabric here in people with significant personality disorders?

Indeed, yes. For years, there has been this debate: Is the person psychopathic? Psychopathy traditionally implies some constitutional, biological disorder of personality. Or is she sociopathic? This refers to a different system—the social cause—and implies that the society has induced the evil behavior. There are degrees of psychopathy or sociopathy, from mild to profound. At times, we use more sensitive terms like "dyssocial personality". However, we still define these dyssocial behaviors as "disorders of conscience". Even within this level there are differences in good and evil. For example, the "creative psychopath" is always getting himself or others into trouble. Such a creative non-aggressive psychopath must be different from the high-grade aggressive evil person without any conscience, whom we sometimes see in a prison population.

Should the fact that a psychopath commits evil because of his illness lead us to conclude he isn't responsible?

No, it shouldn't. Evil to me cannot be condoned by illness.

By the same token, couldn't it be said that everyone who commits heinous evil acts is psychologically ill, even if we conclude that they're responsible?

This is another area for philosophical debate and is dependent on definitions of psychologically ill.

So overall, do you feel that meaning more than religion plays a role?

I think a positive belief system that involves an awareness of others at a moral level is important. If a belief in a higher being becomes part of it, some would argue that's then a personal religious attitude. Some psychologists may argue improvements occur because religion is psychologi-

166

cally substituting for a sense of inadequacy and replacing it with an all-powerful sense of control. I suspect this attitude demeans real religious meaning and the positive opportunity for the growth of personal potential in religious experience. However, irrespective of the deeper meanings or inner individual motivations, the awareness of a person's inherent good and potential can sometimes change the life of a previously lost soul.

For example?
One of my patients was a cocaine addict for years. Then he "found" religion. He has now settled down with his wife and continues the work that he enjoys, but which his drug lifestyle had threatened to destroy. Moreover, the identification with the formal group that many religions provide and the social bonding they cultivate may be an added advantage.

Our discussion at Wendy's next appointment, after a month, focused on another albeit related therapeutic advance, her own practical meaning to life. New endeavors had become important to Wendy.

All she needed to ask was this:
Doctor, what can I do now to help my life and the life of my family? I wish my husband would say how much better I am, but then I can understand him being unwilling to talk much because before, if he said anything, I might have attacked him and beaten him up. But at least now, I'm willing to open up to him, and I think it will make a difference in our relationship.
Wendy, you've said it all. You've provided your own therapeutic insight.

After about two months, Wendy had fully stabilized with her Tegretol treatment. Again, there was progress. She seemed more self-assured, rested and pleasant than ever. When I asked her how she was doing, she responded by saying:
Doctor, there's something I'd like to share with you.
And what's that?
It has something to do with our conversation about guns we had a couple of months back.
I'm interested to hear this.
Well, even though we got the gun out of our house like I told you we would, I knew that I could always have my alternative plan. I'm attractive to men, and even though I was married, I knew that if I needed to, I could go down to the local rifle range. I would pretend to half-seduce one of the men there, and say, "Let me try to shoot that target."
And what would you have done with the gun once he gave it to you?

167

I would have used it to shoot my brains out right in front of him. When I think about it now it's so crazy, but strangely, that's why I could give up the gun. I knew I had that plan in reserve.

And now?
I would never even contemplate such a stupid act again.
So you feel much better?
In every way. I actually look forward to seeing my husband, even if we still have many disagreements to resolve; and I look at the love of my children. I see that they're looking up to me now, and it means so much for me to be with them and be a part of their life again, or maybe for the first time in my life. Thank you so much for saving my life.

It's now four years since I first met Wendy. She qualifies for six monthly follow-up appointments. Just this past Monday, she saw me.

I feel fantastic, Doctor! Did I tell you? I haven't smoked for two and a half years. I've never been closer to my children and my husband and I seem to have worked out our problems. In fact, we have a very active life together. I cannot imagine life, or even existing, without the Tegretol. I must tell you, I did try to go off it once—it just lasted three days—and I could see that I started to go back to my old tricks, so I got back on track again. It's amazing. I might still become a little angry now, but it's a completely normal anger, and I have none of those other symptoms at all. It's like everything has been controlled. It's a miracle!

I looked at Wendy with tears in my eyes.

You know, my biggest difficulty is that the patients I see regularly are draining. I don't mind, because this is part of my way of contributing to them. Gradually, as they improve, I see them less and less often. Eventually, they achieve the ultimate, qualifying for that 6-monthly review to ensure that everything is consistent, and that the broader, detailed plan for the future is running on the right road. You've reached that 6-month goal, and it's positively reinforcing for me to see my 6-monthly patients, because they put the gasoline back in my tank. You, and all those who have succeeded so beautifully and demonstrated how you can become bigger and greater persons, impact on so many precious lives: You make my medical practice worthwhile. So, Wendy, you need not thank me. I thank you. You have made all our worlds a better place.

Chapter 7

Sugar and Spice

Drug interactions.
Absorption, metabolism, distribution and elimination of medications; cigarettes, jet lag, panic, Parkinson's disease, receptors, serotonin.
Sinemet, Theophylline, Vitamin B6, Lasix.
(Victor); (bathtub analogy), (boat analogy)

It was well timed: I had just completed my consultation with Wendy. My pager with its soft music summoned me. I ran up to the ward to respond to the emergency call. There he was, screaming and sweating profusely.

Do something! Do something! I'm dying!

He began to shake.

It's like I'm in a witches cauldron of molten lead and being whipped at the same time! Do something about this pain!

What pain?
This psychic pain, Doctor! It's overwhelming!

I examined him. Pulse high, 108. Pupils: unusually dilated. Profusely sweating. Tremulous. Heart: regular. Breathing rapidly, 26 per minute and shallow. Somewhat cyanosed—blue. No other physical signs. His screening lab tests were all within normal limits. His ward doctors had thought it was a panic attack.

A nurse asked:
Do you want us to give him some Ativan, Doctor, to sedate him?
Not yet. He seems to be settling a little.

I probed a little further, and I began to wonder: Why now, four days after Victor checked into the hospital, does he suddenly start suffering this "panic attack"?

Oh, Doctor, it's been going on for the last day and a half, and it's been getting worse. I didn't sleep a wink last night. I kept waking up having horrible nightmares and a sensation in my chest that made me think I was going to die. They hooked me up to an ECG monitor and told me it was all normal: All my tests on the heart came back negative so I hadn't had a heart attack. But you sure could have fooled me! And with it all, I've just been feeling tense and agitated and restless the whole time.

This seemed to be the reason why Victor had been diagnosed as having a mixed generalized anxiety disorder and panic disorder. Here was the psychiatric consultation to confirm this rather obvious diagnosis.

Andrew followed my examination with great interest.
So he's psychiatric. What proportion of the USA population has some kind of psychiatric problem during their lifetime? 50%?
You're right! The figure is about half the population though studies vary enormously. "Half" is much too high if including only the severely ill but may be on the low side if minor difficulties are included.[56]

Then what proportion of the population over any year period requires psychiatric medication?
Again I'm simplifying and these figures are even more in doubt, but possibly about a quarter of the population.
Let's see if Victor fits within that statistic.

We can see he does, Andrew whispered.

I looked Andrew straight in the eye.
But maybe he has a medical cause for this psychiatric presentation: we must evaluate him properly.

I turned my attention again to Victor.
You've been in the hospital five days now?
Yes.
And I've noticed you have chest problems.
Yes. I came in for my chest. You know, Doctor, I've have bad emphysema.
No doubt you're a smoker?
Yeah, I'm afraid I am. I tried to give up once, but I've never really succeeded.

How much did you smoke?
Well, about a pack a day, up until I came here, but I have to tell you, I haven't had one smoke since then.
That's no wonder, given that this is a non-smoking hospital and you've been confined to your bed.
Doctor, I can assure you it's been absolute hell.

> The first clue had surfaced. I suspected the villain was Victor's medication.

Let's do a theophylline blood level.

What's that?
Theophylline is the medication you take for your breathing. It's a powerful beta-adrenergic stimulant drug. In other words, it stimulates the bronchi—the tubes leading into the lungs—to widen, allowing you to breathe better.

You know, Doctor, now that you mention it, I remember having a level of that done a while back, and it was quite normal. So you probably don't need to bother.
That may be the whole point: let's wait for the results, and I'll tell you why.

> The urgent theophylline level came back within an hour. It was high. Instead of being 10 to 20—the normal therapeutic range—the level was 24. Ten days before, it had been 14.

What's happened Doctor?
I suspect this is why you had your episode of severe anxiety: You've been toxic on the theophylline.

How could that be?
Because cigarettes speed up the metabolism of theophylline:
Actually, it's not the nicotine in the cigarette, but the smoke that cigarettes give off. This contains about 200 different complex organic chemical compounds, which we call "polycyclic aromatic hydrocarbons". Just a few of them speed up the liver, and one area they speed up is the so-called 1A2 component of the P450 cytochrome enzyme system that breaks down theophylline.

Wow, that's a mouthful!

171

It is, and it reflects simply this. At a certain wave-intensity of light, these special metabolism systems in the liver can be analyzed by a complex measure of degree of pigment—the P in P450—linked with the maximum wave length absorption when exposed to carbon monoxide. This turns out to cluster around the 450 unit wave zone. There are at least 31 different systems like this, all involved in the breakdown of a large number of prescribed drugs and even foods. For example, a food that inhibits the system for the drug, theophylline—this 1A2 system—is cabbage. So cabbage theoretically will increase your theophylline blood level a little.

You mean I've got to be careful about what I eat, too?
Indeed you should, but you don't need to worry too much about it because it generally averages out. However, in your instance, your liver was speeded up very much by your cigarette habit, and then suddenly, after a few days of cold turkey in the hospital, it wasn't speeded up at all. This meant the theophylline that was being broken down quickly before was now being broken down more slowly.

That's why I became toxic, Doctor?
Yes, that's why you became toxic, and that's why you developed symptoms that looked exactly like generalized anxiety disorder with panic disorder.

You mean, I could easily have been given Ativan when I didn't really need it?
Yes. Or Valium, Xanax, or even Klonopin: These drugs wouldn't have done you much harm as an emergency measure, but hopefully you wouldn't have been maintained on them.

But aren't those drugs addictive?
Yes, they may cause dependence, and we see withdrawal phenomena from them, and we sometimes even question whether this group of drugs, the benzodiazepines, maintain their efficacy—their effectiveness—over time. They also may have depressed—suppressed—your breathing. I don't like to prescribe them unnecessarily, and as we have likely isolated the cause, I don't think we will need them now or in the future.

Victor suddenly smiled.
It sounds like, in a sense, it was my cigarette habit that was preventing me from getting an attack all those years.
Do you recommend I start smoking again?

I certainly don't. What happened to you was a drug interaction which suddenly stopped when you ceased smoking. All we need to do is lower your dose of theophylline. Now that we know, it's no big deal.

But I want to give up cigarettes, yet I know as soon as I leave hospital I'll be back to that wretched habit. I'm addicted.

Obviously, you have to resolve to give up otherwise you won't succeed.

Any advice?

Exactly, how many were you smoking a day?

Before I came into hospital, maybe 20.

One useful way is to get rid of one cigarette a day. Take your pack and actively remove one more each day. First day nineteen. Second eighteen. Trash one the first day, two the next, three the following. Some people speed this process up and trash three more each day.

How does that work?

If you trash your cigarettes, you're saying to yourself, "I'm getting rid of an item I've paid good money for." If you go and buy them again, you're saying, "Hold on! Why did I trash them?" So you can't buy them without guilt. But you have to actively trash your cigarettes to experience this conflict.

Any alternatives?

As an alternative, I recommend nicotine gum. I prefer the gum to the patches since your mouth is active when smoking, and this way it's actively chewing instead. Remember all this comes to naught without motivation to give up.

I have that, Doctor. I want to live.

I know you do. You may want to arrange with your wife to give up smoking together. It's much more effective to break this habit as a couple. You can give each other moral support this way, you become part of a team, as well, and as an added incentive, you're competing with each other.

We dropped down Victor's dose of theophylline, and suddenly, like magic, within a few hours—because that was the duration of action of the major component of the theophylline—his anxiety began to diminish, and within a day, he was much better. Victor had had a close escape from being launched on a benzodiazepine career.

I evaluated Victor's condition further. We were ready to deal with another difficulty Victor had: He had **Parkinson's disease**. As is so common, he was taking Sinemet—the levodopa/carbidopa combination that awakened my catatonic patients. The Sinemet wasn't working particularly well.

This piqued Andrew's medical student level curiosity:

Do you suppose he has the so-called "on-off phenomenon"?
The on-off effect is certainly something to be considered.

And addressing both Victor and Andrew, I added:
This phenomenon is like a switch on and a switch off: The side-effects begin and end suddenly. Even worse, the Sinemet starts working for shorter and shorter periods. This is linked with acute changes in the dopamine balance. But there is even more to this on-off phenomenon.
What is that?
Sometimes other involuntary movements occur as well.

Andrew could not suppress his pride at having recalled the symptoms of Parkinson's disease:
Are you referring to the stiff rigidity that's sometimes seen with the Parkinsonism, as well as the slowness, the loss of motor expression, the tremor, and the special kind of slowed, careful stepped gait?
Not, actually. The signs you describe are those of Parkinson's disease itself. Instead of the symptoms you listed, with this on-off phenomenon, patients sometimes exhibit what are called "dyskinetic phenomena"—little movements of strange kinds: rhythmic movements of the limbs and, sometimes, even of the mouth. These movements vary from hour to hour depending on when the Sinemet is taken.

Victor did not exhibit any on-off phenomena. However, I evaluated his Parkinson's disease by repeating my examination over a period of six hours so I could see differences in his condition. The Parkinson's was not well controlled. It seemed that the Sinemet had just suddenly stopped working.
I used the first trick medical students, like Andrew, learn: The most valuable method for a physician to obtain information is actually to ask the patient!

Why do you think, Victor, this has happened? Your Parkinson's disease seemed to have been under control.
No idea at all, Doctor.

Well, tell me something: do you take vitamins?
Yeah, I take vitamins every day! In fact, ever since they told me I had emphysema, I started to take vitamins.
Did they warn you about anything with the vitamins?
No, not at all. In fact, I just started a new preparation three weeks ago.
Tell me, what happened to your Parkinson's disease then?

174

It's interesting that you ask that, Doctor, I didn't associate it, but it seems to have gotten worse over the past few weeks!

Would you like to show me your vitamins?
     He reached for his gym bag next to his bed.
Here they are, Doctor.
I see it contains pyridoxine phosphate.
Yes, that's right, Doctor, I think it's one of the B vitamins.
Yes, it's vitamin B6. Did anyone ever tell you that vitamin B6 will interfere with the absorption of the Sinemet?

First time I've heard that, Doctor.
Well, I think this may be one reason why your Parkinson's disease got worse.

Why do you say that? What exactly do you mean?
If you were taking vitamin B6 in tablet form, you were getting an interference with the working of the levodopa, the main component of the Sinemet. The levodopa and the vitamin B6 combine so that the levodopa is destroyed before it passes into the brain. Usually, levodopa forms dopamine in the brain. This helps your Parkinson's. Now it cannot. It's like not taking your Parkinson's medication.

Victor's medication adjustments were the major interventions we achieved with Victor during his hospitalization. The rest of his time as an inpatient went smoothly, and within days, he was due to go home.

We spoke on the day of his discharge from the hospital:
Doctor, I feel I have a new lease on life, because I understand more about my medications. I now even read the package inserts of my medication.
That's good, Victor. Remember, the package inserts mention everything—sometimes relevant, sometimes irrelevant. It's hard to tell the difference so you should, if necessary, consult your physician or pharmacist on that.
I'll remember that.

But Doctor, I wanted to update you: I'm not taking my brand of vitamins anymore. In fact, I found a specific group of vitamins to take, which doesn't contain any vitamin B6.

And, as if, to reinforce his hospitalization, he added:
It's much easier doing this adjustment in hospital, isn't it Doctor?
You're right and wrong, Victor.

Inpatient hospitalization is like a one-act play, intense, sometimes with only one chance to make sure we're correct. The worst part about this one-act play is we often find there are errors and we have to make what I call a "mid-course correction."

What's that?
It means that because changes occur gradually we can only guess at what's most likely the best course of treatment while you're in hospital. This means we should review the situation on several occasions once you're discharged.

Do you want to see me after I leave hospital?
If possible, I do, Victor. I think continuity is important.

So that's why I should fo llow up as an outpatient?
That's right. Attending regularly is relevant because we're able to perform time-based evaluations.

What's that?
Seeing how you're doing over a period of weeks or months. This gives us a perspective to your illness.

Is that the only advantage of outpatient evaluations?
No. I spoke of the mid-course corrections in which alterations of medications or of dosing are almost invariable. The only way we're able to regulate this is by feedback. However, most important, we cannot obtain the correct control for many medications that take weeks to work while you're in hospital.

W*hy do these medications take weeks to work?*
I suspect, Victor, the best way you can appreciate that is by understanding the concept of jet lag.

Andrew, who was with me, interrupted:
Jet lag? You can't be serious!
Yes I'm being serious. One of the problems with theories which sometimes are so obvious but true, is that they're so self-evident, nobody ever thinks of them. I wrestled for some time with the problem of why antidepressants take many weeks to fully kick in. Why is there a whole literature on the use of neuroleptics—antipsychotic drugs; also called major tranquilizers—saying that when these drugs were used in the schizophrenic as antipsychotics, they take several weeks to really fully kick in? Why does the anti-anxiety drug, buspirone, also take three or four weeks to kick in?

Victor listened with a clear interest. I prepared for a long teaching session—Andrew, Victor and myself.

Andrew began:
Is this delay in action a function of these drugs, or is it a function of something else?
I think it's a function of something far more fundamental: physiology. Let's examine jet lag as the only equivalent physiologic model: Depending on time zone, when we shift across from the USA to Europe, we might shift anywhere between six to ten time zones. This takes six days to six weeks to totally psychophysiologically readjust. Jet lag is the physiologic equivalent of the pathophysiological abnormality that we see in anxiety, depression, and psychosis, and all of these take time to re-regulate because body rhythms have been destabilized.

Victor added his few words:
Certainly, when I've flown to Europe, I've tested myself out as a guinea pig. I've noticed that the total adaptation takes me about six weeks, even though much it might happen in the first two weeks.
Well, I draw these same parallels with medication.

What parallels?
Antipsychotics, antidepressants and buspirone take prolonged periods of time because these drugs require physiologic adaptation. You can look at a gradation of improvement over time, but full redeployment of your biological cycles takes many weeks or even months. Basically the body requires a certain stability, and you're more and more stable as time progresses.

And when we shift six or even ten time zones, it takes six days to six weeks to totally psychophysiologically readjust. This is because jet lag is the physiologic equivalent of the delay in action of the antidepressants? Am I using the correct idiom, Doctor?
You have expressed yourself remarkably, Victor; and your point is correct: People gradually improve over a several week period, but it varies individually depending on the person. The same applies with antidepressants.

Andrew was clearly enthralled by this concept and, at this juncture, moved in to join the conversation.
So antidepressants are rather like the phenomenon of jet lag: We fly and shift many time zones. For every hour we shift, it takes variably one to seven days to totally psychophysiologically readjust?
Yes, and the progression through that period over several weeks has a parallel equivalent in disturbed physiology in depression and anxiety. The

177

circadian–daily cycle–dysregulation takes several weeks to appear and also to renormalize as well.

I assume this is the reason for the delay in action of three or four weeks for several physiologically normalizing groups of drugs?
Yes. This is my theory, anyway.

Which drugs are involved?
The groups I've listed: All the antidepressant medications in depression, buspirone in anxiety and the antipsychotic drugs in psychosis.

But how can you say there's a delay with antipsychotics? I've seen how when you give them, a day later, the patient is not hallucinating.
You're right. That's so, just like after a few days with buspirone, we see an anti-irritability effect. Also, after a few days, with the more sedative antidepressants, the patients are sleeping better; while with the more activating ones, the patients have a little more energy. However, it takes several weeks to fully restabilize pathophysiology.

You mean these delays in action are from our body in certain conditions, not due to the drugs prescribed?
Yes, with the medication we have discussed: I like to perceive them as physiological psychotropic agents–drugs which work in tandem with the normal functioning of our body. The delay of several weeks to full efficacy is not due to the drugs themselves, but associated with the time taken for the markedly destabilized pathophysiology in the body to restabilize.

Victor had had some of these medications in the past and interjected:
Is that why I noticed antidepressants work a little in the first week? Is this why the three week delay is not a void period?
Yes, I believe so. Changes are occurring all the time.
Yes. I noticed that I was less worried and less irritable in the first week. I was also concentrating a little better, sleeping a little better, and I didn't have as much fatigue, when I once was taking Elavil.

Andrew nudged in.
How is this rhythm regulated in the body?
This circadian rhythm re-regulation is modulated through the neurotransmitter, serotonin–the major tonic regulator of the brain.

But why does Xanax work straight away for anxiety? Doesn't this contradict the theory?
No. Because using this model, these benzodiazepine drugs–like Xanax, as well as Ativan, Valium, Librium or Klonopin, for example–are not

acting physiologically. They are benefit now, pay later medications. They relieve anxiety using a completely different chemistry from the physiological regulation which goes through serotonin.

V̇ictor had never missed a beat. He had clearly followed everything.

Doctor, you mention serotonin and this interests me a great deal. My doctors had suggested I have a serotonin drug for this panic and anxiety I was having. That was before we realized it was due to the theophylline toxicity.

Which medications were they suggesting?
Two names had come up. Paxil was the one. BuSpar was the other.
You're right. Paxil is a so-called selective serotonin re-uptake inhibitor or SSRI drug so it raises up serotonin level considerably; and BuSpar also acts selectively on serotonin but it regulates the levels.

So could we talk more about serotonin because my doctors had mentioned these medications could still be possibilities for me in my further treatment.
By all means, Victor. Let's do so.

There must a lot of serotonin in the brain.
No, there isn't. It's amazing how a tiny amount of serotonin, 10 mg or 15 mg in an 1100 gram brain, can impact on so many functions. This neurotransmitter originates in a series of nuclei—large cell clusters—in the midline brain stem and impact in every direction—up, down, back, sideways—on all parts of the nervous system and the body itself.

I only heard of serotonin recently. Is it a new discovery?
No. Actually, it's quite old. The story begins back in the 1850s when a substance was discovered that contracted smooth muscle in the gastrointestinal tract. Nobody thought too much about that substance at that time, but a hundred years later, it was discovered—or rediscovered—in Cleveland, and identified as 5-hydroxytryptamine—5HT. Serotonin was reborn, and the research impact for this rebirth was in 1950: A certain substance had been causing weird and sometimes spectacular happenings in the brain. This chemical also impacted on smooth muscle in the gut, and had a structural similarity to serotonin.

This compound became a focus of interest: It was lysergic acid diethylamide—LSD, today recognized as a dangerous, recreational hallucinogenic drug. So the LSD research fostered serotonin research in the hope that we could solve the mysteries of psychosis. Instead, we solved some of the mysteries pertaining to anxiety and depression and fluctuations of mood and maybe obsessionality. It's only now that we're beginning to examine the links of psychosis and serotonin.

179

How does serotonin work?
Serotonin has become a fashionable neurotransmitter. It's a chemical that acts, like all other neurotransmitters do, by shifting across a tiny, microscopic channel—the synaptic cleft—and stimulating the post-synaptic areas.

The conversation had particularly engaged Andrew's interest.
What exactly does "post-synaptic" refer to, concretely?

I was surprised he did not know:
Basics are always more difficult.
The neuron—the nerve cell—allows for transmission of its chemical down its outgoing pipe—the axon. It gets released into a tiny hole—the cleft—and there attaches to a receptor on the other side. This is the "post-synaptic" area and it implies the domain that results in the action once it receives the signal from the transmitter.

Andrew persisted.
Is there a good concrete analogy?
Yes. Do you recall the analogy of boats moored at a dock, to illustrate the role of the receptors? [57]
Yes, I remember.
Well, it's a similar principle here: It's like a boat that arrives and is moor ed to the pier that contains the so-called post-synaptic level. The small space between boat and pier is the cleft. When it's moored, it stimulates a whole series of steps—a whole cascade of events—causing the boat's passengers to disembark and walk a great distance into the town. This serotonin substance is exactly the same at every one of fifteen different serotonin receptor subtypes—so serotonin impacts at fifteen different piers. However, there are essential differences between these receptors. Firstly, they're located in different areas. Next, they have different end-point commands producing a string of reactions—the cascades—that look entirely different: The passengers arrive in different parts of the town— different body parts or biochemical reactions are impacted. Finally, the receptors are so distinct that each has a specific gene determining what the receptor subtype does and where it's located—which specific dock is occupied.

Doctor, the location of the hormone glands doesn't seem to have much to do with the specific function of the hormones?
Right. They work far away. Thyroid hormone or insulin influences the whole body.

Now, does the location of the synapses in the body actually have a concrete spatial significance, unlike the hormones?

180

An important differentiation, Andrew. Yes, synapse location is important. Different receptor subtypes are situated in different places, though the same neurotransmitter might stimulate several sites and produce entirely different results. It's like electricity in the kitchen. At the stove, it may act as a heater; yet if located at a fridge, the same transmitter may cool down the refrigerator; the stove and fridge may be different receptor subtypes for the same neurotransmitter and so act differently. A frozen cake from the fridge can be thawed out on the stove: Regulating is relevant. However, strangely, neurotransmitters don't have a specific location in another way as their influences sometimes are distant to their source by the indirect means of cascades—the numerous steps leading into the different parts of the town.

And could we say, Doctor, that the receptors are those little piers on the dock where the serotonin boat can moor itself?
Very good, Andrew! No receptor is an island entire of itself. Each continually feeds back to other receptors.

I̶t was Victor's turn again to ask a question.
What does serotonin do?
Serotonin is the great tonic regulator, and it controls all the pathophysiological distortions linked with behavioral, physiological, and psychological functions: It modulates fundamental physiologic functions: circadian rhythms, pituitary and endocrine gland control, heart, blood flow and temperature regulation. Serotonin also regulates such fundamental behaviors as appetite, sleep, sex and aggression. Furthermore, it impacts psychologically on irritability, depression, anxiety, lability of mood, obsessionality, memory, stress and even psychosis. So, it's no wonder that the drugs that modulate serotonin have enormous influence, sometimes good, sometimes not so good, on fundamental aspects of human experience.

Can we apply these effects to any medications?
Yes. Understanding what receptors do allows us to have an excellent appreciation of the potential therapeutic uses and side-effects of drugs which act on these receptors.
The converse also applies: We can examine a serotonin active drug and understand serotonin receptors better. For example, let's look at one of the most well known antidepressant groups which act powerfully, raising up serotonin markedly but non-specifically, the selective serotonin reuptake inhibitors—the SSRIs. With these drugs, we commonly see the effects—good, bad and paradoxical—of serotonin excess.

I thought the more serotonin we had the better?

181

Unfortunately not. The correct amount of serotonin is best, not excessive amounts: That's why a regulating medication like BuSpar is so useful.

So there are "bad" effects, presumably side-effects, of serotonin excess?
Yes, there are, particularly if the brain does not adapt properly. The "bad", excess serotonin symptoms commonly involve the following: sexual difficulties; sleep disruption, with increased awakenings at night, sometimes producing heightened dream recall; appetite suppression; and headaches.

What about the paradoxical effects?
On the "paradoxical" side, we usually encounter an anti-irritability effect, but occasionally people become more aggressive. Frequently, we see an anti-anxiety effect yet sometimes we see people more anxious; and infrequently instead of being activated, people feel sleepy on these SSRIs.

And what about the good side of serotonin?
On the "good" side, we consistently see stabilization over three to four weeks of body rhythms; moreover, the SSRIs have anti-depressant effects and they also potently relieve obsessive thoughts.

So the Paxil I may be taking as an SSRI antidepressant drug could result in excess serotonin and this may be useful or problematic?
Exactly, depending on how the brain adapts. The SSRIs, therefore, reflect serotonin excess–good, bad and paradoxical–at the physiological, behavioral and psychological levels of functioning that serotonin influences. It's fascinating that we can actually use medications as a model for the functions of neurotransmitters. In like fashion, we can predict the impacts of a drug by knowing its receptor properties.

It was Andrew's turn.
It sounds as if paradoxical effects can occur in different people even with the same drug?
Yes, that's true. We've mentioned how drugs like the SSRIs, which raise serotonin greatly, can produce what is usually an opposite effect such as worsening of anxiety and irritability, or sedation in some people. Similarly, this paradox even works this way in basic neurotransmitter research.

For example?
One of the paradoxes about serotonin research is that superficially you can prove anything. So, for example, when a patient with depression is analyzed, most of the time you find a deficiency of serotonin, but occasionally you find an excess. With aggression, these same, apparently paradoxical findings occur. Sometimes with anxiety, an excess of serotonin is found, but occasionally a deficiency.

182

How can we have these contradictory phenomena?
Possibly because there are so many different confounding variables. It's difficult sorting cause and effect, and even when we do, it's hard to know what's a direct and what's an indirect cause or effect.

Is there an example I can understand?
Yes, let's measure a critical breakdown product of serotonin—5HIAA—in the watery tube that runs through the brain and spinal cord, in other words in the CSF—the cerebrospinal fluid. Let us say we find a low level. What does this mean? It might imply that a deficiency of serotonin in the brain produces less breakdown product. On the other hand, it could also result, paradoxically, from an excess of serotonin in the brain. In this case, if the serotonin is prevented from being broken down, the CSF level of the breakdown product would also be low.

How could that occur?
Simply by stopping the serotonin flowing away from the receptor where it was working. One way is by what we call "re-uptake inhibition" and this incidentally, is the major mechanism of action of most of our antidepressant drugs, not only the SSRIs. Thus, if this occurred, there would be less breakdown of serotonin and for a completely opposite reason there would be lower CSF levels. So, we always have dichotomous explanations.

But can we prove all this?
Yes, for example, animal researchers can take a peace-loving rat and deprive that rat of tryptophan which is a chemical involved in producing serotonin: The rat becomes aggressive and warlike. If they give the rat some tryptophan again, it resorts to its state of peace; it stops fighting. All these differences in serotonin have animal models and deficiencies in the diet are important. Similarly, added stress will produce change and these therefore are reasons for variations. Moreover, in basic research, as indicated, there are difficulties in interpreting what our accurate measurements reflect like cause, effect, direct impacts, and indirect involvements of pathways.

So these are the major reasons for the strange results in serotonin research and with medications?
These are some of them. To me, the major problem for these strange results in research on any neurotransmitter and in medical practice using brain chemistry drugs is the bathtub.

Victor sat bolt upright in bed. He looked perplexed.

The bathtub? Did I hear right? What's a bathtub got to do with complex chemicals?

Let me introduce you to the special bathtub. It's a bathtub made not of water, but filled with serotonin. One of the problems we have in serotonin research is that we came to conceive of all our serotonin in one bathtub: deficiency with an overall too low a level, and excess with an overall too high a level. In fact, it's more complex than this: We have fifteen different serotonin bathtubs—receptor subtypes—all connected up by a series of pipes. So, we might have an excess in one, the right amount in another, and deficiency in a third. These bathtubs all communicate through these pipes with one another creating even greater complexity. [58]

I could see Victor looking a little overwhelmed.

Don't worry, Victor, if you cannot follow all the details. From your perspective, it may be adequate to know that there are different amounts of chemicals in bathtubs and that these can be used as an analogy to explain how complex the chemistry of nerve cells are. We also use these bathtubs to understand how drugs work: they produce new levels and temperatures in the bathtub.

Andrew was not outdone.

So understanding that there are receptor subtypes allows us to understand subtle side-effects and therapeutic effects?

That's right. The principle is important here: Communications and controlling mechanisms occur even in subgroups of receptors which serve different functions. Each subtype has an overall level and the brain strives for this level to be the correct quantity. We can use the metaphor of a bathtub to better imagine the amounts.

Now is the bathtub analogy different from the boat and pier analogy?

You've asked an important question, Andrew. I don't want to mix metaphors and don't even listen to this if you already understand both analogies. That both have to do with water is coincidental. But this may help put their relationships into perspective.

Yes?

In effect, you can regard the serotonin bathtubs as like the several serotonin piers. That's where they're equivalent. Similarly, serotonin molecules reflect the passengers who populate the boats in large or small quantities. This number of neurotransmitter molecules parallels the level in the bathtub. That's the major common factor of the two analogies. The rest is different.

Go on!

184

I needed to introduce the bathtub analogy because it's broader. The boat analogy does not easily cover several concepts we'll introduce into the bathtub analogy, like temperature—receptor responsiveness; the impact of the individual in the tub—individual variation; leaks in the tub wall—other biochemical abnormalities; or bath-plugs—receptor subtypes that antagonize.

And do the boats cover areas the bathtubs don't?
Yes. The bathtub analogy is also limiting: It cannot portray how the messenger systems walk to different parts of the town—like the passengers climbing off the boat do. This is why I have come up with both metaphors. The boat reflected one series of basics: understanding neurotransmitter mechanisms—how it attaches and impacts even at a distance. Our focus, in general, from hereon out, will be on the bathtub metaphor—how patients need the correct kinds and amounts: quality and quantity of neurotransmitter. You will gradually see how we can apply these principles, and how the bathtub can be applied not only to serotonin, but to other neurotransmitters like norepinephrine.

These are difficult concepts.
Yes, they are. The important point is to understand what you can; make notes, if necessary, and come back to these basic principles. Even physicians have difficulty with them so don't worry if you can't master them fully.

And so, Victor was educated about drugs and serotonin, learning about SSRIs like Paxil and applying the bathtub metaphor. In effect, he had learnt a little about "pharmacodynamics"—the influence of the drug on the organism, in this instance, on the brain. This proved a useful complement to his previous initial short lesson in "pharmacokinetics"—the influence of the body on the drug—learning about the theophylline and the vitamin B6.
But Victor's lessons were not yet over. He was proving to be an exceptional patient, who wanted to learn and learn and learn even more.

At follow-up a month later, Victor's Parkinson's disease was much better. However, I cannot say that he was any different from the "blue bloater" I had seen a month before:
His emphysema was still as bad; he still had chronic bronchitis with a bad cough; and his color was abnormal. He was cyanosed—a little

blue–reflecting the limited degree of oxygen his nearly destroyed lungs would allow him to breathe; unfortunate, but true.

Doctor, I just wanted you to know, I finally gave up smoking.
That's marvelous. Congratulations!

> I was glad, of course, but it was a case of shutting the barn door after the horse had long escaped. In my heart, I wept for Victor. I cried for this beloved patient who had destroyed much of his life, but who was now trying so hard.

But there's something else, Doctor. I don't know how important it is.
Yes, what is it Victor?

You know, I get physically exhausted, and it's been happening ever since I left the hospital. I'm really tired all the time and I have no energy.

> I had heard all this before, and I now realized it wasn't a simple consultation. I had to play the role of medical detective, again.

Can you think of anything that changed during your hospital stay?
The only change, Doctor, was a new drug I was put on after I left.

What medication?
Oh, it's called Lasix.
Lasix is a potent diuretic–a tablet to help pass more water from your body.
Yes, I know, Doctor. It sure works!

Are you aware that this water tablet depletes your body of potassium, and that you need to replace your potassium because of it?
Yeah, that was mentioned to me by my doctor: he asked me to get potassium chloride and I haven't yet acquired some.

> I had arranged for Victor to have some routine blood tests performed a few days before his appointment with me. I wanted, inter alia, to check his theophylline blood level. The results had come in just before Victor's appointment. His potassium was only 3.2: the lower limit of normal is 3.5 and some even feel 4.0. Victor was hypokalemic–he had a low potassium.

Victor, this was something we had already picked up in your blood results. We know that your potassium level is low. Whether or not you had symptoms, I was going to correct this. It's an important consideration because it can put you at greater risk even for heart disease. We don't like the potassium to be low or high.

What does this mean, Doctor?
With you on Lasix—the most potent diuretic we have available—the first modification you should look at is adding more potassium. Sometimes we cannot easily measure the potassium when we do a blood level. This is so because we're actually interested in the potassium in the cells and the blood levels of potassium measure the potassium outside the blood cells in that liquid part of your blood called the serum.

So this can sometimes come out normal?
Yes. Low normal because there has to be a big lack of potassium for the potassium to start dropping in the serum. This is especially so as sometimes the blood cells are slightly damaged during the blood draw and this can produce a major distortion in the potassium level.

What then do I have to do, Doctor?
I want you to increase your potassium intake enormously. You must take the potassium tablets. Because you will be taking them by mouth and your kidneys are functioning normally, it would be difficult for you to take too much. I want you to take four of these potassium tablets a day.

So the important lesson is to jump in early and not late?
True: Prevention is always important. Here, we're treating and also preventing this from happening again.

Andrew had been quieter than usual through my consultation with Victor. After our patient left, Andrew looked up in the quizzical way I had come to recognize over these many months we had worked together.

I don't understand one thing, Doctor. I was reading that Parkinson's disease is not as common in smokers. Yet, here we have an example of these two conditions coexisting.
You're quite right. Parkinson's is not as common in smokers and there may be a causal reason why it's probably the only condition which smoking actually aids.

What's the reason?
The reason is simply this.
The nicotine in cigarettes acts on two areas that will help Parkinson's disease. First of all, it has what is called an anticholinergic effect. In other

words, it blocks the neurotransmitter acetylcholine, and you may remember that because this occurs, we actually have an anti-Parkinsonian effect.

Do the medications we use against Parkinsonism also have this impact on acetylcholine?
Yes, many of them do: That's how some of the milder drugs like Artane and Cogentin work. They block this acetylcholine neurotransmitter.
That's why these drugs are called "anticholinergic". This lowering changes a rather sensitive balance increasing the relative amount of the neurotransmitter dopamine to the acetylcholine. This alteration is a key equation in the treatments of Parkinson's. disease.

And what is the second reason why cigarettes help Parkinson's disease?
The second one may not be linked to this anticholinergic effect. Cigarette smoking also has impacts on the dopamine receptor.

What has dopamine to do with Parkinsonism?
That's the receptor where, in Parkinsonism, there's a deficiency, which we try to raise up with drugs like Sinemet.

And so the nicotine stimulates that dopamine receptor?
Yes, it does, a little, either directly or indirectly, and we think this might be part of the mechanism.

That's interesting, Doctor. What about those people who have Parkinson's secondary to the antipsychotics they were taking? The kinds of patients we spoke about before—patients on Trilafon or on Haldol? Does nicotine work there also?
Yes, it probably does, in lowering the degree of drug-induced Parkinsonism. On the other hand, you'll remember that the cigarette smoke is involved with breaking down these different antipsychotic chemicals. This means that the patients have to have more drugs, and because of having more, their tendency towards Parkinsonism is increased.

You mean so it's a wash—it's a balance?
It's not as simple as that. Nothing in medicine is purely a balance. It depends on the exact dosage, on the particular medication, and on the way specific metabolism of drugs in the liver, and on their own sensitivity towards particular diseases.

Again, Andrew was fascinated.
Can't we learn more about these different drug interactions? They seem so important!

They not only seem important, Andrew. They are critical, vital, and extremely relevant in the practice of medicine, even though they are, at times, difficult to determine.

At that moment, there was a knock at my door. In walked Victor, again.

By the way, Doctor, I'm sorry to worry you, but I just wanted to ask you one other question; I forgot to mention it.

This is not at all an unusual occurrence: I call it the "by the way syndrome". It often happens that, as the patient is leaving, they proceed to talk about the most important facets of their condition. This time, it was just a "delayed by the way syndrome". Victor had already left, but came back to ask the question that had obviously been worrying him all along.

Yes, what is it, Victor?

I was worried that some other medications might also be interacting.

Well done, Victor! You've become aware of an enormously important area. In fact, Andrew and I were going to talk about this area, right now, focusing a little on the drugs that act in the brain. You could sit in if you like and ask questions, as well.

I'd really like to know more about these drug interactions, Doctor, so thank you, I think I will.

*A*nd so we took a look at certain principles behind how the psychiatric and neurological drugs, or for that matter almost all other medications, interact. I began the education process:

Every change we make in introducing medications potentially affects the other medications because of interactions that are occurring at four levels: Absorption, metabolism, distribution and excretion.

Victor immediately responded:

How can I apply the absorption side? I remember the Vitamin B6 story!

Absorption usually occurs from the stomach and duodenum. Medications taken together with liquids and solids influence absorption. For example, interactions of coffee with your drugs should be expected.

Oh, I sometimes actually take my tablets with my morning latté.

Victor, you've introduced then another problem.

What?

When you take your medications with a cup of coffee instead of water, some of it will precipitate out–this means you won't be absorbing as much.

So the caffeine causes the problem again?
It's probably not the caffeine because it's only one of many chemicals that interact when we drink beverages such as tea or coffee. I would guess this would even happen with decaffeinated coffee.

Can you give me an example of what happens?
Yes. This is not so well researched so I will take an example studied years ago: About two-thirds of a medication called Stelazine precipitates out with a cup of coffee. This means if you take 3 mg, you only absorb 1 mg. We think this is so with many medications.

Is this only with coffee?
Not at all. It's so with most liquids. Antacids precipitate out or diminish absorption of alkaline substances and acidic fruit juices act similarly on bases.
And even antacids have an effect?
Yes, and interactions of drugs and food should be evaluated. This means it's best to take your medication with water. Occasionally, certain medications need to be taken with other drinks like milk, but this is rare.

Do absorption problems happen with anything else?
Yes. When you take your medications with antibiotics or with antihistamines or special stomach medications for nausea or pain, the same result may happen.

How can I avoid it?
You ought to make sure you're taking your medication at the same consistent time and in the same consistent way.

In practice?
It is often best taking your medications with breakfast, lunch and dinner. This way you should avoid side-effects pertaining to irritation of the stomach and you may provide some level of consistency in absorption.
If new temporary medications like antibiotics or anti-inflammatories are prescribed, you should, if possible, take those at a different time. However, if they're going to become regular long-term medications, your system has to get used to it, so you may as well take it with your other medication, if your pharmacist or doctor says that's okay. They may then need to adjust doses of your medications a little to take into account drug interactions.

Could you give me an example of when this may not be okay with chronic medications?
Yes. Some cholesterol-lowering medication may produce side-effects, such as diarrhea or constipation. This may have to do with the medication causing deliberate non-absorption of cholesterol in foods. So, sometimes, when you take cholesterol-lowering medication your symptoms could come back—not because of the medication, but because the other medications you're on are not being absorbed. This means that you may lose the cover against your Parkinson's disease that you had before. This must be watched for and doses adjusted accordingly.

This sparked a series of questions from Andrew.
Is this our first principle, absorption?
Right. The first rule about drug interactions is interference at the level of absorption.

What about the second rule? I remember the cigarette and theophylline problem Victor had. Is that relevant here?
Exactly. The second level is the metabolism in the liver—the major drug breakdown factory of the body. You can imagine if there's competition for the same metabolic excretion, the levels of medications will rise. You may remember, that there are at least 31 different ways just within one major system—P450—to break down drugs, and there are other systems as well. Each time we prescribe a new medication, interactions potentially happen. This is particularly so if that medication contains many milligrams: The liver obviously handles a 1-mg drug more easily than a 100-mg compound. It, of course, does not discriminate whether the medications are so potent at the brain level that they require only 1 mg instead of 100 mg. The liver is like a paper shredder. It treats valuable certificates and scrap paper the same, the limiting factor being the quantity.

So there's always competition?
Yes, and just to add in one more complication with the liver, some of these medications, instead of competing, actively inhibit the liver's breakdown, slowing breakdown even more. On the other hand, other drugs actively speed up the enzymes that are involved, increasing breakdown. So with each medication change, there may be many subsidiary changes that go along with it. A side-effect on a new medication may not only reflect that new drug, but it might be withdrawal or toxicity of another drug already in the body. There's not always an interaction, as these depend exactly on the route of breakdown—but it is even more complex because most times we don't know for certain what exactly is happening, as many drugs have not been tested. Fortunately, we can often estimate when interactions may take place, but it requires a solid foundation in the complex principles of hepatic—liver—enzyme systems.

191

You mentioned a third level?
The third level is **distribution** in the body: for example, drugs becoming bound to protein or ending up in adipose tissue—fat cells. So some medications don't only go to where they're supposed to go—for example, the brain—but they bind to protein, or get deposited in the fat cells and end up not doing anything initially. This is another reason for the fluctuation in dosage.

What would be an example?
Protein binding is important, but not as relevant as the liver or absorption. However, sometimes it makes our lives more difficult. For example, some antidepressants, like Paxil and also for that matter another SSRI, Prozac, bind strongly to protein. This means that 95% of the drug may be bound to the protein. The interaction is accentuated by drugs like Prozac, because it and its metabolite, norfluoxetine, last so long in the body. Consequently, interactions may be significant even a month after stopping the drug.

How relevant then is protein binding?
We don't know exactly. The biggest difficulty is this area has been largely unstudied so we're unsure of the exact consequences.

Andrew saw a chance to shine.
But at least we prescribe Prozac in doses like 20 mg, so only small amounts are binding.
You're right. Many other drugs bind strongly to protein and are prescribed in higher doses: So imagine what 500 mg of Serzone can do? However, it's amazing how ignored the area is.

And are there any more principles?
Yes. Just one more major one—**elimination** of drugs. The kidneys purify the body by eliminating fluid through urine. Usually small molecules like salt play big roles in determining exact quantities. This becomes relevant with poor kidney function. But, Victor, you've seen its importance with certain medications such as diuretics—water tablets, where you've lost too much potassium. Similarly, some compounds go via the liver through the biliary system and are eliminated in feces. Again, these are more relevant with disease processes like bile obstruction.

Victor showed he had been listening well:
With all these interactions, Doctor, I sure realize the need to be careful.
Yes, you can be amazed that medications can do so much damage to supposedly unrelated organs, tissues and cells. You can understand now how drugs can work even on basics like your potassium.

192

S pring had shifted toward summer.

Victor attended his follow-up appointment with me.

You know Doctor, it's exactly ninety days since I left the hospital.

You've been counting, Victor.

Yes I have, because I've also been thinking.

About what?

Well, you know, Doctor, it's amazing: My whole experience could have been so different.

In what way?

You know, Doctor, when you came to consult with me, I fully expected to be put onto all sorts of extra medications. In fact, it seems that all that has happened is that I'm taking less.

Yes, Victor. What we did was to rationalize your medications.

I was having a great deal of nicotine and hundreds of different chemical compounds in my cigarettes; but I'm still off cigarettes.

That's wonderful, Victor.

And then there was the diuretic that was depleting my potassium. I'm feeling much more energized now since I've been taking six potassium tablets a day, and my internist has allowed me to cut down my dose of diuretic by half as well.

That's good.

And then there was that strange phenomenon of my taking the vitamin tablets that were keeping my Parkinson's disease medication from working, so I'm no longer taking B6 vitamins. As you know, I found a special preparation which does not contain vitamin B6.

That's excellent, Victor.

What I have learnt, is that I need to be extraordinarily careful about drug interactions. I can ensure that my medication is being consistently absorbed.

And what techniques have you found help you, Victor?

I do that, Doctor, by taking my medication regularly at the same time and under the same conditions—after meals, or just before bed, always with water. I also make sure there are no interactions with every new medication I am prescribed, even an antibiotic. I always check with my pharmacist to ensure that the levels won't go higher or lower, or will not cause strange reactions on my organs, like the brain.

So you're very careful?
I even read the package inserts, though I won't let them frighten me because I know many of the problems listed in them will never happen to me and I certainly don't want to become a hypochondriac!

Andrew sat there amazed at how well Victor, the patient, had integrated his vital lessons.
Victor, you sound as if you're the medical student, not me. I'm sure you would have mentioned the pharmacodynamic interactions as well: for example, how the nicotine at the brain level was actually helping the Parkinson's disease.

Victor did not miss a beat.
Yes, I would have. Speaking of that, I've had to take slightly more Sinemet since I've gone off my cigarettes. But now I feel in control. I understand what I'm doing, my theophylline is well controlled and, in fact, I'm breathing much better. I know I don't have much lung left, but at least I have a little.

If there's a success story with somebody who had significantly damaged his health, Victor is such a tale. His awareness of interactions, both kinetic, at the liver level, and dynamic, at the brain level, did any lay person proud. This education was serving Victor well in his quest to regain as much health as he could. Victor reflected the prototype elderly patient with multiple medical conditions, who could easily have been wrongly labeled "psychiatric".

Victor understated his skills, which he had proven were considerable.
Doctor, I'm not a clever man, but sometimes I like to see links.
That's clever in itself, Sir.

Well, the link I see is: All of these interactions affect everything.
No longer will anything I take be the same. It's like "Sugar and Spice". Doctor, are we going to get rid of "Everything Nice" as well?

194

Chapter 8

And Everything Nice

Herbal remedies.
Absorption, Herbs, Vehicles. Caffeine,
Drug development and marketing, drug regulation,
MAOIs, Melatonin, St John's wort, Vitamins.
(Ryan); (bathtub analogy)

Ryan had arrived for his first appointment.
Doctor, I get agitated at times. I feel just awful. I don't sleep well. My head aches, particularly when there are things going on at work. I want to get better.

Well, Ryan, what are you currently taking?
Nothing really, Doctor. My family practitioner suggested a little bit of anti-depressant, but I've just been on it for a week or two.

Are you aware that antidepressants take a time to work?
Yes, he explained that it might take three or four weeks, but I haven't noticed very much change. In fact, I've been feeling rather strange during this time.

Are you sure you're taking nothing else?
No, nothing, Doctor. Well, you know, besides my regulars.

Your regulars? Which ones?
Well, I don't know, I like to take a lot of vitamins, and I take these anti-oxidants. My wife gave me this St John's wort, and I've been trying that.
Do you take anything for sleep?

195

Yes, Doctor. I like to go natural, so I have some Melatonin, but it doesn't seem to really help.

And that's all?
Yes Doctor, that's all that I take.

What about coffee?
Oh, yeah, well you know, obviously I like my coffee. In fact, it's my favorite beverage. I have maybe two or three cups to get me going in the morning, then I have another two or three in the afternoon to get me over the mid-day slump.

And you're a non-smoker?
No, you know, I've tried to kick the habit, but I vary. Some days I have five, some days I have twenty-five; mainly a pack a day I'd say, on average.

I assume you drink no alcohol.
Well, you know, when I get home after a hard day's work, I like to have a whisky or two and maybe a brandy sometimes over the weekend. Also, when I go out with the boys or watch the games, I drink a lot of beers. We can have a 6-pack each on some nights, maybe two or three days out of the week.

And what about recreational drugs?
Well, Doctor, you know, I don't know if I should be telling you this, I find marijuana really relaxes me and so I have it sometimes, you know, occasionally.
How occasionally?
Well, maybe two or three times a week.

Anything else?
No, Doctor. It used to be that we would sniff a little bit of cocaine, but I've stopped that for the most part much of late.
You say "for the most part." When was the last time?
Well, I'd say about two weeks ago.

What about other things?
I've had a few dots of LSD in my time.

Can you think of any other substances? Medications, non-prescribed drugs?
Oh, absolutely nothing, Doctor!

I see.
Do you always have your medications with water?

No, you know, I drink it down with a soda or coffee sometimes. I really like grapefruit juice, too.

What else do you drink for beverages?
Oh, I love my latté in the morning. One more at lunch and in between plenty of Coke to cool me down.

*T*here were so many places to begin with this patient, but I decided the coffee would be a good starter. Ryan was taking so much and, I suspected, with significant side-effects, that I was concerned for this beloved mind. Possibly, he would improve with some education, which may in turn lead to more rational understanding of herbs, alternative medicine, and medication.

I analyzed his **caffeine** consumption. By the time I had elicited everything, he clearly was drinking the caffeine equivalent of about six cups of coffee per day. I launched into education mode aimed at behavioral alteration in pharmacological habits, in other words, getting him off his caffeine.

Is caffeine the same as coffee, Doctor?
Not exactly. Caffeine occurs in its most potent form in coffee. However, also significant amounts of it occur in tea and soda pop drinks. We regard it as the most commonly used non-prescription drug in the world.

Really?
Did you know that if you averaged it out for the world's population, every person would drink 70 mg a day–that's about half a cup of coffee per day.

Andrew took off the plastic lid to his styrofoam cup of coffee and added:

I heard it's even more in the United States.
True, the average American uses caffeine equivalent to about one and a half cups of coffee per day. This may be from tea or soda pop drinks. A cup of tea or a can of soda pop like Coke or Pepsi contains about half the amount of caffeine as a cup of coffee.

This made Ryan wonder:
But is coffee drinking a recent habit?
Actually, it dates back thousands of years: Tea was apparently made in China 5000 years ago, and coffee beans were recorded 1500 years ago in Africa. Moreover, coffee was popular in Arabia 800 years ago.

What does caffeine do?
197

Pharmacologically, caffeine belongs to a brain stimulant group of alkaloids called the methylxanthines or simply the xanthines. Tea contains a similar drug–theophylline–but in tiny doses, like 1 mg, so it produces little effect. There's also a xanthine in chocolate called theobromine, but it's not potent at all.

Yes, I heard that the coffee bean is the major source of caffeine.
I could see Andrew was about to impress: Medical students need to demonstrate their knowledge.

Did you know coffee is from the Coffea arabica plant, and soft drinks, like Cola drinks, derive from Kola nuts?

And just to emphasize his special knowledge, he added.
And tea leaves are from a plant called Thea sinensis, and cocoa from the seeds of the Theobroma cocoa plant or cocoa beans.

I looked at Andrew direct in the eye.
Impressive. You've been reading up, Andrew. Incidentally, only 5% of the caffeine in Cola drinks actually comes from the kola nut.

Where does the rest come from?
You can imagine that caffeine extracted in the making of decaff does not go to waste: That is where the other 95% of the caffeine in cola drinks comes from. Also the extracted caffeine in making decaff coffee is recycled into the caffeine in chocolate, chocolate milk, hot cocoa, and various other candies.

This stimulated more questions from Andrew.
Do we know how caffeine works in the brain?
Yes, but it's complicated. Technically, caffeine enhances secretion of norepinephrine, one of our most important neurotransmitters. Linked to this is its effect in slowing a special complex pathway relating to energy systems, and it even increases production of cortisone type compounds in the adrenal gland. Strangely, its most relevant effects may be on another related brain system–it antagonizes adenosine receptors. This chemical, adenosine, is an important neuromodulator: it sedates people, relieves anxiety and even diminishes seizures.

Is this why caffeine makes people wired and activated, and why it impacts seizures?
Exactly. Caffeine diminishes this sedative action of adenosine which means it activates. It blocks the relief of anxiety so it's simply the most common anxiogenic–anxiety-inducing agent–in our society.

Isn't this just theory? Is it relevant in practice?
Yes, it is. In fact, seven or eight cups in a day is enough to produce anxiety in almost everyone. Many people are exquisitely sensitive to much smaller doses like a half or one cup. So, often, the first treatment for anyone who is anxious, is to taper coffee. The same applies in people with sleep problems: It may impair sleep in sensitive individuals: so if you're an insomniac, don't use it at night.

And why does caffeine work in headaches? Is it through that same receptor adenosine, as well?
It's disputed whether caffeine even helps headaches. Many drugs prescribed for headache make patients sleepy. The caffeine simply negates the sleepiness. If it works, it could again be through adenosine because this chemical makes the blood vessels in the brain wider, so caffeine would, in theory, constrict down a throbbing blood vessel.

R̲yan was worried at this point.
Let me get back to myself because what I'm going to say is serious: Doctor, I think I may be addicted to caffeine. How would I know?

Do you find you need steadily increasing doses over short periods?
No, Doctor, but my caffeine use increased gradually over my college years. It also has waned. I drank it much more in college with my friends and also, I'm afraid, to enhance my alertness and to stop falling asleep so I could learn late at night.
This is the typical story. You can see it's different from abuse of barbiturates for example, where your tolerance changes a bit over relatively short periods.

But Doctor, I know I'm addicted because when I try to stop, I get caffeine withdrawal headaches and I also become irritable and anxious.
This, too, is a dependence feature: you have typical withdrawal features. However, you can get off caffeine much more easily than say the barbiturates or alcohol. Usually you can taper your caffeine in coffee drinking by a quarter of a cup every second or third day: All you do is add in the equivalent amount of decaffeinated coffee instead.

Doctor, when I miss my coffee during the day, I need my fix.
Yes. This shows the pattern of psychological need for it. So you show patterns of dose increases, dependence and withdrawal.

It looks like I'm in trouble Doctor. Should I give up coffee?
Yes, that may help; but remember that this must be gradual.

I'll drink tea instead.
Wait. Remember tea also contains caffeine, albeit about half the amount as in coffee. So if you increase your tea or Pepsi or Coke, the effects on you are additive: a cup of coffee plus two cups of tea plus a can of Pepsi all enhance the caffeine effect. So if you drink beverages besides coffee, you must still be careful of all your caffeine intake. Also, you should know that if you also take an over the counter preparation containing caffeine, you may become toxic with for example, anxiety, insomnia and irritability.

Ryan became quiet for a moment, clearly pensive.
Then denial began:
What's so bad about coffee, anyway?
Coffee is an anxiogenic, which means that in certain amounts, it induces anxiety. At three cups—400 milligrams—it might not be much of a problem. By the time you drink six or seven cups it will induce anxiety in everyone. Some people are exquisitely sensitive in this regard—a half a cup is enough. It's important for us to remember this because, before we start looking at medications to treat symptoms, we should eliminate the cause. This time we will do it with your caffeine. People sometimes forget that with all of these seemingly harmless beverages, they're actually prescribing medication for themselves.

Nobody's ever told me before that my coffee is like a bad medication. So what should I do, Doctor?
I want you to cut down your caffeine. This should be the only instruction that I give you today, so you can realize, "Hold on, this doctor is serious!" If I were to prescribe two different medications and then say, "Oh, by the way, cut down the caffeine," you might not realize the importance of what we're talking about. We're talking about a dependency—an addictive chemical change in your brain—and we have to re-modify and re-modulate that. As it happens, we have already spoken about other issues, but I want you to remember the caffeine taper as a key instruction.

*R*yan chose his words carefully:
Because caffeine activates like this, is that why people use it to sober up from alcohol?
I wish it were so, Ryan. Caffeine can speed reactions and increase concentration, but will not really help people "sober up" too much from an alcohol binge because the mechanism of action of alcohol may be different.

Andrew, too, was not satisfied.

But why can some people drink coffee with impunity? My middle-aged professor seems to spend his life drinking coffee: He'll be up late at night drinking two or three cups of strong espresso, and it might be as late as eleven PM. Then, he'll start drinking coffee again in the morning. I can tell you, he never looks anxious. He's alert, he has energy, but he never seems to be "hyper". He looks well rested and, as far as I know, he's healthy.

You've asked a testing question. It might be that he's not absorbing some of that coffee. On the other hand, it might be that his receptors are different from somebody else's receptors.

How so?

When we talk about any chemical compound, be it caffeine or be it some prescribed drug, we have to put it in this context: how does the end organ, the actual receptor that's receiving the stimulating chemical, respond? Maybe it's only responding 40%. Maybe it reflects a certain deficiency. Maybe the person who eats and gets fat is just demonstrating a very efficient metabolic system as opposed to the person who can eat and eat, who has so-called "luxus consumption". Maybe the metabolism of the person who can eat ad lib is so good that they're metabolizing everything. Or maybe their metabolism is faulty in a good way: Their receptors are not responding to the actual energy packets of calories that they're receiving in the extra carbohydrate and fat they're eating.

In other words, are you saying that people are fundamentally and qualitatively different?

Indeed so. I suspect it's great simplicity to try to use simple psychiatric labels on each patient, because everyone pharmacologically responds in a special way. There are even those who respond to absolute minuscule doses of a drug, responding in the same way as others respond to high doses of the same drug. It might be that their receptors are simply sensitive.

Is that what we mean by down and up-regulation of the receptor?

Well, these are difficult concepts. In fact, we can talk about it at a later stage.

But Andrew pressed the issue further.

I think my professor is abnormal, Doctor. I think that he needs to be brought back to a normal state of functioning, because if he can have so much caffeine without these strange side-effects, that must be abnormal. Maybe we ought to treat him, so that he will not be able to tolerate more coffee than the rest of us.

You're asking a bold question. He doesn't need treatment because he doesn't have symptoms. In other words, he's functioning normally at every level.

201

Ryan took his turn:

Since Andrew mentioned the middle-aged professor, I want to ask about the other age group: My kids don't drink coffee or tea, but they have plenty of soft drinks like Coke and Pepsi. What happens to the caffeine in them?

Children are not more sensitive to caffeine than adults. In fact, it may be eliminated from the body twice as quickly in children so they may even be less sensitive.

So you regard caffeine as like a drug, Doctor?

No, Ryan. It's not "like a drug." It is a drug, a powerful one.

*B*ut Doctor, am I unusual then in my caffeine use?

No. Your story is typical. Often, people forget that they're on caffeine. I ask them what they're taking, and they say, "Oh, I'm not taking anything!"

Then I say, "Hold on. As far as I can see, you're on 300 mg of caffeine a day, you're on 60 cigarettes a day, and you're on two shots of whisky a day, and you say you're not taking any medications?"

But are those really medications?

They are, and what's more, so are vitamins and different herbal supplements. Those are also just as much drugs as the rest.

Ryan suddenly flushed. He began to sweat. He then quickly regained composure and a little sheepishly protested:

Surely you don't count my little vices, Doctor?

Unfortunately, I do. Caffeine, nicotine and alcohol are probably the three most widely used psychoactive chemical agents in the world. Additionally, other chemicals besides nicotine are relevant when we smoke. We inhale several other chemicals, technically called polycyclic aromatic hydrocarbons, but more colloquially referred to as tar smoke designed to mess up your lungs, heart, liver metabolism and vital functions. These chemicals are drugs that can cause harm.

So what are you saying, Doctor? You mean you want to cut out everything?

Well, Ryan, we will want to look at each and every one of these drugs and try to understand what every one of these does for you. Do remember that just because something is natural does not mean that it necessarily is good. Snake venom is natural. Studies on these herbal products are not being done through FDA approval. That something is "natural" often means that it hasn't been adequately researched using the stringent criteria that regulatory bodies such as the American Food and Drug Administration require drugs to go through.

Well, can we deal with my herbs? Surely, they're all as safe as the bank?
I wish this were so. The first problem I have with herbal remedies is this: They're not single preparations. Presumably there's an active chemical inside them, but we may not even know what it is. Different amounts of that herbal remedy might have different levels of that active chemical, so you might be taking 20 mg one day and 30 mg another day, and that might make a big difference.

Is that the only difficulty?
No, we have a second problem. Because the active ingredients of these herbal remedies are as yet inadequately studied chemicals, we don't know what interactions will occur with your other medications.

Why can't I just take them at a different time from my other medications, Doctor?
This will help with absorption at the stomach level, but not at the liver level. At the liver level, the new herb could increase or decrease or not change levels of your medications: We don't know. Unfortunately, with many vitamin, mineral and natural herbal products, we simply are unaware of how they're going to interact with medications, because we're uncertain whether they're going to affect absorption or metabolism.

That doesn't sound too bad so far, Doctor. Is there more?
That's just the beginning. With many of these medications, we're not even sure that a placebo would not work as well.

Does that mean you're against all the wonderful panaceas that we can buy?

> I detected a hint of sadness tinged with challenge and maybe even subtle sarcasm in Ryan's voice.

No, Ryan. However, I think that people should be careful and aware that they're entering the realm of the unexplored, and that this may be remarkable, but it could also be dangerous.

Any tips for those of us in this realm?

> Ryan's affect had changed to genuine concern.

If you're going to take supplements you have two options. Firstly, you can take them consistently at the same time as your medication, so that both will be malabsorbed or absorbed to the same degree. But then you must be aware that you may so change the absorption of your other medications that they may be wasted. Alternatively, you could swallow the supplements at a different time from when you take your other medications.

This way, you can largely solve the problem of possible impaired absorption. However, protein and liver interactions might push up the levels of your other medications.

Anything else?
Yes. Another problem is that the herb or special over-the-counter chemical might have side-effects.

Don't we know, for example, that vitamins are safe?
Not always. Some vitamins are toxic in too high a dosage: be particularly careful with the fat-soluble ones, like vitamin A and vitamin E. Moreover, the side-effect may not be due to the active chemical. It may be due to the vehicle—the wrapping around the drug—and not the herb or prescription medication or vitamin itself.

*W*hat *exactly do you mean by the "vehicle", Doctor?*
The vehicle is the "concrete" the medication is put in so that it gets absorbed, and this, in and of itself, might cause side-effects. What we're talking about is, if you like, the filler—the chocolate shell or wrapper: This can vary greatly even from one medication to another. The stomach or duodenum will take a longer period of time to uncover a well wrapped drug compared with one that's only mildly wrapped.

But surely this is more general?
Right. This applies not only to herbal medications, but also to generic and brand name drugs. Besides the chemical inside in a generic drug or in any other tablet, there is always a vehicle—the substance that sticks it all together—which may be inert, but can cause its own problems.

Why?
Well, that vehicle might increase or decrease drug absorption. If it absorbs too quickly, unpleasant side-effects may occur because the blood level increases precipitously. But if it is absorbed too slowly, it could cause nausea or diarrhea, especially if the drug is not absorbed, and then the medication will not work, to boot!

Yeah, you know, Doctor, I've also been taking a little bit of chromium and potassium, and maybe the vehicle might be causing me a little stomach trouble.
You've now learnt that any time you find side-effects in the stomach, they may not be dependent on the supplements or drug you might be taking, but rather on the capsule or the glue or vehicle that's carrying it. For example, a generic or for that matter a vitamin or mineral preparation or

herb sometimes causes nausea, yet the real trade name preparation or another vitamin doesn't. So you just change the preparation, and you suddenly find the nausea is gone.

Is the stomach always involved?
No. Different medications are absorbed from different parts of the gastrointestinal tract. This partly depends on the actual vehicle in which the medication is contained. How acidic or how alkaline it is? Also, a capsule might be absorbed differently from a tablet, or a particular long-acting preparation will vary from the shorter-acting one.

Do we see these problems with prescription medications as well?
Yes, we do, but these at least are controlled. Moreover, the pharmaceutical manufacturer generally has a reputation to maintain, and most produce extremely high quality and consistent products as a consequence.

But it's difficult?
Yes, manufacturers try to walk a balance by saying, "We will make this long-acting, slow-release drug." However, all medications are also, in part, dependent on what is eaten and drunk. New preparations must be taken under the same consistent circumstances.

Would you say that we're still ignorant?
Certainly, we don't know about specific interactions as well as we can. We realize that absorption might vary depending on whether the stomach is full or empty; that a generic medication may be a little different from an ordinary non-generic medication, that vehicles may be different and that herbal preparations seem less stringently controlled and certainly less well researched.

So herbs should not be taken?
Not true. Fundamentally, I don't have problems with people taking herbal medications, provided they sensibly observe the changes that are happening to them and exhibit as much care and respect towards potential problems as they would while taking a prescription medication. Another provision exists: They must realize that the well tried and trusted researched prescription drugs may also have been herbs in their primitive days, but now are refined and their benefits have been shown to outweigh their risks. The herbs they're taking may ultimately be shown to be food or poison.

Ryan shifted gear and returned to his medication.

Doctor, I don't even want to be treated. I don't like medications.

Do you think you're alone in this regard? You're not. We encounter this philosophy commonly.

This is why I thought I'd take herbs instead.
But herbs are medications as well, although they're not controlled medications. We don't know the right doses, we don't know their appropriate indications and we don't know the purity of the preparation. They are still medications because they have potential pharmacological effects–they're just inadequately studied drugs. In fact, they may even be more dangerous than regular prescribed drugs because of the many unknowns, impurities and variabilities in potentially toxic compounds.

Are they even worse than medications?
In that context, yes, because many approved medications are the active ingredient of herbs, but they're well-controlled and studied. The difference is that we no longer regard those medications as "natural", yet we know the approximate milligram dosage the patient is receiving. With approved medications, we know the exact active chemical compound. We don't find inconsistencies involving numerous mixtures of substances, which could cause problems not only because of unstudied compounds, but because of variable combinations. We also have good scientific reasoning as to what their effects will be, what their potential side-effects will be, and what interactions may occur with other drugs.

I wanted to resolve an apparent paradox.
But despite your attitude towards not taking medication, you say you're taking no medication other than a little bit of antidepressant?
Yes, Doctor, that's right.

Which one?
I mentioned it, actually: My doctor said it's okay and my wife got it for me; it's another one of those herbal remedies, Doctor, St John's wort. There can't be too much wrong with this natural stuff I'm taking and I find it's much cheaper.

The fact that it's natural does not mean that it's automatically good. We'll have to take a look at some of your medications.
But they're not medications, Doctor. They're herbs and vitamins.

It seemed Ryan was a hard sell.

No, that's what they are–herbs are medication. They're just as much medications as your prescription drugs. Some people are very much into the herbal treatments, and for one reason or another they don't mention to their physician that they're taking this herb or that, because they don't think it will matter.

So why does it matter?
It matters because they may also produce problems. Alternative medicines using herbs have become a great practical option amongst ordinary people, and we doctors recognize this. Approximately one out of three of our patients are estimated to take alternative medicine, either alone or in addition to their current medication, so it's important for us to be aware of the alternatives. Sometimes these work, but it may be difficult to separate their action from a significant placebo effect as much as 25% or 30% of the time. At other times they don't work, but this does not mean to say they will not work for other indications, so the whole area needs scientific control and scrutiny as well as empathic understanding.

> We seemed to be regressing. I had a distinct sense of déjà vu, but not really so: I had in reality said it all before, so it did not qualify as a déjà experience, which involves only *inappropriate* familiarity! [59] But, be that as it may, my message was worth repeating.

Doctor, I don't want to interfere, but I like natural substances and I worry about medications.
Again, because something is supposedly a "natural" substance, like a natural herb, doesn't mean to say that it's completely harmless. Also, as I've mentioned, many prescription medications derive originally from plants, though today synthetic preparations are easier and often better.

But all the magazines tell us the information for herbs. They must obtain it from a reliable source, surely?
Surely, not! Non-medical magazines are not authoritative sources of data. In general, we don't have well researched information for herbs or some of these other natural substances, and sometimes, these medications are even dosed wrongly.

For example?
A drug like Melatonin was marketed for sleep and as a panacea for young age. It's generally produced at much too high a dosage—3 mg or 6 mg a day—when the physiologic dose may be half a mg a day. The problem, however, is absorption: Different preparations may vary enormously. In one preparation most of the 6 mg a day may not be absorbed; in another, almost all may be absorbed so that we may have great variability in dosage. Similarly, with St John's wort the dose seems to be variable, although the claimed appropriate dose may be about 600 mg per day. However, the dose depends on the particular preparation that one takes; presumably these preparations are not equivalent.

Well, why don't they try to make the doses equivalent?
It's difficult to create equivalency when we don't even know what the active ingredient in St John's wort is. Some have said it's hypericin, but we don't really know. There are several potentially active ingredient components in St John wort, and more than one may be acting. [60]

How does St John's wort act?
That, too, is uncertain. One idea is related to increasing certain levels of neurotransmitters, and a common hypothesis is that maybe it acts on an enzyme system called monoamine-oxidase—MAO—which it inhibits, so it's a MAO inhibitor.]

What's the relevance of this?
Simply this: Way back, half a century ago, before antidepressants, it was found that the mood of tuberculotic patients receiving a drug called iproniazid began to improve quite dramatically. This iproniazid was found to have monoamine-oxidase inhibitory effects. This is an example of a prescription drug with a different impact to what was expected. Because of this discovery, a remarkable prescription group of drugs for depression, the monoamine-oxidase inhibitors—MAOIs—were born. The most common drugs in this class are Nardil (phenelzine) and Parnate (tranylcypramine). These drugs seemed to have a remarkable activating effect, particularly on the "atypical depressions".

What are "atypical depressions"?
These are the depressions that are non-endogenous and non-melancholic. In other words, they're not the typical biologically based sadness episodes. These MAOIs raise up the mood by blocking the breakdown of certain chemicals such as norepinephrine and serotonin, and by so doing, cause the levels of these chemicals to go up, and this provides relief of depression.

> Andrew had gone through a quiet phase, but was listening intently, as his question attested.

Would these drugs then prevent the breakdown of the chemicals, norepinephrine and serotonin, by preventing other chemicals from destroying them?
Well done, Andrew! However, a strange phenomenon happened: It was found that, at times, there could be a dangerous food reaction, which has been called the "tyramine effect".

How so?
Well, for example, when a patient on these monoamine-oxidase inhibitors eats aged cheddar cheese or broad beans or certain wines, they may,

208

raise their blood pressure so high because of this combination that they could literally stroke out and die.

Clearly, that's an interaction to avoid!
In addition, when these patients were given antidepressants of other kinds with the MAOIs, similar events could transpire, because these also would raise up the levels of the chemicals we spoke of—the neurotransmitters norepinephrine and serotonin—by different means. There could be an interaction that could cause death. Consequently, we're careful when we use monoamine-oxidase inhibitors.

But didn't you say that St John's wort is a MAOI?
True. At least one of the chemicals in it inhibits the MAO enzyme system; and this action is irreversible and involves both main MAO receptor subtypes—MAOI-A and MAOI-B.

So drug interactions could happen?
Exactly, Andrew. For example, although it's debated whether its actual antidepressant effects have to do with monoamine-oxidase inhibition, this drug still has MAOI properties. Should we be use dietary controls of a special MAOI diet like we do with our regular prescription MAOIs? Not many people worry about this but then relatively few of its advocates may be psychopharmacologically sophisticated. Are the effects of St John's wort too weak for us to worry about MAOI? But then why use it? The likely answer is that its antidepressant properties are not MAOI related.

Some patients are on regular antidepressants as well, aren't they?
Yes, Andrew. Although nothing like this has been demonstrated, the potential for such side-effects must always be considered. Certainly my own patients, may of their own accord, take St John's wort in combination with conventional antidepressants, sometimes not even bothering to mention this to me. Some of these conventional antidepressants are actually directly contraindicated in the presence of MAOIs because of this danger of hypertensive crises. So I caution them.

W e shifted off the MAOIs, but Andrew continued our discussion of St Johns wort.
And yet, St John's wort has become a new panacea. By all accounts it's the most popular so-called "antidepressant" in Germany.
Yes, and it's becoming increasingly important among my patients.

Well, what do you think of it, Doctor?
It's not my place here to discuss detailed opinions about it, because USA psychiatrists have not yet studied it in sufficient detail.

We're probably not dealing with the panacea that some argue it is: St John's wort has been claimed to have antiviral effects, pain relief effects and anti-inflammatory effects. However, some double-blind studies suggest that, under certain circumstances, it may have significant antidepressant and anti-anxiety effects. Such studies have several problems like population selection and drug dose. We should also remember that the preparations that were used in research were consistent and homogeneous. On the other hand, what we buy may be inconsistent and heterogeneous in quality because of the limited degree of regulation of such substances.

Ryan added his dollar's worth of information.
They say it helps the immune system, too.
Yes, and it's been touted as a component of herbal dieting–it's used even in weight reduction. Paradoxically, it has also been used in anorexia, to increase weight. Each one of these effects sounds marvelous, but when we encounter a drug that is supposed to do all these things, we're entitled to have a degree of skepticism.

Well, why?
A big problem is to figure out whether it's doing these marvels initially, and whether it's maintaining its effects later on. There are many other questions. What dosage would be appropriate and how would we tailor the dosage?

But only about one in every forty patients have side-effects?
True, though we should distinguish "side-effects" from "reported side-effects." The low figure may be due to the selection of patients taking the drug, the expectations, report bias, inadequate monitoring of side-effects, limited awareness of what an adverse effect is, and even problems in diagnosis of such effects. St John's wort may turn out to be valuable. However, the important component here is to bear in mind that it's not a substitute for regular, well-established medicine, that has been properly regulated and researched.

Andrew already knew it all.
That's what I thought.

Or did he? He reverted again to his pursuit of extra knowledge.
Do you have an opinion about St John's wort?
Yes. St John's wort is a fascinating substance. It has become extremely popular as an antidepressant in Germany. The active ingredient is uncertain. People talk about hypericum as the plant and hypericin being an important ingredient, but this is uncertain. You're not getting a guaran-

teed milligram dosage; you're not getting a drug that has been studied properly; and you're not knowing the interactions in relation to it.

It was time to steer the conversation away from St John's wort.

Do you have any recommendations?
We ought to always be on the lookout not only for side-effects with drugs such as St John's wort, but also for adverse interaction effects of any of these vitamins, minerals or herbal preparations with our more conventional pharmacological agents. The vitamins and the minerals in this regard are generally regarded as safe, because we have adequate data on appropriate dosing.

So we can take vitamins?
Vitamins have been around a long time, but preparations vary depending on what manufacturer you use. The problem is, just because a preparation may be beautifully packed and cost three dollars for five instead of fifty cents for ten doesn't mean it's any better, and it's difficult to know which preparations are superior. Probably it's a question of looking at how reputable the manufacturer is, at your own comfort level, and whether the specific preparation causes any problems like gastric irritation.

I turned to Ryan. We needed to get back on track.
Now, let's go into your vitamins.
Which ones do you take?
Well, I take vitamin C and E and A and some Bs.
There is a place for vitamins, and there are several different vitamin preparations that have proven useful. Conventional medicine suggests the use of such preparations in cases of vitamin deficiency. Given that we do not usually measure levels of vitamin, although these can be done, for example with vitamin B12 and folic acid, it has become a common practice to supplement treatment with appropriate vitamins.

Yeah, and I also take folic acid, because I heard it's good for the heart. Is that true?
Probably. Folic acid, one of the B vitamins, supposedly lowers the incidence of heart attacks. As many as 70% of the American population may be deficient in it if we assume we need more [800 micrograms] than what was thought was the adequate daily recommended allowance. Folic acid helps to break down certain toxic chemicals into less toxic chemicals which could otherwise accumulate. The latest information is that the risk is higher if one is folic acid deficient than even if you have high cholesterol. People who were deficient in folic acid seem more at risk for hav-

ing myocardial infarction—heart attacks or coronary thromboses—though we don't know if this is causally linked or just coincidence. Consequently, I routinely suggest to any adult male, particularly those in their middle years and beyond who are at risk, to take supplemental folic acid in doses of at least 800 micrograms a day.

But you said we have to be careful taking vitamins?
Yes. True. A problem arises whatever you take. Ryan, you should take medication at the same time each day, consistently, with the same food substances, either before, during or after a meal, for example, or unassociated with meals, as long as it's done consistently. If the medication is being taken with fluid, that fluid generally should be water. The main point is a consistent habit.

Ryan, do you take the same brand of vitamin or mineral all the time?
No, Doctor.
It's important to maintain stability there: Give the body the opportunity to consistently develop a new baseline.

Andrew renewed his unflagging pursuit of knowledge, which proved to be helpful:
By the way, Doctor, how does St John's wort get broken down by the liver? Through which systems does it go?
We don't know.

And what about Melatonin? How does that work?
We don't know.

Well, then, what about Echinacea, it's become a common herbal item?
We don't know.

What about Ginseng?
We don't know.

What about Gingko?
We don't know.

What do you mean you don't know about all these? Surely they've been researched?
No, they haven't been adequately studied.
We don't know about the interactions that these various herbal remedies will cause in our patients.

But why hasn't the FDA already demanded the research? Surely there has been enough time to do so by now?
That's part of the problem with these herbal remedies. They are not as regulated as our conventional prescription medications. This means we don't have the knowledge that will allow us to practice as safe a form of medicine on it.

Andrew, with his great desire for knowledge, then asked a particularly important question.
Why don't the pharmaceutical companies just market these as prescription drugs?
It may sound simple, Andrew, but, in fact, it's complex. To **market a drug** in the United States at this time costs about 400 or 500 million dollars, on average.
We should also bear in mind the number of drugs that have failed. Only about 9% of drugs overall that even are studied at the earliest experimental—preclinical phase 1—level are marketed.

So, it's about one-tenth of all drugs that are developed?
No, Andrew, unfortunately not. Literally, today, hundreds of thousands of compounds are being looked at by computer model. The numbers of chemicals that can be processed per second on computer are absolutely mind-boggling. It may even be an understatement that we can process chemicals at 100,000 times the rate that we were doing twenty years ago.

What do you mean by processing?
Well, at this point, it means computer analysis.

So what's the problem, Doctor?
Simply this, Andrew: The patent begins at the time the drug is developed, not the time the drug is marketed. Because of the seven or even twelve years of research that happens before the drug is approved, the patent may be half over or two thirds over at the time of FDA approval. This means the pharmaceutical company may have seven years, or ten years, to recoup their expenses on the drug and make almost all their profits.

Are you saying that the brand name drug starts out expensive?
Exactly.

Does this produce conflicts?
Potentially. One solution for a pharmaceutical company would be to focus the use of a drug on a specific diagnosis only and do the minimum amount of research on that condition so that the drug could be approved quickly. If the drug were studied before marketing for a second condition,

for example, in pregnancy, the costs would escalate. Also, the researchers may discover a dangerous side-effect, and even though it would not be used in pregnant women, it may not end up marketed because totally controlling its lack of use in pregnancy could be an overwhelmingly large endeavor.

For example?
Thalidomide went off the market world-wide because of its specific dangers in pregnancy. Ironically, it's now marketed in the USA, although strongly regulated for the specific condition of leprosy.

Can you give another example besides pregnancy of what may not be tested for?
Let's imagine there's a dangerous side-effect of a particular antidepressant in liver failure. This may not be detected before approval because it's not usually relevant to test under those circumstances, yet alcoholics may be depressed and conceivably some with severe liver damage may receive the new drug. So, there are always ethical dilemmas in relation to the prescription of drugs because in reality they're marketed in a real world not a controlled ideal, experimental setting.

Are there other ethical problems?
Probably many. An important one is the balance that researchers and pharmaceutical companies must reach, between profits and the humanitarian value of a drug.

Example?
Sleeping sickness is a terrible and common killer in central Africa, but basically an extremely rare condition in the USA as only travelers from Africa could acquire it. A new drug for this condition has little potential for revenue as the profits are made only in the richer countries. Should pharmaceutical companies research such an agent where they're likely to actually lose large amounts of money?

Yes, they should!
Well, do they? Only sometimes and to their credit maybe even more than we would expect.

Andrew remained puzzled.
You've mentioned how drugs are approved for certain indications.
Yes, Andrew, and generally the approval, because of this whole expensive process, is for the narrowest of indications.

But then how come drugs are used for other uses?

Well, after approval begins real exploration and the real experience with the drug. You can imagine that certain standards of practice develop amongst physicians. This is well recognized, accepted and appropriate in this context. So, for example, in psychiatry, maybe as many as one third of prescriptions are not for the specific approved indication; in an inpatient environment in psychiatry, it might even be two thirds. For difficult neuropsychiatric out-patients, it might be three quarters. The major principle is that the standards of practice are set by the treating physician. He uses his skills based on experience and knowledge of the literature as well as the particular patient's condition to assist in this regard. The physician treads the careful line of not poisoning and actually trying to help. Sometimes, there are no drugs available for a particular condition: Of those you're familiar with Andrew, no medications are specifically marketed for aggression or irritability, for catatonic stupor, or for tardive dyskinesia. So every time we prescribe for these conditions, we are applying innovative psychopharmacotherapy.

So what role does the FDA play?
The FDA, in effect, is the ethical gatekeeper that tries to make sure that medications are safe for the public and that there are clear guidelines as to when these medications should be appropriately used. Of course, as I've indicated, further guidelines develop after the drug is marketed, based on the physician tacitly using the latitude of appropriate discretion.

I t was twelve weeks later. Ryan was much better.
How are you doing, Ryan?
You know Doctor. I hate to say so, but I've never felt better.

Well, what are you taking?
Zilch. Doctor. Nothing!

Ryan, we have discussed numerous different non-prescription compounds. Which of those are you using?
I told you Doctor. Zilch, Nothing!

Nothing? You mean no caffeine, no cigarettes, no alcohol, no herbs, no Melatonin, no St John's wort, no vitamins, no marijuana?
Yeah, that's right, Doctor. Nothing. I tapered these off slowly, and went off every one of them after our conversations.

Let's just run through your initial symptoms.

215

How's the agitation?
That's gone.
What about that awful feeling?
No more. I feel real good.

And the headaches?
I haven't had one in fo ur weeks.

And are you sleeping better?
*Like a log. Doctor, I gradually went off everything. Actually, I confess I
wanted to show you up. But in the end, I feel much better.*

I looked at Ryan, and I thought: our consultations have been a little
different from most. We haven't been dealing with specific problems
that Ryan has in relation to pathology caused by disease. We have
been dealing with education about all those extras that he has been
taking, and with it solutions to the problems these non-prescribed
drugs have caused.

Well, Ryan has it been worthwhile?
*Most certainly. You know, Doctor, I never realized I was on six different
medications—the cigarettes, the caffeine, the alcohol, the marijuana, the St
John's wort and the melatonin, not to mention the five different vitamin
preparations. I thought these were all extras, that they didn't count. I now
realize how I have to be careful, even with herbal preparations.*

It was, indeed, an important lesson: "First, not to poison."

Once again, I looked at Ryan.
It's excellent that you're not taking *anything* because at this point you
don't need anything. If the situation changes please let me know. I'm
ready to assist. Medications do help, but only when they're properly used.

I thought to myself. Ryan is healthier off medication. I knew this
would not be the case with my next patient, Jim who needed to have
his lifeline restored with appropriate antidepressant medication.
Sometimes it's not so much a matter of everything nice, as of some
things necessary.

Chapter 9

But It Was Working

Recurrent depression.
Agitated and retarded depressions, Alzheimer's disease
and pseudodementia, history of antidepressants,
ideal antidepressant, serotonin and norepinephrine.
Effexor, Paxil, Serzone, SSRIs, Tricyclics.
(Jim); (bathtub analogy), (computer analogy)

He sat there, puzzled. Should he phone the doctor?
Something is different. I don't feel as good.
Jim had noticed this insidiously over a period of several weeks. He
was not concentrating as well as he used to. He picked up the
phone.

*Doctor, I don't know what it is, but I'm feeling sadder. I realize it's ridicu-
lous, because everything was going for me. Yet, I can't help but see my
situation as hopeless. I've been thinking a lot about dying lately. I even
weep for a half an hour on end. I have no interest in things. My wife's upset,
because we no longer have sex. I've been losing weight. It's awful getting up
in the morning: I'm waking up before the sun comes up. Could it be, Doctor, that this Paxil you gave me is no longer working? It was working so well,
you know. I felt fantastic for six months.*

Jim was a sprightly 75 year old, and had certainly had his episodes of
depression in the past. He remembered back to the 1960s, when he
was given the then "dream" drug, Elavil. He remembered, too, its
side-effects, and how, just a half a year before, he had started another
"miracle" drug, Paxil.

Jim came to my office, his arms a little shaky, clearly distressed.
Doctor, I don't want to go through it all again.

Then came the outpouring, the rationale behind his traumata. He
remembered so well back to that day in June, six months before,

when he had been referred with a diagnosis of dementia. He flashed back to that time, and it became vivid. He was losing his memory. He couldn't remember many things. People had told him to use a note-book, and he had tried it, but didn't have the motivation to do so. He found he couldn't concentrate well, and he was always weepy. He had been labeled as having an early Alzheimer's disease. We had performed a detailed series of several separate evaluations over a week, and indeed, he showed no features suggesting an Alzheimer's condition. He did not have conventional features of dementia with impairments of memory itself.

Jim remembered with relief my words at that time in June:
My suspicion, Jim, is that underlying all of this, you do not have Alzheimer's disease. You have what we call "depressive pseudo-dementia."

What's that, Doctor, and how do you know I don't have Alzheimer's?
That's two questions.
Let's look first at what pseudo-dementia is, and then we'll link it briefly with the frameworks of understanding Alzheimer's.

So we did this. I had explained:
Pseudo-dementia is a condition which looks much like conventional Alzheimer's disease. It's commonly missed because, at times, doctors are unaware that it exists.
In fact, I have an important practical rule: I regard people with early signs of deterioration in thinking as having an underlying depressive condition because they may well respond to antidepressant medications.

How come?
Imagine the brain as a human computer with storage capacity. Let us say the brain needs only a thousand gigabytes (1000 GB) to function, yet most people have plenty of reserve with a total of, say, 2000 GB. As people progress in age, they may have less reserve dropping to 1500 or even 1300 GB, but they still perform as well as ever as they only need 1000. Then they become depressed and the computer that is their brain functions poorly, at say, only 70% efficiency. So even though they, in theory, are okay with 1300 GB, with the lowered efficiency of 70% function, they drop below the critical level of 1000.

Suddenly, they start noticing that they are impaired. They think they have Alzheimer's disease. The previous latent intellectual compromise with the added depression leads to impairments which look like Alzheimer's. You can imagine the vicious cycle that results.

What vicious cycle, Doctor?
More frustration; more stress; worse functioning. This aggravates the stress and may cause a further drop to 60% functioning. Something else happens. As the depression progresses, more worry and agitation requires even more compensatory functioning. 1000 GB is not enough for someone under stress; 1100 is needed because there is more stress to cope with. But by this stage the patient only has 800 as the brain is functioning at less than half-pace. More impairment results: The patient can't concentrate and worries even more, and the vicious cycle continues. Apparently, this is why, Jim, you have been labeled with a possible dementia condition. We must break the vicious cycle.

But how do we know that I don't have dementia?
We cannot know for certain until we observe the progress of the condition. However, there are several elements supporting pseudodementia. Clinically, your depression is in proportion to your impairment of higher brain function. In real Alzheimer's, the most common of the dementing conditions of the elderly, we should see more memory and intellectual deterioration compared with the emotional depression. Also, studies of your brain are reasonable: We looked at the anatomy of your brain by performing a MRI–magnetic resonance imaging–of the head. We found that there was minor loss of brain cells and that the ventricles–the central brain watershed that houses the cerebrospinal fluid–might have been minimally larger than they should have been for somebody age 50; but both these findings are fine for somebody aged 75, like you are. If you had Alzheimer's disease, Jim, we would likely (but not always) see marked cell loss with enlarged ventricles on MRI.

Anything else?
Yes, Jim. You have a previous history, family history and the clinical symptoms of a biological depression. These are positive symptoms supporting the diagnosis of depression as opposed to Alzheimer's disease:
The major condition that needs to be treated is your real depression. Given your previous side-effects on the tricyclics, we will start you on one of the newer antidepressants. You have a family history of a brother and an aunt who have done well with Paxil. Consequently, I have chosen Paxil for you.

I had looked at Jim with some pleasure. True, here was a beloved mind with a depression that was compromising brain function. Yet there was no need to cry. We could act, and he could get better.

And now Jim was back in the present, in December.
Doctor, with the Paxil not working, what drugs are available for me?

There are twenty-one different antidepressant drugs marketed in the United States.[61]

Could we look at them, briefly, one by one?
Yes, let's start at the beginning. It's a lengthy and complex story.

I'm ready to begin, Doctor. I need a perspective on medications that could help me, and to feel informed about your eventual medication choice.
You will be, but understand that this whole area of antidepressants is very complex. We'll approach it historically, gradually approaching the most recent advances.

Andrew, Jim and I launched upon a lengthy discussion, both theoretical and practical, of the **history of antidepressants**, all the way through to the present. We distinguished the slowed depressive from the anxious one. We concluded with a discussion of what may be the ideal antidepressant when applying the metaphor of the bathtub.

I began by answering Jim's question broadly.
If we analyze them from a historical perspective, there were several transitions: The early MAOI phase; the tricyclic age; the post-tricyclic era; the SSRI revolution; and what to me is the current phase: the post-SSRI period.
So there have been different antidepressant fashions or ages?
Exactly. When we look at these ages, we pay homage to the early antidepressant ages—the 1950s and 1960s. The medications at those times are not only still used today, but also created an atmosphere for research on newer, even more useful drugs.

What were some of these early antidepressants?
First, came the monoamine oxidase inhibitors (the MAOIs) in the 1950s: drugs like Parnate, and later Nardil, and Marplan, which is no longer available.[62] We still use these MAOI drugs in the atypical depression patients. The problem is their side-effects of potentially causing a stroke by occasionally raising the blood pressure enormously when people eat foods such as cheddar cheese, which contains the chemical tyramine.

What drugs were making the real impact, given that the MAOIs were dangerous?
The first major impacts were made by the family of tricyclic antidepressants. These still remain the standards to which we compare all other antidepressants. They include drugs such as the two major bastions amitriptyline (Elavil) and imipramine (Tofranil), as well as nortriptyline,

desipramine, doxepin, clomipramine, trimipramine and protriptyline. These drugs are the foundation for the management of depression. Even today, we do not have any antidepressants that are more potent than the tricyclics. We use them as a standard to demonstrate in the double-blind studies whether any new, experimental antidepressants are equal to them in how well they work in depression. None are more efficacious than the tricyclics.

Why did the tricyclics work?
The tricyclics acted as antidepressants because of their special actions. I like to use an analogy of two major "bathtubs": one filled with the neurotransmitter serotonin and the other with a second neurotransmitter called norepinephrine. Five years after we had prescribed a tricyclic like imipramine for depression, it was still working well.

Jim reached for the past.
They worked for me.
Yes. You'll remember, Jim, how you took a small maintenance dose of 25 mg of Elavil for eighteen years, and your depression was under control all that time without any loss of therapeutic effect.
Yes, I remember. And then when the newer drugs were developed, I took others, the latest being the Paxil. And now, Doctor, my Paxil stopped working after only six months!
Right! That may be because it has only one bathtub, serotonin, not norepinephrine; but we're jumping the gun.
The attempt to use the newer antidepressant drugs was not therefore an attempt at raising the efficacy of the earlier antidepressants; it was an attempt at diminishing their so-called "anticholinergic" side-effects.

Do you remember why you went off the Elavil, Jim?
I do. There were minor side-effects like "Doctor, my mouth is dry," and "I cannot read because of the blurring," and "My memory is not so good." Even worse when my dose had increased one time during a period of stress, a big problem arose: "I cannot pass urine." But I must admit these effects included sedation and that actually helped. I remember explaining: "I've had an uninterrupted night's sleep!"

Do you remember any other side-effects to the Elavil, Jim?
Yes, I remember once after only three weeks on it. I think I was taking about 150 mg a day for depression. I began to feel fantastic, and I jumped up out of bed, only to feel dizzy—my doctor at the time told me my blood pressure dropped on standing up because of some blockage of ... I forget.
Technically, Jim, its called "hypotensive tachycardia due to the alpha-adrenergic blockade associated with the tricyclics." Don't worry about the

big words, but we still see this side-effect today with drugs like trazodone, Serzone, Remeron and the tricyclics.

I know the main reason I was taken off the tricyclics was safety.
Very likely. Your urinary retention episode was unpleasant. However, the second major side-effect of the tricyclics, which you didn't have, is cardiac. The heart occasionally became irregular due to conductive abnormalities, but this potential was particularly relevant as the depressed patient could potentially overdose.

Did this prompt the new antidepressants?
In effect, yes. It was elimination of these adverse effects that motivated development of the newer antidepressants: The newer drugs are not more effective in treating the depression than the tricyclics. The difference was their side-effects; the newer drugs tried to eliminate the anticholinergic and cardiotoxic side-effects.

So what happened next?
The next stage was finding drugs with much less cardiotoxicity and also little anticholinergic side-effects: The 1980s saw the development of the "heterocyclic non-tricyclic drugs"—what I call the "post-tricyclic era". This consists of several different groups of drugs not commonly used today for depression itself, but which are interesting.

Were the tricyclics all bad?
No, they were certainly not all bad. The tricyclics were, and still are fantastic drugs. The major aspect of tricyclic antidepressants that's so impressive is that they maintain their effect. We have seen patients on tiny doses of tricyclic maintenance therapy for thirty years. During this whole period, the efficacy of the drug did not diminish.

The newer drugs have their own side-effects, don't they?
Certainly. For example, as you have experienced, some drugs sometimes don't work as well after a period of time.

But isn't there one more issue here? Cost?
You're right, Jim. Cost is a major issue. You must understand that the tricyclics are like good solid small cars. They take people where they want to go, and generally they work well. The newer antidepressants are the luxury vehicles. They also take you where you want to go and work well, but they cost much more.

Why do they cost more?
One reason they cost so much is that they are still patented—there are no generics available. This means there's no competition and makes them

more expensive. This cost issue is relevant. Many patients at times abandon their medication because they cannot afford trade name drugs.

Surely, Doctor, the newer drugs are better?

Yes and no. The newer drugs are often better, but we should be cognizant that, besides being more expensive, they have their own side-effects as well. Moreover, we don't have thirty years of experience with them. But you should always understand there are not only direct costs of a medication, but indirect savings sometimes: a day saved from hospitalization may allow a year's prescription of drugs. A real issue is therefore whether or not patients will be hospitalized. Or if they were in the hospital, will it even be one day less? The costs incurred by one day of hospital stay may be equivalent to approximately six months of treatment as an outpatient on the new drug. Consequently, any minor subtle change which increases the quality of the patient's life is of enormous relevance.

It's not only an issue of hospitalization, but of functionality. If somebody is able to be third, as opposed to 780th, in his company because he's taking one of these newer drugs, can we measure this in terms of cost? Probably not.

So the newer drugs may ultimately be a cost saving?

Yes. The newer drugs came out not because they were more efficacious, but because they had less side-effects—those horrible anticholinergic side-effects we mentioned, such as difficulty passing urine, constipation, memory impairment, and blurring of vision. Also, the tricyclic drugs could potentially cause irregularities in heart rhythm, particularly in high dosage. These new drugs therefore can save money, but even more so they can also save lives.

Tricyclic drugs acted on many different levels. Is that right?

Right. The levels actually relate to chemicals called neurotransmitters. Suddenly, with modern "receptorology"—studies of neurotransmitters—we've become aware that we were using "polypharmacy"—literally, multiple chemicals—all the time even when we were prescribing one drug. That's a major admission, because for many years polypharmacy was regarded as "that dirty word", and now we find we were using "dirty drugs" all the time.

How so?

Because these tricyclic drugs act on several neurotransmitters: serotonin, norepinephrine, histamine, acetylcholine and the quinidine-like receptors in the heart. You can imagine each of these neurotransmitters has effects and side-effects—perceive each as being a series of bathtubs, each requiring the correct temperature and level.

So the newer drugs are better in this respect? They act only on one receptor?

Unfortunately not. In effect, we're using combination polypharmacy with virtually every psychiatric drug.

Any exceptions?

Only buspirone (BuSpar) of our common psychiatric drugs works exclusively on one receptor subtype in therapeutic doses: It acts on serotonin-1A. All the other drugs are multiple receptor subtype drugs.

Andrew, now a young physician, had listened in silence. He addressed Jim briefly.

Jim, you asked for a historical perspective on this. Do you mind if I proceed?

Jim nodded. Andrew then turned to me.

And so the post-tricyclic era came about?

Indeed. This era, from the mid 1970s, is epitomized by one of the earliest of that group, trazodone (Desyrel), which has as its major action, serotonin-2 blockade. This receptor action causes its own side-effects, sedation. In fact, our major use today of trazodone is for its side-effect: We use it as a sleep inducing agent, a hypnotic. Strangely, another drug that best belongs in this group is the latest marketed USA antidepressant, mirtazapine (Remeron). This acts on several receptors and is therefore a lesson in analyzing clinical impacts based on particular receptors.

Could you illustrate that?

Yes. Possibly Remeron's most powerful effect is as an antihistamine and it therefore causes weight gain as well as sedation. The latter is accentuated by its added serotonin-2 blockade. A special quality it has is called "alpha 2 adrenergic effect": some say this is how its antidepressant effect works. It's also antinauseant due to a serotonin-3 blockade effect. A problem unrelated to neurotransmitters is that it has been linked with bone-marrow depression effects, but fortunately, this is rare. Thus, Remeron is a prototype new heterogeneous non-tricyclic drug. It has no re-uptake inhibition—in other words, it doesn't raise the bathtub levels.

Any other drugs of this particular era?

Squeezed historically between trazodone and Remeron, we saw several drugs, such as nomifensine, which were discontinued because of dangerous side-effects. Still others, such as mianserin, were not marketed in the USA, but were sold overseas. This drug is interesting as it has four rings in its structure, not the three that we see with tricyclics, and, therefore, it's similar to another major drug in this non-tricyclic class, maprotiline.

How so?

Ludiomil acts predominantly on norepinephrine, but produces significant weight gain. To round out this heterogeneous post-tricyclic era group is another unique agent, amoxapine. This drug blocks dopamine, and has broad serotonin and norepinephrine actions. This implies a theoretical risk of tardive dyskinesia—that dopamine movement condition—but it could also potentially have antipsychotic effects.

How do we summarize this post-tricyclic era?
It was one of transition. For me none of the drugs in this group are the major players in treating depression today.

A*nd then what happened?*
> I turned directly to face Jim. I did not want to lose his participation.

Jim, do you follow so far?
Yes, I do. I recognize many of these drugs. But it's gratifying to get a historical perspective.
Then came the whole new major era of the selective serotonin re-uptake inhibitors—the SSRIs. This includes your current antidepressant, paroxetine (Paxil), Jim. Others in the SSRI class are sertraline (Zoloft), fluoxetine (Prozac) and fluvoxamine (Luvox). These antidepressants were different because of their serotonin as opposed to norepinephrine specificity—they only have a serotonin bathtub.

But don't the other drugs also raise up serotonin?
You're correct, Jim. In fact, fifteen of the twenty-one current antidepressants, including these four SSRIs, act at least in part by the mechanism called serotonin re-uptake inhibition.

What's that?
You remember our boat metaphor? Re-uptake inhibition means preventing the passengers in the serotonin boat that's moored at the pier from leaving the boat permanently. Although they cannot officially disembark, they are at least allowed to go onto the pier. Whenever they go across to the pier they walk through the pier turnstile: The space between boat and pier is the synaptic cleft, so each time they climb onto the pier they stimulate the receptor. They repeat this repetitively, and each time they do so, the turnstile—receptor stimulation—registers one more hit.

What's special about the SSRIs in this model?
Two aspects. Firstly, the four SSRIs act *pharmacologically* by raising up serotonin levels powerfully.
This implies that in their usual prescribed doses, the patient probably receives far more than he or she needs—the passenger turnstile counter goes to thousands when it only needs hundreds.

Secondly, there are no norepinephrine piers with these SSRIs, only serotonin piers. The lack of a second pier mooring the norepinephrine boat may have caused your experience because this lack eventually created an imbalance.

What imbalance?
What seems to be a common complaint with the SSRIs: Six to nine months down the line, "Doctor, I was taking this drug and it was working, but it's no longer working!" The lack of a norepinephrine balance may have done that.

Jim perked up despite his sadness.

So what about the latest era. Doctor?
We're now witnessing the new era–I call it the post-SSRI era of heterogeneity: The SSRI era had one bathtub: a bathtub with serotonin, while this era looks also at the second bathtub, norepinephrine.
For example?
The first post-SSRI drug, bupropion (Wellbutrin), involved norepinephrine re-uptake inhibition alone. It's an interesting drug, because we didn't originally know how it worked. The drug is active, we now know, not because of the chemical bupropion itself, but through it's breakdown product, "hydroxybupropion" which acts as an irreversible norepinephrine re-uptake inhibitor drug, as opposed to selectively acting on serotonin.

And now?
We have now entered the era of the mid-1990s, and we could call this in depression research, the "post-SSRI era with SNRIs" epitomized by drugs that have the two critical bathtubs: *serotonin*–the S and *norepinephrine*–the N in SNRI. These drugs are selective for S and N. They don't have any other major bathtubs, so their side-effects are restricted to the two major antidepressant receptors, serotonin and norepinephrine.

What drugs fall into this category?
The two drugs in this group are venlafaxine (Effexor) and nefazodone (Serzone). They do not hammer the serotonin receptor as hard as the SSRIs, so they have less side-effects at that level. The two drugs are also different from each other because Serzone blocks components of both receptors and Effexor does not. This means Serzone is more sedative and Effexor is more activating.
Do these represent the state of the art?

Possibly. We are in the age where serotonin and norepinephrine are both specifically involved in re-uptake inhibition—raising the bathtub level—but without the original anticholinergic and cardiotoxic and antihistaminic consequences of the tricyclics.

How effective is this art?
Possibly less than we would hope. Overall, antidepressants work well only in about two-thirds or three-fourths of cases.

Why?
Maybe one reason is that studies in general have looked at major depression as a group instead of splitting the patients into two important groups: "retarded depression"—the slowed, apathetic, retarded movement depression—as compared with the "agitated depression"—the internal restlessness, marked anxiety type of depression. With the newer agents, the double-blind studies were generally done on all cases of biological depression against a standard tricyclic antidepressant, like imipramine. All these drugs are equal to the standard, but not better than the tricyclic, although they are, of course, better than placebo.

Is there a way to make these results better?
I suspect so. The conventional management of depression has been rather disappointing because many researchers and also clinicians have usually not differentiated whether an agitated depression or a retarded depression existed. To me, the most important choice of antidepressant is applying this major dichotomy: Is this depression in the agitated, anxious patient or is it in the slowed person?
For example?

> This time I turned to Doctor Andrew, but I made sure Jim
> still felt part of the conversation.

If you're going to give activating antidepressants like the SSRIs or bupropion or venlafaxine in a so-called agitated depression, where the patient is both anxious and depressed, you're at times potentially going to agitate the patient even more. This is not always so, however, because everyone is different and it probably is only true in maybe a third of such cases.

But...?
However, if you use these same activating drugs in a retarded depression, where the patient is slowed in behavior and thinking as well as depressed, you're going to activate the patient. This use would be logical.

Does the converse apply?

227

Of course. If you give more sedative antidepressants like trazodone, amitriptyline or nefazodone, or tricyclics like amitriptyline, imipramine and trimipramine in retarded depression, you might slow the patient even more, which you don't want to do, but you would use these drugs in an agitated depressed patient. [63]

So in summary?
The retarded depressive patient maybe should be receiving activating antidepressants, such as Effexor or the SSRIs or desipramine. The agitated depressive, on the other hand, should be receiving sedating antidepressants, such as Serzone, trazodone or Remeron or amongst the tricyclics, Elavil or Tofranil.

How much do these rules apply?
They're general rules, always with exceptions. For example, the more activating antidepressants sometimes produce paradoxical sedation—maybe about one in every seven people respond with sleepiness; so we see activation usually, but sometimes some sedation. If you find a drug sedates you, take it at night, and if it activates you take it in the morning.

Andrew then asked an important question reflecting a strange research status.
You mentioned the newer antidepressants were compared double-blind with tricyclics. In what kind of depression?
Congratulations, Andrew: I suspect by the twinkle in your eye, you've detected an odd trend. The antidepressant drugs were generally studied in *major depression*, which implies the biological form of depression, yet generally they're approved by the FDA for *all kinds* of depression. So we find that patients with many other varieties of depression, like the common neurotic depressive—reactive depression which is now called dysthymic disorder—as well as the depressive with schizoaffective disorder or bipolar disorder, may be using drugs studied specifically in a different kind of depression. We seldom find niches where these drugs have been specifically studied and approved for these specific indications.

But is it purely serotonin that affects all these amazing functions?
No, Andrew. We cannot talk about serotonin as if it occurs in isolation from the rest of the neurotransmitters. Clearly, ongoing bodily adaptation occurs all the time through feedback loops, reinforcements of certain behaviors, and automatic processes.

It all sounds extremely complicated?
It is. Many links to biochemical adaptation happen. Improvements occur in those first two weeks, but it takes longer, certainly many weeks, for people to feel totally well, not fatigued and not out of sync. A great deal

228

of chemistry and physiology is ultimately involved. This goes against the grain of the demands we as physicians feel to make our patients better with the "quick fix".

Jim had been listening carefully.
Why do some people readjust quicker than others?
Possibly their systems adapt quicker. We can use the parallel of eating. Some people are stable in their weight despite enormous variations in eating habits. Incidentally, eating and weight are also regulated through serotonin.

So you take into account these biological rhythms with your medication prescriptions, Doctor?
I try to. I far prefer medications that will normalize and stabilize psycho-physiological rhythms; these will, therefore, to some degree give the person the opportunity, after a period of time, to restabilize.
Most rhythms that are in any way destabilized take several months to re-stabilize, which is one of the reasons that antidepressants take several weeks to kick in. I believe it has nothing to do with the antidepressant, it has to do with your rhythms. Three weeks is just the beginning, because then you've established a foothold of stability, but down the line, maybe several months later you'll have even greater stability.

How long then should I take the antidepressants?
When we decide to use an antidepressant, we have to be aware that if we don't use it for at least four months, and probably six months, we will in-crease the incidence of relapse quite considerably. If we have someone like you, Jim, who has had two or more episodes of depression in less than ten years, it's likely that we ought to use lifelong treatment, based on the statistic of 80-90% chance of relapse. That's why you've taken medi-cation these last twenty plus years.

Andrew was clearly intrigued. His well of questions was far from dry.
When should a patient ever begin to taper?
After about six months, one's risk of relapsing into a depression, for ex-ample, is less than if one had been taking that medication only for shorter periods. Only then should you contemplate tapering, if this were a first episode of depression.

Does this apply also to benzodiazepines, such as Xanax, which can be used in anxiety?
Not really. I like drugs that allow appropriate body adaptation so this is one cogent reason why I do not like to prescribe drugs such as Xanax for

prolonged periods as the body does not adapt as physiologically as it does for the antidepressants. When they are prescribed, we often see a withdrawal cluster of symptoms, sometimes over weeks. This is not surprising because these drugs work chemically in an entirely different way. Xanax and all other benzodiazepines work mainly through an entirely different and compound combination receptor, the subtypes of what's called the "GABA–chloride ionophore–benzodiazepine receptor complex".

So it's not through serotonin?
Only indirectly. As with all drugs, benzodiazepines certainly have connecting feedback pipes.

Andrew finally appeared in his element. He began to ask the questions he had been curious about for years.
How does the regulation by serotonin work?
Serotonin's tonic regulation of behavior, physiology and of psychological function occurs mainly because "conversations" occur between the serotonin receptor subtypes so that numerous controls occur to maintain appropriate chemical levels.

What's common to these serotonin receptor subtypes?
Simply this: If you take one drop of the chemical serotonin and put it over a receptor subtype, you're going to get a response. But that response can be anything; it might be increase or it might be decrease. Every one of these receptors has its own special organization. In fact, these serotonin receptor subtypes are so unique that there's a particular "genomic clone"–a specific complex chemical genetic DNA code–that will manufacture each receptor subtype. This produces a consistent physiology–the way it works, pharmacology–the way it interacts with drugs, and anatomy–the localization in the brain. This allows us to apply principles. Consequently, serotonin-1 receptors are broadly similar but different from serotonin-2 receptors. Similarly, a subtype of serotonin-1 called serotonin-1A receptor is different from the serotonin-1B receptor, but closer in its properties to this 1B than to another family like the serotonin-2 group.

Do these different receptor subtypes work with and against each other?
Indeed, they do. One controls the other. The technical term, in fact, is "cross-talk".
For example?
Serotonin-1A talks to serotonin-2A, in a special way. They have an inverse relationship with each other. Thus, the effects resulting when serotonin-1A–the "captain" of the team–stimulates (technically acting as an

"agonist"), is roughly equivalent to serotonin-2A—the "quarterback"—inhibiting (technically acting as an "antagonist").

Vice versa also applies?
Yes: antagonism at 1A is roughly equivalent to agonism at 2A.

> Even Jim seemed interested despite the conversation becoming more complex. Reassurance was necessary.

Jim, you may not follow all the technicalities about serotonin, bathtubs and cross-talk, but do not worry. These are areas even physicians have difficulties with. So whatever you glean here can be an advantage. You're welcome to sit in as I talk to Andrew about these matters.

I'd like that, Doctor, because after all these years of depression, whatever I glean could be useful.

> I turned to Andrew who was ready to continue the discussion.

Do you have a practical example of the 2A quarterback acting as an antagonist?
You're getting the terminology right, Andrew. Yes, I can give an illustrative example, but with a pharmacologically "dirty" drug, trazodone. This is because we don't have any "clean" drugs acting purely on the serotonin-2A—or simply the serotonin-2—receptor. Like almost all our psychiatric drugs, trazodone acts on multiple receptors. I choose it in this example because the major receptor that trazodone antagonizes is serotonin-2. This drug is marketed as an antidepressant, and has some anti-aggressive effects in some studies, and it also relieves anxiety.

So that's serotonin-2. What about serotonin-1A? Is it the opposite?
To some degree it is: We have said that BuSpar is the only commonly used "clean" drug in psychiatry. This means that pharmacologically, at the usual therapeutic doses, the drug acts specifically on one receptor subtype. Its action at this level is partly stimulating serotonin-1A—partial agonism. BuSpar is marketed for its anti-anxiety effects—what I like to call its "anxioselectivity" because this occurs by gradual modulation over several weeks. It also has mild antidepressant effects and a potent anti-aggressive effect.

Are there opposite effects?
Exactly. You can see the reciprocity: 1A stimulation is the same as 2A inhibition in relation to anxiety, depression and aggression. So we see how some impacts are inverse between 1A and 2A.

Does this apply to all effects?

No. This is a simple model only. For example, an important clinical effect of serotonin-2A blockade is sedation: Trazodone is sometimes used as a hypnotic to induce sleep.

But isn't it sedative because it's an antihistamine?
I don't think so. This is often incorrectly stated in books. Trazodone is only a weak antihistamine; the sedation is directly related to its 2A blockade.

Now does serotonin-1A cause sedation?
No. This is why the reciprocity theory is simplistic. Serotonin-1A agonism does not produce sedation at all. So BuSpar seldom causes problems with sleepiness. On the other hand, it has other effects: An anti-impulsivity effect and, I suspect, a mood stabilizing effect. Sometimes, cross-talk conversations do not occur between specific neurotransmitters, but there are often impacts through other regulation means.
Like passengers walking into the town from the boat?
Exactly.

Andrew was encouraged. He lifted his left hand vertically into the air. It was an act that corresponded with a sudden flash of knowledge. He had integrated his lesson.
I think we can apply this to the paradoxical effects of the SSRIs.
And I think you're right, Andrew! From a side-effect perspective, we can now understand why the SSRIs usually relieve anxiety and yet in other patients, possibly a third, cause anxiety-like symptoms. This is really strange, since the SSRIs are sometimes used to treat anxiety. In the one instance, serotonin-1A has been raised: anti-anxiety effect; serotonin-2A raised, however, would produce a pro-anxiety effect.

Theoretically?
In theory, through the inverse relationship of some of these receptors, we can see the potential for paradoxical results like anxiety or anti-anxiety effects arising depending on levels in each receptor subtype bathtub.

But aren't the SSRIs by definition "selective"?
No, the so-called *"selective serotonin re-uptake inhibitor"* drugs—SSRIs—are actually "non-selective" for serotonin as they apparently impact relatively non-specifically on all the different fifteen serotonin receptors. There may be subtle differences, but these are unexplored.

Why then are they called "selective" if they're non-selective?
SSRIs are selective for the neurotransmitter, serotonin, when compared with other transmitters like norepinephrine, dopamine, acetylcholine and

the opioid receptor. They're not selective within the subtypes of the neurotransmitter, serotonin.

Are there connections to these other receptors, too?

Very much so. There are pipes connected up chemically right across the whole network, across receptor subtypes and across receptor families, all talking to each other. We have an internet of fibers, a network of communication, and a string of service providers. There are also incidentally smaller electrical impacts across the individual cells or nerve pipes (axons) and nerve junctions (synapses).

I turned towards Jim.

What other symptoms do you have, Jim?

I must tell you, one of the problems with the Paxil was it helped my depression, but particularly now I feel so agitated. It's like my blood is boiling and I just want to shout, but I don't.

From examining Jim, he indeed showed features of increased anxiety with a fast pulse and dilated pupils, and he was sweating.

It could be, Jim, a medication side-effect relating to anxiety, but this is unlikely given that you've taken the Paxil for so long. Alternatively, it could be that you had an agitated depression, in which case the Paxil was not as good a choice as a more sedating antidepressant.

Andrew was keen to know more.

Could you give an example of how you can apply this to the bathtub that you previously spoke about?

You're spot on. I think this is the best way to understand depression management.

So there's a bathtub model for depression?

Yes, there is. I developed one as a useful metaphor to understand such areas as depression, anxiety and receptor interactions. If we look at our single bathtub, we would say, "depression is a serotonin-deficiency disease."

How do we know that it's a so-called "deficit" disease?

We apply our principles of antidepressants. Most marketed antidepressants in the United States work at least in part by raising the levels of serotonin in one way or another. Moreover, there are complex models to demonstrate this in animals. So serotonin deficiency is depression in our bathtub. However, there are other complex models showing serotonin excess is linked with anxiety.

Andrew was beaming.

In our bathtub, then, it could make perfect sense. We prescribe an SSRI, we raise the serotonin level, and 25% or 30% of the time, the patient becomes anxious.

It makes perfect sense, sometimes, but mostly no sense at all.

Why?

Because about 80% of patients with depression have coexistent anxiety, and about one-third of patients with anxiety have coexistent depression.

How come the difference in incidence?

Anxiety is more common and yet less diagnosed than depression when the two exist together.

But how can we have depression and anxiety coexisting in the same patient at the same time, if the one is deficiency and the other is excess?

Aha! We have already said why. We have fifteen different bathtubs all connected up, and for some maybe we need a deficiency, and in others maybe we need an excess. The two most important of these fifteen serotonin receptors in psychiatry are the major—1A and the quarterback—2A. Analyzing their effects we see they're almost opposites: Serotonin-2A agonism will produce anxiety, but serotonin-1A agonism will produce an anti-anxiety effect. Certainly that's one component of the explanation.

Are there other metaphors in your bathtub analogy?

Yes, indeed! But I'm going to introduce you to another one in the context of a single serotonin bathtub. You already understand this is a simplification because actually fifteen or more serotonin subreceptor tubs are connected by pipes to each other.

Why do you bother to have a single tub analogy, anyway? Why not use fifteen tubs?

Because our antidepressants generally have not become specific to single receptor subtype bathtubs when it comes to raising up the level. They raise them all, as though, practically speaking, there were only one tub. So it's not me. It's our drugs.

So then why bother to talk about subtype tubs?

Good retort! But you've seen when it comes to inhibition—antagonism—that there's some specificity, like serotonin-2A. Moreover, drugs like buspirone are specific in relation to agonism. Also, understanding that there's more out there allows us to appreciate specific therapeutic hypotheses and practical side-effects.

What other metaphor in the bathtub is important?

I have a low level of water in the bathtub, and I climb into my bathtub, but I jump right out: It's boiling hot! Those receptors are too hot—they're "up-regulated" and this doesn't depend on the height of water in the bathtub. Or, alternatively, I put in more water. I raise the level in the bathtub to a good high level, I climb in and "it's ice-cold!" Those receptors are "down-regulated".

And clinically this translates to what?
We have two frameworks here—quantity and temperature. The parallel of level is the number of serotonin receptors in the bathtub—we can refer to this as "sensitivity": too much would be supersensitivity, too little "subsensitivity".
I see. The level is the metaphor for number of receptors—sensitivity?
Correct; and the metaphor for temperature is the degree of serotonin receptor responsiveness—"up or down-regulation". Metaphorically, the temperature could be ice-cold with too much down-regulation or there could be up-regulated hot bathtubs if all the receptors are responding to their maximum to any stimulation.

W e had been enjoying bathing in the tub. Jim pulled us out, back to reality.
How can we apply this to me, the depressed patient?
Let us imagine you're in your bathtub and the bathtub score is 70—you're depressed. We want to fill it to the right level, to 100, so you can feel much, better—the normal level.
But when we gave you an SSRI like the Paxil you took, we didn't fill it to 100: Maybe it went up to 400 or maybe even 900! This is because, in fact, we're using what I called a "sledgehammer" drug—it's so powerful that it fills the bathtub too high. Sometimes in other areas of medicine, we use the phrase "pharmacological doses" as opposed to "physiologic doses". In this instance, the SSRI drugs—20 mg of fluoxetine, 30 mg of paroxetine, 50 mg of sertraline—seem to go well beyond the level that we need.

So the serotonin level goes too high in the brain?
Yes, and the brain says, "Hold on! I wanted some serotonin, but this is too much!"
What happens then?
The brain adapts, and the patient feels better. The brain adapts by cooling down the serotonin in the bathtub. Let's say the level in the bathtub is 70. We raise it say to 400 with our SSRI drug. The brain adapts by responding appropriately to the sledgehammers that are hitting its receptors. It responds only 25% and the appropriate adaptation produces a synaptic score of 100. When we multiply the level and the temperature, if there

235

are no side-effects and pure alleviation of depression, you can imagine the combination in the bathtub would make 100 "synaptic units" again.
Now how do we know this?
We don't for certain, but it seems likely: Pharmacologists recognize this diminished response by the brain and call this mechanism "down-regulation" of the serotonin receptor. I believe it to be an adaptation to too high a serotonin level produced by the antidepressant. This explanation is historically important as this brain adaptation to excess chemical—down-regulation—takes several weeks to kick in. There was even a time when psychiatrists were thinking this was why antidepressants worked—the adaptation effect was interpreted as the cause of action.

Jim had quietly absorbed this information and surprised me with a very astute question.
This adaptation must be difficult for all these receptor subtype bathtubs to be almost exactly spot on, right?
I believe so; and sometimes in some patients, they're not always exactly spot on. This is why we sometimes see different side-effects in different people taking the same dose of the same medication and why therapeutic results may be inconsistent.

So the object is to provide the correct amount, not the most amount?
Excellent! Increasing serotonin is not the goal. It's not too much that you want. What you want is the right amount. More is usually not better. Correct amounts are always best.

I could see where Jim's questions were leading.
Is that what happens to me sexually, Doctor? Even without the Paxil I still had no real sexual interest because I was sad, but at least when it was initiated before the Paxil, I felt something. I knew this was partly linked up with worry about performing.
And once you started worrying more about it, the tougher it became.
Exactly.
So, from that point of view, it's not easy, but it's psychological and not medication related.
But I got over that. Since the Paxil, even when I was well, it's nothing anytime, no interest, no feeling, Doctor; and this is distressing. Is it my receptor subtypes that are imbalanced?
Very likely. The problem is we don't yet know which receptor subtypes are specifically involved with sex.

Andrew added an excellent suggestion.
Logically, if we develop drugs that act not as sledgehammers, we could avoid some serotonin excesses in the bathtub?

236

Yes. We should avoid serotonin overblow so to say. Instead, we could use "chisels" maybe.

Chisels? That's a remarkable thought.

Yes. We push up the bathtub level to 100 or 110. Chisels do not have to rely on the brain appropriately adapting to a level of 400, as occurs with sledgehammers.

But are there such chisels?

Yes. There seem to be. This would imply a less potent drug, but one that does its job maybe more physiologically, raising the level to 100 or 110 rather than 400 or 1000.

> Jim was listening intently, even nodding at times. I addressed
> both Andrew and my, by now, highly erudite patient.

You'll notice, in practice, that the highly potent drugs generally are prescribed in single doses, like 20 mg of Paxil, probably because they have many times exceeded the 100 level they need.

Surely one solution would be tiny doses of SSRI like 10 mg of Prozac, not 20 mg?

You're on the right track, Andrew. Lower doses would theoretically be more physiological. However, that could possibly be as low as 1 mg of Prozac or Paxil, or say 2 mg of Zoloft. The introduction of some SSRI liquid formulations has been an important milestone.

Have we solved it then?

No. Unfortunately, because of the potency of these sledgehammers, as well as varying absorption through the stomach, and "first pass metabolism"—breakdown in the liver before even reaching the brain—these lower doses may vary quite markedly for people. Moreover, the studies in depression were done on much higher doses so we don't even know whether these lower doses would work and how the brain would respond.

What can we do instead?

This is why we spoke about the post-SSRI era. We can use antidepressants that are more chisels than sledgehammers.

So more physiological than pharmacological?

Maybe, that's a parallel. Chisels would bring the tub level to 100 or 110 not 400. So they should help the depression considerably, but with less potential to side-effects.

But would they be able to help in those conditions requiring a high level in the bathtub like 400?

Possibly not, because even in the highest doses, chisel drugs may not go beyond a level of say 150 in the bathtub.

Consequently, possibly in conditions like obsessive compulsive disorder, where the fashion is to use even higher doses of SSRI than in depression, these chisels would not work well.

Please, give me examples of chisels.
In my opinion, the two most important currently are Serzone and Effexor.

Are those weaker SSRIs?
No, they're not SSRIs at all. SSRIs are selective for serotonin. Both these drugs work on serotonin and norepinephrine bathtubs.

And they're chisels at both?
Serzone is. Effexor is and isn't: It causes nausea in lowish doses so it may be a sledgehammer in the serotonin-3 receptor bathtub, but otherwise it probably is a chisel based on its other dose-related side-effects.

So these less potent drugs raise the depth level only to 100 or 110, and by these means avoid the adjustments, the down-regulation, that the brain must make?
Theoretically, anyway.

What about the down side? Is there one?
Yes and no. There is another side: more work. Using such a lower potency drug—using a chisel—the dose would need to be adapted to the individual so patient and doctor must labor harder to use this lower potency drug. We actually have to work to adapt to the appropriate dose for each patient, but in this context, it's possibly more worthwhile, because we're taking into account a more physiological effect on the two major depression receptors—serotonin and norepinephrine.

It was the following day. Andrew arrived early, obviously excited.
I have another easier regulation model, Doctor.
Let's hear it.
We drink a cup of coffee. It's hot at the beginning and then we somehow adjust to the heat and it doesn't seem to feel so hot. The vocabulary that would describe the phenomenon of somehow adjusting to a dose of a medication would be the adaptation to the coffee or the down-regulation of the receptors—the response to the same amount is diminished. Using our bathtub parallel: We get used to the high level of the bathtub by feeling the water is colder. Our body is jerked into a new level of response.
You've got it! Adaptation is the essence of it all. But let's stick with our bathtub. We don't want too many metaphors!

Jim, too, had returned to complete his evaluation.

So what happened to me, Doctor?

Maybe, when you took the Paxil, an SSRI sledgehammer, we filled the bathtub to 400! The pharmacological dose of just 20 mg of paroxetine raised the bathtub well beyond the level that we needed.

Andrew was listening carefully to all this and could not resist quoting my metaphor again.

And the brain said, "Hold on! I wanted some serotonin, but this is too much!"

Right.

I turned to Jim.

The brain adapted appropriately for six months and you felt better. It cooled down the serotonin in your bathtub at several levels; maybe it didn't do a good job on the bathtub linked with sex: hence, your side-effect.

Did the brain use the mechanism of "down-regulation" of the serotonin receptor?

Exactly. There's an important component here. As I see this, it's a response to the antidepressant—to the overflow of the too high a level in the bathtub. This is not the mechanism of the antidepressant action, it's the consequence. For six months, your brain experienced the scenario, "*Doctor, I feel better.*" The brain appropriately adapted as it does in the great majority of patients,

But six months down the line it was no longer working and I felt depressed again.

Yes. Presumably something happened to this adaptation.

Is there a way that we can now treat this, Doctor, since the Paxil has started to lose its effect? Could it be that we could just increase the dose because I'm having another depressive episode?

But why did it happen now? If you were manic-depressive or gave a history of several previous discrete depressive episodes maybe I would do that. But you don't and the Paxil failed to hold you.

So do we look for another cause?

Yes. We did that. I checked you physically and with blood tests to see if there was a physical clue like an underactive thyroid. There wasn't. So this is not the solution.

Maybe we should try to readapt that brain model?

Andrew's interjection was spot on.

239

Yes. You have a knack for understanding what to do, Andrew.

Could it be the bathtub level is high, but maybe it's ice-cold; but I don't think so, because why now?

I addressed at both Jim and Andrew.

Let's look at the course of Jim's improvement for our answer. If the tub became ice-cold why now? It makes little sense because Jim did not require gradual higher doses early on. I think Jim's slide after six months had to do with the lack of another main receptor bathtub.

What do you mean?

I suspect Paxil stopped adapting because the Paxil worked only on the serotonin, not the other great depression bathtub.

Which one?

The norepinephrine bathtub that we know historically was so important. Tricyclics, like Tofranil and Elavil, worked on both receptors generally in non-sledgehammer, physiological doses. These drugs worked for years.

But Doctor, why did they seem to maintain their effects, but the Paxil didn't?

Because the Paxil was a sledgehammer only at the serotonin level with no compensation at the norepinephrine level, instead of acting as a chisel at both these neurotransmitters.

Should we use a tricyclic here?

We could, but then we will have all the tricyclic side-effects instead, like difficulty passing urine which in someone like you, with your large prostate, is not a good idea. So let's use a chisel and also a drug that acts on both serotonin and norepinephrine selectively.

Which means Serzone or Effexor?

Exactly. I'm going to choose nefazodone–Serzone–here.

Why?

Because, Jim, you have exhibited symptoms of agitation.

I turned to Andrew.

You'll remember Andrew, when we treat people with agitated depression, it's logical to use a more sedating antidepressant.

And that would mean Serzone?

Yes.

Why is it more sedating?

Because it has something special in its bathtub.

What's that?

It has a bath-plug.

A bath-plug?

240

Yes, possibly to let out the excess serotonin; this bath-plug is convenient.
How so?
The serotonin bath-plug is serotonin-2A blockade.

Wait a minute! If we get serotonin-2A blockade, this ought to lead to a profound anti-anxiety effect. That's good for the agitated patient.
Right.

And the serotonin-2A antagonism also would produce antidepressant effects?
Right.
And could it be anti-aggressive?
Theoretically, but that's unstudied.
So this would theoretically produce anti-anxiety and anti-depressant effects?
Exactly. In practice, we find Serzone effective in anxiety and agitation associated with depression.

But we ought to see somnolence—sleepiness—and some sedation from the 2A blockade?
Yes, this is a potential side-effect which occurs quite frequently, particularly as we give it in a twice daily dosage; but patients sleep better.

Surely adaptation to it occurs, using our physiological idea?
Generally, yes. People adapt to their hot coffee by it seeming a little cooler. Here, after several weeks, the sedation wears off.

Moreover, because its a chisel, we shouldn't see the serotonin excess effects that we see with SSRIs?
Correct. Its modulating effects imply far less side-effects such as agitation, anxiety, sexual-related pathology, headache and nausea—the typical SSRI effects reflecting presumed serotonin excess.

This approach provided the logical opportunity to teach Andrew more about choice of antidepressant drug. He already had a good solid background from his student and early residency days. My task was to consolidate this knowledge and add in a new twist—the concept of the **ideal antidepressant** using my bathtub analogy.

It sounds like the bathtub analogy could be used to produce a model for the ideal antidepressant, Doctor?
Yes, as I see it, the answer to this question can be applied by using the bathtub analogy.

We fill the bathtub a little, we drain it out a little. We control the temperature and the level: This implies chisels with the possible more exact control of dosage due to a lower potency drug. So chisels become the first principle in the ideal antidepressant model.

Just a serotonin chisel?
No. We would want bathtubs at the serotonin and norepinephrine level.
Like the serotonin-norepinephrine drugs?
Yes. Two bathtubs.
Which means the old ones like amitriptyline (Elavil), and the new, like nefazodone (Serzone), and venlafaxine (Effexor)?
Exactly.

Anything else?
It would be useful to have bath-plugs to let out excess neurotransmitter. A little up and a little down would provide an easier controlling balance when the patient's bathtub level is slightly exceeded. However, there is an important stipulation: the bath-plugs must be receptor-specific.
Why?
Because if they hit all the receptors they would just negate the uptake of the drug.
Which receptors?
Serotonin-2A blockade is perfect on the serotonin side. 2A antagonism is associated with antidepressant effects and also anti-anxiety effects and maybe even some anti-aggressive effects at the same time, with the side-effect of sedation, of course.

What about the norepinephrine side?
So-called alpha-adrenergic blockade is one possibility.
Why?
Because we don't want beta blockade. We see a problem in "beta-blockers".
What?
This drug group might produce depression in too high a dose.

Will the alpha effect be better?
It won't cause depression and that's the only option if we don't go beta. I don't see specific positives otherwise, because it just will produce more side-effects like dizziness due to low blood pressure.

Any particular alpha subtype?
No. It could be alpha 1 or 2. I just want as much specificity as possible for our bath-plug at the adrenergic level. So bath-plugs—selective blockade of receptors—are critical to this model as well.

Any other features?
Obviously, we do not want the side-effects of tricyclic antidepressants.
So?
The ideal antidepressant should be specific for norepinephrine and sero-
tonin, without the extra effects on acetylcholine, histamine and the heart
that the tricyclic antidepressants have.

Could you summarize?
As I see it, the ideal antidepressant should not be a potent sledgehammer
which will raise the level of the bathtub extremely high and have to rely
on the brain's natural adaptation, with possible loss of efficacy later. In
other words, single dose drugs, such as the SSRI sledgehammers, are not
ideal. Drugs that require dose adjustment and are much lower potency
drugs, the "chisels", are more logical.

What a hassle! It seems very elaborate.
Elaborate, yes; but not really a hassle. This attention to detail will help
your patient get better, Andrew. It requires the extra effort.

What will the chisel do?
It will raise our bathtub up to a metaphoric 100 or 110, where we're not
going to overflow the bathtub. If we go with the chisel route, our ideal
antidepressant would have several components. It would act on both serotonin and norepinephrine, but to an order of magnitude less than the
SSRIs. It would raise the level, but not too high. This should lower the
risk of side-effects and later lower the risk of receptor non-
responsiveness.

*But what should be the proportion of serotonin and norepinephrine in the
ideal drug?*
This is a hard one, but I think we ought to have a serotonin to
norepinephrine ratio of four to one, because most antidepressants have at
least some serotonin re-uptake inhibition effect. The impact on
norepinephrine is not as frequent, so maybe more serotonin is needed.

What about the bath-plug?
We have already spoken about a depression receptor-specific serotonin
bath-plug at the serotonin-2 level, and we have chosen an alpha adrenoreceptor bath-plug at that adrenergic level, the alpha 1 adrenoreceptor. We would want the same ratio of balance, serotonin-2A to alpha 1,
as we have with serotonin re-uptake inhibition to norepinephrine re-
uptake inhibition—so four to one.

What would this ideal antidepressant produce?

Theoretically, we would see a therapeutic effect usually, although not necessarily so, in obsessive-compulsive disorder, where we may need a very large bathtub.

And Andrew added, with confidence:
We would maintain the effect over time, we would have physiologic modulation with few or no extreme therapeutic results, and we would theoretically have a lower incidence of side-effects.
You're spot on, Andrew. You've learnt this lesson well.

Andrew smiled.
Which one is the best?
Well, clearly we need to go to the post-SSRI era drugs. Wellbutrin (or its breakdown product, hydroxybupropion) acts as a norepinephrine re-uptake inhibitor drug.
Then it's the opposite of Prozac—not on serotonin but on norepinephrine?
Roughly, since it's one single bathtub. However, because its dose adjusts, it's likely to be more of a chisel.

Back to the original question: what theoretically is an ideal antidepressant?
Well, Effexor comes close because it works selectively on both serotonin and norepinephrine, generally as a chisel. However, it does not have bath-plugs. In practice, this implies why we can use Effexor very effectively in the retarded depressive with their slowing which requires activation.

So it fails a little. Any others that pass your test?
Serzone comes close. If we look clinically at Serzone's profile of therapeutic effects and side-effects it's a chisel. Also, lab animal data on the dilution at which Serzone links up with the various receptors support the chisel theory. For example, Serzone is an order of magnitude less potent in serotonin re-uptake inhibition than the SSRI drug group. That confirms it is a chisel. Moreover, if we look theoretically at ratios of serotonin to norepinephrine, they appear in the right ballpark. All these elements make it the ideal antidepressant. It should encompass all of this, but ...
But?
But there's one added requirement, a rather obvious one.
What's that?
The bath-plug should be small in relation to the bathtub.
That goes without saying.
Yes, but strangely the drug nefazodone (Serzone) fills the ideal antidepressant model perfectly except for this requirement.

What do you mean?
Its major effect is its bath-plug at the serotonin level.

How come?
If we look at the proportion of serotonin-2 blockade to its degree of se-rotonin re-uptake inhibition, we find the bath-plug is much bigger than the whole bathtub! So it fails there, but this failure may be an advantage in one subtype of depression.

What does that mean?
It means, in effect, that Serzone's predominant effect would be in patients who were agitated or anxious with depression as these are the ones who would need sedating antidepressant.

And does it have the side-effects of the tricyclic antidepressants?
No it doesn't, but then none of the newer antidepressants have much of the acetylcholine or antihistaminic effects of the tricyclics.
Except Remeron, which is potently antihistaminic, right?

Andrew certainly had passed his test!

Jim spoke up.
So you're giving me Serzone?
Yes, it fits our profile using the bathtub analogy of a chisel that acts on both serotonin and norepinephrine with bath-plugs. This means it would be my choice drug for your agitated depressive condition. I would have stayed with the Paxil had it been working, but it's not, so we will change you around from Paxil to Serzone.

We will stop the Paxil and start the Serzone?
Not quite. We need to taper you carefully and slowly off the Paxil. This is most important.
Why?
You can imagine that if you have a bathtub score of 400 on your Paxil, and you go off it suddenly or even within a week, your physiologic re-regulation will lag as it takes several weeks. You're putting yourself at major risk, because you're dropping the level to say 100 in that bathtub—the level Serzone will produce, and yet the bathtub may be very cool or ice-cold, it's only responding say 20% or 25%. The Serzone or other drug you go onto may raise or keep the level at 100, but with 25% re-sponse your overall bathtub score would be 25 synaptic units. You may become profoundly depressed or even suicidal under those circum-stances.

Why?
Because the bathtub will remain cold during the psychophysiologic re-adjustment which could take several weeks. Many people will find this is not a problem—their brains may adapt quickly—and they may or may not

245

be the same people who adapt quickly to jet lag: We don't know. But you're placing yourself at unnecessary risk if you go off the Paxil or any other SSRI too quickly.

What kind of risk?

You may become profoundly depressed. I believe you might also encounter the same side-effects as another patient would have when initiating SSRIs—nausea, agitation, anxiety, headache, insomnia or restlessness.

Why?

Because this balance of your fifteen different serotonin receptor subtypes has been disrupted. The only solution is to go slow. Whichever antidepressant you're changing to, taper the SSRI over a period of at least one month. I actually prefer three months and at times, I've even had patients taper over four to five months when they've been given high doses of SSRIs over long periods of time.

Andrew had the chance to demonstrate his knowledge.

Well, you obviously don't need to do it with Prozac (fluoxetine).

Why not?

Because fluoxetine and its active breakdown product, norfluoxetine, together have a half-life of three weeks. This means Prozac will do its own slow taper over months. So we don't need to worry.

It is true, Andrew, that Prozac and its active metabolite sit in the body for ages. This means a steady state level theoretically may take even three months. So it seems this would be an exception, but in practice it's not. Strangely enough, you still need to taper.

Why?

I'll give you two parallels in this regard. If you were giving Zoloft or Paxil every hour, you would taper it, right?

Andrew nodded.

Well, you're in effect giving Prozac like that, because, with its metabolite, its half-life could be something like 20 times longer than Zoloft or Paxil.

Wow!

But there's more. The second facet is that you're not dealing with interactions and drug breakdown—pharmacokinetics. You're dealing with pharmacodynamics—what's the drug doing at the receptor level and is the restabilization of the brain going on? Of course it is, and it's taking two, three or four weeks to fully kick in each time. If stopped immediately, the Prozac bathtub score may be 1000 the first week, 800 the second and 600 in the third week. Each one of these gradations takes a significant period of time for the brain to adapt its temperature upwards from ice-cold—10% responsive.

246

Should Jim wait before you add the Serzone till he's fully tapered off the Paxil?

No, no, no! This is an important error not to make. When you add in any new antidepressant, other than MAOIs which, of course, are contraindicated, you add it in immediately. You cannot wait three, four, five or six weeks: Jim is depressed. If you add in the antidepressant immediately at least you're assisting the new physiological restabilization.

> Jim nodded but looked uncertain. I gestured toward him, as if to invite a question. It came.

So why do we need to taper the Paxil? I want to make sure I understand.

Because the bathtub level is still extremely high and we're still requiring a physiologic readjustment over time. When changing over to any other antidepressant—other than another SSRI—the same would apply: Taper gradually and start the new drug immediately as if not on the SSRI at all.

How should I start the Serzone?

With nefazodone, add it in the same way as if there were no Paxil. Start with 50 mg twice a day and build up every fourth day by 50 mg unless you become sleepy or have other side-effects. Watch out for adverse reactions, but realize that strange effects may be more withdrawal from the SSRI than related to the Serzone.

Isn't tapering your philosophy, anyway?

Yes. I believe in physiological tapers, where we go very slowly, even if we think there's no need. The body has previously adapted to the changes in brain chemistry caused by most medications. We want to give the brain time to re-adapt. It's rather like going off coffee or cigarettes very slowly. We should treat our beloved mind kindly.

> Andrew smiled and showed that, although he was now a doctor in residency, his days of learning were not past.

Now, what would you do with the Serzone side-effect of sedation, presumably from serotonin-2A?

Sleepiness and fatigue can be a little problem, particularly when we give this drug at its recommended twice-a-day dose. It reminds me a little of a benzodiazepine action, as if they were on Xanax, since patients often don't mind the sedation, preferring the anxiety relief. Also, we have mentioned how they seem to attenuate to sedation over several weeks—you'll remember the jet lag analogy again.

But if it's a problem...?

If it's a problem, I give the drug predominantly at night. So, if they're on 300 mg a day of nefazodone–the average dose–I might give them 250 mg at night and 50 mg during the day.

What about the dizziness on Serzone?
Strangely, I do the same with this other side-effect of the bath-plug–an alpha-adrenergic blocking side-effect. This produces possible postural blood pressure drop, dizziness and sometimes a sense of confusion. Sometimes, I combine the Serzone and Effexor to establish the correct neurotransmitter balance. However, if I still want to go with Serzone without dropping the dose initially, this would be another time to use more drug at night. However, Serzone once daily might not last the whole day.

I turned to Jim.
In other words if you start feeling badly on the Serzone, it might be because your blood pressure has dropped. You have taken too much and then you will feel in bad shape. So Jim if this happens to you, stand up slowly from a lying down position. Remember, with chisel drugs, the side-effects are invariably worse with higher doses, and this is so with Serzone. So let's use this to track the dose. Jim, I don't want you to have side-effects if we can avoid it.

And, I assume, as with all the other antidepressants, we don't see abuse, dependence, addiction, tolerance or craving?
You're using the correct terminology, Jim. No antidepressants cause people to become addicted to them.

I looked Andrew straight in the eye inviting his participation, again.
Just one more question, Doctor. Are there any side-effects that we don't understand based on our knowledge of these receptors?
Yes, there are. No doubt we will comprehend them one day. There are several side-effects that we cannot easily explain yet using receptor subtypes. I mentioned the sexual problems on SSRIs that are linked with serotonin: We don't know the exact biochemical mechanism, but fortunately Serzone, if anything, assists sexual functioning.

Anything else?
Yes. We sometimes see dry mouth and constipation on many of these serotonin drugs and we always thought these were the anticholinergic effects of the tricyclics. We don't know where they come from, but maybe it's due to one of those other serotonin receptors–5 or 6 or 7.
Then there's tinnitus–buzzing in the ear. This sometimes happens with high doses of Serzone: again why is unknown, but by the time it occurs,

we know we ought to be dropping the dose; to me, this reflects pharmacological overdose.

I again turned towards Jim.
The most fascinating side-effect that we encounter with Serzone is a strange vision experience occurring maybe in one in ten patients. When shifting gaze from one point to another, you have the impression of not losing the previous image, so it can be distressing.

I gestured towards Jim, pointing out the back wall.
Jim, look at that picture over there of the lake. Shift to the picture hanging up—the portrait. On Serzone you may track all the way through. It feels almost like a visual hallucination experience. Don't be frightened by it if it happens. It's of no relevance. It just relates to a serotonin receptor in the retina: Again, we don't know which one. Instead... enjoy your technicolor! You can, because it's a rather benign symptom. If it happens to you, you may get used to it over time, or dropping the dose may also help.

How often do all these side-effects occur?
If we look at how much more often they occur than a placebo—a sugar tablet with no therapeutic value—we're not talking about major common effects. We're looking at about 1 in every 7 or even 1 in every 14 people depending on the symptom. Also, these side-effects are dose-related—lower doses produce less than higher amounts: You would expect that because of the chisel idea.

Anything else?
Yes. You've already understood a little about drug interactions. If you take grapefruit juice it's going to interfere with your Serzone.

Andrew was intrigued.
Why?
Because the nargin bioflavinoid in grapefruit juice competes and actually inhibits one of those P450 liver enzyme systems we spoke about, Andrew. In this case, it's the 3A3/4 system, and Serzone does the same—marked slowing of other compounds going through this system producing an accumulation of the drug and a higher amount in the body.

For example?
Xanax is an example: We sometimes halve its dose because its breakdown is slowed; the same happens with certain antihistamines like Seldane and Hismanal. In fact, Seldane was withdrawn because too high a dose could cause irregular and dangerous heartbeats—arrhythmias—and this could theoretically happen as a drug interaction. Actually, about a third of our

249

psychiatric drugs are broken down by 3A3/4, so these interactions are important.

And so Jim took his Serzone and tapered the Paxil.

I t was four months later. Jim had consulted me on several occasions during this period. We had been careful with regard to this Paxil taper, and we had built up his dose of Serzone to 250 mg twice a day. We had watched carefully for side-effects and, in fact, at one point, Jim was taking 550 mg a day, but developed the tinnitus—the buzzing in his ear. I had dropped his dose back, and it had appeared that he became stable. He was now off the Paxil for a month and had been on this stable dose of Serzone for six weeks. Jim's eyes beamed. It was not necessary to ask him how he was doing. I had seen this beautiful progression from a desperately depressed patient with no hope to a retired gentleman who was happy, sleeping, eating and yet maintaining a consistent weight. He was concentrating and focusing, and working well and hard at home on his own business.

It's fantastic, Doctor! I didn't make much of a fuss about it, this time when the Paxil stopped working, because it wasn't as bad as the previous time and I had been through it before. But now I can tell you. I thought my memory was gone for good and that I must have Alzheimer's even though you had tested me and told me I didn't. But I kept reading a note you had written for me about pseudo-dementia: I kept it in my pocket, so that I could reinforce to myself that I wasn't crazy. My memory is so good now, all that seems like something of the past!
That's wonderful, Jim!

Doctor, I have one other piece of good news.
And what's that?
You know, you might think I'm an old man, and I am. But I just want to tell you that, in some ways, I'm very young, and my wife and I enjoy each other twice a week, sometimes even more often.

I shared in Jim's happiness. One of the great pleasures of my practice is seeing the hopeless become hopeful, the impaired becoming functional, and the desperate reaching out to the world to participate and contribute—a crying beloved mind laughing instead.
Could Jim improve even more? His follow-up a year later was a resounding "yes": This was still more gratifying for me.

250

Chapter 10

The Deep Dark Pit

Chronic refractory depression.
Adjunctive antidepressant therapies:
anticonvulsants, benzodiazepines, lithium, thyroid,
estrogen, ECT, Visken, BuSpar, antipsychotics;
detailed pharmacological evaluation, hospitalization.
Effexor, Codeine, Prozac, Serzone.
(Katie); (bathtub analogy)

Don't do it, Katie! Don't do it!

She shook her head, as if coming out of some deep slumber. There it was, this twelve inch sharp bread knife, against her chest. Katie knew how it had got there. She remembered walking into the kitchen, seeing it there on the counter, picking it up and proceeding to try to stab herself. But why? She had no idea. She could not explain it. Lately, she had been feeling so much better, and yet, just moments before, she had tried to do this terrible act to herself. These past few days, Katie had felt so proud that she was finally improved, after only three or four days on this new antidepressant, fluoxetine–Prozac. She had been taking 20 mg and her mood had changed, the world had become a bright light and she was feeling happy. Just this morning when she took the Prozac, she realized that even the early morning sadness was much better.

And yet, now, this sudden change. If her husband had not awoken her out of this strange state where she had suddenly noticed this bread knife in her kitchen and become preoccupied with it, goodness knows: She might have killed herself.

This was the story that Katie related at our first meeting.
Doctor, what do you think caused it?
Could it have been this new medication?

I looked up and scratched my head. I truly did not want to answer this question. Yes indeed, I was worried that it had been the fluoxetine, the Prozac. But should I tell her this? For, she and others may lose perspective on one of the wonder drugs of the 1990s. I was going to say,
"Prozac is like New York: Wonderful, marvelous, exciting, but also sometimes with an unfortunate side," but I resisted the temptation.

The parallel of the extremes was something that I felt was highly relevant. Katie was not the first patient I had seen who had impulsively wanted to kill herself on the fluoxetine. The most distressing aspect to these patients was that, often, they were feeling much better; they had been on the drug for two, three, or four days, and with each day had felt brighter and less depressed. Then suddenly, almost impulsively, they had acted or wanted to act to cause deliberate self-injury.

I looked directly at Katie, smiled reassuringly and
replied:
Katie, you must understand that Prozac is a remarkable drug. It was one of the major advances in the pharmacology of depression. I believe, however, that many other drugs have now supplanted it. Because of this, I seldom choose it as my drug of choice unless I obtain a history of a previous dramatic response to the drug or a biological family member has done much better on fluoxetine compared with other agents. So I may consider Prozac under specific circumstances. In general, though, I don't, because I tend to want to go more physiologic.

You're avoiding my question, Doctor. What about this suicidal preoccupation that I suddenly experienced?
It's highly controversial. Some argue it's no more common than with the other antidepressant drugs: We know that there's a phase in the management of depression, where motivation may be activated before the mood is elevated. So patients might be energized enough to act out their sadness with a suicide attempt. We try to be careful in that regard. So, for example, if people feel agitated initially, we may restrict using an activating antidepressant, although, in most instances, such choices may make little difference.
But this has not happened to me before on other antidepressants.
So you're saying this was a new different experience?
Yes. I was feeling very good before the incident with the knife. Despite my depression, this is the first time I've tried to hurt myself. Isn't that different from what you're talking about?
Yes, you're quite right. What you describe is different. What I was talking about is the recovery phase of the depression, where drive is activated

252

maybe before mood, particularly with an activating antidepressant, and the patient might feel suicidal. You, on the other hand, were feeling excellent, even better than you had felt for many periods of your life. So this is different. An explanation that I have that would fit this framework is, maybe the Prozac was different: It worked too well in you.

Too well? What do you mean?
It raised the level of the serotonin in your metaphorical bathtub too high. It needed a level of only 100, not the 300 or 400 that the Prozac was producing. Then when you took an extra dose, this accumulated and the level went to 500 or 600, and the brain, in your instance, did not have time to adapt. Strangely, when some feel distressed by Prozac early on they describe an internal restlessness: "I'm climbing out of my skin!" Their bathtub level overflows. These people sometimes feel acutely agitated and may be at risk for self harm.

But I didn't feel that way. I felt fantastic this morning and yet tried to impulsively stab myself this afternoon.
Your experience is possibly another variant of the overflowing bathtub: maybe your bathtub boiled over acutely, producing an impulsive obsession. You did this only taking the Prozac?
Yes. That's right.
You know we have to be rather careful interpreting your impulsive suicidal attempt because there's such a detailed history of failure before.

Maybe this was just frustration?
Certainly not, Doctor! I was feeling better this morning. I acted on impulse!
That's important to know. Either it was or it wasn't the Prozac. It's almost impossible to separate out the changes that have gone on in your brain with everything that has happened to you before. However, clearly, you should not be taking this medication, because until I can prove otherwise, I must regard you as at further risk.
That seems logical, Doctor.

But please bear in mind that it does not mean to say that the great majority of people will be at the same kind of risk.
Yes, I know. My sister-in-law's best friend has been taking it for a couple of years now, and she's had no problems.
Many people swear by it. It has changed their lives; and yet, there are some, a minority, who describe strange reactions ranging from this suicidal behavior to unusual movements, like jerking. The problem is, we cannot easily delineate out that minority subpopulation. My suspicion is that the initial dose of 20 mg per day is too powerful: It filled up the level in your bathtub way past what was needed, and your brain did not have time to adjust.

Why would my brain not be able to adjust, whereas the brains of all these other people, like my sister-in-law's friend, had no problem adjusting?
Because people are biologically different. Some people over-adjust, in which case drugs stop working—their bathtub became ice-cold. Others like you may not adjust appropriately. Your bathtub remained hot. Consequently, let us look at alternatives.

But how are you going to choose an appropriate antidepressant for me?
Good question. First, we're going to go through all the usual procedures. We're going to take a detailed medical, neurological and psychiatric history, and see if we can tease out any facets that are relevant: any clues in your particular case. This is going to include looking at how members of family have responded to different medications and their particular course of illness, to see whether or not we're dealing with a genetic condition.
Well, that side's easy, Doctor. I was adopted so I don't have any genetic information. I don't know of a single biological relative.

What else are you going to do?
We're going to evaluate your previous responses in great detail, not only to all your different antidepressants, but to any of the psychiatric medications you have taken in the past. Also, we're going to look at any unusual responses to other medication you have taken, as well as non-prescribed agents, such as recreational drugs, like marijuana. All these will give us some perspective.

Ever alert, Andrew, now a physician involved in his neurology residency program, at this point interrupted:
In other words, you're going to take a detailed pharmacological history?
Right, Andrew. Ironically, this is often the most neglected part of the medical evaluation despite being the most important.
And after that?
Actually, before that! We look at the main complaint in a great deal of detail and try to understand what other symptoms may be relevant.

Anything else?
Yes. We will use the typical approach to psychiatric history-taking: For example, we will look at biographical data, beginning at day 1, at birth, and follow the history through childhood, adolescence and adulthood. We will try to understand any specific periods of trauma. If we feel it's necessary, we may also do some personality testing and maybe even look at particular checklists of psychiatric symptoms, so that we can obtain a full perspective.

We will take a detailed medical history to see whether there are any other causes for the depression and whether there are related symptoms like lowered resistance or headaches. These symptoms may also be occurring independently of the depression, but would still be important to know about. For example, the possibility of heart disease may eliminate several drugs, like the tricyclic antidepressants, which may heighten the risk of arrhythmias.

We will then do a detailed physical, neurological and mental status examination and do whatever blood tests, psychological evaluations and other investigations we deem necessary.

I turned to Katie.

After this comprehensive survey, we will be better able to assess your condition, Katie.

So this can take some time?

Yes. It may take several lengthy appointments depending on the complexity of what we're looking for. Thereafter, we will allocate some time to educating you about your condition and your treatment options.

Can we do this on one long day?

It would be remarkable if we could. However, it's not a good idea. Firstly, making several discrete appointments allows us to develop a time-based perspective which is often valuable. Secondly, such a time block allocation is generally impractical: besides anything else, the medical insurances are not generally set up to understand such lengthy appointments.

But what if nothing shows up on all these tests?

If that should happen, we would still have major clues. The fact that you did not have any specific medical condition gives us more opportunities to safely use different medications. We will know that we do not have to treat an underlying medical condition for you to get better. For example, if you had diabetes, unless we treated this underlying condition and you were stable in that regard, you might find that your depression is "refractory" or non-responsive to conventional antidepressant treatments. So we have to know that.

All the same, Doctor, how do negative findings help?

The fact that these findings are negative does not necessarily mean that we have no information. We can still put together the jigsaw puzzle that is the cluster of positive and negative features we have. This should enable us to make a diagnosis. By virtue of your not feeling well, the evaluation will yield positive results even if all the extra tests are in the normal range because we can exclude otherwise relevant information.

255

Katie nodded. It was clear that she understood. Task number one was to ensure that she went off the Prozac, and was adequately covered during this period of time. Task number two was to make a diagnosis and ensure appropriate treatment.

Katie, given what happened to you today, how do you feel about spending a short period of time in the hospital?
I don't know.
Do you really think it's necessary?
I don't particularly like to hospitalize people, but there's one major condition that requires hospitalization, and that's when people are a danger to themselves or to others. Now in your particular instance, you tried to kill yourself, which means you were a danger to yourself. You're looking so much better to me now, and yet, I know that you impulsively acted out. I believe it may be safer to put you in the hospital for a few days while we taper you down on your Prozac medication: as you have taken it only for days, we can do this quickly.

Andrew, always looking to learn more, asked:
But what about other indications to hospitalize psychiatrically beside a suicidal or a homicidal potential?
Some people find that they need to be hospitalized chronically—as in Alzheimer's—because they cannot care for themselves and others are unable to care for them. Then there are those who are out of touch with reality and require a safe haven. Sometimes, of course, patients are chronically suicidal over a period of years, and it's not easy to justify such lengthy hospitalization, nor is it logical, so that we must apply appropriate clinical judgment on this high-risk population.

So when do you hospitalize for short periods specifically?
At times, we hospitalize to make quick but important medication alterations, to give ECT, or to solve recreational drug problems under controlled conditions. Other times, we need to psychiatrically hospitalize as an emergency because the patient is becoming progressively out of touch or agitated. This kind of hospitalization is often to prevent unacceptable consequences in the community or to protect the patient from harm.
Finally, we sometimes need the controlled hospital conditions to make evaluations. Examples are sleep monitoring for sleep apnea, video monitoring of seizures or doing specialized blood tests requiring continuous or repeated monitoring, like measuring oxygenation in arteries.

And so Katie was hospitalized. The important rule in depression is to be safe, not sorry: If the patient is actively suicidal as a consequence of her depressive disorder, hospitalization is usually indicated.

We evaluated Katie in detail: No specific physical abnormalities; and she was healthy and functioning well, physically. However, she continued to exhibit the classic symptoms of major melancholic depression.

Doctor, you don't need to bother, really. It's hopeless. I know that everything out there is black. There's no help anywhere. I can't get better, almost as if I'm sick all over. I'm a nothing. I'm worth absolutely zilch, Doctor. There's no point trying to save me.

She exhibited the typical cognitive—thinking—features pertaining to depression. She felt like Joseph, thrown into a deep, dark pit, but her pit was eternal. She was in a bottomless, black hole that showed no exit for her, with time being lengthened and existence droning on.
She was also showing the typical classical symptoms of the "vegetative shift"—the biological features that go with a major melancholic depression:

I'm very sad. I cry a lot. It's worse in the early morning as I'm waking up. In fact, that's real early now, long before the sun comes up, maybe 4:30 in the morning. It lifts a little during the day, but I never feel well at all. I can't concentrate. I just can't focus on things. I have absolutely no energy.
What's worse? The concentration difficulty or the sadness?
The sadness is really the worse of the two. But it doesn't help to not be able to concentrate and to feel fatigued all day.
Invariably people who are depressed have problems with both, but find the sadness worse than the depression, as you do, Katie.
And yet at the same time I feel extremely agitated and anxious and restless and distressed. It's like a burning fire in me that can't be put out.

How is your husband taking this?
He's been upset with me because I've had no interest in sex for the last two months. In fact, I haven't had much interest in food, either. He's happy that I've lost fourteen pounds, but I wish it were for a good reason. I've lost the weight because I just don't eat. I can't even stand the sight of food. Maybe that's why I'm so constipated.

Katie's symptoms meshed because our whole work-up had shown little, except for a slightly raised morning cortisol level in the blood. This is a common finding that seems to correlate with biological depression. In fact, a biological test, the dexamethasone suppression test—the DST—was at one point fashionable: A potent form of steroid, a cortisol type compound called dexamethasone, would not suppress the secretion of cortisol in people who were depressed. In the normal population, this load of dexamethasone would suppress the production from the adrenal glands of its usual hormone, cortisone. This occurs via a feedback loop to the pituitary. This would not happen in depression, almost as though the feedback loop had been disconnected, further illustrating the biological element.

Andrew, always keen to pick up on the paradoxical, wondered:
But Doctor, why is the suppression of steroid a normal function?
It's normal because the body works by feedback loops. If it receives some steroid from outside, it realizes it has enough, and so suppresses secretion.

How do you think this figures in depression?
In fact, strangely enough, this cortisol feedback loop is linked with the disturbance of what is, in theory, referred to as our "two internal oscillators" which control our daily rhythms. The first is the cortisol-temperature axis whereby temperature varies a little as do cortisol levels in the day. The second is the sleep-wake cycle: this may ultimately be linked with the terminal insomnia—the early morning awakening—in depression. In turn, this may be linked up with an increased quickness through one's first dream cycle sleep, called "diminished REM latency" because REM—rapid eye-movement sleep—is the correlate of dream-related sleep. So you can see how biological depression is truly biological.
Is that the same as melancholia, or endogenous depression, or the depression in manic-depression?
Yes, largely the same.

What then, Doctor, is the role of antidepressants in this cortisone system of the body?
At one point, it was felt that the antidepressants actually acted on increasing this first phase of rapid eye-movement sleep, shifting it backward in time and normalizing it.

Could this be a cause of depression?
That's unlikely. It may, however, be linked up as a consequence of the particular antidepressant, because there are at least two antidepressants that do not do this. One is marketed in Canada, but not in the United States, called moclobemide. The second is possibly the most physiologic of all our antidepressants, the drug nefazodone—Serzone.

258

After Katie had left, Andrew and I reviewed her chart notes together. In fact, her description of depression was not a typical one, but the existential meaningless she exhibited was an all too common phenomenon. Her self-esteem clearly required working with, and so did her potential toward suicidality. I realized that Katie required treatment rather quickly, because she was at high risk for suicide.

You say her description of depression was not typical. Are there any ways she is typical?
Yes. Katie is the typical patient in whom the detailed comprehensive history, mental status, neurological and physical examination, and special investigations may, in fact, prove helpful. She's not the first of her kind presenting as she does with a refractory depression. At one point, Katie was labeled as having a chronic major melancholic depression. She had received every known antidepressant up to the middle of the 1990s. It's remarkable how many different interventions colleagues have attempted.

It sounds like Katie has received numerous interventions.
Yes. But let's get a perspective on this. Katie is very much the exception, not the rule. Most patients require only one antidepressant for their depression and do well on that one drug. We need to examine Katie's pharmacological history in detail because it's complicated and she is refractory—non-responsive to conventional medications. But it will give us an excellent perspective on what adjunctive—extra, non-approved—drugs are available to work with antidepressants.

I felt Katie's case review required extra preparation for Andrew because of its complexity.

Andrew, this discussion is going to be complex in parts, because of the sheer wealth of pharmacological information. You can learn a great deal about drugs for depression by following this. And, in fact, patients too could benefit from Katie's story. But they would have to concentrate a great deal to do so. Don't be concerned if you don't follow all the ramifications because they're not easy.
If you need to stop at any point, let me know. It's easy for me, familiar as I am with all these treatments. But for you, starting out as you are in evaluating depression, this may be overwhelming.

I assume you will do your own psychopharmacological evaluation?
Yes, Andrew, you anticipate me. But to do so, I need to obtain detailed information on what Katie has taken over many years, in what doses, for how long, in which combinations, and finally for which symptoms.

I'm ready. Let's begin.

And so we began the lengthy review of Katie's pharmacological history.

What antidepressants has Katie taken?
You name the antidepressant, Katie has had it—in low doses and in high doses. For example, at one point, she was taking 500 mg of Elavil a day, a very high dose because she had not responded to lower doses, and her psychiatrist had hypothesized that maybe she wasn't absorbing some of it. Eventually, a blood level was done, and she was three times above the upper level for the therapeutic range of the drug, potentially at marked risk for toxicity. However, it was only on those extremely high doses of Elavil that she had seen even the beginnings of a change. In fact, Elavil was one of several tricyclic antidepressants she took. She failed sequentially with imipramine, nortriptyline, desipramine, doxepin, trimipramine and protriptyline.

Then what did she take?
Following this, she had been given one of the earlier non-tricyclic antidepressants, trazodone. This helped her sleep disturbance to some degree, but she had a hangover from it and found it difficult to function during the day. It seemed that whatever was available, had been tried. Other heterocyclics followed: Even amoxapine, which is seldom used, was tried; so was the tetracyclic drug, maprotiline.

Did she even have MAOIs?
Yes, Andrew. As you know, this is an unusual group of drugs, but during the late 1980s, she tried Parnate and Nardil, the two most common monoamine oxidase inhibitors.
Unfortunately, the monoamine-oxidase inhibitors, although they had helped a small amount, did not answer her quest. These drugs most commonly help atypical depressions, which are different from the classical melancholic ones. She did not have them so that was not unexpected.

Andrew was fascinated by this historical approach.
What happened then?
The era of the early-1990s was reached and with it she started the wonder drugs of the early 1990s, the selective serotonin re-uptake inhibitors—the SSRIs.

Which ones?
260

Her doctor put her onto Paxil. She never felt suicidal on the Paxil, although experiencing a significant loss of sexual interest. The dose was pushed up, from 20 mg to 30 mg a day and if anything, she felt a little better. Her mood lifted. This lasted several weeks. Then she began to slide again. The dose was pushed up again, this time to 60 mg a day, and the same events recurred—improvement followed by a slide. She tried valiantly with the Paxil for another seven or eight months, finding each time that in order to improve, the dose needed to be pushed up, but then would seem to lose efficacy.

Was any other antidepressant tried?
Katie also gave a history of the third in the SSRI triad: Zoloft. With this, she developed some nausea and her headaches became much worse, but she didn't notice much effect otherwise. It had been used shortly after the Paxil, so it was difficult to establish the causes of the symptoms. It was clear that Katie was non-responsive to conventional antidepressants alone. This had been recognized.

Did Katie show the side-effects that were special to SSRIs?
Well, Andrew, nothing is special, although we see certain facets more commonly. Excess serotonin is often linked up with valuable therapeutic results like antidepressant and anti-obsessionality effects; but the downside is that side-effects can be significant, as well. Because of the potency of the SSRIs, serotonin-excess adverse effects frequently occur. About two in three patients experience sexual problems and these seem to persist; nausea occurs be in a third, but this usually disappears gradually over time. Many patients report headaches, but most don't link these with their SSRI. Katie experienced all three of these cardinal problems on the SSRIs—sex problems, nausea and headache. But we must always realize there are confounding factors: Are the side-effects directly attributed to the SSRI drug as opposed to coincidence or other medications or part of the illness?

What about the paradoxical effects of the SSRIs?
There are potentially several paradoxical examples: Anti-anxiety effects usually occur, but pro-anxiety effects happen sometimes; SSRIs usually relieve aggression, yet occasionally patients report increased irritability. Thirdly, the patient might report, "I've taken my Zoloft at night, it helps me sleep." In other words, for them, they're having some sedative effect as opposed to an activating effect. These adverse effects are minimal compared with the loss of efficacy over time. This is sometimes reported six or even nine months after starting treatment. Alternatively, as in Katie's case, the need for escalating doses over weeks produced the same effect of the drug stopping to work.

261

Did Katie only receive antidepressant medication for her depression?
Not at all. She took antidepressants during most of this time, except for some months when she was off medication, and a period when her psychiatrist deliberately and individually tried numerous medications. Her story not only is filled with virtually every marketed antidepressant, but also reads like a course in **adjunctive antidepressant therapy**—the appropriate use of extra medications used for other indications, but not approved by the FDA specifically to manage depression. These adjuncts, in fact, do not have the efficacy of antidepressants in biological depression, but they work well with antidepressants, correcting the other chemical problems the patient has, that the antidepressants may not impact on.

What significance do adjunctive treatments have?
Technically, the choices that were tried read like a "Who's Who in Antidepressant Adjunct Therapy". They failed, but given the appropriate indications could have succeeded.
These adjunctive interventions are speckled through Katie's medical record. They started even before she had tried all the antidepressants available up till 1995, but historically they make up an extremely important lesson in the combined thoroughness of many physicians who tried to leave no stone unturned.

Katie's story, then, although not typical, may be valuable to learn from.
Yes. You should listen carefully to this, Andrew, because even the failures illustrate paradoxically how we can move closer to a solution by knowing to what people are not pharmacologically responding. We need to truly hear what our patients are telling us. We are discussing medications; but remember, Andrew, part of your success will be the caring Doctor-Patient relationship that will support your patient through such traumata.

W e continued our important didactic discussion.

So what was the first adjunctive drug tried?
It was **lithium**. A very common first choice in "refractory depressions"—depressions that don't get better on conventional antidepressants.

How did this come about?
Early on one of her psychiatrists had hypothesized:
"Maybe you have manic-depression. We have never seen the mania, but we sometimes use lithium for pure refractory depression."
Indeed, this was a useful try. Katie did not look like the classic major depressive. Her psychiatrist, steadfastly and in graded steps, proceeded to give her lithium carbonate. She built up the dose gradually from 300 mg

daily, and eventually she found herself on 1750 mg a day of a long-acting form, Eskalith.

How did she do on this?

All she found it did was dull her senses. She developed the typical shaking tremor reflecting possibly too much lithium, and her blood lithium came back 1.1 milliequivalents per liter (mEq/L). This is a high therapeutic range for manic-depressive illness. Her mood, in fact, became a little worse and she found that she still could experience no pleasure–she was anhedonic.

After three months of lithium, regarded as an adequate trial period, the drug was stopped, but not before the dosage had been dropped by two-thirds, so that her blood level was in the 0.4 mEq/L range. This is the conventional level that much research has suggested is needed for patients with depressive episodes without highs; and, in fact, in patients with real refractory biological depressions, there's a two-thirds responsiveness.

S*o did this psychiatrist give up after the lithium?*

No, Andrew. He prescribed another logical option. The anticonvulsant drug, Tegretol, which research and clinical experience had shown was a useful choice in manic-depressive illnesses resistant to lithium.

And did it help?

No. It had no effect; and not surprisingly: There was no evidence of temporal lobe disease clinically, no dyscontrol, and the brain waves on EEG were absolutely normal.

What then?

The doctor was persistent. "If lithium and Tegretol don't work, let's use another anticonvulsant, Depakote instead."

He went to the next major option in manic-depressive illness—otherwise known as bipolar disorder?

Yes. That's right; and, of course, Katie had never exhibited any features of bipolar illness. She had a chronic resistant unremitting depression with no cycles.

The Depakote failed?

Unfortunately. It was a situation where medications were being tried with reason, but the wrong reason. If A fails, let's try B. You don't have the condition for B, but what else can we do?

And so we continued to examine her notes and I synthesized the information for Andrew.

So at this point the doctors were battling to find a solution?
Right. You must remember we're condensing years of Katie's medication history into one small session.

Did anyone try to target anxiety, maybe?
Yes. That, in fact, was the next intervention.
"Maybe there's some anxiety we haven't treated!" one of her psychiatrists had said.
And so she went through a similar story, taking several different **benzodiazepine** medications—Ativan, Xanax, Valium, and Librium. Her doctor had told her about "this phenomenal new medication, Klonopin," and this, too, was tried. All of these sedated her a little, and made her sleep better initially. At one point, she decided to stop taking all her medication and she went through a difficult withdrawal period, involving significant anxiety, agitation, headache, palpitations, and feelings that she was going to die. At one point, she restarted her benzodiazepine and settled but found it did not maintain its positive effect after a few weeks and she was gradually tapered off.

*T*hen *what?*
By this stage, poor Katie was on her 9th doctor. Once again, based on the history of this refractory condition, a physician recognized the solution: "Let's use thyroid medication!" Her thyroid function tests had been evaluated, and they appeared well within normal limits. The particular indicator that was used was her thyroid stimulating hormone, a hormone deriving from the pituitary gland, which regulates the level of the actual two major thyroid hormones in the thyroid glands, namely thyroxin—T4—and tri-iodothyronine—also called T3. These levels were normal as was a key test, the thyroid stimulating hormone level was in the highish normal range—we usually like to see levels below 7, and this was 5. These findings suggested that biochemically the thyroid was statistically average.

Why did he go with thyroid supplementation?
Katie's physician felt she could still potentially benefit a little based on her clinical symptoms. Her physician made the decision to use thyroid supplementation to help her fatigue. She was begun on 50 micrograms of T4, the thyroxin.
Why T4 and not T3?
I note you've been reading, Andrew. There is actually debate as to whether the T3 compound is better. We certainly know that it's at least twice as potent. In my experience, I have also tended to use T4, although

I will restrict usage to patients who look like they may have clinical hypothyroidism. I will not use T4 or for that matter T3 randomly just because my patient may be suffering from a refractory depression. I like to have clinical justification for all my decisions.

Please elucidate.
For example, I use T4 possibly if there's not only fatigue and tiredness, but the pulse is slowed—generally in the 60s. Sometimes, there may even be some complaints of hair falling out, skin being dry, and not tolerating cold weather. Under those circumstances, I believe we have excellent pointers to use thyroid supplementation in patients who have what is commonly labeled as a "refractory depression"—a depression that has not responded, despite the fact that the patient is on adequate doses of anti-depressants for an adequate period of time like three or six weeks.

So what happened to Katie?
Not surprisingly, Katie did not respond to thyroid hormone either. She did not have the clinical or biochemical profile we would expect for her to respond. However, if she had had the correct profile, she would have had possibly a two in three chance of response.

I assume Katie went to her next psychiatrist?
No she didn't. This time she consulted her gynecologist. Katie had actually entered the gynecologist's office with her solution. "It must be my hormones!"
But there was in reality no fluctuation in her moods during the month and, in fact, she had absolutely no premenstrual variations. So we could expect failure.

But estrogens were tried?
Of course. Katie used the next major option for adjunctive treatment for depression—estrogen supplementation in women who are usually going through certain phases in their life—pre-menopausal, menopause or even post-menopause. But Katie at that stage was 33, and she was not going through any of those phases. However, at times, supplementation of estrogen, for example, beta-estradiol, or maybe the less pure Premarin, does wonders in these kinds of patients. However, Katie did not respond.

What do you think of hormone therapy?
Hormones play a role in all sorts of symptoms, and they sometimes help considerably. One ought not to think, "I'm just taking this like a vitamin." To a certain degree, it might be playing a significant role in normalizing mood. You know, female hormones do have their role in normalizing.

Who does well on these hormones?
Many women do well on small amounts of female hormone supplementation. There's a great deal of research that progesterones are usually ineffective in helping mood, except that some people find they do a great deal, particularly if they're natural progesterones. Consequently, the focus has generally been on estrogens.

What has your experience been with hormone therapy?
I have told several patients: "Given that you did well in your pregnancy, and you have these terrible times when your hormone levels drop before your periods, it's clear to me that unless you have a little bit of hormone, you're not going to improve."

So what do you do?
Certainly, regular estrogen supplementation frequently makes a critical difference, but dosage, not too high or too low is often the determining factor. Some patients do well on beta-estradiols like Estrace, others do better on broader estrogen mixtures such as Premarin. In general, when women still have a uterus, they need progesterone supplementation with the estrogen; if they're hysterectomized, they don't. And occasionally, we find patients responding dramatically to progesterones alone.

What exactly is the relation between the two, Doctor?
Estrogen and progesterone go together: they are the hand and the glove. When you take the one without the other, you're getting only half your cycle. Some people have side-effects from the estrogen, and apparently Katie did, and some people have side-effects from the progesterone. If the estrogen is taken without the progesterone, it builds up in the uterus and there's a slightly increased risk of endometrial cancer, so doctors usually give the progesterone if the patient has a uterus. If you take the progesterone alone it probably will have some oral contraceptive effects, but you may not menstruate. Of course, it depends on exact preparations.

But we digress. Back to Katie.
Yes, I was going to ask: then what happened?
The next stage was inevitable. Her eleventh physician decided that the treatment of a refractory chronic unremitting depression was ECT.

What did this physician base this on?
Her logic was simple. What do we do with an atypical, and, in fact, rare, patient, who does not respond to all of the conventional treatments? Do we fall back to the final common resource and give electroconvulsive therapy (ECT)? For the refractory depressive, ECT is an excellent treatment. Whereas with antidepressants in general, we may be talking a

three-fourths responsiveness if we're lucky. With ECT, we're probably talking about a degree of responsiveness of the order of about 95%. In fact, my suspicion is that it's basically 100% if the appropriate patient type has been selected to receive ECT.

Who is the appropriate patient?
One with true major melancholic depression with significant degrees of agitation.

Have these appropriate patient types not responded to conventional anti-depressants?
Exactly. This is so as conventional antidepressant therapy has invariably been the treatment prior to the ECT. Occasionally, the ECT has been performed as an acute emergency treatment to get a patient who is extremely depressed and highly suicidal directly out of their depression, in which case the rare patient may not have been treated with antidepressant drugs.

So was Katie the correct patient?
It was a logical try, but it turned out Katie was not. Somehow, something was missing. The biology of her particular refractory condition was not being addressed, and hence not being corrected.

Did ECT at least help?
Yes. As always, ECT helped. Katie received the customary seven ECT treatments. As always these were performed under anesthesia. By treatment number three she was improving. After treatment number four, she was much better. Three more ECTs were given as is the custom to ensure maintained improvement.

And then?
Katie left hospital taking maintenance antidepressants. Within three weeks she began to slide.

And so?
Psychiatrist physician number twelve re-admitted her and gave her fourteen, not seven, more ECTs.

And did she improve?
Of course, but it was the same story again. She began to relapse after three weeks, but this time the difference was the decision to give so-called "maintenance ECT". She received an outpatient ECT two weeks after leaving the hospital and thereafter four more at two weekly intervals in association with antidepressants. But in the long run, it didn't help. So the psychiatrist gave up.

Ironically, in taking the history from Katie, ECT had been previously contemplated on prior occasions. However, two psychiatrists had pointed out how atypical her condition was, how partly physically based it was, and how she was not the typical prototypical case to respond to ECT. They had predicted that initially it would blur her memory a little, and even produce a period of response for days, but that they would not have been able to perform the psychotherapeutic interactions that they were doing.

At this point, Katie arrived as we had previously arranged, allowing us the opportunity to have her continue her pharmacological history in person.

Then this doctor of mine tried me on something called Visken, but I was never really sure exactly why she thought it would work.
Visken (pindolol) is something rather new in its use in depression. It has become fashionable to use this "beta-adrenergic blocking agent" because it's thought that it might speed up the action of whatever antidepressants you're taking and the theory is that it helps facilitate the antidepressant.

Doctor, what do you mean by "beta-adrenergic blocking agent"?
That's another way of saying beta blocker. These drugs essentially block the action of norepinephrine, which means it diminishes the so-called "fight, fright or flight response."

Andrew interrupted with a simple question, but one that showed he was determined to fill any gaps in knowledge.
I'm sorry Doctor, but what does "beta" mean?
You've learnt about serotonin receptor subtypes like 1A or 1D, Andrew. Beta also refers to a subtype of the norepinephrine receptor. Beta is contrasted with alpha; and, just as serotonin-1 breaks down to A through E, there are beta-1 and beta-2 receptor subtypes.

Was Visken the first beta-blocker used to help depression?
In fact, historically, the use of beta-adrenergic blocking agents in depression goes back a quarter of a century: Dr. Mosey Suzman in South Africa, used high doses of propranolol (Inderal) in conjunction with tricyclic antidepressants. Inderal is a non-specifically acting beta blocker, blocking up the two different receptors, beta-1 and beta-2, and blocking them relatively equally. Also, being very fat-soluble, it passes into the brain far more than any other beta blocker. In addition, because it does not stimulate any of these beta receptors, we're able to titrate the dose according to pulse, bringing down the pulse to the mid 60s per minute. Inderal

worked, maybe partly because of drug interactions, but it certainly is more logical than the new Visken fashion. Unfortunately, Visken slightly stimulates the receptors as well as markedly blocking them. Also, it's far less lipid-soluble so it means it passes only somewhat into the brain. Consequently, I don't believe Visken should be the first choice in this class of beta-adrenergic blocking agents. However, we should discuss it further, because it has become fashionable.

What's your opinion of Visken, Doctor?
I see little role for Visken, at present, given the availability of another drug, BuSpar. Visken is thought to work by blockade through the serotonin-1A system, but usually it has less advantages than buspirone (BuSpar), the only specific serotonin-1A drug. BuSpar is safer and has less potential towards side-effects. But most of all, BuSpar is more flexible and physiological in that it modulates receptors instead of blockading them even if they are already too blocked, like Visken does. BuSpar stabilizes by adjusting physiologically: too much, it blockades; too little, some degree of stimulation.

So Buspar sort of knows how much the body is needing and adjusts accordingly?
You could say that. However, we should pay great homage to the beta-blocker group of drugs, as well: They're used because of their beta-blockade in numerous important conditions ranging from high blood pressure to heart irregularities to thyroid disease. But they also have important side-effects.

What side-effects of beta-blockers are you talking about?
For example, beta blockers are dangerous in asthmatics and patient with heart failure, as well as in Raynaud's disease—a blood vessel disease with cold extremities and poor circulation. These side-effects may occur with Visken or with the several other beta-blockers.

Andrew interjected and I responded noting Katie's distress.
What happened to Katie on the Visken?
Basically, it didn't work. Visken was tried and failed as the umpteenth adjunctive option in Katie's refractory depressive condition.
Again, however, it seems clear, Katie, that you were not the right kind of patient expected to do well with Visken.
What would you characterize as the right patient?
I would see this as somebody with many autonomic features, where the pulse is in the 80s or 90s, despite having normal thyroid functions. These patients easily sweat and develop palpitations in response to stress. With

269

these patients, again we would expect a two-thirds response, but Katie, you were not one of those; and so, as expected, it, too, failed.

W e–the three of us–continued to go over Katie's voluminous notes.

What else had been tried with Katie?
Katie's next to last intervention was small doses of BuSpar–30 mg a day. However, when it did not help, she was tapered off it. The use of **BuSpar** is based on two different hypotheses: either treating the anxiety linked with the depression or the idea that it might stabilize the receptor in those who have lost Prozac or Paxil efficacy. In these patients, we see a two out of three response, so there was a logic to this treatment.[64]

As a long shot, had anyone thought of trying antipsychotics?
Good thinking, Andrew. In fact, in the mid-1980s, one of her physicians had thought, "Well, maybe this whole kind of thinking, despite her functioning, is a little psychotic." Small doses of the **antipsychotic** drug, trifluoperazine, had been added. Despite the fact that she was taking only 2 mg per day, she developed severe extrapyramidal symptoms. She became stiff as a board and looked as if she had Parkinson's disease to the extent that she began to drool. This required further treatment with the antidote, benztropine, a so-called anticholinergic agent, which raised up the proportion of dopamine to acetylcholine by diminishing down the level of acetylcholine even further. This quickly relieved her symptoms and after about ten days, she went off trifluoperazine as an antipsychotic agent.

Were any other antipsychotics which may have had less side-effects tried?
Yes. In fact, one final common adjunctive antidepressant treatment was tried, showing how thoroughly Katie had been worked up in the past. This involved the administration of small doses of antipsychotic medication together with her antidepressant. In this instance, her doctor chose perphenazine [4 mg a day], again a logical antipsychotic medication choice because we seldom see major side-effects, either extra-pyramidal ones or sedation on perphenazine.
What was the result?
Perhaps Katie could summarize.
Well, I didn't notice any side-effects on the Trilafo n. I did notice a little bit more tranquillity...
These drugs are major tranquilizers.
... but I didn't notice that it was causing any relief.
In fact, you complained of the typical features that we sometimes find in people given these major tranquilizer antipsychotic medications unnecessarily. Your thinking became a little bit blurred and not as clear, and you

couldn't concentrate as well, and you had a bit of fatigue during the day. So the perphenazine, too, was discontinued.

Andrew interrupted:
Were any more adjunctive antidepressants tried?
No. This was the formal adjunctive antidepressant list. However, during this time, you can imagine other methods were also used. This included light therapy, vitamins, naturopathic remedies, and to activate her she was even given the psychostimulants, Ritalin and Cylert. None of these worked, either.

And so this takes us up to the present?
Yes. And for the past few months, psychiatrists have not been giving her adjuncts, only antidepressants alone. This led to her Prozac prescription, which began our description of you, Katie.

And so, finally, we had reached the consultation phase. I very much wanted to help poor Katie's suffering. It was obvious, it was not going to be easy. It was clear that we needed to be innovative. We were still missing that vital clue: What biochemically was wrong with Katie?

Katie sighed:
So now that I am consulting you, Doctor, what is your initial impression?
I know that you, Katie, have received all the available major groups of antidepressants. I know too that you have received at various times during your resistant depression every available major adjunctive treatment group. You've taken lithium, thyroid supplementation, pindolol as a beta blocker, benzodiazepines like alprazolam, buspirone, estrogen and progesterone, Tegretol and Depakote as anticonvulsants, two antipsychotics—trifluoperazine and perphenazine; and of course you've received ECT.
Additionally, I am aware that you have also taken high doses of the antioxidant vitamins C, E and A. All of these have not altered your status as an atypical, non-responsive, refractory depressive. But I am not giving up with you, Katie. We must look deeper for the solution.

Katie had sat through much of this detailed review, contributing occasionally, but usually sullen, withdrawn, shaking her head and clearly distressed at each failure. It had been only the week before that I had begun seeing her, yet it seemed an eternity for her.

Do you remember, Katie, what you said to me at just last Monday?

Yes, almost word for word: "But why, Doctor, have others not got it right yet? I've taken so much. I confess that I've given up hope, although if I had completely, I suppose I wouldn't be seeing you."

Yes, that's right. And I'm not about to let you give up hope.

To me, one of the most important points in psychopharmacology is what I call a mid-course correction: I'm not all-knowing. At certain key points in time, I can only say, "this is the direction I think we ought to pursue, this is what we ought to do." We examine data, then we evaluate; later we re-evaluate: "Aha! She's had a paradoxical response to medication X or we find the patient doesn't respond to medication Y."

Often, strange responses are due to organic reasons: a structural or physiological abnormality in the brain sometimes relating to uncorrected biochemistry. But I'm persistent in finding out what's wrong. So we're going to win.

If we found the right biochemical abnormality, we could treat it?
Usually, Katie. If we have the antidote.

Do you always rethink about medications?
Yes, when responses are different from those I expect. Because of this, I have to reformulate ideas, and this I cannot contract into one day. Sometimes evaluations take some weeks to obtain information, particularly the many physiological type medications which, fortunately or unfortunately, take a few weeks to fully work. The important point is to detail exactly what has been taken before. If we do, we understand both the positive and negative biochemical facets.

A ndrew added, almost rhetorically:
Does this imply a time-based evaluation?
Exactly, Andrew. We're dealing with a process, sometimes right, sometimes wrong. We test out limits when we need to, and each time we do, we learn from the information. We're learning about your own biology now, Katie, and it's complicated even more because there always are drug interactions, as well.

So failure is relative?
Right! Every response gives an index for future biochemical improvement. We're ultimately tracing psychopharmacological responsiveness as an underlying indicator of response and non-response.

Katie showed she was taking all this in, and could see her relevance to our discussion.
Is it then okay, Doctor, not to respond?
All it means is that biochemically you respond somewhat differently. That's why I think psychiatric diagnoses are so simplistic: They don't take

pharmacological response into account. We'll get closer and closer to the truth even at times when things are not working, or when side-effects occur, because we develop further biochemical and electrical conceptions.

But will you stick with it, Doctor?
I'm very persistent, okay? I like to see people better; and as I said before, sometimes I need mid-course corrections. It's possible you might have the same kind of reaction as before, but that would be good information biochemically to me. It helps me because it says: "Hold on! You're not plus that, it's minus this," and it begins to steer me around to change the framework. It's important for you to understand that.

Am I going to get better?
Indeed, Katie. Your faith doesn't need to waver in relation to this. We will find a clue and I'm going to get you better; and I want you to stay better, and this is why I'm not prepared to accept even a 10% improvement. I want to see a big jump, and so we're going to have to balance these good sides and these bad sides.

At that moment, I gazed at Katie rather wistfully, thinking about those several antidepressants and related medications that are not marketed in the United States, but are available in other areas of the world. Drugs such as dibenzepin (Noveril) or moclobemide (Aurorix), which potentially, in difficult cases, have helped absolutely enormously. My regret in this regard was that the pharmaceutical companies fail in their attempts because of the enormous costs—hundreds of millions of dollars—involved in marketing a medication in the USA. These companies have to balance what proportion of the market they can corner with recoupment of expenses and profit. Sometimes, perfectly legitimate therapeutic agents are not marketed because of the usual requirements of studies having to be repeated in the USA. This is a good and a bad requirement: good because of the added levels of precautions, controls and standardization required to ensure safety and efficacy for the medications; bad because sometimes there's a reinvention of the wheel.
I felt wistful, too, as there came to mind some of the other superb antipsychotic medications that we did not have available: drugs such as pipothiazine palmitate (Pirportil Depot) or sulpiride (Eglonyl), each with their own unique special qualities. I thought: *"Make do with what we have."* Fortunately, we have plenty, and we can usually be pharmacological magicians, even without these extras.

Our history-taking session had taken us to the present, where we were still seeking the most valid and appropriate treatment for Katie. However, there was an immediate problem I wanted to solve, and I introduced it on her next visit.

I looked Katie straight in the eye.
I sometimes tell people this and they look at me, yet they just don't understand. So I want you to listen to this and heed this advice. You have to understand that you can be helped. You have a condition that's treatable. This is very useful to know. It doesn't help if people kill themselves before they're helped.

She nodded, but in an unconvinced way.
When people feel depressed and down, it's like they're in a black pit and they don't think they will ever come out of this pit, and they feel terrible and feel there's no point to it all.

There was a little sparkle maybe in her face.
I hope you're listening, because I think it's very important for you to understand that one of the consistent things we know about deep, black pits is that people come out of those dark pits and they do okay. This is very, very important for you to understand. If you don't understand that, you won't realize that you can get better, and you're going to get better. There is no doubt about that. I don't like to see you suffering like this.
Even though you don't know me?
What do you mean, "even though you don't know me?" I've seen you on a few occasions and I don't like to see you suffering. My object is to try to prevent suffering and help end the suffering.

Her nod was still uncertain, but her face reflected some hope. I handed her a sheet of paper.
I want you to remember this, Katie.

Katie read the sheet:
Remember when you're depressed everything feels hopeless and bleak. But your condition is treatable—completely.
It may be difficult to believe this while depressed, but you will get better.

Fortunately antidepressants can and do help. They take time because, biologically, your body is out of rhythm. Usually you will see changes over three to six weeks.

You will take three steps forward. You may take a step back because your body needs to readjust: don't worry if you do.

274

You don't make major decisions while depressed.
You can look forward to being well again.

Remember the symptoms you have are symptoms of biological changes. We should be able to correct your problem chemically so you can be happy again.
These symptoms will improve as the medication works:
> *Early morning waking.*
> *Worse in the morning.*
> *Terrible sadness.*
> *Concentration poor.*
> *Loss of interest in sex.*
> *Constipated.*
> *Feeling hopeless and helpless.*
> *Feeling inadequate, like a nothing.*
> *Low self esteem.*
> *Guilt and self-blame.*
> *Feelings of self-destruction.*
All these are biologic feelings of depression.
These biologic correlates of depression happen.
But they will get better.

There is only one certainty in depression, and that is that you will get better. Okay? And that's very important to know. When you're depressed, it's like being in a big black deep dark pit and you cannot even see the top of that hole. It's a terrible feeling. It can suck you in. It's not any way to live.
But conquer it you can and you will.
Read this and believe it. Getting better is worth it!

It was the next day. Again, Andrew and I were reviewing Katie's case.
What then have you decided to do, Doctor?
I realized early on that our options were limited.
Fortunately, in our detailed investigations, we have been able to demonstrate that there is probably no abnormal electrical firing in the brain. The EEG was normal despite the numerous previous ECTs, the last more than a year ago, suggesting but, of course, not proving that Katie does not need any anticonvulsant medication either. She has no major clinical symptoms of seizure disorder and no episodic features. In short, she has no obvious biological cause for her illness. For example, our blood tests show no evidence of vitamin B12 deficiency, hormonal imbalances or underlying chronic inflammatory disease. Her blood count is normal as are her electrolytes, kidney and liver function as well as her blood sugar.

What then?

Katie is a high-risk patient to kill herself. The risks of her future existence are at stake. Consequently, I recognize the treatment may need to be radical enough to support such an approach.

So, the next stage is ensuring that we have excluded other medical conditions. I have re-analyzed my detailed physiological investigations, physical examinations after appropriate histories, and psychiatric history.

Any medication probes?

Yes. You're right to ask, Andrew. I also examined the classic indices of response to a specific antidepressant agent:

We know Katie has not previously responded to a specific antidepressant but we cannot obtain a biological family history because of the adoption. These extra probes do not, therefore, produce any further yield.

Are there any clues along the way?

Yes, Andrew. I have found there was one period in Katie's life when, in fact, she had felt normal.

When was that?

After a minor surgery to repair a broken leg, she received hydrocodone medication (Vicodin), a mild narcotic.

Katie entered for her appointment. After the usual pleasantries, I keyed in for what I hoped would be the critical clues.

What happens when you go to the dentist, Katie?

Don't talk to me about the dentist, Doctor. I loathe going there! Do you know that even when they just give me a teeth-cleaning, the pain is terrible, it's awful!

Have you ever needed fillings?

Yes, but they have to give me nitrous oxide for that!

What happens when you get the nitrous oxide—the laughing gas?

You know, Doctor, it's interesting that during those short periods, despite the fact that they're working on my teeth and giving me a filling, I feel normal.

Andrew was as intrigued as I was.

What do you conclude from this, Doctor?

Nitrous oxide has been demonstrated to be a pure opiate agonist,[65] which implies that it's working through the same endogenous opioid pathway that the body uses. Drugs like morphine, heroin and codeine, in effect, supplement the pain-relief. This usually comes about as a result of the added production in the body of these substances where, most times, the body responds appropriately to its pain need, by producing its own opiate compounds. This seems to be the major physiological clue. It seems that with Katie we are dealing with someone who may have a deficient endogenous opioid system.

That's interesting, Doctor. What made you think that?
Well, Katie had had very short periods in her life where she experienced herself as normal. All of these periods related to taking some kind of drug which would increase her opioid system. Could her lack of experience of pleasure, which is very much linked up with the pain experience, be something that we can correct by giving her a mild drug that would help enhance her opioid system function?

It seemed clear that this was the direction to take with Katie. I discussed this with her and indicated the potential risks of dependence.

Wouldn't the fact that she needs this drug to be treated mean that some dependence is involved?
Not necessarily so. All it means is that finally we have located the key. The historical link that's been missing so long may be the deficiency in the opioid system.

How do you distinguish her authentic physiological need for opioid from the need of an addict?
Firstly, her pattern of behavior through numerous medications has never shown any physical dependency or addictive quality. Secondly, her personality profile shows no such features either. Thirdly, the history is clear: she has a different endogenous opioid system to most. This is clearly a rare condition, but it's an excellent reason why Katie has not responded till now.

So how do opioids compare to the other antidepressant medications?
Andrew, we're not talking about comparing opioids with antidepressants here. They're to be used as adjunct to an antidepressant. At any rate, the comparison to make should be with the benzodiazepines.

How so?
Surprisingly, the risk of dependence with opioids is probably lower than the risks of dependence in drugs such as the benzodiazepines. Some have argued that the risk of dependence with the opioids may be as low as a few percent. It's extremely difficult getting any of these patients off benzodiazepines—drugs such as Valium, Ativan and Xanax—although they may not be formally regarded as dependent.

What opioid medication did you have in mind?

I discussed the dependency risks of opioids with Katie, and as always focused on the drug I was about to prescribe, namely codeine phosphate.
What can you tell me about it, in relation to how it acts in the body?
Codeine phosphate is generally broken down in the body into morphine, with the consequence that we have to be particularly careful of drug interactions. The particular liver enzyme system involved in such drug interactions is the 2D6 system. For example, if Katie had taken codeine specifically with potent inhibitors of that liver enzyme like Paxil or Prozac, it would not easily have been metabolized properly so the codeine wouldn't have worked well.
Anything else?
Yes. Incidentally, this 2D6–part of the P450 cytochrome enzyme system–is a major pathway of breakdown of psychiatric, neurological and other drugs. Approximately one-third of all those compounds go through this system, which is extremely complicated because there's a genetic variability as to how much each person has.

I wanted to obtain one last key piece of pharmacological history from Katie.
Katie, has anyone ever given you a so-called "non-steroidal anti-inflammatory agent" like ibuprofen (Motrin)?
As it happens, I sprained my ankle last year, and I took some ibuprofen for three weeks; my doctor told me he had put me on high doses.
Well, what did it do?
It helped my ankle settle, I assume. But if you're asking about my mood, I'm afraid it did absolutely nothing.

Katie nodded her head in affirmation.
I remember telling my sports medicine doctors that even though they had relieved my ankle and also incidentally my headaches a little, they hadn't really affected my mood at all.
In fact, Katie, they hadn't affected your mood like the codeine would. You needed to have your opioid receptor stimulated.

I had completed that last piece of the puzzle. Non-narcotic pain relievers had not helped Katie.

I planned three different medications for Katie, but I knew it was important to prescribe one drug at a time and make one change at a time. We were dealing with a road-map for Katie's whole future. There was time for us to be patient. Despite my pressured desire to see Katie well, to give her the whole combination that I knew she would likely require all at once, this was clearly illogical. Instead, I

278

realized I should establish the correct dosage of each medication individually, and assess side-effects and therapeutic outcome stepwise.

　　　I turned to Andrew.
We will make only one change at a time, Andrew. This way we will know what's going on every step of the way. It's likely we will need to use a mild narcotic like codeine, an antidepressant which we will discuss, and another drug which stimulates the opioid system, Ultram. We will do this all, if necessary, sequentially.

We embarked on our next step: We began Katie on codeine.
First, we built up the dose of the codeine gradually over three weeks to a 120 mg plateau. For the first time in her life, Katie began to feel normal. She was thinking more clearly, she was more motivated, she was suddenly able to experience pleasure, she was concentrating, she felt that she had more energy.
And yet, there were still these frustrations that she had, and some symptoms of residual sadness. It was clear to me that she still needed the second intervention, an antidepressant compound. Clearly, Katie had a residual depression. Consequently, it was logical to add in an antidepressant. I wanted to be as physiologic as possible and use an antidepressant that would act on both the serotonin and norepinephrine receptors. We had to find the ideal antidepressant for her.

A̲ll this time, Katie had listened quietly.
Doctor, I need an atom bomb to explode me. I need activation.
You're right. Because you're fatigued, I want to use an activating antidepressant.

So what do you suggest?
Let's look at the candidates for the ideal antidepressant for you.
What do you think, Andrew?
What about venlafaxine?
Yes, Effexor.
　　　Katie perked up.
Why that one, Doctor?
Effexor is particularly logical in you, Katie, because it will raise the level of the serotonin and the norepinephrine, but not to a profound degree. Moreover, it does not markedly change the levels of the various chemicals that are broken down by the liver so that we would not expect significant drug interactions. For example, codeine is broken down into a more active form, morphine, by the liver. Effexor has little influence on this or any other drug interactions we know of, for that matter.

What side-effects should we look out for?
It's interesting that, when it was initially marketed, the major side-effect people encountered was nausea, to the extent that maybe two-fifths of patients would report nausea, and many would discontinue. The initial starting dose recommended [37.5 mg twice a day] is much too high. The logical dose to begin with, as we will with you, Katie, is 12.5 mg twice a day. Recently, incidentally, a long-acting Effexor medication has come out, with the consequence that we can give it as a once-a-day dose. This is an enormous compliance advance. In addition, we find that patients can now begin on the 37.5 mg daily of the slower-acting Effexor.

> Andrew was intent on deepening his new found knowledge
> of pharmacology, and saw his chance.

And so how will you treat Katie on Effexor?
I will begin Katie on Effexor and gradually build up the dosage. The important component is to establish the most appropriate dose for her. As I've indicated, I prefer to choose the "chisel" not the "sledgehammer" effects of these drugs, this way producing a possibly less overwhelming impact on the receptors.
Because the sledgehammer effects of the selective serotonin re-uptake inhibitor (SSRI) drugs raise up the level of the serotonin too high in the bathtub: higher than what the patient needs?
Right, Andrew. You've learned well. The brain will usually adapt appropriately, but it may have difficulty doing so, because it must adapt to at least fifteen different serotonin receptor subtypes—fifteen different bathtubs being filled too high. Consequently, we may see side-effects.

What sledgehammer effect does Effexor have?
The major sledgehammer effect of Effexor seems to be on one of these receptors, serotonin-3, which produces nausea. The rest of its effects are far more physiologic, raising up the bathtub level more gently, with the consequence that I use symptoms such as headache as a potential index that the patient is receiving too much Effexor. So, in building up the dose of Effexor gradually with a previous patient, we were able to settle on 150 mg a day. When we would go higher, to 225 mg or even to 187.5 mg a day, his headaches would become much worse. This is a useful practice—monitoring side-effects and using these as an indicator of appropriate dosage in the event of a response having occurred.

> Katie, listening carefully, demonstrated a grasp of the subject
> and its pertinence for her.

But Doctor, is this logical?
Yes indeed, Katie, it's logical. It's a useful way of adapting dose to the actual physiologic demands of each individual. Sometimes side-effects may not specifically be correlated with the receptor we're looking at, so

we have to be innovative in our response. In my experience, monitoring side-effects of Effexor allows a good index of the appropriate dose.

What side-effects should I be watching out for?
One major component is that it might minimally increase your blood pressure, which is why we like to ensure that your blood pressure is monitored at regular intervals. This can be done in our office or in your family practitioner's office. Recent research has suggested that a good proportion of the population raise up their blood pressures when they visit the doctor. We call this "white coat hypertension". It's far more logical for you to either visit your pharmacy or one of those blood pressure machines in stores and take it yourself.

Or I could look into buying one of those automatic blood pressure machines. That way, I could just take it at home.
That's a good idea. Incidentally, if you decide on one of those, make sure you don't get one which is a watch or one you hook up around your fingers. There may be models out there which are reliable, but I haven't found as good a correlation of blood pressure with these models as I have had with regular blood pressure machines which take blood pressure automatically.

It was three months later. Again, Andrew and I were reviewing Katie's follow-up.

And so how is the prescription of codeine going for Katie?
It has been very satisfactory. I wanted to give her physiologic doses, and so we began very low. Ultimately, she was stabilized on about 120 mg of codeine daily–30 mg four times a day–as she had been after three weeks. To lower the risk of abuse even further, the codeine was at times prescribed with an analgesic compound, with acetaminophen in combination medication. This is a rather clever way to prevent drug addicts from mainlining or utilizing inordinate amounts of the codeine itself, because with the added acetaminophen, it's toxic when injected intravenously.

How did you maintain her on physiological doses of the codeine?
I wanted to be sure that Katie got the lowest possible dose of any opioid that she could, even if we had her ultimately on a stable dose.
Fortunately, we have the drug Ultram available. This is a fascinating chemical which will stimulate the opioid system. It therefore acts in the central nervous system as a synthetic anti-pain medication. It is not an addictive opioid drug, but it is complementary to them because it stimulates opiate secretion by binding to one of the many opioid subtypes, the "mu opioid receptor".

And so when did you add the Ultram?
After we stabilized Katie on the Effexor for a month on what turned out to be 225 mg daily, we started her on the Ultram. I perceived this as our insurance policy for the opioid system; you'll remember, it stimulates opioid production.

Giving Katie 200 mg daily, we were able to lower the dose of the codeine. However, Ultram has not been adequately tested for long-term usage. As with so many areas of pharmacology, we were, of necessity, entering the realm of the unknown, a piece of information I explained to Katie. We knew that Katie would not respond to drugs like ibuprofen.

> Andrew wanted to return to the previous thread of Katie's unfolding treatment.

This Ultram intrigues me, Doctor. Tell me more about it, pharmacodynamically speaking.

I see you've picked up on the pharmacological terminology, Andrew! An extra bonus with Ultram is that it not only has effects on the opioid receptors, but it also has effects on serotonin and norepinephrine, and raises them up slightly. Hypothetically, therefore, Ultram also ought to have some antidepressant properties. So pharmacodynamically, the drug impacts on the brain by acting on the opioid receptors.

> To Andrew, who had not seen Katie for two of these three months, she presented quite differently on this occasion, and the difference was entirely positive. Katie delighted in updating Andrew.

You ask me how I am. Let me put it this way. With small exceptions, on a scale of 10 using 0 as worst, for the last eight years frankly I have been at best a 1, and often a minus 5. I know that's not allowed on the scale, but that was my suffering. There were short periods where I felt better, but not often. Even so, I can't remember ever being more than a three, except under two circumstances. The first were the times inhaling nitrous oxide at the dentist; the second was when I had those narcotic pain killers for a few days. Both times I would score myself as a five or six. Now I'm consistently a seven at least, some days an eight, and on rare days a nine.

> I still wanted to ensure we had taken care of any side-effects.

Katie, do you have any down sides to this treatment?

Absolutely none, Doctor. I have no side-effects to any of the medications; and I know you mentioned my blood tests and blood pressure have been fine. Incidentally, those headaches I've had for years have all but disappeared, as well. Strangely, Doctor, I know you mentioned to me about constipation possibly being a problem, but I've never had that difficulty.

Four months later, on a return appointment, Katie thought she would surprise me.

You know, that really sustained me, that note you wrote on hope in depression, with the assurance I would get better: Now I understand, but I couldn't comprehend it then because I wasn't in a position to appreciate it. So do remember that for other patients.

I remember. You're not the first who has told me this. It's very important to know you're going to get better.

Well, I just want to tell you: I am better.

It was a year later. Katie had continued to do extremely well. She was functioning in a high pressure job and her family, too, was delighted. However, six weeks before, we had decided to taper the Ultram slowly. Katie was no longer the consistent "eight or nine" she had been for the past five months, but a "six or seven."

I had been concerned with keeping Katie on Ultram unnecessarily so I had ventured to taper her dose.

Doctor, it's been ten months now on the Ultram, and you've had me gradually tapering it down these past six weeks. You know, I just don't feel quite as good as before.

I turned to Katie.

Katie, I'm wondering whether or not our diminution of Ultram, which was perfectly logical, has not in a way paralleled this small slide you have experienced lately, so we have to look at the two bases. I've been keen to diminish the Ultram because of the lack of data available on its long-term impacts on the liver: As you know, most medications are studied for rather short periods. On the other hand, we can say that more important than anything else is raising up your mood again—in other words, improving your quality of life.

I agree, Doctor. What shall we do then?

Katie, We're making the assumption that the risk is not a high-level risk, but it's there all the same and we don't have sufficient statistics to gauge it exactly. It might not even be there; we don't know. In other words, it's almost as if you were taking it as an experimental medication at this point, with regard to its long-term long-range potential side-effects—whether it can impact on liver function. Based on the lack of reports, it's likely that it would impact only a small proportion of people. Clearly, however, you need the Ultram.

We built the dose back quickly over a week from the 50 mg daily she had been taking to 300 mg per day.

283

O n Katie's follow-up appointment three weeks later, she was already better.

It's interesting Doctor. It took these three weeks to fully return to a 9 out of 10. I was able to see it gradually happening, but I knew it would, so that was okay.

Yes. Psychophysiologic stabilization takes time. You may rank yourself a nine now, but it's possible you may feel even better in a month or two.

In fact, Katie did begin to hit the odd ten in the next few months. It wasn't every day, but she kept a record and it seemed to be six or seven days a month with no specific pattern to them.

You know Doctor. I remember how concerned you were about the codeine. Do you know there has not been a single day I have taken an extra dose? Sometimes I've been tempted to do so when situations that were stressful were coming up, but I never did. I stick strictly to your prescriptions. I use one of these pill boxes and in a year, I don't think I have once missed a dose. My life is too important to mess around now that I've had a new lease on existence, on pleasure I should say!

A nd so it was with Katie that suddenly a patient who was extremely impaired, listless, and had no interest in life, in effect, came to life. She began to have interests, and this grew, because she realized her need to interact at a community level. She avidly devoured books pertaining to positive facets of life.

We were able to hook her up with a psychotherapist who would accentuate and support her cognitive progress exemplified by her thoughts becoming more reasonable, more logical, more positive and more directed towards the future.

Katie was maintained on her regular dose of codeine with acetaminophen, along with Ultram, which would stimulate her opioid system a little more, as well as Effexor.

Today, two and a half years later, we're dealing with a highly functional individual, instead of a walking corpse. Katie is the embodiment of lost hope, found again; of a mind, crying in pain, that has become belovedly wholesome once more.

Chapter 11

Three Steps Forward, One Step Back

Depression in adolescence.
Loss of efficacy, meaning, prescription education.
BuSpar, Zoloft.
Voyage of new discovery.
(Suzanne); (bathtub analogy)

She fell to her knees, looked up, and prayed. There was little else Suzanne felt she could do. Things were hopeless. Her world was destroyed; and the worst part about it was that she didn't understand why. She just knew how incompetent she was and how hopeless she was in all things, and she felt entirely helpless. She might as well lie down and die.

Then from above, she was hearing the voice of her mother. *"No, no! Let's try one more time. Let's seek help!"*

It was so perplexing. Suzanne had gone through it before. Each time she would take this Zoloft in higher dose it would help. She would be fine for a week and then the slide would begin; a rapid slide over days, back to the severe depression.

During my multi-session comprehensive evaluation of Suzanne, I was able to look in greater detail at the person behind the complaint. Suzanne was a young adolescent and life had been so easy until two months ago when she started to develop the symptoms of her first major depressive episode. There were no obvious environmental triggers. The illness seemed based on this being time for her biological clock to enter into overwhelming despair. It seemed that she was following in the footsteps of her maternal grandmother, who had committed suicide in her late twenties.

Andrew was waiting for me in my office in typical education mode.

I think, Doctor, that Suzanne's case will educate me a great deal about depression.

You're right: Her story is instructive, Andrew, so please listen carefully. Suzanne is a sixteen year old female who has dropped out of school these past seven weeks after suffering, and I mean suffering, her first major depressive melancholic episode.

I'm listening.

Her family practitioner—her FP—started her on sertraline (Zoloft), 50 mg daily. Three weeks later, she returned: "Doctor, I'm better." She went back to school for a week, but then she returned to her FP, with a familiar SSRI complaint, "Doctor, it worked, but it's no longer working."

So her FP pushed up the dose to 100 mg again, "It worked for a little while, but in a week it's no longer working." Again, he pushed up the Zoloft to 150 mg, then 200 mg. Same story. "Doctor, I'm better." But a little after that, "It worked, but it's no longer working."

At that point, Suzanne consulted with me.
She had again dropped out of school, despite taking the 200 mg of Zoloft a day.

Doctor, I cannot go on. In fact, I don't want to. There's not much point in coming here, because I know you can't do anything anyway. My mother persuaded me to come, but she's wasting your time and my time, so let me go. My family will get over it.

It was clear that Suzanne had had enough. Although there were times when she felt a little bit better, it was so much lower than her expectations that she saw absolutely no point to life. In fact, her description of depression was not a typical one, and the existential meaningless she exhibited was an all too common phenomenon. I realized that both aspects required treatment—the meaninglessness and the biological element which was likely largely responsible for the impediments—and rather quickly, because our risk of losing Suzanne in the long term was high, and our short-term risk was enormous.

I don't sleep so well, Doctor. I wake up two or three times in the night, then I go back to sleep, only to wake up early in the morning. I know I'm supposed to feel worse early, and my sadness does; but as an extra, my anxiety seems to build up during the day; and then well, it sounds like a little detail, Doctor, but it's uncomfortable: I'm constipated. I don't want to complain more, Doctor, but my concentration could be better; but that's minor: it's this draining feeling of sadness that really hits me. Doctor, don't waste your time. It's hopeless. I feel downright helpless. I'm a nothing.

> Her self-esteem required working with, and so did her potential toward suicidality.

I've been wasted, Doctor. There's no point in going on. I don't experience any pleasure.

> It seemed to me that a major facet was her anhedonic presentation—this inability to experience pleasure—no matter what she did.

Yeah, I watch the ball game sometimes, but it doesn't really interest me. I've been encouraged to support our local teams and I try hard, but I can't experience any pleasure when they win; and yet, at times, I feel sad, like weeping, but it always relates to when I'm inactive. Certainly, when I'm at school, I'm actually a bit better because I'm doing something, but I cannot get up to go there. It's when I've got time to think about myself that I'm pretty lousy.

> And again I heard the awful plea: the cry to save her beloved mind.

Doctor, I cannot go on. I don't want to. Just let me go, my time is up.

> It was clear that Suzanne had reached her nadir, and although there were times when she felt a little bit better, these periods were so much lower than her expectations that she saw absolutely no point to life.
>
> She had also hit the typical age of adolescence where everything is in black and white—no tones, no shades, everything either wonderful or terrible, awesome or boring. In her case, this was augmented by her depression.

Doctor, there's no point in you trying to make me better, because there's no relevance to life anyway. Every last bit of life is worthless! I don't know why you're bothering. Everything in life is pointless and stupid.

> She was the prototype iconoclast, possibly the product of our modern era, where even the most fascinating of phenomena becomes something ordinary and uninteresting for our new youth. I recognized this as a special kind of problem.

287

Suzanne, I would like somebody to work with you in relation to your thoughts. You can meet with a therapist, possibly once or twice a week if you want. You can tell this person your innermost thoughts, and she can support you with your ideas. I am recommending a particular therapy called "cognitive therapy" or thinking therapy, and I'm suggesting it be directed towards looking at your future endeavors and the relevance of life. Linked to this cognitive therapy, I'm going to suggest a positive approach, and it may best be obtained by reading classical books on life and meaning—for example, Viktor Frankl, Abraham Twerski or Norman Vincent Peale.

To her credit, Suzanne, with some trepidation and after a great deal of encouragement, devoured these books over the next few weeks, and these certainly gave her some meaning. But, fundamental to all of it was a lack of pleasure, and this needed handling.

I realized that treating her biochemical imbalance was a critical facet. However, running, peri passu, was the rehabilitation back to the healthy phase of normalcy, where she would be able to see a meaning and a relevance to life. And so I planned the two together—therapist plus books of meaning plus activity on the one side, pharmacological intervention on the other.

I can understand and I feel for you. But it's action time: When you encounter a boulder, you can either become bigger or you can get smaller. You can either trip over it or you can use it for support.

Do you think there's hope?
Things are always hard; nothing is easy. The world consists of a series of boulders which you can either stumble over or use to reach greater heights. Life is a beach speckled with a pile of rocks. Some are small, some large; and the very same rocks that would trip you up, you can use for support—getting to where you want to go. When you use adversity positively, you climb to higher levels, and you will actually be developing as a human being on this beach.

Suzanne was listening, but with a wistful sadness in her voice.

Whose beach?
Sometimes those rocks are your own personal beach and sometimes those rocks are others' beaches. In your case, it's both and it's your life that's involved with both beaches.

How so? Surely my beach is not their beach.
It is. All our beaches share the same ocean.

288

So how do we do it? How do we go on and up?
Sometimes you miss rungs on a ladder, and you slip. This is frustrating, but it can also encourage you to be more careful as you proceed. What we're trying to do is help you get up those rungs.

But how do medications help these problems?
You have to separate biology from psychology and the environment from your constitution. Certain biochemical aspects underlie even the most obvious of environmental stresses. Does it make sense to understand that your bathtub level needs to be 105 units, not 95, because the chemicals have to compensate for your added stresses?

Yes, that makes sense.
And we want to correct and restabilize those biochemistries. If we did this, we would find that you would feel better.

Rather dramatically, Suzanne changed the subject. She had had enough of talking about herself at a personal level. I was surprised by the content of her questions, but I was more intrigued by the process taking place—the shift to something about her which allowed greater security from any further intrusions into her thinking. I picked up on this using words like "case" and shifted my discussion towards concrete discussions like spinal taps not psychological symptoms. It was interesting that Suzanne picked up this facet spontaneously with her next question. This way she became more comfortable.

Maybe I have something organic. What about a spinal tap or an MRI of the head?
It's not clinically indicated, in your case. On the other hand, statistically there may be a chance that one of those would pick up something. It might be at the same level as the general population, or, because you have symptoms, there might be a slightly higher incidence. We have to balance the risk of the procedure and the costs involved compared with the potential yield in benefit.

Are there dangers?
Sometimes. For example, spinal taps involve removal of a small amount of cerebrospinal fluid. This means there's a perforation into your spinal canal, and the potential for a leak dropping the pressure. This is not common, but it's something that has to detected. Consequently, we take precautionary measures like hospitalization for 24 hours. This increases cost, trauma and inconvenience. On the other hand, blood tests generally have minimal risk.

So we don't need to investigate everything at the moment?
Right. We have to balance the benefits of a test against its risks, necessity, costs and inconvenience.

> Andrew, uncharacteristically refraining from questions, had been taking notes, and only now interrupted with a quick question.

Does that mean that without such tests, psychiatric diagnoses are simplistic?
I think psychiatric diagnoses are simplistic, but not because an MRI or spinal tap are omitted.

> I turned back to Suzanne to continue her participation. I realized she could handle the illness model more easily than the psychological limitation one; the passive would be easier to accept than intrusion into her mind.

MRI and spinal tap are low yield tests for your condition as they would be normal. Relatively few people with depression or anxiety have brain problems using formal tests like these. However, it's not the absence of these hard line tests, like MRI, that make the difference. Psychiatric diagnoses may be simplistic because we classify them only into a small number of illnesses. I suspect that we should be conceiving of a far more complex biological system of illness: Major advances will come about but only when we use new measures, like response to medication, as part of our basic diagnostic assessment. Then we will see how varied single conditions like depression are.

I had entered phase two: We were ready to discuss Suzanne's medication. However, Andrew's characteristic questioning began to come to the fore again: In his innocent, but typically engaging fashion, he was ready to plunge into an unknown cesspool. Fortunately, despite prematurely mixing psychological and medication issues, his questions could ultimately be used for therapeutic advantage, by involving Suzanne in important facets of her own treatment.

Doctor, if I may ask Suzanne: Maybe you become depressed each time because of lack of meaning in life? Maybe it has nothing to do with the medication?
Interesting hypothesis, Andrew.

Then, not wanting Suzanne to be embroiled in Andrew's provocative question at this time, I courteously but deftly brought the discussion back on track.

And this is an important aspect I want to address, as well, because there certainly is an existential lack of meaning. However, the pattern of what happens has been repeated four times: add more medication—increase the Zoloft—feel better for a week, slide over days. This has a biological feel to it. So Suzanne, we must now make a decision about your current medication of 200 mg per day.

Why not just push the Zoloft from 200 mg to 250 mg a day in Suzanne's instance?

I turned from Andrew to Suzanne.

Suzanne, because if I did, it's likely you would again respond for a short while and a week later not respond again. You would first improve and then become depressed again. To act, we must understand what's happening.

Is there an easy physiological explanation for this? Or even better a metaphor to understand?

Yes, Andrew, we'll go with the metaphor. You're by now familiar with the bathtub analogy of depression.

Again I turned to Suzanne, the key player, whom I wanted to educate.

I call what happened to you, Suzanne, the "subacute overadaptation model". The level of serotonin in your bathtub kept rising: on 50 mg per day maybe it was 300; on 100 mg per day, maybe 500; and on 200 mg per day maybe 700. But the brain kept overadapting. The responsiveness was ultimately, say, only 10%, making an overall score of 70 synaptic units instead of the 100 that you need to stay better. We can imagine this by using a temperature analogy; although your bathtub was full of serotonin, the temperature dropped maybe originally from 75°F to 57°F; then from 54°F to 45°F; or even 32°F to 23°F. It's ice-cold in your bathtub. This phenomenon took several weeks. If the level went up even more, the temperature would have maybe become even lower using this analogy of the even more frigid, very tall bathtub.

I had Suzanne's participation.

Why not then just drop the level of the bathtub down by using only 50 mg of Zoloft a day?

Because under those circumstances, you could harm yourself significantly, or become intensely depressed.

Why?
Because after the level of the bathtub was raised very high, it would drop down precipitously with the much lower dose. However, your bathtub would still have remained ice-cold despite the level dropping. You may become acutely depressed under those circumstances, or you might rather bizarrely see the same side-effects that we would sometimes see when we add in an SSRI.

Why?
Because you actually have a whole series of different serotonin bathtubs all controlling each other.

What could I experience?
Theoretically, nausea, headache, irritability, agitation, fatigue or insomnia. These side-effects are all side-effects of serotonin excess which we sometimes see when we initiate SSRIs in different patients. However, because of the different balances of the different bathtubs, we might see these on acute withdrawal of the SSRIs.

Andrew felt neglected.
So what's the bathtub neurotransmitter metaphor here?
We have the two variables at the neurotransmitter level: an increased number of molecules in our bathtub and a diminished responsiveness at the receptor—the water level is too high but ice-cold. This is our bathtub parallel: SSRI overdrive. With the ice-cold bathtub, the brain over-adapts to the overfilled bathtub—in effect, too much down-regulation of the receptor occurs. This is the key: The SSRI has worked, but it is no longer working because the sledgehammer—very powerful serotonin effect—pushed the level too high and the brain cooled the tub too much in response.

This is the subacute overadaptation model: in effect, what has happened is that the bathtub score keeps going up and the brain keeps adapting or over-adapting by cooling down that bathtub.

Andrew remained a little puzzled.
I understand logically what you say, Doctor. But may I still ask a question?
Go ahead, Andrew.
How do you know Suzanne actually even needs antidepressant medication? If Suzanne's thinking is hopeless and helpless, why can't this be an adolescent crisis? Maybe, we should be treating this solely with psychotherapy?

I saw Suzanne nodding.

This is a most important question. In fact, psychotherapeutic interventions may be very valuable in your case, Suzanne. However, you would partly respond to an antidepressant irrespective of the biological basis of the depression. In addition, medication does not negate other interventions like support, counseling or psychotherapy. We need to find the appropriate combination of the two, and certainly medication is part of that.

It was Suzanne's turn to actively speak.

But Doctor, you're saying the antidepressant medication would also help if this was not a biological illness?

Indeed it will. It will even help with psychological difficulties when there is no obvious chemical imbalance. However, you may need lower doses than you would need for a biological illness and, in addition, we must then treat the underlying cause—the psychological difficulties; this submerged cluster may be personality linked.

Andrew took his turn at this critical discussion.

Do we really know whether there's a biological element here or are we guessing?

No, Andrew, we aren't guessing. We have important pointers about the need for antidepressant medication.

Once again, I turned to Suzanne.

Firstly, Suzanne, you have the classic presentation of a biological depression. You have symptoms of regarding yourself as worthless and helplessness—the cognitive cluster. These feelings are combined with what we call the vegetative shift—the biological symptom cluster. These include early morning waking, feeling worse in the morning, appetite and weight loss but with no obvious precipitator. Second, your response reflected pharmacological patterns. For example, Suzanne, you responded to the Zoloft over the classic restabilization period of three weeks, and we saw the gradations of response with you having more energy, concentrating and focusing over that period of time. So there was the typical biological pattern of response.

Which means I probably needed the Zoloft?

Right, but even if you did not need antidepressant medication, the fact is that your receptors have been modified by the Zoloft, which means that we have to taper down that dose of Zoloft over a period of time.

You want me to take medication, Doctor, but I don't want to poison my system. I've already had experience with medications and I don't like it.

You must understand, Suzanne, that what we're attempting to correct is underlying biochemical disturbances, in the same way as a patient with diabetes needs to have his or her biochemistry corrected.

You know, I'm frightened to take medication. I was scared before I started the Zoloft, and now I'm cynical.
I can understand that, and that's perfectly legitimate. In a way, it's good to be suspicious about medications. But we have to look at their appropriate use to help you.

Medications won't deal with the most basic problems that I have. I've come to recognize that there are many psychological difficulties that have come about through my life, and these need treatment.
Yes, and medications then can be perceived as a component of the overall treatment plan. It's vital to treat the whole person. It's important to understand that certain psychological dynamics exist.

These emotional difficulties can be better handled over time if you're not profoundly depressed or profoundly anxious. The object is to handle the symptoms that may be overwhelming for you during your therapy so that your therapy can work to allow you to improve as well.

So does this exclude certain medications?
Not, absolutely. However, certain medications would not be preferred. For example, I do not want to knockout the motivating, mobilizing anxiety–this is the good anxiety of the fight, fright or flight response. I want to hit only the immobilizing anxieties–the bad ones that cause difficulties. Moreover, I prefer the immobilizing anxiety to be treated without sedation. So this would be an example of when we would use buspirone as opposed to the benzodiazepine group of drugs, like Xanax and Valium, which knock out all kinds of anxieties–abnormal ones as well as normal, and also sedate. I want you Suzanne to remain alert.

Yes, I don't want to be a zombie.
And I promise you, that you will not become one.

But then, if I were treated with both therapy and medication, I wouldn't know which was helping me?
In fact, Suzanne, we know that improvements on placebo can occur in a quarter or a third of cases, so that medication or psychotherapy may not be the reason for your getting better. But even if your improvement related to such a placebo response, you would be better, and frankly, Suzanne, that is the important aspect. You're not part of a scientific experiment. You're a real person who is suffering, and we're trying to alleviate suffering with medications and with support.

I smiled and continued:

But incidentally, we're talking about more than just the one third response to placebo. We should see a very high success rate with proper treatment, so we know that appropriate medication, and psychotherapy in your case, should do something. It is not just the sugar pill response of placebo medication.

Andrew had a thought at this point.

Doctor, please use the bathtub model again to help us understand why both medications and treatment are important.

Very well. In effect, you climb into the bathtub, and now there's a body in there that's changing the shape and levels of that bathtub and even influencing its temperature. Your organism is influencing the drug and creating a new experience. That component could be perceived in terms of the psychotherapeutic aspects and the support aspects, and may not necessarily be directly related to medication, although obviously there are some influences of your shape on the serotonin in the tub. On the other hand, we discover in this bathtub that there are certain leaks, and leaks not going into the appropriate piping linked with the bath-plugs.

These leaks are in the frame of the tub and they go in wrong directions, into the wall. We have to patch up those leaks. These are the biological abnormalities or dysfunctions or imbalances that we're correcting by using appropriate chemicals, just as we're using medications in psychotherapy. I recognize it as important to treat the whole person.

Suzanne began to move about a little in her chair.

Doctor, I'm beginning to understand that there are two facets to my recovery: my chemistry needs to be fixed; and my thoughts about myself and the world need to be more in order.

You've summarized it perfectly.

Well, I've been talking to my Mom about what we've discussed, and although she doesn't usually talk about it in public, I know she also went through something like I am going through.

Suzanne's mother had assiduously brought her daughter to her appointments. Yet, she had never said a word except when directly spoken to. At Suzanne's request, this time, she had sat in for some of our consultation. I had wondered why? Now, I understood. Suzanne wanted to have a double re-enforcement and support: her doctor on the one hand, her mother on the other. I saw this as a positive change.

Suzanne's mother spoke up:
Doctor, yes there is something I want to share. Suzanne, told me about the boulders and the beaches and I realized it had happened to me as well.
I'm listening.

When I was young, I used to drink a great deal: every night and on the weekends; three or four times a week, maybe, I was drunk. I did some stupid things while in that state, including an arrest for drunken driving. When I'd stop, I'd go through terrible withdrawals; I'd be all shaky and agitated, and I'd have to drink again just to get over it. At one point, I checked into a rehab place for a month and I got off alcohol while I was there, and they were giving me strong medicine to help.

Did you find that rehabilitation helped you?
Yes, Doctor, I did. But I must tell you, I think I did it myself. I got rid of that alcohol habit on my own. I kicked it. I haven't touched it now for sixteen years!

How did you kick it?
You know, some would say you can learn about religion, and some would say you're born into it, and I don't know which is true. One way or another, I began to realize that there's a meaning to life.

You did well. That's one facet that I find to be possibly the single most important determinant whether or not people will get off their alcohol, or their drugs of abuse, for that matter. Not only do they have to have the removal of the negative side—the removal of the alcohol or the drugs—they have to have a positive substitute to take its place.

I was pleased Suzanne's mother had ushered in this new voyage of meaning. It was critical to Suzanne's recovery.

I looked Suzanne directly in the eye.
Do you think there are any principles you can apply here?
No. I don't have an alcohol problem.

What about meaning and positive substitution?
What do you mean?
Are you doing much community service?
Our school requires that, Doctor, but as you know, I dropped out of school, and anyway, I haven't the time for that.

She didn't have the time?! All she had done these past three weeks was in effect lie on her bed moping. Her parents could not list one productive act she had performed even for herself. However, at least, I knew she was not using non-prescribed drugs. Not only was this vehemently denied by Suzanne and her family, but a urine toxicology screen had come out clear. I wanted to tell her what was on my mind, but I kept the words to myself for now, until three weeks down the line when I knew she would be on the road to recovery.

Maybe if you started looking outwards, away from yourself, and began performing kind deeds for others, you would find that you're performing the sweetest of actions for yourself.

Instead, with Andrew's new question, I returned to the pharmacology of hope. I focused on how to handle an imbalance in receptor chemistry using the bathtub analogy again, but this time through the mechanism called partial agonism, and using the drug, BuSpar.

And as quickly, as we had shifted to the psychological, Suzanne shifted back. I had come to recognize this pattern in her. She needed small bites of psychological information, of shifting away from herself, and of biochemical re-assurance.

I want to get back to the bathtub, Doctor. I've been surprised, but I find I can understand the bathtub well. What principle can we apply to handle this overfilled, ice-cold bathtub?
We apply a remarkable principle of the partial agonist group of drugs—we renormalize the receptor. This is where the whole idea of buspirone combination therapy with SSRIs has its theoretical base. Theoretically, we can extend the action of the SSRI drugs by adding in buspirone—BuSpar—because it acts as a partial agonist—the most important new concept in the pharmacology of the brain.

What do partial agonists do in this context?
There is one fundamental principle of partial agonists: In the presence of supersensitivity of the receptor, we can subsensitize that receptor back to normal. In English, we can re-normalize that receptor, from a tall ice-cold bathtub to the right level and the right temperature.
The correct balance is restored.

When did you first describe this finding?
In 1990. I presented this idea to a conference. Subsequently, people have been using buspirone as adjunct to antidepressants, particularly SSRIs, but they never fully seem to have appreciated this simple principle.

> I saw a sparkle in Suzanne's eye: momentary, but real phar-macological hope!

How do you apply this to me?
With you, we will apply the principle of partial agonism. We will diminish the number of supersensitive serotonin receptors back to the right amount—there are too many molecules of serotonin and the many bathtub receptors are therefore becoming overwhelmed. Fortunately, we can re-normalize by restoring the right balance between number of molecules and degree of response. We will use the drug BuSpar, a medication that acts as a partial agonist on a receptor subtype called 1A—the captain of the serotonin team.

> Andrew wanted to know still more about the interplay between BuSpar and the SSRIs.

When do you add the BuSpar to the SSRIs?
We add in buspirone to the SSRIs when the SSRIs *were working*, but then stopped working: When the Zoloft in your case, Suzanne, ceased helping, then it was time to augment with—add in—buspirone.

How does augmentation of the BuSpar work when you're taking SSRIs?
Basically, I think the mechanisms are complicated, so I will give you my perspective. Most important is buspirone's action as a partial agonist. It "subsensitizes" the receptor back to normal—it creates the right balance of the level of the bathtub and the temperature of the bathtub.

So the bathtub model has two main variables, temperature and water level, right? Briefly, what concretely and precisely do these two metaphors correspond to?
Temperature reflects responsiveness; level reflects number of serotonin molecules which corresponds, in effect, with number of receptors.

What does the BuSpar do?
The partial agonist property of buspirone regulates the SSRIs. [66] Using a different analogy to the bathtub: When it's completely bright, the partial agonist will actually lower that light; when it's too dark, it will make it tolerably lighter. Partial agonist drugs restore the equilibrium rather like the brain adaptation tries to do. When the brain fails in this regard, we use BuSpar to re-adapt the serotonin chemistry.

I was pleased that, with this technical diversion, Suzanne was listening intently and seemed to have understood. I was clearly winning the medication compliance battle, and I knew that Suzanne had needed scientific persuasion.

In my case, then, how will you dose the buspirone?
For the BuSpar to assist the Zoloft, we need only go to thirty or more mg per day: This is what we can call the "post-synaptic dose"—the dose that stimulates the nerve connections in the higher brain areas—the cerebrum. But, I also want to give you added advantage, so we also will utilize some of the mild antidepressant effect of the BuSpar as well. This is best found at higher doses—between 45 mg and 60 mg per day. We'll gradually build the BuSpar dose from 15 mg daily to 20 mg three times a day. But we're going to use the BuSpar combined with the Zoloft.

But why?
Because the Zoloft helped you before. It will again; but this time we will cover you with BuSpar so it doesn't overblow your bathtub.

I turned to Andrew.
So this is a good example of rational combination polypharmacy: the rational use of more than one drug together to create the best effect for Suzanne.

Andrew was back in the discussion and beginning to show a real caring for the patient.
Suzanne, would you mind if I ask the Doctor a question?

She nodded her head, indicating that it was okay and Andrew proceeded.
Is there a parallel metaphor for partial agonism in the brain?
Yes. The principle of partial agonism is too little, raise it up; too much, lower it down; the right amount, probably further stabilization and further regulation. Technically, the brain is probably doing this all the time, as regulation is clearly a very important function.

If the brain is controlling on its own, where's the problem?
Sometimes the brain can and does fail in its self-regulation, and my theory is that when the brain has failed a little bit in that regulation, some dysregulation occurs. So the buspirone is, in a way, paralleling the brain. Neuromodulation is the phenomenon that we're seeing in the brain, and the pharmacological equivalent, which we have used here is partial agonism.

When buspirone is acting as a partial agonist in relation to an SSRI in the patient's system, is it actually altering, on a chemical level, the body's way of responding to that SSRI?
Yes. As I see it, it's controlling the extremes, the job the brain should be doing. So it's regulating and normalizing.

Would you say buspirone acts like a crutch that substitutes, more or less temporarily, for a disabled limb?
You can draw parallels, certainly. But crutches imply psychological or physical support. BuSpar normalizes like insulin does in diabetes. Is that a crutch? I don't think so.

It's not really a crutch, then, but a corrector of biological imbalance?
Exactly, Andrew. As I see it, buspirone is the most physiologic of all our psychotropic compounds. This is really a great advantage. We can contrast this a little with the SSRI drugs, which we're trying to normalize. You'll remember that Paxil, Prozac, Luvox and the Zoloft, which Suzanne has been taking, act like sledgehammers: "The serotonin is low, boom! We'll raise it way up!" Where we might need to raise it up to 100, the SSRIs may raise it up to 300 or 400, and the brain will say, "hold on, I've got too much," and it usually adapts appropriately—it regulates. This time the system failed, a problem which buspirone is meant to address.

> Suzanne impressed me. Despite her sadness and concentration difficulty, she was still following the thrust of the conversation.

So how long will restabilization take for me?
The physiologic restabilization will not occur within hours. Jet lag takes weeks and so does this. It will take three, four, or maybe even five weeks to fully restabilize that receptor.

> And so we began the necessary educational process about the medication I was about to prescribe. Suzanne was free with her questions. [g]

*W*hat is BuSpar?
I regard BuSpar as one of our safest medications. It's so safe, we even use it a great deal in the elderly. Like the antidepressants, BuSpar, of course, is non-addictive, and doesn't induce dependence. However, it's one of the few medications that's generally safe to use with alcohol and therefore

---

[g] This short large letter section discusses how to use buspirone, but non-technically. It can be skipped over, losing detail but not perspective.

even in alcoholics. Overdose alone has never killed anyone, and although it's a stabilizer more than anything else, it's FDA approved only for anxiety. BuSpar also has mild anti-depressant effects, and profound effects on helping irritability. This medication to me, par excellence, is the normalizer. The brain itself is a stabilizer, but sometimes it fails. Once you're normalized on buspirone, you might be able to come off it after say six or twenty months. This is so only if there's no recurrent cause for destabilization.

How long does it takes to work?
Buspirone takes three or four weeks to fully start working because of the physiologic regulation. The delay is not due to the medication. The same principle applies as for the anti-depressants. It's the body that takes the time to adapt–like our jet lag example. So you will find a gradual improvement over time.

However, many people notice changes early on, in the first week or so. The early changes you might notice are improvements in concentration, less worrying and some improvement of irritability. BuSpar handles the build-up of irritability due to frustration. You may notice other improvements like less agitation and better sleep.

For a moment, I turned to Andrew.
It won't handle the second level of irritability: the explosive irritability– Tegretol is needed for that.

I faced Suzanne again.
So BuSpar helps which symptoms?
It helps anxiety, irritability, depression and concentration.
With anxiety, we see gradual improvements over several weeks.
The irritability begins to improve in just days.
Concentration has a similar time course to the irritability.
And although BuSpar is not as powerful as the antidepressants in depression, people don't need a powerful antidepressant unless they have a major biological depression, as in your case, Suzanne.

And the side-effects?
It does not usually make people sleepy and it usually produces few significant side-effects other than the "good" one–I call it "NVD".

What's NVD?
NVD or a mouthful "non-vertiginous dizziness" is an important side-effect with buspirone.
This special BuSpar symptom involves au unusual kind of dizziness where you don't feel like falling over.

301

How will I recognize this side-effect of NVD?
NVD starts about half an hour after taking the BuSpar. It lasts for a twenty to forty minute period. You may experience a strange sensation in your head which my patients variably describe as:
"a kind of dizziness, Doctor, this horrid, funny feeling, I've never had anything quite like it. It's a dizziness, but it's not really a dizziness. It's almost a headache, but it's not really a headache; and then it melts away like butter after about half an hour."

I believe that this side-effect of NVD can be used as a special dosing indicator. When NVD happens, you usually don't need to stay at that dose, but can drop down by 5 mg a day; if you still have the symptom, you drop down further. If you experienced the side-effect at 15 mg a day, which is uncommon but can occur, you will drop to 10; if you still have it at 10, drop to 5 mg per day. Similarly, if you experience NVD at 55 mg per day, you lower the dose to 50 mg. In other words, NVD is an extraordinary indicator of serotonin-1A function as BuSpar acts only on one receptor at those doses: This unpleasant, but benign side-effect seems directly linked up with the appropriate dosage.

Will this affect my dose?
If we don't encounter NVD, we're going to build up the dose from 15 mg a day to 60 mg a day. But if NVD happens, give me a call, just to make sure that the side-effect is NVD and not some other form of dizziness. This way we can be more certain that it really relates to the medication.

> Suzanne despite her suffering was beginning to enjoy sharing humor.

But surely you shouldn't tell patients exactly about NVD? They might imagine it?
Good question! At one point in time, I was reluctant to tell my patients, in detail, about any side-effects of any medication, because I thought they might imagine they have it. I carefully selected with whom to discuss side-effects.
However, my experience with patients is one of great respect: They don't imagine their problems, and if they know what to look for, then this extra information helps them. With NVD, it's useful for us to check that it's the right side-effect. If NVD happens, it's an advantage because we have the exact index.

Any other side-effects?
You will find in the package insert the mention of headache, but I think this headache is really the funny NVD sensation that people can't describe. In fact, we have found BuSpar helps many headaches.

Why?
You can imagine that if you're going to normalize biochemically and begin to have less anxiety, it will help to prevent headaches.

What else?
You only seldom see nausea because the nausea seems to be at a higher dose level than the NVD, so that dose should not be attained.

Suzanne was now on a roll. She was asking questions freely. I was particularly pleased because she was asking general questions. This meant that even her mother, who was on other medication, could benefit from the answers, although I took care to caution her that these were principles only, and that there were always exceptions to the rule.

Should I take my medication at any specific time?
Usually after meals would be best to allow consistent absorption. Some people take it twice, others three times per day. If we go to higher doses like 45 mg per day or above, I prefer thrice daily.

What if I miss a dose?
Missing a dose of some medication will make an enormous difference. With BuSpar, missing a dose generally won't make that difference although some people notice subtle changes quickly. I generally suggest you make up half of your missed dose with your next dose, but not more.
You may be able to learn how your body responds and work out your own special regimen based on that.

How am I going to take it?
We'll start low at 5 mg three times a day.
We'll build up to 60 mg a day by increasing by 5 mg daily increments every third day. So the first three days you'll be taking 15 mg per day; the next three days 5 mg-10 mg-5 mg making it 20 mg per day; then 10-5-10 mg resulting in 25 mg daily on days 7 through 9; and so forth.

Can I drive with it? I started learning shortly before I became depressed.
BuSpar is one of the few medications that has been tested in a simulated driving environment using normal subjects, and it doesn't seem to impair psychomotor responses. In other words, it won't impair driving—in fact, volunteers drove minimally better on BuSpar than they did with placebo; but exceptions always apply. I cannot directly recommend driving and you should always be particularly aware of any fatigue or sleepiness.

303

Sometimes, this could be due to drug interactions, not even the specific medication you're taking. In general, BuSpar is relatively safe.

But if I go off it, can I just stop it?
If you went off it, incidentally, you would, like everything else, taper it gently. I even taper placebo, for that matter, because placebo produces certain fundamental changes in your body—you might secrete some endorphins, for example, under certain circumstances.

Will I have to be taking it forever?
Not likely. The object is to normalize your receptor biochemistry. If we can do this, you can taper gently indeed. However, sometimes relapses into depression occur recurrently. If so, it's safer to take your medication for prolonged periods unless the condition is mild.

And so Suzanne began her medication regime. First, build up the BuSpar, then start the taper of the Zoloft. Her responses were typical.

After a week, she came back to see me:
Well, are you feeling any better?
No, Doctor, I'm not. It's not doing anything!

The only way you will know it's doing something, is to record what you feel, so every day you should record something like:
"I have difficulty with concentration, I just don't feel right."
Then you compare that with what you will experience down the line. You may even want to assign yourself a score for each symptom. During these first several weeks, you ought to be noticing early changes. If there's some irritability, or worry, or concentration difficulties, these should improve.
I hope so, Doctor.

But her mother noticed something significant.
Doctor, she's back in school.

Then the second week, Suzanne was still unconvinced.
No, Doctor, I'm still not better.

Her mother, however, was quick to mention a relevant detail.
She got an A on her math test.
304

And a Suzanne retort.

Yes, I do feel a little better. Then I try something new and I feel worse; it's very frustrating.

I call it "**Three steps forward, one step back.**" I expect this to occur. Progress is not a straight line. There are mainly good periods, but also slides and you shouldn't worry about that.

Sometimes you are trying something new in your quest for health and you go too fast. But sometimes your body must just catch up and you feel you're sliding. Remember, three steps forward, one step back is the rule not the exception.

The third week, finally, Suzanne announced:
Doctor, I'm feeling a little better.

To this her mother responded:
It's about time you recognized it. It took making it on the cross-country team to finally realize you're better!

The patient is sometimes the last to know about their improvement or, for that matter, their deterioration.

Suzanne was happily, but mildly indignant.
But I noticed my improvement! Like you told me, Doctor, I analyzed myself inwardly and I compared. I said:
"Listen, this is how it was, and this is how it's become," and:
"Wait a minute! I have less worry ; I'm less anxious."

Excellent, Suzanne, you can see how psychophysiologic stabilization takes weeks, just like the action of the antidepressants and jet lag. BuSpar normalizes, so you're not getting a lift; nor is it giving you the surge that recreational drugs do for those poor people who take them out of ignorance or as their own cry for help.

And to reinforce Suzanne's real involvement, I added:
And, Suzanne, you knew about your improvement in your heart, because you followed my suggestion and monitored the changes, even if you could not feel it early on.

Then, it happened: at 50 mg per day.

Doctor, it's a strange dizziness. I've never had anything like it before.
It's a strange sensation that goes behind my ears, it's an uncomfortability,
it's indescribable. This occurs, I specifically noted, about 30 minutes after I
take it and it generally will last about 30 minutes.
Congratulations, you have achieved serotonin-1A neuromodulation! We
know this because you have the "NVD" symptom we spoke about. What
this means is that we can drop down the dose. We will not stay at this
dose of 50 mg per day you're taking, but we will drop down by 5 mg a
day to 45; if you still have the symptom, we can drop down further.
When no NVD occurs, this will be your indicator that that's your appropriate dosage.

Suzanne began taking 45 mg a day of buspirone. This proved to be
her dose: no special dizziness–NVD, and the beginnings of feeling
more stable.

I started the big operation: Taper down Suzanne's Zoloft, but very
slowly according to a regimented scheme, over a period of three
months, from the 200 mg daily, cutting down each week by 25 mg
daily. At week 4, Suzanne and I reviewed her previous responses to
the Zoloft taper, and set up an even slower taper. We went from 125
mg daily, down by 12.5 mg per day every week until by week 10,
she was taking 50 mg per day. At that stage, Suzanne, took upon
herself to taper a little further.

The Zoloft felt a little too strong, Doctor.
She tapered under my supervision to 37.5 mg daily. Finally she
achieved 25 mg on week 12. She then held her dose there.

Suzanne's depression was long gone, she was performing well at
school, socializing and solving her problems with her therapist. Andrew and I had seen an example of appropriate restabilization of the
receptor using the correct combination of therapy.

I had whetted Andrew's curiosity, and after Suzanne left, he
asked.

What proportion respond to this adjunctive treatment of BuSpar with
SSRIs, Doctor?
About two out of every three patients; but, of course, the correct clues
must be there.

And the clues are?
Simply, has the patient lost a response which existed previously on the
antidepressant?

If yes, did this occur after the patient had taken antidepressants for weeks only and was the loss of effect rapid over a period of days?

If yes, has it been corrected with escalating doses of antidepressant in the past?

If all the above are present, I guess that we're dealing with a nine in ten success rate. If only some of these criteria exist, I estimate on two in three patients responding.

What's the difference between Suzanne's depression and Jim's. Jim found his Paxil was not working after seven months? Is there a difference?
I suspect there is, Andrew.

With Jim, his bathtub may have been eventually overadapting, in which case he, too, should have responded to BuSpar. However, given that he did not require escalating doses, and that his deterioration was insidious—slow and hardly noticeable on a day to day basis taking months—I suspect what he needed was a proper balance of his serotonin and norepinephrine bathtubs. Hence, we prescribed a drug which worked on both serotonin and norepinephrine. In his instance, we used Serzone because he happened to be agitated. We would have used Effexor if he had a retarded depression; and he could equally well have responded to tricyclics which were acting on norepinephrine drugs, but then he may have had anticholinergic side-effects.

So the essential difference is?
With Jim's depression, there was gradual loss of effect over months after half a year of stability on the same dose of SSRI. This meant we needed to compensate with a second, new norepinephrine bathtub.

In Suzanne's instance, escalating doses of SSRI produced repetitive quick loss of efficacy after only weeks of treatment. This implied the problem was in the serotonin bathtub: This imbalance was repaired by renormalizing with BuSpar.

Suzanne returned to see me for her one year follow-up. By this time, she was a confident young lady.

Doctor, I really enjoy school now. I've been doing volunteer work twice a week. I concentrate better. I think much more clearly: I got four As; I still got a B in physics, but I've never enjoyed physics anyway and never had any real aptitude for it; but I feel so much more confident.
That's great!

I

t was two years later. I received a call. Suzanne was again in distress. She came to see me.
She had gone off her medication.

Doctor, I did taper; I had learned the lesson about slow tapering, so I went off my antidepressant and off my BuSpar over a period of two months. Now I feel like a mess. I recognize all those symptoms, although they're not as bad as they were before; but I still feel helpless and hopeless.

The lesson about *how* to taper was one useful facet. Unfortunately, Suzanne had clearly not learnt *when* to taper. She had wanted to go off medication but she was not ready and, in fact, had she consulted me with her intention, we would have worked together, going far, far slower with any taper than she had.

Suzanne was having a second depressive episode. It hadn't occurred immediately. It had occurred about four months after she of her own volition went off her medication.

Of course, I was disappointed. However, it was not unexpected. Suzanne had given clues about her potential towards later non-compliance.

But I could use this new psychopharmacological information as an index that she needed to receive medication for a prolonged period of time.
Furthermore, I knew the dose that should control her. This was not necessarily the same dose as before, and sometimes patients tragically lose their response the second time around, but it was likely that the new dose she would need would correlate reasonably well with the older one.

You know what's interesting Doctor. I remember from before how you wanted me to work with positive facets and my own self-esteem.
Yes?

Well, I find I expect so much of myself.
This is common in depression. There are always two components:
The first is reality as it exists for everyone.
The second is the expectations each individual has. In your instance, as I see it, we have frequently dealt with some tension between these two—and that's something many people have. In your reality versus expectations

308

profile, your expectations are very high for yourself. You can't change your eye color, and, you cannot easily lower your expectations, but the reality is that if you didn't expect so much of yourself, you wouldn't find yourself pushed so hard.

So what should we do, Doctor?
Again the solution is primarily biological although you're welcome to receive support from your psychotherapist.
I'm going to start you again, Suzanne, on the 25 mg of Zoloft a day that you were taking. To cover the brain's adaptation to the bathtub, and also to help with the anxiety, I'm going to give you small amounts of buspirone.

> And so we carried out the plan.
> Suzanne re-started on the Zoloft to 25 mg daily, and added in 45 mg of buspirone, beginning as always at 15 mg per day after three days on Zoloft.
> She built up her buspirone every three days and within three weeks, Suzanne was stable again.

It's now four years after I initially saw Suzanne. This time she's a blooming young lady.

Doctor, I have a boyfriend—nothing sexual, just platonic—but we're getting to know each other more and more. I told him about my depression and he understands. In fact, it's not a problem any more. I take this medication and I have no side-effects.
That's wonderful.

But there's something more. You know, Doctor, I've been trying to help individuals. I'm doing community service at our local food bank. I really feel for those poor people. I never would have expected it, but it's rather remarkable that this has helped me.
Yes, Suzanne. To quote the contemporary British medical ethicist, Lord Immanuel Jakobovits:

> "We live not to have a good time, but to make the times good."

Our lives necessarily involve putting something in, to get satisfaction out. We cannot be takers rather than givers, because by giving, in certain ways, we're taking.

309

Andrew, the young physician, was with me, and posed a
most apt question.
Is this the essence of medical practice. The helping profession?
Yes, Andrew, it is. You have been granted a great responsibility, but also
a remarkable opportunity to be a person.

*You know, it's interesting. When I started studying medicine, I thought it
was a prestigious occupation where I would not want financially.*

And now?
*Now, I have learnt that those two factors are secondary. My special mission
is to help and contribute.*
Good, Andrew. This is the core of what it is to be a doctor. Most understand this. Some never do—and they cannot be successful human beings.

Suzanne's mother had come with her, and was clearly grate-
ful at the change that had come over her daughter.
She's a different person, Doctor, the real Suzanne I always knew was there.

I looked at both of them.

Thank you to you both. I'm so pleased you're better, Suzanne.
It's gratifying to see the whole family functioning. Your improvement is
my pleasure. The world has become a slightly better place, as well.

Once again, a tormented mind had been helped.

Chapter 12

Curing The Incurable

Tardive dyskinesia.
Longitudinal history perspective, mechanisms of action,
social history of psychosis and antipsychotics.
Corgard, high dose buspirone.
Voyage of new discovery.
(Kim, Queenie); (bathtub analogy)

Her tongue protruded out an inch then moved back into her mouth, continuously, rhythmically, ten times a minute. It looked deliberate, like a dog drooling for food, but unfortunately, her movements were not under her control. Her mouth writhed, taking half her face with it, creating strange masks, almost like a child willfully pulling faces. Kim's speech was distorted because these movements continued through her whole waking day. She had difficulty eating, spilling her food down her clothes where it ran in trails to the floor. She looked like a victim of cerebral palsy or a spastic disorder. Yet in a strange way, she was unaware, as are many patients with this condition, of her awful chewing movements. Kim presented the most severe case of tardive dyskinesia (TD) any of us had ever seen. Her symptoms were so pathetic, they were traumatic even for the psychiatric staff who routinely worked with TD patients. She was a fifty-two year old woman who looked seventy. She was a woman destined to make medical history.

Of all the cases Andrew had seen, this patient seemed to spark the most interest in him. The first time he had sat in on one of my early follow-ups, our search for an answer to the riddle of the condition that so tormented her had not yet born real fruit.
Nevertheless, I had hope that Kim's suffering embodied a summons for us to begin a voyage of exploration into uncharted waters, toward a land of promise.

One gateway there would involve, as Andrew realized, a longer look at the patient.

I think this case, Doctor, is as fascinating as it is disquieting. Do you think it would be worthwhile to understand the whole framework of our patient here? Could we discuss the "longitudinal perspective"—her case history, right from the beginning through to her present?
Of course that's worthwhile, Andrew. It's valuable with every case, and particularly in the context of psychiatry, we should trace chronologically—over a period of time—these various historical parameters.

I noticed that you do that every time, but the aspects that you've been talking to me about have for the most part fo cused on the pharmacological.
Yes, you're quite right that we have been working largely on a psychopharmacology course; but let's embark on an extended view of our patient, Kim, over a period of many years.

And so I began Kim's tragic story:
As a child Kim had been untroubled, artistically talented, and socially adept. When she graduated from High School in 1963, she enrolled immediately at a University in Minnesota with the hope of working toward a degree in Sociology. Her artistic bent served her well in her first year of college. To make money, she designed a line of embroidered toy animals that she sold at street fairs and craft shows. Her dress and behavior were as colorful and flamboyant as her stuffed animals. This made her later psychological decline just that harder to detect. At the time of her first episode of what initially was labeled "schizophrenia", later revised to a diagnosis of "schizoaffective disorder", Kim was completing an internship at a social service center in downtown Minneapolis. There she was learning counseling skills and helping at an occupational therapy unit.

When did she first become ill?
Her supervisor first noticed that Kim was late for work. Then she began to miss entire days, although she had clients to see. When he eventually went to her apartment to check on her, he found her in a deep depression, but at the same time in an oddly combative mood.
Although he was forced to fire her from the internship, he persuaded her to visit a community clinic. She failed to continue seeing her first psychiatrist, because she suddenly realized that he was trying to kill her. She had to keep quiet about it, however, because his staff were all part of the elaborate plot. They did not want her special mission to save the world to succeed. These were among the paranoid elaborations typical of schizophrenia that possessed her.

Strangely and ironically, she would make her mark on the world. But this would occur only many years later and not involve saving the world.

Kim would play the more modest but no less significant role as a patient who was contributing to a break-through in medical science that would, in a sense, save her. But Andrew did not know that at the time. I had a semblance of awareness.

How did her condition progress?
Kim seldom keeps appointments, even now, so it's difficult to reconstruct the complete chronology of events. However, the next phase for Kim seems to have included a combination of hearing unseen voices at all times of the day and night. She would hallucinate sounds of both men and women, known and unknown, dead and alive. These communications, at times, would torment her and at other times comfort her in her isolation.

But she had not yet been formally treated?
Correct. One Saturday morning in the spring of her junior year, she piled most of her possessions on the sidewalk in front of her apartment and began to give them away. Later the same day, she went to a female friend's apartment and began to make sexual advances to her friend's husband. Over the next week, she had a succession of affairs with men she picked up around the university and at crafts events, displaying a pattern of behavior more typical of extreme mania.

Did her life get even worse?
Unfortunately. She failed to complete any of her courses that year, flunked out of the university, and stopped all contact with her parents and friends. To pay her rent that summer, she took a job at an open air vegetable market where she worked as a cashier at a stall. Soon customers who touched anything got an earful of abuse.

About the time she was fired from this job, it seemed that she yelled not only at real customers, but that she also talked to people who were not there: She was experiencing auditory hallucinations. Picked up by the police one night for chanting naked in a park, she was kept in jail for twelve hours as a drunk and then released.

What happened then?
A week later she returned to the vegetable stand and began to unpile and re-pile all the food. Her former employer called for the security guard. Kim threw herself onto a pile of strawberries and smeared them on anyone who tried to subdue her. She was eventually restrained and arrested

313

on a charge of vandalism and brought to the city jail. The following morning, she was in a deep depression. The judge assigned to her case tried to talk with her for ten minutes, but Kim was unable to return a coherent response, so the court committed her to a psychiatric ward for evaluation.

Her formal treatment career began only at that point? Rather late.
Exactly. Kim was diagnosed as a schizophrenic and put onto two standard antipsychotic medications—Stelazine and later Haldol. Her career with medications had begun. The Haldol, particularly, was enormously useful. She became functional again. The voices disappeared. She did not worry about her special role in society and she was not afraid of her persecutors.

And then what happened?
Kim was released to a community clinic, the first of fifteen she would attend in four states.
Psychiatrists followed her progress monthly when she was well, admitting her when she was ill and losing her to follow-up countless times. Kim did not trust her doctors fully, and she would stop her medication. This would lead to repetitive admissions, and she once even spent a year in a mental hospital. During all this time, she was too fragile to receive indepth psychotherapy. She would have disorganized and disintegrated had any therapist tried to probe her inner secrets.

Why?
The onion of her consciousness was kept as intact as possible with no peeling of layers. Her average visits to doctors lasted minutes with less attention to content than process: *"How are the voices?" "What's your concentration like?" "How are you sleeping, Kim?"*

So the psychiatrists recognized this fragility and left her "onion" intact?
Yes.

Or were they just being cursory with her treatment?
I hope not. Many psychotic patients cannot tolerate anything longer than cursory face-to-face interactions.

Please continue, Doctor.
From that summer of her junior year, in 1966, Kim never returned to college, she never held a steady job, and she never saw the friends of her past. While her family made a few attempts to communicate with her, she steadfastly broke off those ties, becoming more and more isolative.
For their part, her parents finally decided to break relations, yet they did so without understanding Kim's problems, which Kim was unable to

explain. Kim's lack of insight into her condition persisted over many years. She kept secret the awareness that actually her voices were real. She discovered a special unseen male friend who would talk to her at night and tell her to do things that she did not understand. Once she almost burned down her apartment because "he"—and he never had a name—told her that God had commanded her to turn her curtains into beacons for the Messiah. Fortunately, a neighbor found Kim behaving bizarrely, and she ended up spending two months in the hospital.

Was she keeping these voices a secret out of paranoia or out of a more normal embarrassment?
Probably out of paranoia. Somehow she knew that others would not believe her even though they were clearly true.

And then?
Over the next fifteen years, she was admitted to the hospital twenty five times for care, sometimes for suicidal behavior, at other times for bizarre conduct. Not infrequently during this time, she would become wildly elated only to crash horribly. Even when her hallucinations and mood swings were well under control she couldn't keep a job. She made faces at people, she spoke nonsense, and she was told that she was rude and smelt offensively.

How did Kim respond to what was happening?
When Kim heard these criticisms, she thought people were just looking for reasons to fire a mental patient. She became increasingly paranoid, fearing that if she left her apartment people would kill her.
At the same time, she became more convinced that she had a special power and only she could understand what it was. Kim discovered amazing connections to her thoughts and would make elaborate drawings of the future of the world that seemed to rest on a series of numbers, 9612227772883.

What was her condition labeled as?
Kim's diagnosis of schizophrenia was revised over time by various doctors who favored one category or another of the standard clinical system. Her auditory hallucinations were characteristic of schizophrenia.
However, her manic highs and weeks of depression were characteristic of manic-depressive illness—bipolar disorder. Over the years her physicians also prescribed lithium carbonate (Eskalith) to control her mood swings. This seemed to stabilize Kim, and provided she took the haloperidol, she did not hear the voices either. At that point, she learnt that her combination of schizophrenic and manic-depressive symptoms was being labeled "schizoaffective disorder."

315

Her condition must have been very frustrating.
I'm sure it was; but despite this, Kim always remained hopeful. She had faith in her doctors, but she could not comprehend what they told her. When she first began to develop tardive dyskinesia, one of her doctors explained the connection between her medications and the strange movements she was experiencing, but she could not make the logical connection.

Why did she have this problem? Just because she was a lay person uneducated about medicine, or because of her pathology?
Because of her illness she had a limited insight into what was real and what was imaginary. She would read meanings into anything including this event.

Did she have anyone to share her troubles with?
Yes, eventually: Fifteen years after she first began attending community psychiatric clinics, she met Tom, the friend with whom she was living when we first saw her. He, too, was severely psychiatrically impaired with severe immobilizing anxieties and fears, but he was not psychotic—he had insight into his condition, was not withdrawn, and was able to live independently and work most of the year. Tom had been part of the mental health outpatient network for twenty years, working irregularly as a janitor but never requiring admission. He became her kindly male friend.

So the relationship lasted?
Yes. He stuck by her. Five or six years her senior, Tom regarded himself as her caretaker, a role that gave him some satisfaction in life. Unfortunately, he, too, gradually became so impaired that, at times, between the two of them they were unable to figure out how to catch a bus.

How did Tom and Kim relate?
There was no sexual relationship between them, at least none that they would discuss with their doctors. Kim's emotional life had become so blunted that she seemed utterly without joy. The only positive experiences in Kim's life were her devotion to her friend, which was returned with equal fervor, and her childlike hopefulness.
Kim would seldom leave the house because she did not want to be stared at, or even worse, see people turn their heads away in avoidance, sympathy or disgust at her visual agony. Tom would buy the groceries, Kim would do the cooking. Television became a life-style, looking at the TV as opposed to talking to each other. At times, Kim would look at herself in the mirror and imagine that she was beautiful and perfect; and then she would weep when she saw the grotesque facial twitching.

She did not imagine that the incurable could be cured.

Tom had been good enough to be with Kim whenever he could, for her comfort, as well as to amplify information we might have needed.

I calculated Kim has endured tardive dyskinesia for almost ten years, Doctor. I'm unsure when exactly it began, because the movements began with only slight twitches of the mouth, which seemed like a habit. Very gradually, I noticed the mouth movements grew worse, finally reaching this extraordinary state of uncontrollable writhing during the last twelve months.

Andrew was engrossed by this lengthy medical history.
I continued Kim's tragic story.
Kim had somehow, finally, realized that her tardive dyskinesia was due to her medication, and she decided to stop taking all her antipsychotic medication about eight months ago.

How did she realize this?
Kim's decision to stop taking her antipsychotics was probably as much a random result of her paranoia as it was a rational choice to stop taking a potentially harmful drug.

Was this the first time she had stopped?
No, she had stopped taking her medications at least ten times before.

I've heard that people suffering from TD also sometimes have arm and leg writhing, and trunk movements. Does Kim have these?
You're right, Andrew: Many times, tardive dyskinesia manifests not only with the awful mouth movements, but with abnormal, uncontrolled arm and leg writhing and even chest movements.
If Kim could gather any solace from the blow her TD had hit her with, it was that, in all her time with this condition, she never had the limb or trunk manifestations. However, her mouth movements were so extreme, she could hardly regard herself as lucky not to have had these other involuntary movements.

So, Doctor, did Kim first come to you with a conscious desire to have her TD treated?
Actually, no. Tardive dyskinesia was not the reason for her appearance at the hospital. In fact, she had all but given up seeking help. She had put up with her psychosis and the stigma of TD for ten years, and despite her general hopefulness, she did not believe that anything could be done to control her unwilled movements.

Then how did this patient come into your life, Doctor?
What happened was that Tom, for the umpteenth time, brought her to an emergency room. Tom recognized she was ill again and needed treatment. At night, she watched television, any television, or listened to talk shows on the radio. She would often have two way conversations with the television. She was agitated and confronted her house-mate over every real or imagined slight, and was so restless that she continually and noisily paced her apartment, making it impossible for both her roommate and her partner to sleep.

Was she hallucinating at the time?
No. Despite this, she was not hallucinating. She looked more as if she was on an irritable manic-like high. But her temporary acute psychiatric presentation was overshadowed by her chronic neurological condition—her TD.

Andrew shifted from Kim's specific symptoms to the more general perspective of TD in the community.

Why is TD so important?
Andrew, to answer that seemingly simple question properly, I'm afraid I will have to take you on a slightly diverging excursion into the **history of antipsychotics** as treatment.

In fact, I'd been meaning to ask you about that since you mentioned it earlier.
Good. I seem to be getting to a point where I'm anticipating most of your questions.

How did it all begin?
When the first effective antipsychotic medications were developed in the early 1950s, psychiatrists throughout the world hoped the way was clear for rapid advances in the care of the mentally ill. Care-givers of all kinds began to draft plans for opening the doors of the dreaded state mental hospitals, and families hoped for the return of loved ones. The way out turned into an ugly dead end. Not only did de-institutionalization leave thousands of ex-patients on the streets as a generation of bag people, but the drugs themselves, one after another, revealed a tendency to create side-effects that the public and family members found almost as troubling as the psychoses themselves.

So this became a political issue?
Yes. Throughout America, many government jurisdictions eventually passed legislation restricting the long-term use of antipsychotic

318

medications–the neuroleptics–for some classes of patients, especially those in nursing care, because the side-effects of neuroleptics were turning people into socially unacceptable spectacles.

In effect, the long-term treatment with antipsychotics had created a new disease—tardive dyskinesia—on a social scale?
Yes, in a sense, that's what happened. The last twenty years have made the problem much more visible and much more widely understood, with American psychiatric hospitals beginning to release large numbers of patients to the streets. As these patients were "mainstreamed", many physicians refrained from prescribing antipsychotics to avoid such a publicly visible side-effect and to avoid the risk of litigation.

This must have created quite a dilemma.
It did, perhaps most of all for public policy. It still raises ethical questions: Do you decline to medicate, releasing ill psychotics without the drugs that would greatly improve their quality of life and even substantially increase the danger to themselves and the public? Or do you medicate, sometimes without consent because the patients are lacking insight into their illness and behavior? Are long-acting depot injections of neuroleptics lasting several weeks the answer? Is it appropriate to create a minority class of "walking wounded" who were visible pariahs, who would stagger, slobber, and jerk with other uncontrollable gestures that make them targets of discrimination and perhaps abuse?

Well what do you think is the solution?
I believe the answer is to medicate appropriately, particularly given that most patients with TD have much milder symptoms, sometimes even almost undetectable except to the expert. Kim is by far our worst such case. I feel desperately sorry for her.

What about TD and the elderly? I noticed that Kim is getting on in years. Is this a relevant factor?
Kim is entering that age–she's 53–where such statistics may be relevant. The fear of tardive dyskinesia has led to changes in medical practice and to what's called the OBRA legislation. This restricts the use of antipsychotic medications for older people in nursing homes, even where there's clear evidence that low doses of these drugs could help to manage aggression or agitation.
Among the elderly, tardive dyskinesia strikes up to 50% of all patients within a year; among younger patients the risk is also high. Five percent of patients will begin to show signs of TD for each year antipsychotics are taken, so that the risk increases year by year to about a twenty percent level.

Is TD dosage related, then?
Yes, it appears that TD is dosage related, with higher doses producing more rapid and more severe effects, but even more so it's directly correlated with length of time on medication. In fact, the elderly may be more severely affected by TD because any dose will stay in their bodies longer. It takes older people longer to metabolize drugs–to clear them from the system–with the result that older patients may carry higher levels in the bloodstream at all times, producing more severe and more rapidly visible side-effects. Elderly patients may also be prescribed more medication than is necessary. In nursing home practice, antipsychotics might be used in low doses to control aggression and irritability. Unfortunately, even these doses may produce TD, particularly because these patients do not usually have the dopamine excess state that would make antipsychotic drug prescription more justifiable.

What about Kim?
Kim is clearly a patient at risk–an older female who has received high doses of antipsychotic medication for many years for a condition that was not typical schizophrenia and therefore was biochemically different.

Why exactly is it called "tardive dyskinesia"?
"Tardive" is simply a form of the word "tardy", or slowly developing. "Dyskinesia" means "disordered movement".
TD involves movements not only of the mouth, tongue, lips and cheeks, but also involuntary movements of the limbs. The first time I saw these uncontrolled limb movements was in a fellow medical student who had destroyed a brilliant mind with hallucinogenic drugs. He developed an unusual paranoid condition, resembling schizophrenia. His persecutory delusions and inappropriate perception of himself as a supreme being were controlled by antipsychotics, but only at a severe price...

He developed TD?
That's right. His TD was subtle at first. He moved his arms slightly, touched his fingers together compulsively and rhythmically rotated his arms at the shoulders. To cover up these effects, he carried a yo-yo constantly, so that he would appear to be playing with it when, in reality, he was unable to control his movements. Despite obtaining a medical degree, he was not allowed to practice medicine.

So TD is a direct result of prolonged antipsychotic treatment?
Tardive dyskinesia is a slowly developing condition that destroys whatever sense of well-being has resulted from a successful intervention by antipsychotic drugs, in that those same antipsychotic drugs also cause the uncontrollable and inappropriate movements.

How easy is it for this to happen?
It's impossible to develop tardive dyskinesia after a single dose of antipsychotic or neuroleptic; it takes many doses, perhaps even many years of medication to develop, and most patients develop few if any symptoms. Many cases, however, develop within two or three years, but sometimes it happens in less time.

What exactly is the chemical mechanism whereby antipsychotics engender tardive dyskinesia?
We think it relates to the model of dopamine supersensitivity. You'll remember the bathtub. This time the level is very high, but no adaptation of the temperature has occurred—it's still hot: Using our other metaphor, there have been more piers—receptors—built, and this allows more boats—neurotransmitters—to or there.

Andrew shifted away from the metaphoric:
Does anything else cause TD?
Yes. The antipsychotics belong to the neuroleptic group because they block dopamine. Some anti-nausea medications also are neuroleptics, for example, metoclopramide (Reglan) and prochlorperazine (Compazine). We're careful with these medications, using them for short periods in small doses, and we're particularly attentive to the elderly and organically impaired.

Isn't it an unusual disease, in that it does not arise naturally, but is introduced from without, chemically?
Good point.

Would a parallel be the so-called "Agent Orange" sickness?
Maybe. The difference is one of intent. Antipsychotics revolutionized psychiatry and made functional the non-functional.

When were these dangers found out?
When Kim started on antipsychotics, doctors did not yet know about tardive dyskinesia. Only in the early 1980s was she first told about the risks of her drugs, although her doctors had some awareness of TD during the 1970s. At that time, it was still regarded as a vague condition not requiring patient information.

You know, Doctor, mental patients already have to go through significant social pain and discomfort, not to mention their psychic distress. This rise of TD only seems to have added insult to injury.
I couldn't agree with you more, Andrew. That successful treatments have not been found for tardive dyskinesia may say something about the spe-

321

cial status of mental patients, who still live under a cloud of blame and misunderstanding compounded by various cultural perspectives on mental illness. Is a psychiatric disorder a crime? A punishment from God? A genetic disorder? A bad habit? Or a matter of biochemistry? Mental patients have a history of being treated in ways similar to criminals and are often subjected to treatments that are aimed more at the protection of society than toward rehabilitation.

What have been some of the impacts of this cultural prejudice on the patient? And on Kim in particular?
In the case of tardive dyskinesia, it's ironic that some patients prefer to avoid certain improvements to their psychosis. We can control their delusions, but they prefer lowering the risk of the distorted facial gestures, because they would rather have a cosmetically "acceptable" result of no movements than be clear of psychosis. This is tragic because we're dealing with a relatively low risk of what's often only a mild TD condition, anyway.

Andrew's brow tightened into a knot of concern.
Faced with the symptoms Kim has presented, Doctor, aren't you tempted to ask, what's the object of medicine? To heal the patient or to put families at ease?
Yes indeed, Andrew; but even such a well-meaning question as that can oversimplify the issues. How is it possible to measure the relative suffering of the patient? Which is worse: to have paranoid delusions of abandonment and jeopardy, or to go through each day writhing, unable to chew, and spilling food all over your clothes? There are no good answers to questions like these. If a patient says that the family cat is a lion, that doesn't necessarily mean that she's as frightened as you or I would be if a lion appeared in our living rooms. Maybe the patient thinks she's the world's greatest lion tamer, or Noah leading the animals to the ark. Maybe, on the other hand, the patient thinks she's a child about to be eaten. In like manner, Kim's thought *content* may be idiosyncratic—peculiar to her alone. I'm more interested in the *process* of her thinking because this allows me insights into her abnormal brain chemistry.

Well, Doctor, certainly I feel for Kim's tragedy, and I hope you will bring me up to date on it as time goes along.

I was determined to help Kim's seemingly baffling state and alleviate her suffering. The sense that psychiatric patients are incurable does not encourage researchers or clinicians, who are often left to their own creativity to seek solutions.

322

Conventional limitations in knowledge encourage innovative clinical approaches to medications in such cases. These drugs are often approved for other disorders, but may produce improvements in other neuropsychiatric illnesses when used out of labeling–for a non-approved indication.

Treating the marginalized patient often leads the doctor into the practice of a deeply caring and careful medicine, representing a grave challenge of the risks of venturing into the unknown that nevertheless proffers incalculable rewards. I knew from the first that I needed to try to alleviate Kim's suffering.

Could it be that high doses of BuSpar would help? There was a theoretical reason for this which I discussed with Andrew, a week later the next time we met. [h]

Andrew! It's good to see you.

Why don't you step into my office, and I'll give you a rundown on Kim?

How have you treated Kim?

Her psychiatric condition is stable at this point without antipsychotics. As you know, we have continued her previous prescriptions for the conventional treatments for tardive dyskinesia–she has now taken Vitamin E, lecithin and magnesium for six months. She has unfortunately continued to experience her tardive dyskinesia even though she stopped taking neuroleptics nearly a year ago. So there's little to lose.

Well, what do you plan to do?

I now want to treat her with high doses of buspirone–BuSpar. Theoretically, this should work.

Buspirone? Why?

It's difficult to tell whether this hypothesis is an intuition, a subtle awareness of the drug's potential, or a conclusion based on a theoretical understanding of this drug. I suspect it's all of these.

Kim's appearance is so extreme that she's an ideal candidate to be the first patient to receive this treatment.

What is it about buspirone that makes you think it's applicable in this case?

It's a long story which I will abbreviate. As you know, BuSpar has been marketed since the mid 1980s as a medication for anxiety. Oddly enough, it was first developed a decade earlier with the hope that it would prove to be antipsychotic.

---

[h] Again, this very short section between large letters has some technical elements and can be skipped over, losing detail but not perspective.

Andrew looked puzzled.

I'm still in the dark about how this relates to TD.

Well, your puzzlement reflects the complex nature of the drug. When I explored the chemistry of this drug, I realized how complicated it was: I knew the actual details were less important than the principles of its action. This understanding led to what I hoped would be a major breakthrough in medicine—not only helping Kim, but the many others truly suffering from tardive dyskinesia.

So what is it exactly about buspirone that makes you think it is logical for Kim?

As you know, BuSpar's distinctive property turns out to be that it acts specifically and selectively at a particular receptor site in the brain called the serotonin-1A receptor. It acts at a special level on this site by a mechanism called partial agonism. In fact, it's the only marketed serotonin-1A partial agonist.

Would you run through what partial agonism means in light of your investigation of BuSpar?

Certainly. You know what agonism means, right Andrew?

Yes. It means normalization—modulation up or modulation down.

Wrong! That's what partial agonism means. Agonism itself is full blown; it refers to stimulation—4 or 6 shoots up to 10, even if only 5 is necessary. "Partial agonists" stimulate somewhat when necessary—4 is raised to 5 or 6, but not more than that. In effect, partial agonists could also be called "partial antagonists" (though they're not called that) as they partly inhibit when there's too much—when the score is 7 they bring it down to 5. They modulate or normalize. So partial agonists act like normal body mechanisms to stabilize.

Normalization is a mechanism we all use, unconsciously, all the time— breathing, the heart beating and regulating blood sugar. The pharmacological equivalent is partial agonism—the ultimate modulation by drugs: If your temperature were 104 degrees, you would be in a state of fever; if your temperature were 94, you would be in equal distress. We know that somewhere in the brain there's a mechanism that modulates temperature, pushing it up or down as needed. Partial agonism is a kind of modulation where it's not simply just up or just simply down, but rather a balancing of the two.

Chemically speaking, how does buspirone's partial agonism work?

Buspirone in the usual therapeutic doses only acts through partial agonism of that single important chemical in the brain, serotonin. It acts on a particular chemical site, the serotonin-1A receptor.

The captain of the team!
Andrew grinned, remembering the phrase.
That's right. Serotonin-1A often dictates what the rest of the serotonin receptors do.

So how does this partial agonist quality of buspirone impact on Kim?
I want it to regulate and balance Kim's system—not too much and not too little—thereby making her movements normal. Theoretically, this is exactly what buspirone could accomplish, but strangely I need to impact not serotonin, but dopamine to do this: I think BuSpar will achieve this.

I could see that Andrew's brow was beginning to acquire that characteristic compression I had come to know.
But Doctor, I'm still a little confused. Buspirone was initially hypothesized to be an antipsychotic, even though it did not prove to be so. How could it now, according to your research, be used for TD, which was the unfortunate legacy of prolonged antipsychotic treatment? Please enlighten me.
I hope I can, Andrew. You see, in the 1970s, we knew nothing about serotonin-1A. It was known that in the early animal studies with buspirone, BuSpar had effects on dopamine: It reversed the effects of chemicals that stimulated dopamine production in the brain like the narcotic apomorphine and amphetamines like "speed". So it was known that BuSpar blocked the dopamine receptors, and it was also known that the antipsychotic drugs blocked dopamine receptors, so here was a link.

Could it be the case that BuSpar would indeed be an antipsychotic?
Many clinical trials were attempted, but they showed that BuSpar had no such antipsychotic effect. We now understand why.

Why?
In very high doses—fifteen or twenty times higher than we use for anxiety—BuSpar blocks dopamine excess like a drug functioning as a *dopamine* partial agonist should.[67] It doesn't work by blocking—by antagonizing—unless there's excess when it effectively partially antagonizes because there's too much dopamine. But, and this is the key, it also reverses drugs that block dopamine, such as the antipsychotics: It may be the only dopamine partial agonist that we know of.

Andrew shifted back to Kim's management.
High doses BuSpar sounds exciting! But what are you after with the buspirone in relation to Kim?
We certainly would not use buspirone to treat Kim's hallucinations or delusions: It won't help those because it's not antipsychotic, although it

may handle her anxieties, but this is secondary. We want to use the medicine to help her mouth movements, and this would require the partial agonism effects on the dopamine receptors in the brain.

Andrew's brow was relaxing, and I think he was beginning to fully understand the exciting situation at hand. A cure was actually in sight for Kim. Could it be that she would change the history of psychiatric illness, as the first individual to be a living testament to the confirmation that tardive dyskinesia is no longer incurable? If Andrew's brow was no longer furrowed, however, his questioning mind was not yet at rest.

So BuSpar reverses the dopamine blockade created by the antipsychotics as well as dopamine excess?
Yes. It works both ways—too much dopamine is lowered, too little is raised—by normalizing. Let's first use the examples you know about: When SSRIs are no longer helping the depression, we can re-regulate serotonin by normalizing receptor supersensitivity, by using buspirone as a serotonin partial agonist. In this case, it's the same, but with dopamine: Buspirone in much higher doses functions as a "dopamine partial agonist."

I remember how with Jocelyn's catatonic state, we pushed up her dopamine by giving her Sinemet.
Good. Well, we don't want to randomly push up the dopamine too high in Kim, as we did for Jocelyn—in other words, cause the bathtub of dopamine to go to 300 or 400. We only want it at 100. If it goes to 300 or 400, we will make Kim psychotic, and we do not want to do that. We want to regulate what is already abnormal and reverse it if necessary. Moreover, if it went too high, the brain would start compensating by cooling down the bathtub, producing only short term results and actually at a later point maybe complicating the TD—the tardive dyskinesia.

Are there any other clues that buspirone will work, Doctor, as you propose it will?
Yes. You'll remember that we have spoken about how the neuroleptics given to experimental animals produce catalepsy—the equivalent of catatonic stupor in humans.

Yes, where patients may hold their limbs fixed in distorted positions for hours at a time and sit like statues, like Jocelyn did.
Right. Well, every antipsychotic drug will produce catalepsy in animals, but amazingly BuSpar will reverse these effects. This is one of the reasons why we know that BuSpar is also partly a dopamine agonist when there's

too little dopamine around. Buspirone, then, has the characteristic of reversing both dopamine agonism and dopamine antagonism.

That's interesting. Buspirone seems to possess an inherent balancing capability. Is this the same as the partial agonism you spoke of earlier?
Yes, and so, I have the hope that this property may prove to be a kind of salvation for Kim, who has suffered for so long. It should normalize her receptor, but will require very high doses—much more than the usual 15 mg to 60 mg per day that we give—to obtain the dopamine partial agonist effect.

What doses are we talking about?
The studies on schizophrenia even tried as much as one gram—1000 milligrams—per day, about six times higher than I anticipate Kim will receive. It did not work in helping hallucinations and bizarre thinking, but it proved to be safe. Doses twenty or thirty times higher than usual are often dangerous, but BuSpar appears to be safe at these levels. Certainly, over ten million persons have been treated with it at the conventional low doses: In doses up to 60 mg per day—the doses it marketed at for anxiety—it's proving the safest psychotropic drug ever developed. There are no instances of death by overdose. We know, too, that it does not produce dependency or addiction, abuse, withdrawal, or cravings.
But, since marketing, no one has used the doses I'm planning to give to Kim.

Well, what do you think? Will it work? And how does Kim feel?
I have high hopes for helping her tardive dyskinesia and we will monitor her condition carefully while Kim is in the hospital. We will evaluate her many times a day to ensure that the procedure is safe and can be monitored. We have already discussed the treatment in detail with Kim and Tom, and received their informed consent to go ahead. They're excited, but I'm trying to hold back my enthusiasm so there won't be a let down.

But is Kim okay to decide?
Fortunately, Kim is not displaying active features of her psychosis as otherwise her treatment would be complicated by the dilemmas of using antipsychotic drugs. This would also potentially interfere with our interpretation of our results. Symptoms such as her hearing voices, or her feeling that beings were plotting against her, may place her in a situation of dangerousness to herself or to others and would limit her functioning.

We were on the brink of possibly curing the single greatest epidemiological scourge since the advent of drugs in psychiatry—tardive dyskinesia—with very high doses of buspirone.

327

Andrew wished to know a little about previous treatment attempts for TD, and I obliged him.

Several drugs were unsuccessfully tried in the hope of improvement. The benzodiazepines, such as Valium and Librium, sedate the patient, but do not reduce the movements. Anticonvulsants were prescribed without effect. Beta-blockers, which work well for thyroid disease, high blood pressure, and anxiety, were also attempted without results. Vitamin therapies have also been tested. Vitamin E helps slightly—when it works at all it may mildly alleviate the symptoms of TD for six or seven weeks. Magnesium also may have a minor effect, as may lecithin and certain fatty acids.

But, as you have more than once intimated, there was one sure-fire treatment: antipsychotics.
Yes, Andrew, paradoxically, they did help—temporarily. Increasing the dose of antipsychotics temporarily *masked* the effect of TD—but at a terrible price. The improvement continues for perhaps a month, and then the patient relapses with even worse and more severe symptoms.

Does this worsening keep spiraling?
If this regimen is continued, increasing doses of antipsychotics will be followed by reversion to still worse tardive dyskinesia. Eventually the patient may disputably develop a still worse condition called "tardive psychosis". In this illness, both the complicating TD and the original psychosis seem intensely dependent on tiny fluctuations of dosage.

How tiny are we talking?
Well, for example, a 1 mg variation, rather than a 20 mg dose alteration of an antipsychotic drug like Trilafon, may produce profound changes. In effect, what's going on is that increasingly smaller doses do what larger doses used to do. TD is the prototype human condition for this dopamine supersensitivity—this high level in a still hot—unadapted—bathtub. With tardive psychosis, not only are the movements involved, but the thinking is as well. The difference, I hypothesize, may be changes in some of the dopamine subtype bathtubs—just like serotonin has at least fifteen, dopamine has several—we don't know how many yet. If only we could reverse this supersensitivity!

Until Kim walked into the hospital with her marked case of tardive dyskinesia, there seemed to be no good treatment for her condition. We could not reverse her supersensitivity with any known drug.
I was apprehensive knowing a new treatment was in sight—buspirone in high doses.

So how much buspirone do you think will be needed?
I hypothesize that Kim would need 120 to 200 milligrams of buspirone daily. This should be sufficient to create sufficient dopamine effect in Kim's case. This would reverse the supersensitivity.

Why not the 1,000 mg per day you spoke about?
Because, TD by its very nature is a supersensitivity state. Consequently, I hypothesize we will only need maybe a quarter of the dose that usually we would use in someone without supersensitivity, but whose dopamine receptors we would be trying to normalize. Of course, we wouldn't have to in the latter case, so I'm talking theoretically!

I see, Doctor. This is exciting.
I'm glad you feel that way, Andrew. We're dealing with not only a treatment to help Kim. We're dealing also with a voyage of exploration to a previously unexplored area. We're literally crying to help a beloved mind. Critical to our success will be the gradual buildup of the dose and the monitoring of response at every level.

How will you monitor change?
That's a very important scientific question, Andrew! No scale has been invented for adequately measuring changes in movements of this severity, so I have developed one in anticipation to be able to mark small alterations. This way we can differentiate between the terrible and the still more profound dysfunction.

But why do you need a more precise scale?
Previous movement scales used 5 point measures like 0 through 4, and descriptions like "mild, moderate, severe, or profound". Now, someone as severe as Kim could be scored as profound even after substantial improvement. Her index of severity is off the wall. Consequently, I have constructed a ten-point scale. This is partly based on a previous measure used in Holland which had a range up to 6, but even this is variation is insufficient. With our new modification, small changes, such as moving from a 10 to a 9.5, can be measured.

W e began Kim on a low dose of fifteen milligrams every day. Gradually, we built the dose up by ten milligrams a day, so that her condition could be watched carefully.

Our initial results were as expected. By 60 mg daily there was absolutely no change: her movements—the writing, the speech defects,

329

the tongue protrusion, were all as bad as ever. She still spilled her food all over her body. We expected no change because dopamine was not yet being involved: I had estimated that buspirone would significantly impact the dopamine receptor itself only at about 120 mg per day.

And then after about a week and a half, the marvel began: a spark of change, a minimal improvement in her movements.

Again, I filled Andrew in:
At 90 mg per day, there was a minimal, but definite improvement.
It led to my ranking Kim not a 10—meaning extremely profound with terrible uncontrolled movements—but a 9.

But, Doctor, was this response because of the buspirone beginning to work at the dopamine level? Or was it coincidence, or even a placebo response?
I thought it was real, but we had to wait and see.

Did the improvement continue?
Yes, it did. At 100 mg daily there was a more visible, but still only slight improvement—she was rated an 8.
This continued. At 110 milligrams, Kim was scored as a 7, and by 120 mg daily a 6. By this time, although her tongue protrusions were still severe at times, she had periods when they were absent. Her speech was improved and she was able to eat with more confidence.
She was so improved that we entertained the consideration that we were dealing with a spontaneous remission, and that the drug had nothing to do with her improvement.

Nevertheless, she had improved, right, Doctor?
Yes, indeed, Andrew.
For the first time in many years, Kim looked happy. She was full of hope. I could see in her eyes the new questions she was finally allowing herself to ask: *"Am I finally going to get better? Is the torment of people staring at me over at last?"*

So have you tried to find out whether Kim had a spontaneous remission?
Yes, we have, because the question concerned us: How could someone who had been so terribly maimed by TD for ten years make such a rapid improvement?

Well, was it possible?

To test the possibility that BuSpar was doing nothing at all, we took her off buspirone for 24 hours. Her movements immediately became far worse, though not as bad as when she first entered the hospital. When the drug was started again, she improved immediately. Buspirone is a short-acting drug that's quickly metabolized and flushed from the system. In Kim's case, she needs her medication every six hours. She's so sensitive to the level of buspirone in her brain that we can see a measurable deterioration in her condition in the hour before she takes her next dose.

Like in Parkinson's patients on levodopa?
Right.

How did Kim feel about this test of withholding medication?
Kim does not know about the changes in her dosing and she did not know that the medication had been stopped for a day.
As part of our consent discussion before we had started, I had emphasized to her that we would not be able to let her know about dose alterations or any withholding of the BuSpar. This way we could obtain a slightly more objective impression when rating her movements. When I told her later about the medication stoppage and its effects, Kim was excited. She knew that the drug was having a real effect; and we knew we were on the verge of a legitimate and dramatic finding in medicine.

Andrew's expressed the keen desire to meet with me again, as soon as something new developed, and we met to discuss Kim's progress on several more occasions.

Over the next week, we continued to build up Kim's dose to 160 milligrams.

This was already perhaps the highest daily dose of the drug ever given since marketing. Was this mere folly, impersonal science, or an intense desire to help a patient? The dose was still comparatively low: only one sixth the amount of 1000 mg that had been used in schizophrenia research prior to the drug being officially marketed.

Andrew was concerned.
But what about side-effects?
As you know, BuSpar has its own side-effects, like non-vertiginous dizziness and nausea. We were concerned that these might begin to appear at any time because this would force us to choose a dosage that would balance her tardive dyskinesia—itself a side-effect of her years on neuroleptics—against the side-effects of BuSpar.

331

Did nausea or dizziness happen?
Fortunately not. However, something much worse did: Kim presented us with a sudden and more dangerous condition–uncontrollable diarrhea–which could dehydrate and even kill her in a matter of days, if untreated. Her diarrhea had developed gradually, but she had kept its initial mild presentation to herself, as many patients would. Kim was particularly concerned that if she mentioned it we would take away the treatment that could change her life.

Presumably you treated the diarrhea rather easily?
We tried to but did not succeed. We actively treated Kim's diarrhea as soon as we learnt about it. She was given all the regular treatments–drugs, fluids and preparations that turn the gut to concrete–but none of them worked.

What was going on?
We wondered whether this could be a side-effect of the BuSpar or something else.

Like what?
We began to explore yet another drug interaction. Kim had stopped taking her neuroleptics more than eight months before. But instead, she had been taking lithium in the hopes that despite her label of "schizophrenia", her illness could be controlled without resorting to the antipsychotic group that would ultimately make her TD worse. We had kept her on her lithium. Could it be that the lithium, which sometimes increases serotonin, was, with the BuSpar, causing her serotonin system to go into overdrive?

So you were linking the diarrhea to the serotonin?
Yes. With these high doses, we wondered whether buspirone's partial agonist effect on the serotonin system was being mobilized by the lithium, resulting in this augmentation of serotonin in her system?

What did you do?
We prescribed a serotonin blocker, Periactin. In this case, the serotonin that concerned us was not in the brain, but in the gut–the source of the diarrhea: As you know, Andrew, serotonin is densely distributed in the gastrointestinal tract and serves an important function regulating bowel movements.

It was a little blip presumably. You solved that problem easily I assume?
Yes and no. The results were striking. Her diarrhea stopped within half a day; but there is now an even bigger problem.

332

What?
Kim's tardive dyskinesia has come back!

But why?
The serotonin blocker seems to have been negating the effects of the bus-pirone on the TD.

Do you mean to say that serotonin balance is somehow integral to curing her TD?
Yes. This means that in some way serotonin receptors as well as dopamine receptors are involved. This unexpected result could reflect a tragic result not only for Kim but potentially for thousands of others who may benefit if this treatment turns out successful. So the stakes are high and this is where we are at the present time.

What are you planning to do then?
Clearly, we have to fix her diarrhea urgently, and yet still maintain the anti-TD effect of the buspirone. We have to find a serotonin blocker that will control the serotonin in Kim's gut. At the same time, we must not interfere with the complex chemistry of her brain, where the buspirone is controlling her tardive dyskinesia by apparently modulating both the serotonin and dopamine.

What will allow us that privilege?
We must find a serotonin blocker that will not pass through the blood-brain barrier and one that preferably hits serotonin-1A, as buspirone acts specifically on serotonin-1A.

So it must not be fat-soluble?
Right. This way it's unlikely to pass into the brain.

> The task did not seem daunting, but somehow I couldn't think of a drug that fitted this bill. I spoke to my local colleagues—clinicians and pharmacologists. No one could make a suggestion. I consulted experts around the country: The animal did not appear to exist.
>
> That night, I went to bed deeply troubled. I needed to find a solution urgently.

Early the next morning, it came to me. Nadolol (Corgard), a common beta-blocker used in hypertension, should fit both criteria. It was not fat-soluble, and, in animal experiments, several drugs in its sub-receptor class—beta 2 adrenergic—had been shown to block serotonin-1A.

However, this property had never been demonstrated in humans and we did not even know for certain if nadolol would act like the four drugs in its class that had already been shown to have this property. These four drugs were either lipid-soluble and so would pass into the brain, or were unavailable in the USA.

Andrew was there the following day, to hear the follow-up.
Well?
It was make or break for Kim. Her diarrhea was priority number one. We gave her nadolol to bring her gut under control, and allow the buspirone to work without complications. It worked. No diarrhea, and her tardive dyskinesia steadily improved!

After Andrew had left me that day in the library study room with a serene brow, a sign of no further questions to be asked, Kim stayed in the hospital for about six weeks. When she left her tardive dyskinesia was almost gone. Her score was a 1 out of 10 and sometimes even a round zero.

That veritable success changed Kim's miserable life.
We published the first successful treatment of tardive dyskinesia, in a British journal, [68] but Kim's follow-up was not completely satisfactory. Patients with mental illness are not the most reliable self-medicators. She returned for a few evaluations, and then her underlying psychotic condition began to worsen as it had on so many occasions before when she was off neuroleptics.

Then one day, she didn't show up for her follow-up. Attempts to phone her and write to her address yielded no response. She had vanished without a trace. We tried without success to trace her. She was lost to us.

Two years later, Kim was admitted to a different hospital in the midst of a major psychotic episode. Regretfully, her tardive dyskinesia was almost as bad as at her first admission. By luck I heard about her, and she was referred to my care.

I discovered that she had gone off her buspirone more than a year before. She had not consulted anyone, and had gradually deteriorated.

All this time, Andrew had assumed that Kim's initial cure was a simple success story, and he was quite surprised to hear of her disappearance and subsequent reversal of her condition.

With genuine feeling, he said:
How unfortunate, Doctor, I'm sorry to hear that. What have you done? Are you simply going to repeat what worked last time?

I could tell Andrew's interest was one of genuine, considerate concern. His question did not reflect a purely academic appetite for knowledge for its own sake, which I knew used to move his questions more in the past.

I was glad to see this progression in him, adding a humane complement to his unquestionably bright mind. Could it be that my mentoring during so many of these voyages in patients' lives had contributed to this welcome character maturation, as a budding doctor and as a maturing human being?

Well, Andrew, I can assure you that our hope in Kim is not at all lost. We decided first to try a different class of medications because her psychotic symptoms were our primary concern this time.

What symptoms?
Kim was fearful that her boyfriend and caretaker was going to marry a woman who had been dead for fifteen years. More realistically, she worried that she would be evicted and kicked out to live on the street, and that she was an embarrassment to her boyfriend, even though he was also impaired.

So did she also immediately begin the BuSpar again?
No. We gave her antipsychotics. On this occasion, however, she was not taking lithium.

And what happened?
We had initially prescribed a mild and rarely used neuroleptic—pimozide—hoping that it would not worsen her TD. When that did not control the psychosis, we tried a "middle of the road" neuroleptic, Trilafon. This helped her psychosis considerably: She stopped believing that her boyfriend was going to marry the long-dead lover. Still, she was

displaying other symptoms of paranoia and thought disorder, although she had some confidence in her doctors. After a few weeks, her psychosis was controlled.

What about the TD? How did you treat that?
I didn't want to muddy the waters with buspirone, so at the time we started Kim on the antipsychotics, we also prescribed the standard dietary approaches to controlling TD—vitamin E, lecithin and magnesium.
I wanted to establish whether these approaches could be as effective as buspirone in Kim's particular case. If they were, we would not have then needed buspirone.

Did the TD improve on that regimen?
Yes, but only slightly. The TD improved by about 20% for a few weeks. This temporary change could have related to beginning antipsychotics drugs again as, strangely, they will temporarily improve TD; alternatively, it may have been due to the magnesium, lecithin and vitamin E she received.

But clearly the improvement in Kim's TD was not satisfactory?
Correct. After a few weeks, we again attempted to actively manage her TD with buspirone as the improvements had already waned. Once more, we built up the buspirone dose.

Did she get the diarrhea again?
Yes she did, at about the same dose as before, around 120 mg daily; but this time the diarrhea occurred off lithium. Once more we gave her nadolol, and once again she was cleared of diarrhea and her tardive dyskinesia greatly improved. Both her TD and her psychosis are now better, and Kim is in really good spirits. In fact, if you can stay for a few minutes longer, you will be able to meet her again and see for yourself.

I would like that very much, Doctor. You know, the last time I saw her was over two years ago.

And so, Andrew was re-united with Kim. Addressing me, she declared:
Doctor, it's so wonderful to be free of my years of suffering! I hope I won't ever have a relapse again!

I emphasized once again the need for medication compliance. This was my great concern about Kim's future.
I'm confident Kim, that you will do well provided you take your medication. This is the key.

Kim's face beamed with a smile at this assurance and, out of a genuine interest which seemed to rise beyond self-interest, asked me:

Am I your only success story, Doctor?
No, Kim. In fact, we have continued to use high doses of BuSpar in tardive dyskinesia. When we reached your dose range, 120 to 180 mg per day, our results have been rewarding: We haven't seen a patient who has taken BuSpar in these high doses, who has not responded.

In addition, several colleagues around the country have used this treatment and given me feedback: They have consistently reported significant success. It seems we have found a solid way to manage TD.

What about the diarrhea?
Strangely, in all our patients, you're the only one who got diarrhea on BuSpar. When others had side-effects, the problem was nausea, usually at about 90 mg per day so that made responses in those patients not as good.

Do you think this nausea may have originated from a cause similar to my diarrhea?
Yes. I think they both are due to the serotonin, but I think the nausea comes from the brain, the diarrhea from the gut.

Doctor, now that we know buspirone is my cure, will I be able to take it as long as I need it? And am I right to assume that will be for my whole life?
Yes, I anticipate lifelong treatment, Kim. However, buspirone is not approved for the treatment of TD. There are no drugs that are. We don't know for certain that buspirone will work forever. We hope it will.

After Kim left the room, I updated Andrew.
I've been treating other people with tardive dyskinesia. The one who has been on BuSpar the longest is Queenie. Her reactions have taught us a great deal about the disease.

Is she psychotic too, Doctor?
No, Queenie is not, and has never been. It's not only psychotics who can develop TD. Queenie also had a very severe case of tardive dyskinesia, but she had been taking high doses of a neuroleptic anti-nausea agent, Reglan, for many years. Her chief problem throughout her life has been recurrent nausea, which had been treated by multiple surgeries on her stomach and other parts of her gastro-intestinal tract.

How did Queenie present?
A year before she came to us, her husband had asked her doctor about occasional bouts of strange chewing movements, but these had disappeared. In the meantime she had stopped taking Reglan for many months. Queenie has become the longest consistently followed patient taking high doses of BuSpar for tardive dyskinesia. Although she was taking as much as 240 milligrams per day, her maintenance dose for some years has been around 120 milligrams.

So have you tried to take her off the buspirone?
It has not been possible to take her off buspirone although on many occasions we have tried to taper down her dose.
However, at one point, she required further abdominal surgery, and because there's no intramuscular form of buspirone she could take while she was unable to take oral medication, she was forced to stop taking BuSpar.
Two days after surgery she ecstatically reported that she was without symptoms of tardive dyskinesia, but within a week the TD was back.
We restarted the BuSpar. The TD disappeared again.

It's now more than eight years since Queenie started to take BuSpar. We have not been able to taper her off it. Her dose has generally been 30 mg four times daily. Her TD is generally perfectly controlled, although stress exacerbates it just minimally. When she drops her BuSpar dose below 120 mg per day, the TD exacerbates a little; and one time when her family practitioner prescribed an anticholinergic substance—a group of drugs we know exacerbates the TD—the TD became worse. Today she assiduously checks before taking any new medications. She has been a remarkable success story and a certification that the BuSpar works permanently in this condition.

Andrew, the neurologist, was again visiting:
Have you tried to research that high dose buspirone actually works in TD?
In fact, we did. To confirm the general finding, I teamed up with a specialist at a distant medical school. [69] This study was therefore carried out as formal research under strictly supervised research protocols—it was "blind" in that the rater did not know the dosage of buspirone being prescribed. Our results confirmed that buspirone is a powerful anti-tardive dyskinesia agent.

What are the implications of your finding?
Enormous, Andrew. Maybe we have a treatment for TD. The findings are even more exciting because buspirone was also used to treat an animal model of tardive dyskinesia developed in the mid-1980s.[70] It's ironic that this important basic research work, by Brian McMillen in Connecticut, only came to my attention after my initial treatment of Kim, when it could have been a special clue for my ongoing inquiry.

What did he find?
McMillen demonstrated that in rats it's possible to prevent supersensitivity to a commonly prescribed antipsychotic medication (Stelazine) by pre-treating the animals with buspirone. We now can understand the full implications of this study: Perhaps buspirone might be used not only to control tardive dyskinesia, but to prevent it.
We have yet to test this hypothesis.

Can we prevent tardive dyskinesia with this treatment?
I don't know yet. In the nine years since high dose buspirone in TD, I have been very encouraged. I get the impression that we can prevent tardive dyskinesia maybe by using high doses of BuSpar, but I cannot prove that.
As it happens, I have never seen or heard of a case of tardive dyskinesia developing with patients who were taking antipsychotic medication as well as prolonged buspirone treatment, not necessarily just for prevention, but for anxiety or irritability.
The BuSpar seems to normalize the whole supersensitivity framework. Overall, I propose that buspirone could provide good protection, but we don't know basics.

Like what?
Can we can use lower doses to prevent TD? The biggest single problem we have is not the dosage—its the cost. This is significant. It may not be viable economically to prescribe it en masse only possibly to lower the risk. I believe it could lower both the incidence and the severity of the condition considerably, but we don't also know about adverse effects at high dose in the population at risk.
It's going to take what we would call a major prospective epidemiological study over many years and with thousands of patients to analyze these results definitively. Funding this would cost a fortune; and you must remember that TD is already a hot potato.

A hot potato? In what way?
In practice, most drugs that impact on dopamine tend to have a warning listing in their USA package insert about the risk of TD. Buspirone does even though theoretically it should diminish the risk!

339

So BuSpar has that warning. Is that not a hot potato, itself?
Yes. But that's apparently a technicality listed as a medicolegal protection. This is the same global warning we may see with other dopamine active drugs. The irony, of course, is that BuSpar only acts on dopamine directly in doses far exceeding the usual therapeutic 15 to 60 mg daily. Moreover, as I see it, theoretically, buspirone could not cause TD.

What then would be the major stumbling block to research?
The biggest problem is that involuntary movements sometimes appear after withdrawal of antipsychotic or even after only slight changes in dose. Consequently, these movements can, in error, easily be attributed to the new drug being prescribed not the withdrawal; this has even happened. Sometimes medical research is difficult to interpret. This means that misinterpretations of data can occur. As such, no pharmaceutical company can sponsor work on any new anti-tardive dyskinesia drug, be it buspirone or anything else, without them enduring considerable risk.
This is one of the misfortunes of USA medicine. Research has become a distorted medicolegal issue—in this instance, to the detriment, potentially, of millions of patients.
There is no officially approved drug for use in tardive dyskinesia in the USA, or for that matter anywhere. Unless thinking radically changes, this situation will continue.

Andrew looked out the window, reflectively, then to me again.
Doctor, these several years have left me with an enduring interest in the voyage of psychiatric drugs. I was wondering about various balances among the receptors. For example, is the serotonin receptor balanced by the dopamine receptor? Is there some inverse relationship between the two?
Yes, indeed. Once we realize that all these receptors are interlinked in this enormous receptor world, rather like the Internet in the world of communication, nothing is separate and uninfluenced by others anymore.

Anything else?
Yes. As part of this receptor world, there are controlling features modulating up and down. We cannot even say that one receptor is actually counterbalanced by another, because each of these sub-receptors might do different things, and they're controlling each other. These controls are very much dependent on the receptor subtype, and sometimes even relate to the particular situation. The brain is always adapting when there's too much chemical at one receptor, adapting by effectively lowering it down.

340

How? Does it simply move the chemical elsewhere where it no longer has an effect, or does it transform it into a neutral "waste product"?
Both. It may break down the product to something inactive. Alternatively, the body may remove the excess chemical out of the area of action; but there's a third way as well.

I looked at Andrew directly in the eyes, something I had done hundreds of times over many years. His skills as a doctor had grown enormously; and he had actualized that ineffable quality of humanness for others in the truest of medical traditions.

But one common factor remained from the Andrew I had known and grown to respect over all these years: his intellectual curiosity. I anticipated Andrew's continued barrage of questions.

What's that?
The degree of responsiveness will change. The bathtub becomes colder or hotter, as we have discussed so many times.

So this fits the adaptation by the body model?
Exactly. There's a person in the bathtub raising up the level, occupying space, contributing his own heat. The secondary phenomenon is the bodily compensation. It's simplistic, therefore, to even talk about just counterbalancing. More accurate is to recognize the complex modulation stages of one receptor with all the others.

Andrew, not only as a physician, but as a human being, had matured immeasurably. I had repeatedly observed with pleasure his progression towards the attainment of caring, a quality that differentiates special human beings and just possibly hurdles through that gap beyond actualization to true transcendence of self, rather like a transmitter across a synapse.

No doubt, there would be other times, but I prepared for Andrew's final flurry of the day.

Appropriately he was trying to apply the medical synaptic model to his broader world.
I did a mathematics major and I like the analogy of one multiplied by the other. Can we boil down the complexity of all this "controlling" and "modulation" to a mathematical complexity?

Do you want to clarify further?

As an example, let's use imaginary figures like twenty receptors averaging ten subtypes all influencing each other and all acting ultimately on a hundred other chemical systems.

I'm listening, Andrew.

Can we then "do the math" and come up with a figure, resulting in, say a complexity of five million possible chemical effects?

I looked at Andrew, puzzled. He was teaching his teacher.

Am I missing a key point here, Doctor? Is the complexity deeper than that?

Andrew, I like lateral thinking and I will not refute your model. But we're dealing with biological complexity using feedback systems: "too much, let's lower; too little, let's raise; more balance, let's involve that other receptor." This is less mathematical and more biological.

So it's more complex?

Indeed. Feedback is often qualitative; mathematics is basically quantitative. So I'm not sure whether complex biochemistry can be reduced to this, but such a calculation certainly begins to transmit the absolute complexity of what we have been talking about all this time.

You don't entirely reject this?

Not at all. Our world is perceived according to numerous systems. We have focused on the biological and to some degree the psychological. We can perceive people at a social or cultural or family level as well. We can use an economic, ethical, political or military model for history. We can potentially apply a physical, metaphysical or mathematical or any other model as well to numerous diverse phenomena. Ultimately, there's too much complexity for one model to maybe deal with everything unless we use the broadest one of all—a philosophical framework based on the thinking of all the other models.

Andrew's voyage of discovery had been completed. I could not answer all his questions. However, further research and even more so, assiduous attention to detail, may make us able to impact on previously untreatable conditions. In the future, the psychotic patient may not face release from the hospital with an unpredictable choice between the risk of becoming a public spectacle or the reality of remaining reasonably sane.

Already, movement disorders and stupor have been re-awakened and re-visited. The refractory depressed patient should recover very well; medications which have ceased working can be jump started. The patient with seizure disorders and atypical spells has numerous excellent options. Those with episodic phenomena can stabilize chemically and electrically; and greater knowledge of medications, even herbs, are leading us to an important awareness of dangers and virtues. We no longer need to cry for our beloved mind.
Help is at hand.

My life had also been modified during this voyage of discovery. My experiences with the movement disorders of Kim, Priscilla and Jocelyn had impressed me greatly, but then so had the presentations and responses of all the others. I had taught Victor, with his drug interactions, but I had learnt from his keenness to learn, as well. Ryan, who thought herbs were not medications, had shown me alternative perceptions of the world.

Then there were others who had made an abiding impact on my thinking. The intractable depressions of Jim, Katie and Suzanne were ameliorated but with that came the special insights of individualizing treatments. Harry, Eileen, Lucy, Steven and Wendy manifested fascinating different presentations of electrical phenomena in the brain and demonstrated to me the diversity of brain-firing.

All these people, and my thousands of other patients, have brought about indelible influences on my thinking, and on my philosophy of life. For that I thank them. They have taught me how precious our being may be. No longer do I cry for the beloved mind, for I travel great distances and achieve change through the voyage that is the pharmacology of hope.

Glossary
Brain
Anatomy (off-midline; schematic)

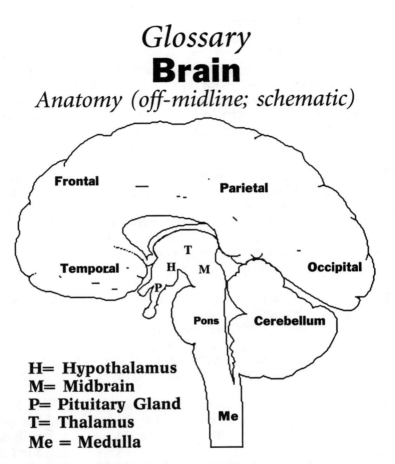

H= **Hypothalamus**
M= **Midbrain**
P= **Pituitary Gland**
T= **Thalamus**
Me = **Medulla**

Simplified Functions

Major part	Brain area	Major function
Cerebral	frontal lobe	executive-motor functi
Hemispheres	temporal lobe	integration
	parietal lobe	somatosensory percepti
	occipital lobe	vision
Diencephalon	thalamus	relay-station
	hypothalamus/pituitary	hormonal regulation
Mesencephalon	mid-brain	(reflex) controller
Rhombencephalon	cerebellum	co-ordination
(Hindbrain)	pons/medulla	vegetative mediator

Glossary
Boat-Pier And Bathtub
Analogies Of Neurotransmission

"BOAT-PIER"	ANALOGY
concept	metaphor
neurotransmitter (NT) **mechanism**	boat-pier analogy
NT attachment NT distant effect	boat analogy essentials
NT at synapse	boat
receptor; (R)	pier (= bathtub)
NT molecules	passengers
NT attached	moored
post-synaptic R	shore
medications	influence on boat NT mechanisms
NT influence	business
2nd NT or drug	competing boat
R subtypes' varied distant impacts	different parts of town
cascade effects	many parts of town
direct NT impacts	shadow
synaptic cleft	between boat and pier
human body	town
R stimulation	turnstile
medications: direct or indirect agonist or antagonist	directly or indirectly help at pier; occupies, stimulates or prevents
agonism, stimulation	passengers doing business on shore
antagonism, blockade	passengers restrained from climbing off boat
re-uptake inhibition effects	same passengers return through turnstiles
different anatomy of R subtypes	dock = exact location of each pier

"BATHTUB"	ANALOGY
concept	metaphor
neurotransmitter (NT) **quantity & response**	bathtub analogy
pier equivalent	bathtub
receptor (R) subtypes that antagonize	bath-plugs
NT amount = sensitivity of R	water level (L)
R responsiveness	water temperature
appropriate adaptation	L x temp = 100 synaptic units
psychotherapy plus individual variations pharmacologically	body—influences shape, levels, temp
excess up-regulation	boiling hot
weaker drugs acting in physiologic doses	chisel raising level moderately
down-regulation	colder
subsensitivity	deficient L
supersensitivity	excessive L
up-regulation	hotter
excess down-regulation	ice-cold
individual variation	individual in tub
other biochemical imbalances	leaks in frame
no messenger systems	limitations
use adjunctive therapy	patching leaks
connections between receptor subtypes	pipes
NT overblow	raising L high
strong drugs acting in pharmacological doses	sledgehammer raising level high
anxiety with serotonin	too high L of water
depressed mood	too low L of water

Glossary
Neuropsychiatric Drugs

This reference list applies only to the broader medication *groups* mentioned in this book. By convention, the trade names—those allocated by pharmaceutical companies—are capitalized. The actual chemical or generic names are in small print. Trade names outside the USA are indicated in italics. In this book, trade names are frequently used, particularly with the anticonvulsants and the newer non-generically substituted medications. This list is by pharmaceutical category, e. g. antidepressants. The generic-brand glossaries on pages 346 and 347 convert names.

Prescribed Medications:

ANTICONVULSANTS:
Monotherapy:[i] carbamazepine (Tegretol, Carbatrol, Epitol); ethosuximide (Zarontin); phenobarbital (Luminal, Donnatal, *Gardenal*); phenytoin (Dilantin, *Epanutin*); primidone (Mysoline); valproate (Depakote, *Epilim*); valproic acid (Depakene)
Add on: [j] felbamate (Felbatol); gabapentin (Neurontin); lamotrigine (Lamictal); tiagabine (Gabitril); topiramate (Topamax).
ANTIDEPRESSANTS:
Tricyclics: amitriptyline [k] (Elavil, *Tryptanol*); clomipramine (Anafranil) [l;] desipramine [m] (Norpramin, *Pertofran*); doxepin (Sinequan)[k] ; imipramine (Tofranil)[k]; nortriptyline (Pamelor, Aventyl); protriptyline (Vivactil)[m]; trimipramine (Surmontil) [k].
Non-tricyclic heterocyclics: amoxapine (Asendin); *dibenzepin (Noveril);* maprotiline (Ludiomil); *mianserin (Lantanon);* mirtazapine (Remeron)[k]; *moclobemide (Aurorix)*[n]; nomifensine (Merital)[n]; trazodone (Desyrel, *Molipaxin).*
Serotonin re-uptake inhibitors: [15] citalopram (Celexa); fluoxetine (Prozac); fluvoxamine (Luvox)[l]; paroxetine (Paxil); sertraline (Zoloft).
Post-SSRIs: bupropion (Wellbutrin) (NERI)[m]; nefazodone (Serzone) (SNRI+)[k] ; venlafaxine (Effexor) (SNRI)[m].
Monoamine oxidase inhibitors: isocarboxazid (Marplan)[n], (also iproniazid)[n]; phenelzine (Nardil); tranylcypromine (Parnate).
ANTIPARKINSONIAN AGENTS:
Dopamine agonist: selegeline (Eldepryl); amantadine (Symmetrel); bromocriptine (Parlodel); levodopa/ carbidopa (Sinemet); pergolide (Permax); pramipexole dihydrochloride (Mirapex).
Anticholinergic agents: benztropine (Cogentin); biperiden (Akineton); diphenhydramine (Benadryl); orphenadrine (Norflex); trihexyphenidyl (Artane).

---

[i] "Monotherapy" anticonvulsants are approved in the USA for seizure use on their own.
[j] "Add on" anticonvulsants are USA approved for seizure use only with other drugs.
[k] Sedating antidepressant.
[l] Both Luvox and Anafranil are not approved for depression in the USA.
[m] Activating antidepressant.
[n] No longer / not manufactured in the USA.

ANXIETY:
Azapirones: Buspirone (BuSpar).
Benzodiazepines: alprazolam (Xanax); chlordiazepoxide (Librium); clonazepam (Klonopin); clorazepate (Tranxene); diazepam (Valium); lorazepam (Ativan); oxazepam (Serax, Serepax); triazolam (Halcion).
Beta-blockers:[o] nadolol (Corgard); pindolol (Visken); propranolol (Inderal).
HORMONES:
ß-estradiol (Estrace); dexamethasone (Decadron); thyroxin (Synthroid).
LITHIUM:[p] lithium carbonate (Eskalith, Lithobid, *Camcolit, Lentolith, Quilonum*).
MIGRAINE/HEADACHE/PAIN, AND OTHER PREPARATIONS:
analgesic nitrous oxide; codeine ± acetaminophen; hydrocodone bitartrate (Vicodin); cyproheptadine (Periactin); ibuprofen (Motrin); morphine (Kadian); tramadol (Ultram).
MISCELLANEOUS APPROVED MEDICATIONS:
diuretic: furosemide (Lasix); bronchodilator: theophylline (Theodur).
NEUROLEPTICS:
Antipsychotics: chlorpromazine (Thorazine, *Largactil*); clozapine (Clozaril, *Leponex*); fluphenazine (Prolixin); fluphenazine decanoate (Prolixin Decanoate, *Modecate*); haloperidol (Haldol, *Serenace*); olanzapine (Zyprexa); perphenazine (Trilafon); pimozide (Orap); pipothiazine (Piportil); quetiapine (Seroquel); risperidone (Risperdal); thiothixene (Navane); thioridazine (Mellaril, *Melleril*); trifluoperazine (Stelazine).
Antinauseants: prochlorperazine (Compazine); metoclopramide (Reglan).
PSYCHOSTIMULANTS:
methylphenidate (Ritalin); pemoline (Cylert); dextroamphetamine sulfate (Dexedrine); mixed [D/L version] amphetamine (Adderall).

Non-approved drugs:

HERBAL PREPARATIONS:
St John's wort, Melatonin, Echinacea, Ginseng, Gingko biloba [Ginkgo]
MINERAL AND VITAMIN PREPARATIONS:
B vitamins: folic [folate, folacin] (Bc); niacin [nicotinamide] (B2); pyridoxine (B6); thiamine (B1); cyanocobalamine (B12).
Anti-oxidant vitamins: ascorbic acid (Vitamin C); tocopherol (Vitamin E); beta-carotene (Vitamin A). Other: Cholecalciferol (Vitamin D).
Trace minerals: chromium, zinc.
Essential cations: potassium, sodium, calcium, magnesium.
SOCIAL USE CHEMICALS:
Nicotine and polycyclic tars in cigarettes; alcohol in whisky, beer; caffeine and theobromine in coffee, tea, cocoa.

---

[o] Not approved for this indication in the USA.
[p] Approved for mania and its prophylaxis.

Glossary
Generic to Brand Drugs

Medications are generally only listed under the name used most in the book, either Brand Name (Capitalized) or generic name (small case). This means that you may see trimipramine not Surmontil. The Neuropsychiatric Drug Glossary lists either brand (more commonly) or generic names. To facilitate easy conversion of these terms, alphabetic conversion of generic to major brand name is listed below.

alprazolam	Xanax	metoclopramide	Reglan
amantadine	Symmetrel	mianserin	Lantanon
amitriptyline	Elavil	mirtazapine	Remeron
amphetamine	Adderall	moclobemide	Aurorix
benztropine	Cogentin	morphine	Kadian
beta estradiol	Estrace	nadolol	Corgard
biperiden	Akineton	nefazodone	Serzone
bromocriptine	Parlodel	nortriptyline	Pamelor, Aventyl
bupropion	Wellbutrin	olanzapine	Zyprexa
buspirone	BuSpar	orphenadrine	Norflex
carbamazepine	Tegretol, Carbatrol	oxazepam	Serax
chlordiazepoxide	Librium	paroxetine	Paxil
chlorpromazine	Thorazine	pemoline	Cylert
citalopram	Celexa	pergolide	Permax
clomipramine	Anafranil	perphenazine	Trilafon
clonazepam	Klonopin	phenelzine	Nardil
clorazepate	Tranxene	phenobarbital	Luminal
clozapine	Clozaril	phenytoin	Dilantin
cyproheptadine	Periactin	pimozide	Orap
desipramine	Norpramin	pindolol	Visken
dexamethasone	Decadron	pipothiazine	Piportil
D-amphetamine	Dexedrine	primidone	Mysoline
diazepam	Valium	prochlorperazine	Compazine
dibenzepin	Noveril	propranolol	Inderal
diphenhydramine	Benadryl	protriptyline	Vivactil
doxepin	Sinequan	quetiapine	Seroquel
ethosuxamide	Zarontin	risperidone	Risperdal
felbamate	Felbatol	selegeline	Eldepryl
fluoxetine	Prozac	sertraline	Zoloft
fluphenazine	Prolixin	theophylline	Theodur
fluvoxamine	Luvox	thioridazine	Mellaril
furosemide	Lasix	thiothixene	Navane
gabapentin	Neurontin	thyroxin	Synthroid
haloperidol	Haldol	tiagabine	Gabitril
hydrocodone bitartrate	Vicodin	topiramate	Topamax
ibuprofen	Motrin	tramadol	Ultram
imipramine	Tofranil	tranylcypromine	Parnate
isocarboxazid	Marplan	trazodone	Desyrel
levodopa/carbidopa	Sinemet	triazolam	Halcion
lithium carbonate	Eskalith, Lithobid	trifluoperazine	Stelazine
lamotrigine	Lamictal	trihexyphenidyl	Artane
lorazepam	Ativan	trimipramine	Surmontil
maprotiline	Ludiomil	valproate	Depakote
methylphenidate	Ritalin	venlafaxine	Effexor

Glossary
Brand to Generic Drugs

This glossary allows easier conversions of brand name drugs such as Tegretol into the generic equivalent such as carbamazepine.

The conversion is useful for the Neuropsychiatric Drug Glossary and the Index.

Adderal amphetamine
Akineton biperiden
Anafranil clomipramine
Artane trihexyphenidyl
Ativan lorazepam
Aurorix moclobemide
Aventyl nortriptyline
Benadryl diphenhydramine
BuSpar buspirone
Carbatrol carbamazepine
Celexa citalopram
Clozaril clozapine
Cogentin benztropine
Compazine prochlorperazine
Corgard nadolol
Cylert pemoline
Decadron dexamethasone
Depakene valproic acid
Depakote valproate
Desyrel trazodone
Dexedrine dextroamphetamine
Dilantin phenytoin
Effexor venlafaxine
Elavil amitriptyline
Eldepryl selegeline
Eskalith lithium
Estrace beta estradiol
Felbatol felbamate
Gabitril tiagabine
Halcion triazolam
Haldol haloperidol
Inderal propranolol
Kadian morphine
Klonopin clonazepam
Lamictal lamotrigine
Lantanon mianserin
Lasix furosemide
Librium chlordiazepoxide
Lithobid lithium
Ludiomil maprotiline
Luminal phenobarbital
Luvox fluvoxamine
Marplan isocarboxazid
Mellaril thioridazine
Motrin ibuprofen
Mysoline primidone

Nardil phenelzine
Navane thiothixene
Neurontin gabapentin
Norflex orphenadrine
Norpramin desipramine
Noveril dibenzepin
Orap pimozide
Pamelor nortriptyline
Parlodel bromocriptine
Parnate tranylcypromine
Paxil paroxetine
Periactin cyproheptadine
Permax pergolide
Piportil pipothiazine
Prolixin fluphenazine
Prozac fluoxetine
Reglan metoclopramide
Remeron mirtazapine
Risperdal risperidone
Ritalin methylphenidate
Serax oxazepam
Seroquel quetiapine
Serzone nefazodone
Sinemet levodopa/carbidopa
Sinequan doxepin
Stelazine trifluoperazine
Surmontil trimipramine
Symmetrel amantadine
Synthroid thyroxin
Tegretol carbamazepine
Theodur theophylline
Thorazine chlorpromazine
Tofranil imipramine
Topamax topiramate
Tranxene clorazepate
Trilafon perphenazine
Ultram tramadol
Valium diazepam
Vicodin hydrocodone
Visken pindolol
Vivactil protriptyline
Welbutrin bupropion
Xanax alprazolam
Zarontin ethosuxamide
Zoloft sertraline
Zyprexa olanzapine

349

Glossary
Neurotransmitter Effects

Effects of common neurotransmitters on different receptors (simplified, as receptor subtypes exist)

Key broad effects of receptors (simplified)
serotonin—tonic regulation of anxiety, depression, obsessions, aggression, sex, sleep, hormone, body regulation (Serotonin-1 through 7 components; 1A, 2 = 2A important)
norepinephrine—acute reactivity with flight, fright, flight (alpha and beta components)
dopamine—movements, psychosis (Dopamine 1 and 2 important)
opioid—pain (includes mu receptor)
GABA, Benzodiazepine, chloride ionophore complex stimulation—sedation, anticonvulsant, hypnotic, muscle relaxant
glutamine—seizures

Side-effects of the receptors (simplified)
alpha-adrenergic blockade—hypotension, dizziness, confusion
anticholinergic—dry mouth, blurred vision; memory & urinary difficulties
antihistaminic—sedation, weight gain
beta-adrenergic blockade—hypotension, cardiac failure, asthma, Raynaud's phenomenon
dopamine blockade—Parkinson's symptoms, tardive dyskinesia
dopamine stimulation—psychosis, dyskinesia, lactation
norepinephrine excess—hypertension, agitation
serotonin-2 blockade—sedation
serotonin-1A agonism—non-vertiginous dizziness
serotonin excess—sex problems, headache, insomnia, nausea, paradoxes

Drug effects on receptors (simplified)
Anticholinergic agents: Anticholinergic
Anticonvulsants: Vary: AMPA, GABA, glutamine, kainate and NMDA receptors
Antiparkinsonian Agents: Dopamine agonist or Anticholinergic
Azapirones: Buspirone: Serotonin-1A
Benzodiazepines: Benzodiazepine-GABA-Chloride ionophore stimulation
Beta-blockers: Beta-adrenergic blockade
Dopamine agonist: Dopamine stimulation
Headache/ Pain: Narcotics: opiate stimulation; cyproheptadine: serotonin blocker
Lithium carbonate Serotonin stimulation, broad action, tremor
Monoamine oxidase inhibitors: Tyramine reaction, hypotension, non-specific
Neuroleptics: Antipsychotics and Antinauseants: Dopamine blockade
Non-tricyclic heterocyclics: Trazodone: serotonin and alpha-adrenergic blockade
Post-SSRI era: Bupropion NERI; nefazodone SNRI+; venlafaxine SNRI
SSRIs: Serotonin excess with re-uptake
Tricyclic antidepressants: Anticholinergic, antihistaminic; serotonin & norepinephrine repute inhibition, serotonin-2 & alpha-adrenergic blockade

Glossary
Medical Abbreviations

For simplification, the convention of not using periods has been used for the medical abbreviations below.

mg	milligrams
ml	milliliters
IU	international units
mEq/L	milliequivalents per liter
5HIAA	5-hydroxy indole-acetic acid
5HT	5-hydroxytryptamine
AMPA	Amino-hydroxyl-methyl-isoxazole-propionate
CFS	Chronic fatigue syndrome
CSF	Cerebral spinal fluid
DNA	Deoxyribonucleic acid
DSM IV	Diagnostic and Statistical Manual of Psychiatry 4th ed.
DST	Dexamethasone suppression test
ECG	Electrocardiogram
ECT	Electroconvulsive therapy
EEG	Electroencephalogram
FDA	Federal Drug Administration
GABA	Gamma amino butyric acid
GB	Gigabyte
GGT	Gamma glutamyl transferase
Hz	Herz; cycles per second
INSET	Inventory of Neppe of Symptoms of Epilepsy & the Temporal Lobe
LSD	Lysergic acid diethylamide
MAO	Monoamine oxidase
MAOIs	Monoamine oxidase inhibitors
MRI	Magnetic resonance imaging
NERI	Norepinephrine re-uptake inhibitor
NMDA	N-methyl D-Aspartate
NVD	Non-vertiginous dizziness
OBRA	Omnibus Budget Reconciliation Act
PCP	Phencyclidine
PND	Paroxysmal neurobehavioral disorder
PTLSs	Possible temporal lobe symptoms
REM	Rapid eye movement sleep
SNRI+	SNRI with blockade
SNRIs	Serotonin norepinephrine re-uptake inhibitors
SSRIs	Selective serotonin re-uptake inhibitors
T3	Tri-iodothyronine
T4	Thyroxin
TD	Tardive dyskinesia
VNS	Vagus nerve stimulation

Glossary
Medical Terms

This glossary of one line definitions of medical terms is for quick reference to terms used in the context of this book. Consequently, wherever possible the definitions correspond with the short phrases associated with the em dash sign (–) that appear in the book.
The definitions are deliberately simplified for easier comprehension.

absence seizures blackouts with transient loss of consciousness due to seizures
accessory symptoms extra symptoms in a condition requiring separate treatment
acetylcholine neurotransmitter with memory and automatic movements roles
adenosine receptor receptor relating to caffeine and many chemical reactions
adjunctive medication unapproved second drug used for a condition
adrenoreceptor adrenergic receptor; norepinephrine
affect emotion
agitated depression internal restlessness, marked anxiety type depression
agonism receptor activation by stimulation or inhibition
akathisia unpleasant subjective sensation of inability to keep still
akinesia loss of accessory muscle use, like non-swinging arms
alpha EEG waves of 8-13 Hz; a variation of adrenergic receptor
altered state of consciousness modified alertness and responsiveness level
Alzheimer's disease dementia associated with specific pathologic changes
ambulatory EEG lengthy special computerized EEG performed at home
anatomy the localization in the body
anhedonic unable to experience pleasure
anoxia too little oxygen
antagonism preventing of action of a receptor using antagonist chemicals
anterior front
anticholinergic drug acting against acetylcholine
anticonvulsant medication to prevent seizures; anti-epileptic drug
antihistamine histamine blocking agent
anxiogenic anxiety inducing agent
artifact noise; EEG distortions outside the brain, usually the muscles
atypical spells strange behavior events in PND due to firing episodes
auditory hallucinations hearing non-existent voices
aura, aurae warning symptoms preceding or heralding a seizure
autism withdrawal into one's own reality
axon outgoing pipe of the neuron
beta EEG waves of ≥13 Hz; a variation of adrenergic receptor
bioavailability extent of availability of drugs in the body
biopsychofamiliosociocultural biological, psychological, family, social & cultural
bipolar disorder affective illness, bipolar mood disorder, manic depressive illness
blackouts absence seizures due to petit mal or temporal lobe epilepsy
blockade receptor antagonism
blunting of affect a diminution in range of emotion
bone marrow depression malfunction suppressing blood cell production

borderline personality disorder character disorder with extremes of view
brain-stem   midbrain, pons & medulla; automatic basic functions
brand name   pharmaceutical company drug name, usually patented
cascade   string of chemical reactions
catatonic stupor impaired responsiveness but adequate awareness
cation   positively charged ions, like sodium, potassium, calcium
cerebellum   trilobed brain structure which co-ordinates movement
cerebral   brain
cerebral spinal fluid   the liquid that runs through the brain & spinal cord
cerebrospinal fluid   cerebral spinal fluid; CSF; runs in a tube
cerebrum   higher brain area: frontal, occipital, parietal and temporal lobes
characterological   personality, fixed portion of behavior over years
chindling   chemically induced kindling-like phenomenon
circadian   daily cycle
clouded consciousness   impaired consciousness
coarse neurobehavioral syndrome   behavior due to hard line brain conditions
cognition   thinking
complex partial seizure   partial seizures with impaired awareness
compliance   habit of taking medication regularly
confusional state   clouded consciousness linked with inappropriate behavior
consciousness   level of awareness
cortex   cell collection on the outside of the cerebrum
creative psychopath   non-aggressive psychopath who is inappropriately creative
cross-talk   conversations between neurotransmitters
cryptogenic   hidden cause
cyanosed   blue coloration reflecting too little oxygenation of the blood
dehydrated   significant bodily fluid loss; dry skin & mucous membranes
déjà vu   subjectively inappropriate impression of familiarity of present
delta waves   EEG waves of ≤4 Hz
delusional episode   episode of delusions
delusions   fixed false beliefs
dementia   memory and intellectual deterioration; chronic brain condition
dementia praecox   old term for schizophrenia
depersonalization   strange sense of feeling not quite oneself
depressive pseudodementia   depression producing a dementia-like picture
depth electrode   electrodes put deep in the brain to detect abnormalities on EEG
derealization   strange sense of unreality about the world
dexamethasone suppression test   test of proper adrenal gland function; DST
disorder in thinking   abnormal linking of thoughts and their special meanings
dopamine   neurotransmitter: psychosis, catatonia and movement disorder
down-regulated   low responsiveness of brain receptors to stimulation
drive-in phenomenon   Landolt's forced normalization of the EEG in psychosis
dysfunction   malfunction
dyskinesia   disordered involuntary movements of limbs or mouth or trunk
EEG   electroencephalogram
efficacy   effectiveness
electroconvulsive therapy ECT, shock treatment, electrical seizure stimulation
electrodes   buttons on the head to receive the EEG brain waves
electroencephalogram   EEG, test to examine brain waves

electrolytes   (medical) sodium, potassium, calcium, chloride, magnesium

encephalitis   brain inflammation usually infection, often viral

encephalization developed brain

enzyme   body protein acting as a catalyst in chemical reactions

epilepsy   recurrent seizures without obvious reason

epilepsy plus patients epileptics with seizure-related behavioral abnormalities

epilepsy standard patient   epileptics with no added psychopathology

epileptic psychosis   heterogeneous group of psychoses in epileptics

epileptologists experts in epilepsy

ethicobiopsychofamiliosociocultural ethical biopsychofamiliosociocultural

etiology   cause

executive   frontal lobe higher motor function

extrapyramidal symptoms rigidity, tremor, akinesia, akathisia; Parkinson-like

filler   vehicle "concrete" in medications and drugs

first pass metabolism   liver breakdown of drug before even reaching the brain

frontal lobe   lobe of cerebrum mainly associated with executive functions

GABA   neurotransmitter predominantly inhibitory in electrical firing

generalized from the start   immediate grand mal or unconsciousness seizures

generic   substituted, not patented, pharmacologically equivalent drug

genomic clone   a specific complex chemical genetic DNA code

gliosis   scarring

glutamine   neurotransmitter, major excitatory seizure linked

grand mal   generalized tonic-clonic seizure

hallucinations   perceptions without stimulus

hallucinogens   drugs that induce hallucinations

hepatic   liver

heterogeneity   non-homogeneity; consisting of dissimilar elements

hyperventilate   over-breathe to produce different acid-base balance

hyperventilation   overbreathing on EEG to provoke a brain wave response

hypothalamus   great regulating hormonal gland of brain; controls the pituitary

hysterical epilepsy   non-epileptic seizures, pseudo-seizures

ictal   events linked to seizures

ictus   around the time of the seizures, peri-ictal

idiopathic   unknown medical cause

indications   approved uses of a drug

induction   speeding up of enzyme metabolic processes

inferior   bottom, lower portion

inhibition   slowed down enzyme metabolic processes; opposite: induction

inpatient   hospitalized

insight   real appreciation of own illness

integrator   temporal lobe higher integrative sensory and motor function

inter-ictal   events linked to the time period between seizures

interictal dysphoric disorder depression between seizure episodes condition

kindling   repetitive electrical brain stimulations to threshold permanently

labeled indications   drug within FDA dose, duration, and diagnoses approvals

labeling   of disease, assigning diagnosis; of drugs, assigning indications

labels   applying labeling of disease processes to patients

laryngeal stridor   spasm of the muscles inside the larynx

lateral   side

light therapy   bright lights or dawn simulation used in morning in depression
limbic system   anatomical area reflecting mainly the emotional brain
malfunction   brain sense: poor function producing adverse effects
manic depressive illness psychotic disorder with highs and lows, bipolar disorder
manic-depressive insanity   old term for manic depressive illness
mesial aspect   midline part
mesial temporal cortex   midline cortex part of the temporal lobe
messenger systems   complex often distant chemical reaction series: results
metabolism   breakdown of chemicals
metabolize   to clear from the system
mid-brain   mesencephalon; between cerebrum and pons
mid-course correction   changes in medication corrected over time
motor   brain: movement both voluntary and involuntary
NERI   drugs preventing norepinephrine leaving by re-uptake inhibition
neural   nerve
neurobehavioral behavior associated with brain function
neuroleptics   antipsychotic drugs, also called major tranquilizers
neurology   medical discipline dealing with the nervous system
neuron   nerve cell
neuropharmacology   discipline of drugs for the nervous system
neuropsychiatry medical discipline; interfaces brain in psychiatry and neurology
neurosis   non-psychotic psychiatric conditions: defenses against anxiety
neurotransmitters   chemicals producing responses at the synapses
NMDA   neurotransmitter electrical, mainly excitatory, kindling linked
non-epileptic seizures   pseudo-seizures, hysterical epilepsy
non-ictal   events unrelated to seizures in epileptics
non-vertiginous dizziness   serotonin-1A symptom: non-rotational dizziness
norepinephrine neurotransmitter noradrenaline; controls immediate responses
normality   coping adequately at biopsychofamiliosociocultural levels
nuclei   large cell clusters
occipital lobe   lobe of cerebrum mainly associated with vision
oculogyric crisis   eye muscle spasm as rare response to neuroleptics
on-off phenomenon   acute movement changes in Parkinson's: lost drug effect
opioid   neurotransmitter in pain control and morphine-like, endorphins
out of labeling   use of drug for indication unapproved by the FDA
P450 cytochrome enzyme system   special liver detoxifying metabolism system
parietal lobe   lobe of cerebrum mainly associated with general sensation
Parkinson's disease neurologic condition: dopamine, acetylcholine; basal ganglia
paroxysmal discharges   episodic brain firing
Paroxysmal Neurobehavioral Disorder abnormal brain firing behavior ;PND
partial agonism drug-related regulation pharmacological receptor property
partial seizures focal seizures, firing is localized to an area of the brain
PCP   a profound hallucinogenic agent
Pellagra   brain nutritional disease due to nicotinic acid deficiency
peri-ictal   events linked round the seizure time; pre-, post-, during seizure
personality disorder   Axis 2 DSM disorder of character
petit mal   generalized blackout seizures with blanks; specific EEG finding
pharmacodynamics   influence of the drug on a body organ like the brain
pharmacokinetics   influence of a body organ like the liver on the drug

355

pharmacological doses higher amounts than the body requires physiologically
pharmacology the way the body interacts with drugs
pharmacotherapeutic psychopharmacological therapy
photic driving photic stimulation
photic stimulation flashing lights provoking brain waves on EEG
physiologic doses estimated amounts that body requires physiologically
physiology the way the body works
placebo drug without direct pharmacological activity
PND Paroxysmal Neurobehavioral Disorder
polypharmacy use of more than one drug together
possible temporal lobe symptoms abnormal temporal lobe symptoms; PTLSs
post-ictal events after the seizure,—headache, disorientation, sleepiness
post-synaptic area the domain of action once after neurotransmitter signal
posterior back
potassium cation essential to life mainly in cell
pre-ictal events linked to the time period before the seizure
pseudo-seizure hysterical epilepsy, non-epileptic seizures; without brain firing
pseudodementia non-dementing condition which looks clinically like dementia
psychiatry medical discipline: abnormal behavioral, thinking, emotional
psychology non-medical discipline dealing with human and animal behavior
psychopath severe disorder of conscience resulting in antisocial behavior
psychopathology abnormal psychiatric symptoms
psychopharmacology medical treatment discipline using psychiatric medications
psychosis conscious out-of-touchness with reality and impaired insight
psychotic someone with psychosis
psychotropic psychopharmacological drug
push-button button pressed during ambulatory EEG
re-uptake taking neurotransmitter away from the receptor action site
recreational drugs non-prescribed drugs of abuse like LSD, heroin, marijuana
receptor receptacles at which neurotransmitter chemicals act
receptor subtype subclassification of receptor family
receptorology study of neurotransmitters
renal kidney
retarded depression slowed, apathetic, retarded movement depression
re-uptake inhibition preventing neurotransmitter re-uptake
rigidity stiff muscles
scalp electrode EEG placement button on scalp
schizoaffective disorder psychosis between schizophrenia and bipolar disease
schizophrenia psychotic illness with disordered thinking and deterioration
sciction science through fiction
secondarily generalize seizure starts focally and progress to grand mal
seizure episodic cerebral neuronal firing producing bodily changes
sensory brain sense: perception and sensation
serotonin neurotransmitter; tonically regulates functions
shock treatment electroconvulsive therapy
silent episodes firing seizure episodes on EEG without clinical correlation
simple partial seizures partial seizures without impairment of consciousness
sodium cation essential to life mainly outside cell, like common salt
somatosensory feeling sensations like touch, pain, position sense awareness

SSRI drugs maintaining serotonin in synapse by re-uptake inhibition
status epilepticus a cascade of seizures each superimposed on the last
sub-threshold stimulations not producing a response
subacute over-adaptation model brain over-responds to excess transmitter
substantia nigra site of production of dopamine for Parkinson's and psychosis
superior top, upper portion
synapses the connection of these nerve endings
synaptic cleft tiny, microscopic channel in synapse linking post-synaptically
syndrome symptom cluster
tachycardia rapid pulse
taper gradually diminish dose
tardive slowly developing
tardive akathisia akathisia which persists due to medication
tardive dyskinesia TD; prolonged neuroleptic induced movement disorder
temporal lobe` lobe of cerebrum mainly associated with integration functions
temporal lobe blackouts staring temporal lobe seizures with post-ictal features
temporal lobe seizures seizures deriving from the temporal lobe of the brain
theta waves EEG waves of 4-8 Hz
thought disorder disorder of illogical linking and special meanings of thoughts
threshold sensitivity range to seizures, low threshold = higher sensitivity
time-based evaluations repetitive assessments of changes in presentation
tinnitus buzzing in the ear
tone degree of stiffness of muscles
tremor shaking, generally of hands
tumor a benign or malignant growth
tyramine effect dangerous "cheese" reaction linked with MAOI drugs
up-regulated high responsiveness of brain receptors to stimulation
vagus nerve stimulation VNS: stimulating the vagus nerve to diminish seizures
vehicle allows drug absorption by holding medications together
volition drive
within labeling specifically approved in the package insert for condition
zero order metabolism liver breakdown overload for specific drugs

357

Glossary
Index Of Concepts

360

liver, 34, 35, 52, 59, 119, 130, 131, 132, 161, 172, 191, 192, 194, 203, 204, 214, 237, 249, 275, 278, 279, 283, 354, 355
local, 46, 47, 62, 86, 113, 121, 124, 125, 168, 287, 309
lorazepam, 347, 348
Ludiomil, 224
Luvox, 300, 346

—M—

manic, 6, 118, 122, 316, 355
marijuana, 140, 196
memory, 3, 20, 49, 52, 68, 83, 90, 96, 97, 141, 218, 219, 221, 223, 250, 268, 350, 352, 353
mesial, 109, 151, 355
messenger, 54, 185, 355
metabolism, 34, 120, 131, 160, 171, 191, 201, 203, 354, 355
metabolize, 320
mg, 33, 34, 56, 57, 59, 83, 103, 106, 116, 119, 122, 123, 130, 132, 134, 179, 191, 192, 197, 202, 203, 208, 221, 235, 237, 239, 247, 250, 251, 253, 260, 261, 270, 279, 280, 281, 282, 283, 286, 291, 292, 299, 302, 303, 306, 309, 327, 328, 329, 330, 331, 336, 337, 338, 340
migraine, 102
milk, 136
mineral, 203, 205, 212
motor, 26, 144, 174, 344, 354
mouth, 32, 61, 173, 187, 221, 248, 311, 317, 326
movements, 5, 26, 28, 39, 70, 73, 76, 77, 93, 117, 174, 311, 316, 317, 320, 322, 325, 328, 329, 331, 340, 352
MRI, 289, 290, 351
muscle, 32, 44, 70, 73, 76, 77, 179, 350, 352, 355

—N—

nadolol, 334, 347, 348
Nardil, 208
nausea, 23, 44, 102, 131, 134, 190, 205, 238, 261, 303, 321, 332, 337, 338
neural, 90
neurobehavioral, 42, 126, 351, 353
neuroleptic, x, 19, 107, 115, 117, 119, 321, 338, 357
neuroleptics, 19, 110, 115, 124, 319, 323, 332, 355

neurology, 25, 254
Neurontin, 100, 349
neuropsychiatry, viii, ix, 5
neurotransmitter, 13, 14, 28, 118, 119, 179, 181, 184, 185, 188, 221, 248, 292, 345, 352, 354, 355, 356, 366
neurotransmitters, 14, 15, 19, 53, 180, 181, 185, 209, 223, 224, 350
niacin, 347
nicotine, 171, 173, 188, 193, 194, 202
NMDA, 14, 53, 350, 351
norepinephrine, 16, 209, 225, 226, 238, 240, 242, 243, 244, 245, 268, 279, 307, 350, 355
normal, x, 9, 15, 50, 62, 66, 67, 68, 69, 70, 77, 87, 89, 90, 92, 95, 99, 100, 104, 111, 125, 140, 150, 153, 154, 158, 163, 164, 168, 169, 171, 178, 187, 202, 235, 255, 258, 264, 269, 275, 304, 315, 324
normality, 27, 66
nortriptyline, 346, 348

—O—

occipital, 344, 355
oculogyric, 149, 355
opioid, 14, 135, 276, 277, 278, 279, 281, 282, 284
overblow, 299
overfilled, 292
overflowing, 253
oxazepam, 347, 348

—P—

pain, 14, 44, 97, 113, 143, 210, 276, 277, 278, 281, 282, 322, 350, 355
parietal, 70, 344, 353, 355
Parkinson's, xi, 13, 14, 15, 22, 28, 29, 47, 119, 169, 173, 174, 175, 186, 187, 188, 191, 193, 194, 270, 331, 350, 355, 357
paroxysmal, 38, 41, 43, 47, 126, 158, 366
partial, 39, 40, 44, 45, 60, 62, 82, 84, 148, 231, 297, 298, 299, 300, 324, 325, 326, 327, 332, 353
Paxil, 179, 182, 185, 192, 217, 219, 221, 233, 235, 236, 239, 240, 245, 246, 250, 261, 270, 278, 307
pellagra, 4
personality, 55, 65, 127, 139, 146, 166, 254, 277, 293, 353
petit, 36, 39
pharmacodynamic, 194

Glossary
ENDNOTES FROM TEXT

1 "Faction" (a rare term) or "docudrama" purposefully combines fact and fiction; "sciction" links with current scientific knowledge but expresses opinions. "Science fiction" involves futuristic, speculative, scientific fantasy; "sciction" involves a modifiable composite present involving current knowledge and techniques.

2 Patient confidentiality has been respected so that any resemblance of any patient to anyone living or dead is purely coincidental: see "Disclaimer and Warning" section.

3 Each chapter header highlights in sequence : Fundamental theme (italics). Important discussion areas. Main drugs. Any historic voyage (italicized). (Patients' names; other names) (analogy– detailed metaphors).

4 The short glossaries –"Neuropsychiatric Medications Glossary", "Neurotransmitter Glossary", "Medical Abbreviations", "Brain Diagram" and "Analogy" sections–combine with a lengthier "Medical Terms Glossary" to further assist the reader's comprehension. Finally, the extensive index allows further linking of major ideas.

5 Short definitions of terms appear in the "Glossary of Medical Terms" starting on page 350; em-dashes (–) in the text reflect definitions.

6 Dialogue with spaces between are used here as an equivalent to paragraphs: they reflect changes of theme. When the same theme is continued, no spaces exist between the answer and the next question

7 See Chapter 12.

8 A simplified list of neurotransmitter effects and side-effects appears in the "Neurotransmitter Glossary" at the back of this book.

9 All abbreviations in this book have been written without periods. See "Medical Abbreviations Glossary" on page 349 for the full text.

10 AMPA and kainate are other mainly excitatory neurotransmitters. Their roles in seizures are poorly understood.

11 "Boat and bathtub analogies" on page 343 clarifies the boat-pier model, which appears several times in this book.

12 Siegel RK: *Fire in the Brain*, New York: Plume (Penguin). 1993.

13 See the classification in the "Neuropsychiatric Drugs Glossary" on page 344.

14 Neppe VM: Management of catatonic stupor with L-dopa. *Clin Neuropharmacol.* 1988; 11 (1): 90-91.

15 Sacks O: *Awakenings.* London: Duckworth (now Harper, Perennial). 1973. Movie: same name, 1990.

16 See "Brain Anatomy and Simplified Functions" on page 342.

17 *Diagnostic and Statistical Manual IV*, American Psychiatric Association, Washington, DC. 1994.

18 Neppe VM, Blumer D: Atypical spells in the non-epileptic and paroxysmal neurobehavioral disorder. See www.pni.org/neuropsychiatry.

19 See www.pni.org/research/anomalous

20 Neppe VM, Tucker, GJ: Neuropsychiatric aspects of seizure disorders, In: Yudofsky SC, Hales, RE, eds. *Textbook of Neuropsychiatry.* Washington, D. C.: American Psychiatric Press; 1992: 397-426; or see www.pni.org/neuropsychiatry

21 Blumer D: Antidepressant and double antidepressant treatment for the affective disorder of epilepsy. *J Clin Psychiatry.* 1997; 58 (1): 3-11.

22 See www.fda.gov. The descriptions in this book simplify a very complex area.

23 Procrustes was a mythical Greek giant who tortured captives by stretching or shortening them to make them fit his rack.

24 Sciction, but see Spotteswoode J, Tauboll, E, Duchowny, M, Neppe, VM: Geomagnetic disturbance as a seizure provoking factor: an epidemiological study. *Epilepsia.* 1993; 34 Suppl 2, 56.

25 See overview in Neppe VM: Anomalistic experience and the cerebral cortex, In: Krippner S, eds. *Advances in Parapsychological Research 6.* Jefferson, NC: McFarland; 1990: 168-183.

26 See the simplified brain function diagram in the "Glossary" on page 342

27 The Inventory of Neppe of Symptoms of Epilepsy and the Temporal Lobe; see www.pni.org/neuropsychiatry

28 The figure 7.83 Hz is usually bandied around, but because it varies, the exact figure 7.83 is purely an academic average.

29 Sciction, but see Wilensky AJ , Neppe, VM. Prolonged stereotyped post-ictal psychosis. *Epilepsia .* 1993; 34 Suppl 2, 135.

30 See e.g. www.pni.org/philosophy

31 See www.pni.org/deja

32 Neppe VM: *The Psychology of Déjà Vu.* Johannesburg: Witw. Un. Pr. 1983.

33 Louw DEL: *A literary study of paranormal experience in Tennyson's poetry, PhD thesis,* Rhodes University, RSA, 1990.

34 Sciction, but links with Neppe VM: Tape recording auditory hallucinations. *Am J Psychiatry.* 1988; 145 (10): 1316.

35 Neppe VM, Wessels, WH: Psychotic toleration of neuroleptic medication. *S Afr Med J.* 1979; 56 (27): 1149; or see www.pni.org

36 Physician's Desk Reference. Medical Economics, Montvale, NJ. e, g. 58 ed, 1998. See also www.pdrnet.com

37 Neppe VM: Carbamazepine as adjunctive treatment in nonepileptic chronic inpatients with EEG temporal lobe abnormalities. *J Clin Psychiatry* 1983; 44 (9): 326-331; originally *Epilepsy International Congress, Kyoto, Japan.* 1981; 149.

38 See Neppe VM: *Innovative Psychopharmacotherapy*. New York: Raven Press. 1990; Chapter 5:123-151. Or see www.pni.org

39 See Neppe VM: Carbamazepine in nonresponsive psychosis. *J Clin Psychiatry*. 1988; 49 (4S):22-28

40 See Neppe VM: *Innovative Psychopharmacotherapy*. Chapter 5:123-151. New York: Raven Press. 1990; or see www.pni.org

41 See Chapter 6.

42 Haase HJ: The purely neuroleptic effects and its relation to the neuroleptic threshold. *Acta Psychiat Belg*. 1978; 78: 19-36.

43 See chapter 12.

44 Chapters 9-11 focus on serotonin and norepinephrine.

45 Neppe VM: *Innovative Psychopharmacotherapy*. New York: Raven Press. 1990; or see www.pni.org/literature

46 See www.pni.org/neuropsychiatry

47 Neppe VM, Bowman B, Sawchuk KSLJ: Carbamazepine for atypical psychosis with episodic hostility. *J Nerv Ment Dis*. 1991; 179 (7): 339-340; or see www.pni.org/psychopharmacology

48 Neppe VM, Kaplan C: Short-term treatment of atypical spells with carbamazepine. *Clin Neuropharmacol*. 1988; 11 (3): 287-9.

49 Shakespeare W: Sonnet CXVI. Circa 1600.

50 See www. pni. org/inset

51 Neppe VM: Carbamazepine as adjunctive treatment in nonepileptic chronic inpatients with EEG temporal lobe abnormalities. *J Clin Psychiatry* 1983; 44 (9): 326-331.

52 Neppe VM. Carbamazepine in the psychiatric patient. *Lancet*. 1982; 2 (8293): 33.

53 FDA rules are complex. See www.fda.gov

54 John Locke's unformed, featureless mind.

55 Freud S: *The Standard Edition of the Complete Psychological Works*. J. Strachey (Ed). London: Hogarth. 1953.

56 Regier, DA, Burke, JD Epidemiology.(in Section 5 on Quantitative and Experimental Methods in Psychiatry). In Kaplan, HI, Sadock BJ: *Comprehensive Textbook of Psychiatry / VI (Sixth Edition)* Baltimore: Williams and Wilkins. Chapter 5.1. Specifically see the NIMH epidemiologic catchment area program comorbidity study.

57 See chapters 1, 2 and 5 or the index.

58 "Boat and bathtub analogies" on page 341 clarify the bathtub model, which appears several times in this book.

59 Neppe VM: *The Psychology of Déjà Vu*. Johannesburg: Witw. Un. Pr. 1983; or see www.pni.org/deja

60 "Wort" is the old English for "plant"; it blooms around June 24th, the birthday of St John the Baptist.

61 Including Clomipramine (Anafranil) and fluvoxamine (Luvox) used as antidepressants overseas but approved only in obsessive-compulsive disorder in the USA.